D094627

A RICH BREW

A Rich Brew

How Cafés Created Modern Jewish Culture

Shachar M. Pinsker

NEW YORK UNIVERSITY PRESS

New York

Central Islip Public Library
33 Hawthorne Avenue
C_____ ___'_ NY 11722

3 1800 00338 3847

NEW YORK UNIVERSITY PRESS
New York
www.nyupress.org

© 2018 by New York University
All rights reserved

References to Internet websites (URLs) were accurate at the time of writing. Neither the author nor New York University Press is responsible for URLs that may have expired or changed since the manuscript was prepared.

Library of Congress Cataloging-in-Publication Data
Names: Pinsker, Shachar, author.
Title: A Rich brew : how cafés created modern Jewish culture / Shachar M. Pinsker.
Description: New York : New York University Press, [2018] | Includes bibliographical references and index.
Identifiers: LCCN 2017034136 | ISBN 9781479827893 (cl : alk. paper)
Subjects: LCSH: Jews—Social life and customs—19th century. | Jews—Social life and customs—20th century. | Jews—Intellectual life—19th century. | Jews—Intellectual life—20th century. | Coffeehouses—Social aspects.
Classification: LCC DS112 .P64 2018 | DDC 305.892/4—dc23
LC record available at https://lccn.loc.gov/2017034136

New York University Press books are printed on acid-free paper, and their binding materials are chosen for strength and durability. We strive to use environmentally responsible suppliers and materials to the greatest extent possible in publishing our books.

Manufactured in the United States of America

10 9 8 7 6 5 4 3 2 1

Also available as an ebook

This book is dedicated to my wife, Amanda Fisher,
and to my dear friend David Ehrlich.

CONTENTS

A NOTE ON TRANSLITERATION AND TRANSLATION

Modern Jewish culture is multilingual, and the sources I draw on, cite, and analyze in this book are in Hebrew, Yiddish, German, English, Russian, and Polish. Three of these languages do not use Roman characters, and this fact creates a major problem, since there are various norms and variations. Creating a perfectly consistent system of transliteration in English across the various languages is doomed to fail, despite the best intentions. The purpose of transliteration is to assist readers of English who are not familiar with the original languages, and this principle takes precedence over the desire for consistency. Nevertheless, I try to be consistent within each language. For Hebrew, I follow the *Prooftexts* journal system of Romanization, which is a modified, simplified version of the Library of Congress system. For Yiddish, I follow the YIVO system. For Russian, I follow the Library of Congress system. For proper names of people and places, I try to retain the form most familiar to readers of English.

When texts from foreign languages have been translated into English, I use and cite these published translations. Otherwise, translations are mine, with much-needed assistance from experts on languages in which I am not proficient.

Introduction

The Silk Road of Modern Jewish Creativity

In January 1907, a young and handsome Jewish man took the train from his small hometown of Buczacz to the city of Lemberg. The nineteen-year-old was an aspiring Yiddish and Hebrew writer by the name of Shmuel Yosef Czaczkes, better known to us as S. Y. Agnon, the winner of the 1966 Nobel Prize for literature. The trip to Lemberg—the provincial capital of Galicia in the Austro-Hungarian Empire—took him only a few hours, but it changed his life. Shmuel Yosef was traveling in order to become an assistant to Gershom Bader, an older journalist and writer of fiction who wrote in Hebrew, Yiddish, German, and Polish. Bader had established a Hebrew daily newspaper with the name *'Et* (Time) and invited Shmuel Yosef to assist him. This was an opportunity he could not refuse.[1] In Lemberg—also known as Lvov in Russian, L'viv in Ukrainian, and Lwów in Polish—the budding writer encountered many institutions that he had never before seen: boulevards, parks, theaters, museums, and an opera house. One urban institution made a particular impression: the café.[2]

Lemberg in the early twentieth century was renowned for its coffeehouses. Bader and other Jewish writers frequently socialized in cafés; sometimes they would also write or edit there, using the café table as their working desk.[3] In spite of the energy and optimism of Bader, the Hebrew daily paper quickly faltered, and he was soon forced to close it down. Shmuel Yosef lost his source of income and returned home. But during the months in which he lived in Lemberg, he visited several cafés and met many Jewish writers, politicians, and intellectuals, as well as people from many other walks of life, Jews and non-Jews, young and old, rich and poor.[4] The polyglot enthusiasm of Lemberg's café, an institution held together seemingly by little more than the desire for coffee and conversation, made a strong impact on him.

A little more than a year later, in April 1908, Shmuel Yosef traveled to Lemberg once again. This time, he had decided to leave his parents' home and migrate to Palestine in the Ottoman Empire. On his way there, he stopped in a few European cities. First, he arrived at Lemberg's railway station and went directly to the café to bid farewell to his old friends and to meet new ones. After his visit in Lemberg, Shmuel Yosef traveled to Kraków and then to the capital city Vienna, where he met other Jewish intellectuals in still more *Kaffeehäuser*. At the end of this trip, he arrived at the Arab port of Jaffa on the Mediterranean coast. He lived in Jaffa for a few years, frequenting Arab-, German-, and Jewish-owned cafés, and became part of a small Jewish intellectual and literary community. He made a name for himself as a Hebrew writer and changed his last name from Czaczkes to Agnon. Then in 1912, he journeyed back to Europe, this time to Berlin, where he joined a thriving Jewish cultural community that again met frequently in cafés. He spent the tumultuous years of World War I in Berlin before leaving Germany in 1924, traveling to Mandatory Palestine and eventually settling down in Jerusalem. In the 1930s, many Jewish migrants arrived there after fleeing Nazi Germany and Austria. As they found their way beyond the trauma that had forced them out of their homes, many of the refugees opened cafés, becoming part of the growing local intellectual and literary community, which had so inspired Agnon.

Agnon's journey took him to many cities and to many cafés. He traversed much of the route that we will follow in this book. But Agnon's café-laden path also tells us something about Jewish modernity writ large. These coffeehouses, way stations for Jewish intellectuals on the move across Europe and beyond, were central to modern Jewish creativity. In order to begin to contemplate the role of cafés in the development of Jewish modernity, we can turn to Agnon's fiction, to texts such as the novel *Tmol shilshom* (*Only Yesterday*), which he wrote in Jerusalem when he was a middle-aged man. In the novel, Agnon used episodes from his own biography to depict the life of Yitzḥak Kumer, a young and naïve protagonist. In one of the early chapters of the novel, Kumer travels to Lemberg, and upon arrival at the train station, he hurries to one of the local cafés. Why the coffeehouse? What, after all, is so important about a local café that Kumer feels that he must go there as soon as he arrives in the city? Agnon's narrator explains:

A big city is not like a small town. In a small town, a person goes out of his house and immediately finds his friend; in a big city days and weeks and months may go by until they see one another, and so they set a special place in the coffeehouse where they drop in at appointed times. Yitzḥak had pictured that coffeehouse . . . as the most exquisite place, and he envied those students who could go there any time, any hour. Now that he had arrived in Lemberg, he himself went to see them.

A few hours later, Kumer finds himself

standing in a splendid temple with gilded chandeliers suspended from the ceiling and lamps shining from every single wall, and electric lights turned on in the daytime, and marble tables gleaming, and people of stately mien wearing distinguished clothes sitting on plush chairs, reading newspapers. And above them, waiters dressed like dignitaries . . . holding silver pitchers and porcelain cups that smelled of coffee and all kinds of pastry.[5]

This explanation of the significance of the café in the big city is simple yet quite accurate. In contrast to the intimate and thoroughly familiar small town from which Kumer—and Agnon—came, the urban environment is inseparable from, and often thrives on, a sense of anonymity and alienation. And yet city dwellers also need a place to meet people and establish a sense of community. Thus, cities have always included some sort of gathering places. For the past three hundred years, one relentlessly popular and profoundly influential place has been the café, offering the city's inhabitants—locals, migrants, and even visitors—an easy place to buy coffee and pastries in comfortable surroundings.

Of course, the items for sale are often the entry for something more profound. The urban café is not just a site of consumption but also an institution of sociability and exchange, where people can meet, converse, read newspapers, or discuss and debate the news of the day or other matters. In Agnon's novel, the Jewish students in Lemberg can do all of this for the price of a cup of coffee, if they can afford it. Kumer's experience as a wide-eyed young migrant who envisions the café as "a most exquisite place" and a "splendid temple" is telling. The café is seen here as a substitute for what has been lost in modern life and at the same time

Figure I.1. Photograph of the interior of Café Central, Lemberg, 1904 (Courtesy of the Urban Media Archive of The Center for Urban History of East Central Europe / Collection of Oleksandr Korobov)

a place that is completely novel and exotic, a place that can open doors to unfamiliar worlds. Thus, cafés embody the search for a space that can be both comforting and exhilarating, both familiar and strange. For Jews in the modern world, whether in Europe, America, or the Middle East, that search took on an even greater urgency.

Agnon and his literary protagonist Kumer were far from alone in moving from a small town to large cities and in gravitating to their cafés. This movement across cities and cafés was very common and was an essential aspect of Jewish modernity. From antiquity through the eighteenth century, traditional Jewish culture was quintessentially collective: to be a Jew meant to belong to the community. Thus, the culture that traditional Jews created was distinct from the surrounding society. Yet what may be "the most defining characteristic" of modern Jewish culture is precisely "the question of how to define it."[6] From around the time of the French Revolution at the end of the eighteenth century, modernity created new possibilities and challenges, which went hand in hand with processes of secularization, emancipation, and urbanization.[7] As Jews left close-knit Jewish communities and migrated to large cities, cafés emerged as significant sites for the modern Jewish experience and for the production of modern Jewish culture, a culture that became difficult to define or to pinpoint as "Jewish" in traditional terms.

Amid the enormous historical, cultural, and economic upheavals of the nineteenth and twentieth centuries, Jews migrated to large cities and found their cafés. Indeed, Jews were often owners of cafés. Jewish writers have written in cafés, and they have written about cafés. Jewish intellectuals have used the café to create a place to argue with each other. Jewish merchants have made the café into a negotiating table. The café, in other words, has been an essential facet of the modern Jewish experience and has been critical to its complex mixture of history and fiction, reality and imagination, longing and belonging, consumption and sociability, idleness and productivity.

Jewish Urbanization, the Public Sphere, and the "Thirdspace" of the Café

Urban cafés, as we shall see, acted as points in a silk road of modern Jewish culture in the mid-nineteenth to mid-twentieth centuries. The "Silk Road" is a modern concept, coined in Berlin by the geographer Ferdinand von Richthofen in 1877, to describe a vast premodern Afro-Eurasian trade network between Byzantium and Beijing, Samarkand and Timbuktu. This nineteenth-century European invention of the silk road—a concept that became widespread only in the twentieth century—was more about the interconnection of modernity through railroads, commerce, and cultural exchange than about describing an ancient reality.[8] I invoke the silk road here as a spatial metaphor to describe a network of mobility, of interconnected urban cafés that were central to modern Jewish creativity and exchange in a time of migration and urbanization. Significant numbers of Jews migrated to cities across Europe and to the U.S. and to Palestine/Israel during this time period, often frequenting cafés and finding them to be places ripe with possibilities for fostering creativity and debate and for negotiating their roles in an uncertain world. The migration of café habitués and their role in moving ideas through global networks had important ramifications for the modern Jewish experience, which reached far beyond the confines of the café itself.[9]

Unlike the synagogue, the house of study, the community center, or even the American Jewish deli, the café is rarely considered a Jewish space.[10] Rather, it is mostly associated with the development of modern urban culture more generally. That broad link—with modernity, with urbanity, and with culture, rather than any specific association with Jewishness—is key to café culture. Although the café is understood as a chiefly European institution, it originated—like coffee itself—in the Islamic Near East. Along with coffee, a new and exotic commodity, the coffeehouse was imported to Europe from the vast Ottoman Empire during the sixteenth and seventeenth centuries.[11] Initially flourishing in London and Oxford, coffeehouses were established, and became popular, throughout European cities in the eighteenth and nineteenth centuries.[12] Jews have been attracted to, and associated with, the coffee trade and the institution of the coffeehouse from its arrival in Christian Europe. Oxford was the location of one of the first western European coffeehouses: the Angel was launched in the 1650s by someone we know only as Jacob, a Jewish entrepreneur of Sephardi origin, possibly from Lebanon.[13]

The historian Elliot Horowitz has shown that coffee and coffeehouses already played a role in Jewish life in the early modern period in such places as Egypt, Palestine, and Italy. Coffee was important for pietists and kabbalists, who used the beverage to enhance nocturnal religious rituals such as the midnight Tikun Ḥatsot. Jews in Venice, Livorno, and Prague were attracted to cafés as hubs of sociability, as places to gather outside the confines of the synagogue or the house of study, to talk, argue, and commune with each other and with their non-Jewish neighbors.[14] In seventeenth- and eighteenth-century Germany, Jews harnessed the new drink of coffee to enrich their personal, religious, social, and economic lives. Robert Liberles has analyzed Jewish consumption of coffee and has shown its commercial importance, as well as how coffeehouses served as sites of integration of Jews from various social strata into Christian society.[15] As we shall see, Moses Mendelssohn, "the father of the Haskalah" (Jewish Enlightenment), made his first significant entry into intellectual circles at the Gelehrtes Kaffeehaus (Scholars coffeehouse) in 1750s Berlin, and those connections launched his publishing career in both German and Hebrew.

The link between Jews and cafés, however, becomes more pronounced starting in the nineteenth century. As modernity, the café, and urban life all flourished, so too did secular Jewish culture. Whether called café, *Kaffeehaus*, *kawiarnia*, *kafe-hoyz*, *beit-kafe*, or any other name, the institution was especially dominant in urban, literary, and artistic life in this period; across many countries, people gathered, wrote, discussed, and debated issues within the café's walls.[16] These urban cafés were especially attractive for Jews in Europe and beyond because Jews did not always find a warm welcome in more exclusive meeting places such as clubs. This was also true in taverns, in which many Jews did not feel comfortable, in spite of the fact that many taverns were also owned by Jews.[17] The relatively new institution of the café—often called a "tavern without wine"—emerged as an appealing alternative. It was usually, but not always, inexpensive, felt exclusive without feeling restrictive, and offered a certain degree of freedom from the increasingly prying eyes of the government.[18]

Cafés, in spite of taking deep roots in various cities and becoming an essential vehicle of culture for numerous countries, always retained an air of "otherness"; both the institution and the drinks that were consumed there did not originate in the local soil.[19] This "otherness," and the mix of the national and transnational characteristics of the coffeehouse, might have something to do with the fact that many cafés were owned by Jews; even more Jews were consumers who frequented these cafés and became their most devoted habitués, or *Stammgäste*.[20] The link between Jews and cafés was evident not only in fin-de-siècle Vienna or Berlin but also in the new Russian city of Odessa and in the emerging metropolis of Warsaw, as well as in New York City—the new center of Jewish migration in America—and the "first Hebrew city" of Tel Aviv in Mandatory Palestine. From the mid-nineteenth until the mid-twentieth century, cafés in many cities were deeply, though never exclusively, identified with Jews and with Jewish culture.

As Agnon's life and novel reveal, these urban cafés—in particular those known as "literary cafés"—were especially alluring spaces for Jewish writers and members of the intelligentsia who were migrants, exiles, or refugees. Many of them were struggling to make ends meet and eager to find company in a new city; the café was often for them a substitute for a home and a community. However, cafés were not only a home away from home or an escape from a rented, cold room; they were also spaces in which complex and often tense social and cultural negotiations took place. The urban café was one of the few places where Jews could become part of non-Jewish social circles and spheres of activity. Thus, it was essential to modern Jewish acculturation. Though the processes of integration and acculturation—the acquisition of the cultural and social habits of the majority group—are both hallmarks of Jewish modernity, repeated again and again in different facets of life, there is still much we do not know about the way these processes played out. As we will see, urban cafés—and their intimate relation to the press, literature, theater, art, and politics—played a key role in the creation of modern Jewish culture and an emerging Jewish public sphere.[21]

The more we look, the more we discover the café's astounding influence. However, we must not be tempted to idealize the café. Jürgen Habermas, writing in the 1960s, declared the coffeehouse as a key example of "the public sphere of bourgeois culture." For Habermas, the coffeehouse—as it arose in early modern, increasingly capitalist Europe—was a space in which private individuals come together as a "public" distinct from the state. He claimed that such a public sphere emerged as a realm of communication that gave birth to both rational and critical debate.[22] London's coffeehouses in their golden age, between 1680 and 1730, provided the individual with access to a wider strata of the middle class than was ever before possible and thus enabled more people to communicate with each other informally, with fewer of the restrictions of class hierarchy that had long dominated British life. Habermas's public sphere is built, thus, on its accessibility to individuals, who come together without hierarchy, through their discussions of literature, news, and politics, a broadened notion of participation that helped to form a new civic and liberal society.[23]

This vision of the coffeehouse as an emblem of the public sphere has been essential and influential, but it is built on an ideal. In Habermas's eagerness to see the roots of a liberal, civic society, he neglected much of the messy historical reality. His assumption that everybody had the same unfettered access to the social and cultural institution of the café is too simplistic.[24] Moreover, the applicability of Habermas's framework to this study is evident but also limited. For him, the coffeehouse as a space of the public sphere reached its heyday in London of the eighteenth century and fell into a state of decline through the nineteenth century, when it was "invaded by private interests."[25] However, the period between 1848 and 1939 was the golden age of café culture across Europe and beyond and thus constitutes the chronological backbone of this book. In fact, the late nineteenth and early twentieth centuries saw not so much a decline but a further transformation of the public sphere.[26]

Such transformation of the public sphere, and of the role of café as a cultural institution, was contemplated by the Jewish thinker Walter Benjamin. In his essay *Berliner Chronik* (*Berlin Chronicle*, 1932), he uses various Berlin cafés as a chief "guide" around which he arranges his "lived experience" in the city as the "space of his life . . . on a map."[27] Benjamin attempts to divide Berlin cafés of the 1910s and 1920s into "professional" and "recreational" establishments, but he quickly notes that his classification is superficial inasmuch as the two categories coincide with and collapse upon each other. Benjamin thus demonstrates an enduring truth about the "lived experience" of the café, defined by a subversion of distinctions between private and public, professional and recreational, bourgeois and bohemian, and literary and consumer culture.

Benjamin's failed attempt to clearly define various types of cafés leads to a more complex understanding of the café as an institution and in terms of a place and space.[28] It becomes clear that the café has been (and perhaps still is) a place of commerce that revolved around consumption, leisure, and the spectacle of commodity—in other words, the epitome of bourgeois culture. At the same time, it was a place of the bohemian and the avant-garde that aspired to undermine the values of that bourgeois consumer culture. The café has been a space in which the enunciation of identity, the celebration of lived experience, and the grappling with contested meanings took place. Thus, it is more productive to study the café as a "thirdspace," a concept that emerged from the work of cultural geographers on the "production of space" and "lived environment." Challenging notions of space as an abstract arena and passive container, cultural geographers posited unified physical, social, and mental conceptions of space by emphasizing its continual production and reproduction.[29]

"Thirdspace," as we will use it as a critical tool to study the café, emphasizes the interplay between subjectivity and objectivity, the abstract and the concrete, the real and the imagined. Thirdspace is crucial to our exploration of the urban café in general and of its role in modern Jewish culture and literature in particular. It functions as a geographical concept that enables us to understand the café in the way it is located at and mediates between the real and the imaginary, the public and the private, elitist culture and mass consumption. In the context of modern Jewish culture, the thirdspace of the café sits on the threshold between Jew and gentile, migrant and "native," idleness and productivity, and masculine and feminine.

As a result, this book pays much attention to the ways in which Jewishness has been contested, enacted, experienced, and represented in the space of cafés. The café as an imaginary and real thirdspace and its perceived "Jewishness" are fluid, constantly changing expressions of Jewish modernity. The thirdspace of the café also is very much related to differences of social class, political ideology, choice of languages, and gender, which we will follow carefully. As we shall see, in the context of modern Jewish culture, the masculinity of the café was very pronounced. Numerous texts point to the fact that cafés served as a modern substitute for the traditional male *beys medrash* (house of study). This common comparison also highlights the fact that the space of the café was gendered in a specifically Jewish way, one that is marked by homosociality, a form of "intense male fellowship."[30] Very few women were part of Jewish literary café culture.[31] At the same time, when individual women such as Else Lasker-Schüler, Leah Goldberg, Anna Margolin, and Veza Canetti became important figures in Jewish café culture, they consciously pointed out the masculine nature of the modern Jewish café and simultaneously disrupted it.

Mapping Urban Cafés, Migration, and Modern Jewish Culture

Mapping these urban cafés and their interconnections, spreading from eastern and central Europe both to North America and to the Middle East, helps us to chart the spatial history of modern Jewish culture and literature in a new way. Using the coffeehouse as our lens reveals Jewishness in the nineteenth and twentieth centuries as a network of transnational migration.[32] Thus, examining the confluence of the thirdspace of the café, the urban environment, and the diversity of multilingual Jewish culture enables us to better understand crucial aspects of Jewish modernity. Previous attempts to explain how Jews became modern often resort to concepts such as Jacob Katz's "neutral" (or "semi-neutral") society of modernity, a public sphere in which one's religious or ethnic identity may be left at the door.[33] As in the case of Habermas's public sphere, the assumption of religious neutrality is problematic and does not describe well the reality of Jews in different places and within variable political and cultural contexts. Likewise, the terms "emancipation" and "assimilation" have been the tools of analysis for scholars of modern Jewish history for generations. But these are contested terms with many different and conflicting meanings. The ideologically fraught term "assimilation" presupposes the existence of static majority and minority groups. Even the more precise one, "acculturation," hardly captures the subtle variations of the various dominant groups to which a given group of Jews acculturates.[34] Ultimately, these terms are often too rigid to illuminate the actual development of modern Jewish culture, which, as we will see throughout this book, is fundamentally diasporic and transnational, no matter where it is provisionally located.[35]

The subtle variations of Jewish acculturation are intimately related to Jewish migration, because it is this fundamental fact—that Jews have been on the move—that became a hallmark of Jewish modernity. Of course, we have long studied and written about Jewish migration. But we have focused almost exclusively on immigration, framing it from the point of view of arrival to a new country or city, rather than on the itineraries of people and institutions as they move and the networks they have created. As Rebecca Kobrin has pointed out, we know a lot about Jewish immigrants in various cities around the world but not about the transnational character of the movements that brought them from one place to the next or about the links forged between those places.[36] As the example of Agnon's life and work in and about the café hints, by exploring the café, we are inevitably exploring how Jews got to that café and where they went after they left. In other words, studying this one very specific place illuminates the transnational cultural entanglements of Jewish migrants. Thus, while each chapter of this book focuses on a particular city in its unique geography, politics, and culture, the interconnected cafés allow us to explore and analyze the migration networks of diasporic Jewish culture created at their tables.[37]

Parallel issues arise as we try to understand modern Jewish literature. Dan Miron's recent attempt to describe what he calls "the modern Jewish literary complex"—in terms of "contiguity" rather than "continuity"—is crucial to apprehend the true reality of Jewish literature, a "vast, disorderly, and somewhat diffuse" body written in many languages and places.[38] The challenge with the concept of contiguity is its abstract nature; in order to be useful, it needs to become concrete. Using the café as a lens both elucidates and makes concrete the spatial history of modern diasporic Jewish literature, in Jewish and non-Jewish languages alike, and illuminates the many manifestations of Jewish culture, as they have been created in the café and clashed in the café and carried forth from the café.

It is clear that café culture and modernism, which flourished in the period covered here, were inextricably linked, in that "literary cafés, journals and publishing houses encouraged the development of new styles of writing to meet new realities and needs."[39] Indeed, "literary cafés"—places such as Café Griensteidl and Café Central in Vienna, the Café des Westens and the Romanisches Café in Berlin, and the cafés of the Left Bank and Montparnasse in Paris—were indispensable for the creation of European modernism.[40] What is often overlooked is the fact that these places, essential for the development of modernism, were not only attractive spaces for many Jews; they were sometimes identified, for better or worse, as "Jewish spaces." Scott Spector has warned that "Jewish modernism" is "a complex field of self-contradictory tensions and inversions," and therefore "its story cannot simply be narrated, but can perhaps best be captured by representing a constellation of moments in its elastic life."[41] By using the café, and writings about the café, as the focal point of such constellations of moments and spaces, we see how Jewish culture and modernism emerged side by side, each shaping and being shaped by the other.

This book offers a wide-ranging exploration of Jewish café culture in Odessa, Warsaw, Vienna, Berlin, New York City, and Tel Aviv. The reasons to focus on these cities are manifold. First, it is true that these six cities are far from the only places in which Jewish café culture was manifest; Lemberg, Budapest, Prague, Paris, Buenos Aires, and Jerusalem surely come to mind.[42] While this book deals almost exclusively with Ashkenazi Jews, there was also robust café culture in urban centers of Sephardi and Mizrahi Jewry: Baghdad, Cairo, and Tangier.[43] However, the six cities that this book explores provide a good illustration of the principal crossroads of Ashkenazi Jewish migration in eastern and central Europe, North America, and the Middle East, and thus of the Jewish modernity that was created there. Second, these cities were at one point or another—and, in some cases, continue to be today—centers of modern Jewish culture in multiple languages: Yiddish, Hebrew, German, Russian, and Polish. In the space of the cafés of these cities, intense exchange between Jews and non-Jews, and between Jews of different political and cultural orientations, took place. Looking at the cities and their cafés helps us to see how Jewish modernity was created along networks of migration, as Jews were pushed out or chose to leave some areas to migrate to others, bringing the cultures they had created within one city's cafés with them to another.

As will become evident, this exploration of the role of urban cafés in modern Jewish culture follows not only a geographic-spatial axis but a chronological-historical one as well. As we journey across continents alongside the Jewish migrants, we will also journey through time to explore the unfolding histories of modern culture, of Jewish culture, and of café culture. In some cases, these histories overlap, and in others, they diverge. Thus, in eastern and central European cities, we will focus mainly on the period between the mid-nineteenth century—following the revolutions that swept Europe around 1848—and the 1930s, when the rise of the Nazis, World War II, and Sovietization eradicated much of café culture and the modern Jewish culture that flourished there. As our narrative spreads beyond Europe, so too does our chronology. In New York City, the development of both multilingual modern Jewish culture and café culture begins toward the end of the nineteenth century with the migration of Jews from European countries and ends in the post–World War II years. In Tel Aviv, these same processes occur between the first decade of the twentieth century and the 1960s.

This book does not present a linear cultural history with clear points of beginning and ending for modern Jewish culture and café culture. Instead, it charts a spatial history and cultural geography of Jewish modernity through the lens of the café, through the embrace of both national and transnational contexts, and through partly overlapping geographies and chronologies. Moreover, while the book is organized around specific cities and the particular geography of each city, much of the exploration highlights the fundamentally transnational network of migration and

Jewish diasporic culture that find their nexus in urban cafés. This migration is core to the story of modern Jewish culture that emerges here. In other words, Agnon was in good company.

Almost all of the men and women who appear in this book migrated from one city to another, or to many others, sometimes for a few weeks or months, sometimes for years. Without fail, they find a café, or more than one, in each of these cities, compare them, take something from one café to another, and create the ebb and flow of the interactions and negotiations that occurred in them. Though they are Jews on the move, between cities and between cafés, they remain Jews, even as they pick up new languages, passports, identities, politics, and sometimes even a new religious identity. The result, it becomes clear, is that urban cafés are at the heart of Jewish modernity, and a better understanding of their crucial position reshapes our understanding of modern Jewish culture.

In order to bring readers into the world of Jewish café culture, this book makes use of newspaper articles, memoirs, letters, and archival documents, as well as photographs, caricatures, and artwork. However, the material that has survived the passage of time is partial. The cafés themselves and the activities that took place in them belong to the ephemeral realm of everyday life. We have no immediate, physical access to these cafés, which is particularly disappointing, since the reason why they were generative was precisely their palpable reality. Alas, most of these places do not exist today, and the one or two that do resemble a museum more than a living institution. As with all history, we must make do with what is available; we must resort to the written descriptions of these places, fictional and factual alike, and to photographs, drawings, and paintings. Like all evidence, these are subjective and yet highly instructive. Each of our sources refracts the reality of cafés in different ways, distorting some aspects, illuminating others. The gaps and imperfections of our sources can be frustrating, and yet they are in some way fitting, reminding us of the fundamental ambiguity and constructed quality of the café—its thirdspace—and its ephemeral qualities.

Literary works—stories, novels, poems—that take place in cafés and that were written by Jews in Hebrew, Yiddish, German, English, Russian, and Polish are a particularly crucial source. Texts such as Agnon's *Tmol shilshom*, which are rife with descriptions of cafés, are important sources because their writers, who were habitués of cafés, constantly employed the coffeehouse as a thirdspace. These literary texts are not to be taken simply as historical documents, but they give us a better understanding of how Jews—locals and migrants, poor and rich, bohemian and bourgeois, as well as the writers themselves—experienced the space of the café as a contested locus of urban Jewish modernity. Throughout this book, we will give special attention to the *feuilleton*: the hybrid literary-journalistic form of the sketch that mixed cultural criticism with storytelling. The feuilleton originated in Paris's newspapers in 1800 but became popular all over Europe in the period covered in this book. The feuilleton also became central in modern Jewish culture all over Europe and beyond, in German, Russian, Hebrew, Yiddish, and Polish languages. As we shall see, the feuilleton was also linked to Jewishness and café culture from the time Heinrich Heine wrote his *Briefe aus Berlin* (Letters from Berlin) in 1822.[44]

The literary texts considered in this book were written by a broad expanse of Jewish authors, including Heinrich Heine, Sholem Aleichem, S. Y. Agnon, Isaac Bashevis Singer, Joseph Roth, Isaac Babel, Theodor Herzl, Else Lasker-Schüler, Sholem Asch, Julian Tuwim, Leah Goldberg, Aharon Appelfeld, and many writers who are not as well known today. In one way or another, these writers made the café a dominant aspect of their fiction, poetry, essays, and memoirs, using this thirdspace as a microcosm of urban, modern Jewish experience on multiple continents. Transnational Jewish modernity was thus born in the café, nourished there, and sent out into the world of print, politics, literature, visual arts, and theater. In this way, what was experienced and created in the space of the coffeehouse influenced thousands who read, saw, and imbibed a modern Jewish culture that redefined what it means to be a Jew in the world.

1

Odessa

Jewish Sages, Luftmenshen, Gangsters, and the Odessit in the Café

In Odessa, the destitute *luftmenshen* roam through cafés,
trying to make a ruble or two to feed their families, but there
is no money to be made, and why should anyone give work
to a useless person—a *luftmensh*?
—Isaac Babel, "Odessa," 1916

In 1921, after World War I, the Bolshevik Revolution, and Russian civil
wars, many Jews left Odessa and migrated to other cities in Europe,
America, and Palestine. Among them was Leon Feinberg, a Yiddish
and Russian poet, writer, and translator. He traveled first to Tel Aviv but
shortly thereafter settled in New York City. In 1954, Feinberg published
a poema, a novel-in-verse titled *Der farmishpeter dor* (The doomed generation), that gave a voice to a generation of Jews who grew up in Odessa
and ended up in America. They experienced from afar the destruction
of European Jewry in the Holocaust, as well as the Stalin purges. The
first part of his novel-in-verse is "Odessa," a poetic representation of
this port city at the turn of the twentieth century. Several of the poems
follow Nyuma Feldman, a character from the poor neighborhood of
Moldavanka, who speaks "Odessan language"—Russian tinged with
Yiddish—and goes between Café Fanconi and Café Robina in the city
center. In these cafés, historical figures mix freely with fictional characters crafted by celebrated Jewish writers such as Sholem Aleichem, S. Y.
Abramovitsh, and Isaac Babel.[1]

What are these cafés, and why were they important for Feinberg and
others who remembered them so vividly in New York and elsewhere
after many years? The cafés played a key role in the development of
modern Jewish culture in the port city of Odessa, as part of an interconnected diasporic network that developed during the nineteenth and

early twentieth centuries. Odessa's history is unique, especially in the half century before the collapse of the Russian Empire and the Bolshevik Revolution in 1917 and the subsequent Sovietization of the city. In this period, the southern city of Odessa was perceived as a center of newfound Jewish freedom from strictures of both Jewish traditional life and the Russian regime. The mythic status of Odessa and its persistent image as a "Jewish city" have been documented by historians and literary scholars alike.[2] Odessa cafés have been part of both the history and the myth of the city and thus are our first example of a thirdspace, that liminal space between the real and the imaginary that can help us to understand both. Examining the confluence between the city's cafés, its urban modernity, migration to and from the city, and multilingual Jewish literary and cultural activity enables us to see the role of Odessa in Jewish modernity in eastern Europe. Through the lens of the café, we can better understand Odessa as an anchor in the silk road of transnational modern Jewish culture in a time of far-reaching urban migration, a period of transition from traditional forms of Jewish cultural expression to modern, secular ones.

Compared with other European cities of distinction and culture, nineteenth-century Odessa was very young. Established in 1794 by the empress Catherine the Great on land conquered from the Ottoman Empire on the site of the Black Sea fortress town of Khadzhibei, Odessa received its name—after an ancient Greek settlement called Odessos—the following year. Catherine sent notices throughout Europe offering migrants land, tax exemptions, and religious freedom. In addition to a nucleus of Russian officials, Polish landlords, and Ukrainians, many non-Slavs responded to her call. Within a few decades, a new city emerged, energetic and quite different from any other in the Russian Empire. With handsome streets laid out by Italian and French architects, a harbor sending shiploads of grain to every Mediterranean port, and the leadership of a series of tolerant and economically progressive administrators, some of whom were foreign-born, Odessa's economic foundations were established alongside its cultural ones. Thanks to its status until 1859 as a *porto franco*—a free port, exempt from taxes—it attracted wealthy foreign merchants and exporters. Within a few decades, it became a sizable city and soon commanded an international reputation as the preeminent Russian grain-exporting center. Thus, from its beginning until the city became known as the capital of Novorossiya, the empire's "wild south," Odessa was multinational, multilingual, and multiethnic. It attracted migrants of all types and creeds, with substantial numbers of Greeks, Turks, Italians, Armenians, Tatars, and Poles as well as some French, Swiss, and English.[3]

The city also attracted numerous Jewish migrants. Odessa was at the southern end of the Pale of Settlement, the area of the Russian Empire to which Jews were confined. This meant that Jews could settle there with few restrictions. Many Jews, both from Galicia, especially the city of Brody, and from small towns throughout the Russian Empire, made their way to the city in search of a better life. In fact, Jews were the fastest growing population in the city; they quickly adapted to the entrepreneurial business spirit of Odessa and became prominent players in internal Russian commerce to and from the city.[4] In Odessa, Jews did not have to "assimilate" to a single set of customs but to an urban way of life created by different groups and ethnicities, including the Jews.[5] Politically and culturally, toward the middle of the nineteenth century, Odessa became a center of Jewish life and attracted many *maskilim*: proponents of the Haskalah, the Jewish Enlightenment that began to take hold in eastern European cities and towns. In the 1860s, Odessa was the empire's center for the publication of multilingual Jewish periodicals. *Rassvet*, *Sion*, and *Den* appeared in Russian-language editions between 1860 and 1871, as did *Ha-melits* in Hebrew and *Kol mevaser* in Yiddish in the same period. By the late 1860s, major Jewish book publishers opened branches in Odessa, promoting, among other publications, books of the Haskalah movement. People such as the writer and editor Aleksander Zederbaum and Yitskhok Yoyel Linetski, a popular Yiddish writer, made their way to Odessa and found there ample opportunities to write and publish.[6]

The result was a palpable sense of Jewish freedom in the Russian Empire, although a freedom represented in highly ambivalent ways in the popular and literary imagination. People hoped to "live like God in Odessa," as one Yiddish dictum declares, but it was also imagined as the place where "the fires of hell burn for seven miles around it," because it was understood as a city of sin, vice, and temptations. This double image of Odessa soon became an essential component of the mythography of the city. The city was experienced both as a cosmopolitan place of enlightenment and culture and as El Dorado, a place in which one might get rich but that was also full of corruption and sin. Midway through the nineteenth century, these conflicting images of Odessa were crystallized around a number of urban cafés. Coffeehouses were not commonplace in the cities and towns of the Russian Empire. Odessa was different. People in Odessa liked calling their city "Little Paris"; the city was often compared to others in Europe and America but rarely to Moscow or other Russian cities. As Oleg Gubar and Alexander Rozenboim write in their survey of daily life in Odessa, one of the similarities between Odessa and Paris was "the presence of cafés, colorful and festive, with graceful verandas or tables simply placed under . . . acacias on shady, picturesque streets."[7]

Odessa's first cafés, like those in other European cities, were Turkish, Greek, and Armenian, regions that were the chief importers of coffee to the city through the Black Sea from the Ottoman Empire.[8] Alexander Pushkin, the great Russian poet of the nineteenth century, lived a short period of political exile in Odessa in 1823–1824 and visited these cafés. He immortalized the city in his verse novel *Eugene Onegin*, in which he wrote, "like a Muslim in his paradise, I drank coffee with Oriental grounds."[9] Later, cafés in Odessa were owned also by Italians, French, Swiss, Germans, and Jews, and their food and drinks, as well as their appearance and ambience, were influenced by all the different places from which the owners came. The warm weather of Odessa encouraged many of these places to be open to the tree-lined boulevards and streets, with verandas that let people enjoy the weather and the sea air and enabled cafés to be experienced as a thirdspace, located between the inside and the outside, the private and the public.

Jewish presence in these multiethnic cafés was first recorded in the mid-nineteenth century. The 1855 Robert Sears's guide to the Russian Empire declared that "there is perhaps no town in the world in which so many different tongues may be heard as in the streets and coffeehouses of Odessa, the motley population consisting of Russians, Tartars, Greeks, Jews, Poles, Italians, Germans, French, etc."[10] Local Jews and Jewish travelers from other parts of the Russian Empire noted the confluence of Odessa cafés and Jewish culture in the 1860s. It was an age of relative tolerance in Russia and a time of growth and maturity for Odessa's Jewish community, which constituted a sixth of the population of the city. In a published letter from November 2, 1861, Z., a traveler from Vilna (Vilnius, Lithuania), wrote about his experience in Odessa, which he called "the capital of Jews" in the Russian Empire. "In the days after I returned from Odessa, I hastened to relate to you," he wrote to a friend, "the impressions I had. . . . I won't tell you about the beauty, the princely life, the freedom and the wealth, which is already more or less familiar to all; I will tell only that I, at least, have never seen a comparable city. . . . But all this is of secondary importance for Jews, as there are many beautiful cities in the empire. I want to dwell only on the situation of our coreligionists there." As an example of what he found so attractive and exceptional in Odessa, Z. gave the city cafés: "When I stopped by Café Richelieu," Z. observed, "I saw that almost all of the customers were Jews, who argued, read, reasoned, and played; eventually I realized that this was something in the way of a Jewish club." What caught his attention more than anything else was that in the cafés, Jews "felt absolutely at home."[11]

The attraction of Jews to Odessa's cafés and the sense of ease and being "at home" in them, without being watched and judged, was seen as a sign of freedom and progress to some and as a threat to others. This ambivalent attitude can be seen in memoirs, letters, and newspapers, as well as in fiction written by Jewish writers. The Russian-Jewish writer, journalist, and editor Osip Rabinovich came from the small town of Kobelyaki and studied at Kharkov University before becoming a notary in Odessa. Being a notary did not stop Rabinovich from visiting and enjoying Odessa's cafés. He also became very interested in the world of journalism and Russian literature and began to publish feuilletons and stories in Odessa's Russian newspapers. In 1860, Rabinovich established the first Russian-Jewish periodical in Odessa, *Rassvet* (Dawn). In a short story published in 1865, Rabinovich described a traditional character named Reb Khaim-Shulim, a watchmaker who has troubles supporting a large family in the city of Kishinev. When he wins a lottery ticket, his appetite for business and wealth grows. Lured by stories he had heard about Odessa and the possibilities of getting rich there, Khaim-Shulim sets out not only to retrieve his lottery winnings but to move to the city on the Black Sea. "I'm going to Odessa for the money," he declares to his good friend Reb Khatskl (Yehezkel), but Khatskl warns Khaim-Shulim's wife, Meni-Kroyna, just as her husband enters the room, that Odessa is a dangerous place, a city of sin: "Temptations for your husband will be legion: in the café, in the theater. . . . It's better, you see, that he has the Book of Psalms with him, so that in his free time he will sit and read. It's edifying and free."[12] Khaim-Shulim does not listen to the warning of his friend, and he ends up losing all his money, returning to Kishinev with almost nothing. Thus, even if Rabinovich himself sat in cafés, for Khaim-Shulim, cafés were also a place of temptation and risk, both financial and spiritual.

We find a similar warning—that Odessa cafés were full of "sinful Jews"—in a novella by the Hebrew writer Peretz Smolenskin. Smolenskin was born in a small town in the Mogilev district, was influenced by the ideas of the Haskalah, and migrated to Odessa. He lived in Odessa from 1862 to 1867, before moving to Vienna, where we will encounter him again. Smolenskin made his debut as a writer in *Ha-melits*, Odessa's Hebrew newspaper. He wrote in and about the city in his first novella, *Simhat hanef* (The hypocrite's joy, 1872). The novella tells the story of twenty-three-year-old David, who lived in Warsaw, participated in the Polish uprising against the Russian Empire (1863), and ran away to live anonymously in Odessa, which Smolenskin's narrator calls Ashadot (Waterfalls). David earns a living by teaching Hebrew, as many *maskilim* did. The narrative unfolds in the relationship between David and his friend Shimon, another Hebrew teacher, who scolds him about his "sinful life." When David protests these accusations, Shimon admonishes his friend, "You still ask me what sin you committed! You are hanging out with lighthearted people who indulge in gluttony, who spend their days in cafés, in places of eating and drinking, with laughter and debauchery all day long. Isn't this a sin? To spend days and nights in folly and to waste the money you earn with the sweat of your brow; isn't that an evil, foolishness, and a great sin?"[13]

Thus, the image of Odessa as "a city of sin" was bound up with cafés, as spaces of eating, drinking, and loitering that attracted Jewish men. This link between cafés and sin or folly in this period seems to be shared by both rabbis and some *maskilim*. As the historian Jacob Katz has noted, "social activity for its own sake, that is, the coming together of people to enjoy themselves simply by being together, was regarded as a religious and moral hazard," especially when the sexes were mixed. But even homosocial masculine activity was viewed by some people with misgivings. It was believed to open the door to "transgressions" such as "gossip, slander, and bickering." In addition, the requirement underpinning traditional and *maskilic* culture demanded of men no less than total dedication to study and thus negated any acknowledgment of the need for "leisure time."[14]

Nevertheless, the attraction of these places for many people was not just the indulgence in food and drink or even the sociability that cafés facilitated. Like Rabinovich, Smolenskin became a habitué of Odessa cafés when he lived in the city, and they were central to his literary and journalistic activities. In the historical novel *Sipur bli giborim* (A story without heroes, 1945), the Hebrew writer A. A. Kabak portrayed Odessa's Jewry during the 1860s.[15] Some of the activities in this novel take place in the Greek café owned by Mitri Chirstopulo on Bazarnaya Street, where "penniless Hebrew *maskilim*, teachers of the Bible and the holy tongue, are spending their free time, together with business clerks who come to bask in the light of the *maskilim*, young men who ran away from their wives, and others." In the novel, Smolenskin visits this Greek café because "he likes to be in a place in which he is the center of attention. . . . They welcome him there, and everybody listens to his discourse and his jokes."[16] Moreover, the character Smolenskin knew everybody in the café, since many of them were Jewish migrants like him: "Almost all visitors hail from Lithuania and Poland, fleeing the darkness and poverty of the Jewish shtetls. . . . In their pockets, a few coins already shake. . . . They still think highly of themselves because they escaped the Yeshiva, and they come from time to time to the café to play chess and enjoy the fragrance of the *maskilim*."[17] Soon after, however, Smolenskin concludes that—in spite of his fondness for the place—in this café, "people bury large parts of their days and nights. If they had a real passion for life, they wouldn't sit there."[18] As these writings illuminate, the thirdspace of the café was experienced by people who enjoyed its sociability and exchange of ideas, both as a place of production and idleness, a tension that became central in Odessa, as well as in other cities.

Reading these Russian and Hebrew texts, it becomes quite clear that by the 1850s and 1860s, cafés were an important and notable part of Odessa's urban space, and migrant Jews—*maskilim* and businessmen—went there to meet each other for business, to play chess, to socialize, and to further their cultural endeavors. It is also evident that these cafés, and the Jewish presence in them, could be understood in two opposite ways: one that equated the cafés with the relative freedom and civility of Odessa's Jews, and the other with idleness and the danger of sitting around and indulging oneself.

The Blessing and Curse of Odessa Cafés

This double image of Odessa and its cafés was intensified toward the end of the nineteenth century, as Odessa became the fourth-largest city in the Russian Empire and, perhaps more importantly, "an interface between Russia and the outside world."[19] Around that time, Odessa was blessed, or cursed, with many cafés. In 1894, the newspaper *Proshloe Odessy* reported about 55 cafés and teahouses, 127 bakeries, and 413 restaurants in the city.[20] Only a few of these establishments became well known for their food and drink, for their visitors, and for the activity that took place within their walls. German and English guidebooks for tourists in the 1880s and 1890s mention the most established and popular cafés. There was the Italian Café Zambrini, which Anton Chekhov visited; the Swiss-owned Café Fanconi, opened in 1872; and the French-owned Robina (or Robinat) and the Jewish-owned Café Libman (or Liebmann), both opened in the 1880s. Odessa also had many *café-chantants* (literally "singing cafés"), a kind of cabaret where singers or musicians entertained the patrons and which dotted both the center and the outlying neighborhoods of Odessa.[21]

"By the end of the nineteenth century," writes the historian Steven Zipperstein, "little was left . . . of [Odessa's] Italians or French influences than a smattering of splendid, popular cafés—Café Fanconi was the best well-known."[22] Many of Odessa's Jews were attracted to these new cafés, as can be attested by Giuseppe Modrich, an Italian visitor to 1880s Odessa. Modrich wrote that he enjoyed the drinks and a wide variety of newspapers at Café Fanconi but claimed that while Odessa's Italians are moving to America, the Jewish merchants, who "have absorbed all commercial resources," are dominating the café and the public spaces of Odessa more generally.[23] What was the nature of Odessa cafés that attracted many Jews and non-Jews in the last decades of the nineteenth century? Gubar and Rozenboim write that the famous Swiss-owned Café Fanconi "existed from 1872 . . . until the last owner immigrated. At first, the café was a hangout for card sharks and shady businessmen, but gradually it became a kind of club for local and visiting writers, artists, actors, and athletes."[24] The memoirs, essays, stories, poems, and plays written by Jewish writers who lived in Odessa during this time show that Fanconi and similar cafés were places of consumption and entertainment that were mixed with business, politics, literature, art, and theater.

The mix of activities in Odessa cafés reflected the diversity of Odessa's Jews. In 1897, the 138,935 Jews constituted over a third of the city's total population. Most of the Jews who lived in Odessa at end of the nineteenth century were migrants, from middle-class merchants to poor Jews, who were living and working as small artisans and middlemen in neighborhoods and suburbs such as the Moldavanka. The number of Jewish intellectuals, writers, and thinkers who made Odessa their home was small, but their presence made the city a major center of Jewish high-minded culture, with politics, literature, journalism, and theater. As we have seen, Odessa was an important center of Haskalah and bourgeoning Jewish press and literature since the 1860s, but toward the end of the nineteenth century, an extraordinary group of Jewish writers and intellectuals made their home in the city. The person who emerged in this period as the most important Yiddish and Hebrew writer in the Jewish world, Sholem Yankev Abramovitsh, who wrote under the name Mendele Mokher-Sforim, settled in the city in 1881, when he was invited to direct a new modern school founded by the Jewish community of Odessa. Around the same time, Odessa became the center of Jewish nationalism and proto-Zionism in the Russian Empire. Leon Pinsker, the author of Auto-Emancipation, was active in the city as the head of the Odessa Committee of Hovevy Zion (Lovers of Zion) until 1891. He was joined by the thinker Aḥad Ha'am (Asher Ginsburg), the historian Simon Dubnow, the poet Ḥayim Naḥman Bialik, and the writers Moshe Leib Lilienblum, Elḥanan Leib Lewinsky, Yehoshu'a H. Ravnitsky, and others. These writers, intellectuals, and political figures formed a loose circle that became known as the "Sages of Odessa."[25] They wrote in Yiddish, Hebrew, and Russian and had followers far and wide.

Some of these "Sages of Odessa" who tried to foster a highbrow sense of Jewish culture and nationalism did not know how to respond to the mixture of consumption, leisure, business, conversation, and intellectual activity that was exhibited in Odessa cafés. Somewhat ironically, this ambivalent attitude can be seen best in a Hebrew feuilleton—that hybrid literary-journalistic form that originated in Paris and became associated with the café and with Jews—titled "'Ir shel ḥaiym" (City of life, 1896), in which Elḥanan Leib Lewinsky reflects on various cultural spaces in Jewish Odessa.[26] In his feuilleton, Lewinsky writes that he passed with sadness a building on Langeron Street, a bustling café that only a few years earlier had been a library. After a few years of absence from Odessa, Lewinsky asks the owner of the building why, in a "city full of men of enlightenment and readers of books," the library could not attract more readers? The proprietor answers that Odessan Jews enjoy "boisterous activity, rich food, and harsh coffee" but not books. The Jews of Odessa, Lewinsky concludes, are happy to pay good money for "the sheer pleasure of having dirty water tossed in their faces."[27]

It should be clear that Lewinsky's feuilleton and his condemnation of Odessa's Jews' love of cafés and "harsh coffee" does not mean that he did not frequent some of these cafés himself. However, it is indicative of a certain attitude of Odessa's Jewish "sages" who were reluctant to frequent these cafés. Reading through their memoirs and what other people wrote about them, it becomes evident that these "sages," especially those of the older generation, preferred to meet behind closed doors, rather than in the café. Throughout the second half of the nineteenth century, there were a number of attempts to create Jewish literary and cultural clubs such as Beseda (Conversation), but they were only partially successful.[28] Some of the "Sages of Odessa" met in "salons" that took place, often on Friday evenings or Saturdays, behind closed doors in the private houses of Abramovitsh, Ahad Ha'am, and Dubnow.[29] These "salons"—an institution that had flourished in Europe since the eighteenth century—were an alternative to the café. Instead of the thirdspace of the café, located between the private and the public, the inside and the outside, salons were open only to a small group of people who were familiar to each other, spoke essentially the same language, and had similar concerns. As we shall see, salons of one kind or another constituted competition for the café in almost every city in which modern Jewish culture was created.

However, Odessa cafés were important for many other, mostly younger Jewish writers and intellectuals, as well as for the development of Jewish theater in the city. The modern Yiddish theater was born in Romania in the middle of the 1870s and was consolidated in Odessa in the late 1870s and 1880s, before migrating and spreading to Warsaw,

London, New York, and other cities around the world. As in the case of Jewish journalism and literature, in the realm of theater, Odessa cafés were part of a cultural network of Jewish creativity in transit. Avrom Goldfaden, the leading pioneer of Yiddish theater, settled in Odessa in 1878, after some years spent in Romania, and established a theater troupe that met, rehearsed, and sometimes performed in Odessa's cafés and taverns. The Yiddish actor Jacob (Yankl) Adler was born in 1855 to a family of migrants to Odessa and began his acting career in the city. The playwright and director Jacob Gordin also began his journalistic and literary activities in Odessa in the 1880s, before he moved to New York City and its cafés. In 1882, the Yiddish popular writer and dramatist Nokhem Meyer Shaykevitch, known as Shomer, opened a Yiddish theater in Odessa in partnership with Goldfaden. Peretz Hirshbein, who arrived in Odessa in 1908, established his own art theater troupe there. Although all these playwrights, directors, and actors migrated elsewhere—mostly to New York City—because of frequent tsarist bans on Yiddish productions, Odessa was crucial for the growth and maturity of the Yiddish theater.[30]

In Odessa, local *café-chantants* staged Yiddish plays, and both cafés and taverns influenced the creation and diffusion of music that was closely related to these theatrical performances.[31] Jacob Adler wrote about his stormy youth in Odessa and how he roamed between cafés, taverns, and the Russian city theater.[32] When he returned from serving as a solider in the Russian army during the 1877 war with Turkey, he started to work as a journalist at the Russian newspaper *Odesski vestnik* (Odessa messenger), but he spent the evenings at *café-chantants* and wine cellars, as well as in Café Fanconi, where he met with other actors and began his theatrical career.[33] Adler soon became more involved in the theater, and his acting friends met at Café Fanconi, as well as in the Jewish-owned Akiva's café on Rivnoya Street, where theatrical rehearsals and performances also took place.[34] When Avrom Goldfaden came to Odessa the following year, there was much excitement at Café Fanconi, where "everybody already gathered, all talking about Goldfaden and the sensation his arrival made."[35] Eventually, Adler acted with Goldfaden's troupe in Odessa and other cities in the Russian Empire, before he migrated to London and to New York City.

The role of Odessa cafés as part of a growing network of Jewish culture can also be seen in the activities of Jacob Gordin, the most important

Yiddish playwright of the late nineteenth and early twentieth centuries. Gordin was born in Mirgorod, a small town in Ukraine, and traveled far and wide in the Russian Empire. He lived in Odessa and, like Adler, published essays in Russian, in the local liberal newspaper *Odesski vestnik*.[36] In the 1880s, Gordin frequented Odessa cafés and knew them very well. Although he started writing Yiddish plays only after his migration to New York City, many of his plays depict Odessa and are infused with Odessa's society. A case in point is Gordin play's *Saffo* (Sappho), produced in New York in 1900.[37] The entire play takes place in Odessa and is based on Gordin's familiarity with the city and its social and cultural life.

The main figure of the play is Sofia Fingerhut—dubbed "The Jewish Sappho"—a figure of a "New (Jewish) Woman," who works in an office to support herself. At the beginning of the play, Sofia is about to get married to Boris, a modern Jewish photographer. Matias Fingerhut, the father of the bride-to-be, is torn between his happiness about the marriage and his fear of the new values that his daughter and Boris share. Mr. Fingerhut declares to his daughter and wife that he is "going to treat himself to tea in the terrace of Café Paris—perhaps the French-owned Café Robina—so everybody will know what sort of man [he] is."[38] In this case, Matias, a migrant to Odessa and a merchant, is clearly torn between his notion of masculinity, Jewishness, and middle-class respectability and his daughter's newfound independence. Soon after, Sofia finds out that Boris really loves her sister, Lisa, and refuses to marry her, in spite of the fact that she has a baby with him. In act 2 of the play, which takes place a few years later, Sofia continues to live and work as a single woman. Boris and his friend Samuel Tseiner discuss match-making in Café Fanconi, and Mr. Fingerhut also visits the café, where he receives much information about the relationships between his daughters and the men in their lives. He finds out that a young Jewish pianist, with the nickname Apolon, fell in love with Sofia/Sappho, but she resisted him. The play ends with Sofia moving out of Odessa with her little daughter.

Although Gordin wrote the play for an American Jewish audience in New York, where it was very successful, it was clear to viewers that modern Russian Jewish figures (Boris, Sofia, and Apolon) were likely to be found in Odessa. These young Jews, as well as their merchant father, could flaunt their modernity in Cafés Fanconi and Paris. But Gordin's play also highlighted an important gender element of Odessa's cafés. Sofia, the modern Jewish woman, only hears about what is going on in the cafés but never participates in their social life. Throughout the nineteenth century, Odessa cafés were developed as homosocial, masculine spaces, where "respectable" women were not to be seen. Thus, Sofia's relative independence as a working, single woman could not be sustained in Odessa's cafés.

Gordin's play is a good example of the importance of Odessa cafés in modern Jewish life, but it also highlights the conflicts and tensions around gender and around the changing contours of what it meant to be "Jewish" in the modern urban environment of Odessa. Indeed, during the final decades of the nineteenth century, Odessa cafés were very popular, but they were also spaces of various conflicts and tensions, not just between traditional and more modern Jews but also between men and women, businesspeople and intellectuals, Jews and gentiles. The vigorous Jewish presence in these cafés attracted much attention, for better or worse. After the assassination of Tsar Alexander II in 1881, when there were waves of anti-Jewish violence in the Russian Empire (even in Odessa), the reaction to the Jewish presence in cafés was sometimes marked with anti-Semitism, real or perceived, as well.[39] On August 10, 1887, *Ha-melits* reported about a story published in *Novorossiysk telegraph*, a regional Odessa newspaper that was known as instigating Judeophobia:

> The Jewish community of Odessa decreed a boycott on the tavern of Mr. Fanconi and made it forbidden to all Jews to step inside the house, because he printed in the journal a letter and cursed the Jews who made it a communal space. On both sides of the coffeehouse Jews stood up and announced this boycott; they took note of anyone who did not obey them and entered the café. Mr. Fanconi is very happy with this boycott because now the huge crowd of Jews, who used to do business there, stopped visiting; instead many Christians continued to frequent it, to drink and eat there to their heart's content.[40]

Less than two weeks after the report, in the same Hebrew newspaper, Ravnitsky, who used the pseudonym Bar-Katsin, wrote a story in order

to better explain what happened and to further report on the latest outcome of this affair in Café Fanconi. Ravnitsky wrote,

> For the sake of the readers who are far from Odessa, I would like to ex-
> plain the meaning of this event, which became a topic of conversation
> for everybody in our city. Fanconi is not a tavern but the largest café
> and pastry shop in the city of Odessa. This is the meeting place of many
> not-so-small merchants, the elite of Odessa who do not care much about
> money. The establishment, which stands proudly in the center of the busi-
> ness district, became a meeting place of every respectable merchant. And
> when one merchant looks for another, he knows that he would find him
> in Fanconi and converse with him over a cup of coffee and sweet pastries.
> It is easily noticeable that almost all the habitués of the café are our Jewish
> brothers. . . . In the checkbook of every Jew in our town . . . you would
> find a nice sum that was payable to Fanconi. . . . With the price one pays
> for a cup of coffee and light delicacies, a poor man with a wife and five
> children can live quite comfortably.[41]

In short, Ravnitsky contended, since the opening of the café, the relationship between the middle-class Jews of Odessa and Café Fanconi was
beneficial to all. What instigated the Fanconi affair was a young and poor
maskil, who used to frequent Fanconi without having enough money to
pay. Somehow he always got by, with one person or another paying for
him, until the waiters of the café had enough and decided to throw water
on him in order to scare him off. This act created a strong backlash, with
many of the Jewish habitués of the café scolding the waiters.

According to Ravnitsky, in response to all this, Mr. Fanconi himself
wrote a letter to *Novorossiysk telegraph*, seeking to defend his workers
and blame the Jews for "turning his café into a tavern, making noise, and
creating mayhem." The habitués decided to do the unthinkable, namely,
to avoid Fanconi, and the café became almost completely empty, to the
chagrin of Mr. Fanconi. Subsequently, he decided to publish a large announcement in the liberal newspaper *Odesskie novosti* (Odessa news)
that, according to Ravnitsky, said the following: "The good relationship
between Café Fanconi and the *maskilim* of our city over many years
forces me to explain in print . . . that all the rumors about Jews refusing
to visit the café are completely wrong, because most Jews, apart from

Figure 1.1. Postcard of Café Fanconi, Odessa

a small minority, continue to frequent the coffeehouse. I ask all those who were insulted by the ugly act of the waiters or by misunderstanding our announcement in *Novorossiysk telegraph* to understand that I never meant to offend the Jewish people."[42]

Mr. Fanconi noted that nobody could accuse him of anti-Semitism and that he warmly welcomed everybody ("and their deep pockets," adds Ravnitsky) with open arms. Ravnitsky's report ends with the conclusion that the outcome of the affair was that most, if not all, of the Jewish habitués returned to their beloved Fanconi, but these events caused "our brothers to raise their self-evaluation as Jews."[43] Thus, we can see that Odessa's prominent cafés were spaces of tensions and contested meanings. The highly visible attraction of Jews to Café Fanconi was so prominent that it made it appear as a modern "Jewish space." Mr. Fanconi and his waiters might not have liked the marking of the café as Jewish, but they depended on it in order to continue to flourish. Moreover, we can see the economic tension between middle-class merchants and *maskilim*, as well as between Jews and non-Jews and even among the owner, the waiters, and the habitués.[44]

These tensions and the fact that Jewish modernity in Odessa was inextricably bound to its cafés became evident to Ravnitsky's friend, the young Sholem Aleichem (Sholem Rabinovich), who was soon to become one of the most beloved and influential Yiddish writers in the world. Sholem Aleichem came to Odessa from Kiev in 1891, after he lost all his father-in-law's wealth in the stock exchange. He lived in Odessa for a number of years, trying to make a living by publishing in Russian, Hebrew, and Yiddish. These years in Odessa were difficult financially for Sholem Aleichem but also very memorable and productive. Unlike some of the "Sages of Odessa" but like Adler, Goldfaden, Gordin, Ravnitsky, and Rabinovich, Sholem Aleichem enjoyed visiting Odessa cafés, eating, drinking, observing, and participating in the activity that took place there. In *London: A Novel of the Small Bourse* (1892),[45] which is the first part of what evolved to become the epistolary novel *The Letters of Menakhem-Mendl and Sheyne-Sheyndl*, Sholem Aleichem makes masterful comic use of the space of Café Fanconi. More than any text written before it, Sholem Aleichem's novel situates Odessa's cafés on the map of modern Jewish literary imagination.

In the novel, the protagonist, Menakhem-Mendl, who arrives in Odessa from his tiny fictional shtetl Kasrilevka, is bewitched by the stock market and the currency-exchange market of Odessa, where he believes he has made a large amount of money quickly and without much effort. Menakhem-Mendl is equally allured by Café Fanconi, the location of the elusive "small bourse" in the novel's subtitle, where business is done over a cup of coffee or tea. As he writes to his provincial wife, Sheyne-Sheyndl, whom he left behind in the shtetl, "If only you understood, my dearest, how business is done on a man's word alone, you would know all there is to know about Odessa. A nod is as good as a signature. I walk down Greek Street, drop into a café, sit at a table, order tea or coffee, and wait for the brokers to come by. There's no need for a contract or written agreement. Each broker carries a pad in which he writes, say, that I've bought two 'shorts.' I hand over the cash and that's it—it's a pleasure how easy it is!"[46]

After a few days, Menakhem-Mendl boasts that he is so successful in Odessa that all the dealers already know him in Café Fanconi:

By now they know me in every brokerage. I take my seat in Fanconi with all the dealers, pull up a chair at a marble table, and ask for a dish of iced cream. That's our Odessa custom: you sit yourself down and a waiter in a frock coat asks you to ask for iced cream. Well, you can't be a piker—and when you're finished, you're asked to ask for more. If you don't, you're out a table and in the street. That's no place for dealing, especially when there's an officer on the corner looking for loiterers. Not that our Jews don't hang out there anyway. They tease him with their wisecracks and scatter to see what he'll do. Just let him nab one! He latches on to him like a gemstone and it's off to the cooler with one more Jew.[47]

It is hard to mistake the target of Sholem Aleichem's biting humor. The provincial Menakhem-Mendl, the quintessential *luftmensh* (man of the air), would soon lose all his money in the Odessa speculative market, as Sholem Aleichem himself did in Kiev and as the character of Khaim-Shulim did in Osip Rabinovich's novel. But Menakhem-Mendl's experience also captures something essential about the Odessa café as a metonym for the contradictions of urban Jewish modernity.[48] Sure, the café gives anyone, even Menakhem, access to a marble-top table and, along with it, to conversations about politics and culture and even to the business that presumably takes place by a mere nod. Moreover, all of this can be done while a waiter in a frock coat will serve you coffee and the best ice cream in the city. However, if you lack the money to order a few servings, you are out in the street, in danger of being picked up by a police officer ready to roust any Jew who might interfere with the life and the business of the café. Sholem Aleichem builds on Osip Rabinovich's Khaim-Shulim and on Ravnitsky's *maskil* in "the Fanconi affair," but his comic genius goes deeper in penetrating into Odessa café life.

We can see through Menakhem-Mendl's letters to his wife that the modern business that takes place in the thirdspace of the café is different from the "old" and more tangible business. It is very much tied to smart conversations about politics and news, which Menakhem-Mendl can only partially follow. He tries to explain to his wife that her "doubts about the volatility of the market reveal a weak grasp of politics." Menakhem-Mendl gets his "grasp of politics" in Café Fanconi by speaking to a habitué named Gambetta, "who talks politics day and night. He has a thousand proofs that war is coming. In fact, he can already hear the cannon booming. Not here, he says, but in France."[49] Thus, one can presumably sit in an Odessa café, where journalists and readers gather, read newspapers from all over the world, follow the news about the war in Paris and London, and speculate on currencies and stocks that are part of the new modes of capitalist economy. This economy is like the ephemeral "market" in the café that people like Menakhem-Mendl cannot really fathom, even if he desperately tries to.

Menakhem-Mendl's wife, Sheyne-Sheyndl, is as essential to the epistolary novel and to understanding Jewish café culture in Odessa as the male antihero is. In spite of the fact that she never leaves the shtetl of Kasrilevke, she is able to mount a critique of Café Fanconi and the conversations and business that go on there. About Gambetta, the source of knowledge about politics and market manipulation, she writes to her husband, "And as for your Gambetta (forgive me for saying so, but he's stark, raving mad), I'd like to know what business of his or his grandmother's it is. You can tell him to his face that I said so. What kind of wars is he dragging you into?"[50] Sheyne-Sheyndl is also highly suspicious about the fact that her husband spends so much of his time at Café Fanconi, instead of doing some more traditional business or work. She also suspects his fidelity when she writes, presumably without even understanding what a café is or what its name is, "And by the way, Mendl, who is this Franconi you're spending all your time with? Is it a he or a she?"[51]

Although the café habitués used to be all men, just around the time Sholem Aleichem wrote his comic novel, modern women began to access the café, which raised the suspicions of traditional wives like Sheyne-Sheyndl. It is also clear that she is correct about the demise of her husband's business activities. Soon enough, Menakhem-Mendl starts to lose everything he gains and more. At this point, he confesses, "I tell you, my dearest wife, I've had my fill of Odessa and its market and its Fanconi and its petty thieves!"[52] In Sholem Aleichem's novel, Café Fanconi can indeed be a dangerous place if you do not know how to navigate your way in this thirdspace of urban modernity. Odessa cafés were clearly both a blessing and a curse to many Jews who migrated to the city and made their home there. While they were crucial to the development of Jewish business, politics, theater, music, press, and literature, they also exposed strong anti-Semitic sentiments, the challenges of modernity, and changing economic and class structures. The café was becoming a site of tense negotiation around consumption and politics, gender, and the widening economic gaps that were part and parcel of Odessa's Jewish urban modernity.

Revolution, Pogroms, and Politics in the "City of Life"

At the beginning of the twentieth century, Odessa's status as a center of modern Jewish literature and culture unparalleled in the Russian Empire was firmly established, as was its role as an anchor in a network of Jewish culture. This did not stop its reputation for being full of wealth and full of sin. The tensions that were visible after 1881 in Odessa cafés and elsewhere only intensified in these years, when the Russian Empire entered a deep recession. Odessa's economy suffered a setback due to the decrease in demand for manufactured goods, a drop in the supply of grain available for export, and the drying up of credit. There were flaws in Odessa's economic infrastructure, and conditions continued to deteriorate, especially following the outbreak of war between Russia and Japan in 1904. All these developments fused together with the political and economic unrest that swept the Russian Empire before the failed 1905 revolution against the tsarist regime; that unrest was especially high in Odessa, in spite of its relative distance from imperial centers and its reputation as a multiethnic, cosmopolitan "city of life."[53]

One of the defining moments of that aborted revolution took place in Odessa: the rebellion that erupted on the Russian battleship *Potemkin* on June 14, 1905, immortalized by Sergei Eisenstein's film *The Battleship Potemkin* (1925). A few months after these dramatic events, Tsar Nicholas II issued the October Manifesto, promising political reforms. A large pogrom, a wave of anti-Jewish violence, erupted in Odessa on October 18–22, 1905, in which at least four hundred Jews and one hundred non-Jews were killed and approximately three hundred people, mostly Jews, were injured. Around 1905, a new generation of Russian Jews—some born in Odessa, others who had migrated to the city—came of age and found their place within the city's cultural life. The October pogrom and several others that followed it thoroughly shaped members of this new generation but did not dim their engagement with the city. Most of them felt thoroughly at home in Russian language, literature, and culture, and they made good literary use of the unique Russian dialect of Odessa, which was tinged with Yiddish and Hebrew and with influences of many other languages spoken in Odessa. Odessa continued to attract young people from the Pale of Settlement who wanted to bask in the light of

the "Sages of Odessa," but many of Odessa's new writers and cultural figures, as well as its merchants and lower-class workers, were born in the
city and proudly considered themselves to be real Odessits. Odessa cafés
continued to play an important role in the city and in Jewish culture in
the tumultuous and occasionally violent years around the revolution.
Much of the writing in and about the café reflected on the changes that
took place in Odessa and the tensions that abounded around the aborted
revolution and the pogroms.[54]

The Jewish-Russian writer and journalist Vladimir Jabotinsky was
born to an acculturated middle-class family in Odessa in the year 1880.
The young Jabotinsky, who later became the leader of the Zionist Revi-
sionist party in Palestine became the chief cultural correspondent for
the prestigious Russian daily *Odesskie novosti*, writing many witty feuilletons. Jabotinsky used to sit in Odessa's famous cafés, writing, observing, and gathering information about cultural events in the city, as well
as in the simple Greek cafés near the port, which he especially liked.
Years later, he wrote about the city in his semiautobiographical novel
Pyatero (*The Five*, 1936).[55] In the novel, Jabotinsky chronicles the lives
of five children in the Milgrom family and their different orientations,
choices, and fates. Many of the events in the novel take place in the center of Odessa, where "one could see the trading terraces" of the two most
famous institutions, Café Fanconi and Café Robina, which were "noisy
as the sea at a massif, filled to overflowing with seated customers, surrounded by those waiting to get in."[56]

The narrator's view of these cafés as sites of "trading" captures well
the mixture of business and pleasure, literature and culture, sociability
and commodity, in the period before 1905. The changes that occurred in
Odessa after the turbulent events of 1905 are also experienced and depicted through the cafés, which according to Jabotinsky suddenly emptied.
In fact, for Jabotinsky and his narrator, after 1905, Odessa would never be
the same city, and the years of the fin-de-siècle constituted the golden age
of Odessa, its cafés, and its other public spaces. Jabotinsky describes in the
novel a literary club that met in a building at the center of Odessa in 1903
as an ideal location for cultural mixture: "I think that most interesting of
all was the peaceful brotherhood of peoples amongst us at the time. All the
eight or ten tribes of old Odessa met in this club, and really it entered no
one's head, even silently to oneself, to notice who was who."[57]

Something of the way Jabotinsky experienced the cross-cultural pollination of the years before 1905 can be seen in the memoir of his friend Israel Trivus, one of Odessa's Zionists. Trivus wrote about his encounters with Jabotinsky in 1904. According to Trivus, Jabotinsky said that in the Greek Café Ambarzaki, "there is an aroma of Asia, . . . but it creates an ambience that takes you up to the sky, where there is no limit to your thought and imagination." Playing on the Greek name of the café, Jabotinsky claimed that when he got to know this "lofty institution" well enough, he finally understood "the ancient Olympus, where one could enjoy ambrosia and nectar," and that "God's nectar is really a fragrant cup of Turkish-style coffee, and ambrosia is *rahat lokum* [Turkish delight] and halva."[58] However, it was not just the divine food and drink that Jabotinsky was attracted to but the conversation with the Greek owner of the café. He was enthralled with the visitors' talk, which, according to Trivus, revolved around Greek and Jewish national movements and the emerging Zionist movement, as well as around the glories of Odessa, Pushkin's poems (which Jabotinsky recited from memory), the city, and its cafés.[59]

The cafés that Jabotinsky's narrator wrote about embody the way he understood the spirit of Odessa before 1905, but things changed drastically after that in Jabotinsky's novel and in reality. During the year 1905, with the aborted revolution and with the pogroms that followed in the next months, the activity in Odessa's cafés was very different. Some cafés were even in the line of fire. The most famous of them was Café Libman, the Jewish-owned establishment in the center of Odessa, which was located within the well-known Passage building.[60] Café Libman was bombed by a group of socialist-anarchists in December 1905. Their mission was to spread propaganda in the factories and organize revolutionary labor unions as vehicles of class warfare. The bombing was a part of their effort to create "economic terror." Apparently, the Jewish owner of Café Libman was blackmailed by the anarchists. They did the same thing to other shopkeepers and café owners, whom they described as "bourgeois bloodsuckers." When Mr. Libman refused to pay them protection money, the café was bombed, which caused much damage to the café, as well as injuries.[61]

These economic and political tensions were a crucial part of Odessa's modern Jewish culture. One of the most important aspects of the "economic terror" in this period was that not only were the owner of the café and many of the visitors Jewish, but so too were many of members of the anarchist group. As the historian Anke Hilbrenner claims, Café Libman might have been chosen as a target precisely because the owner of the café was known to the anarchist terrorists. Moreover, Café Libman was not really the café of the "bourgeois bloodsuckers," as the anarchist sources claimed, but a place where students, liberals, and intellectuals would go. Since many of the guests were Jewish, some of the people injured in the bombing were Jews, including families with children. One of the Odessa anarchists, Daniel Novomirsky, criticized the bombers precisely for bombing a café where the "local intelligentsia" would sit and drink tea and coffee.[62]

If the bombing of Café Libman, which was soon renovated and continued to flourish for another decade, was a sign of the occasionally violent class warfare in Odessa, the pogrom in Odessa was a painful reminder that the city was never immune to anti-Semitism. A number of writers described in their fiction the devastation of the anti-Jewish violence in texts that were centered in cafés and similar institutions. The most famous is Alexander Kuprin's short story "Gambrinus" (1907).[63] Kuprin was not Jewish but a major Russian writer who presented a nuanced portrait of the Odessan Jews in his writing. "Gambrinus" is the name of a real establishment in the center of Odessa. It was not a café like Fanconi, Robina, or Libman but an underground establishment, a mix of tavern and café-chantant, in which music was played every night. In the story, the most beloved musician in Gambrinus was Sashka, an Odessan Jewish fiddler who was steeped in the tradition of Jewish (klezmer) music that developed in Odessa. Sailors and workers would flock to see and hear Sashka because he mesmerized audiences with his improvised response to the most varied requests, from Russian folk melody to Viennese waltz to an African chant.

In this period, Jewish musicians, especially fiddlers, began to dominate. The fictional Sashka was based on a real figure, Sender Pevzner, familiar in Odessa for his violin playing. In Kuprin's story, Sashka volunteers to fight in the tsar's army during the 1904 war with Japan. After his return, the pogrom in Odessa erupted, and the very same people who enjoyed Sashka's playing in Gambrinus were suddenly incited against Jews. One day when Sashka was walking in the streets of Odessa, a stonemason wanted to attack him with his chisel. When someone grabbed the hand and said, "Stop, you devil,—why it's Sashka!"[64] the assailant stared and stopped—and smashed the brain of the little dog that was always found in Gambrinus instead. But then Sashka disappeared, nobody knew where; when he returned to Gambrinus, his arm was broken, and the visitors of Gambrinus realized he could not play his fiddle. The story ends with the triumph of art over the force of anti-Semitism and violence, as Sashka takes up a small harmonica and begins to play one of his beloved tunes.[65]

Thus, the violence of the revolution and the pogroms entered Odessa cafés and became enmeshed in modern Jewish culture in the city. These elements play also a major role in Ya'akov Rabinovitz's Hebrew novel *Neve kayits* (A summer retreat, 1934).[66] The plot of the novel takes place in the summer of 1905 between a *fontan*—an Odessa seaside resort— and the city, with its cafés, restaurants, and theaters. It revolves around the life of young Jewish men. All of them are acculturated to Russian culture; some are from bourgeois families, and others belong to revolutionary movements. The tensions between Jews and non-Jews and the threat of anti-Semitism and violence gradually enter their bohemian life. These tensions can be seen, for example, when one of these characters, the highly sensitive Yitzḥak Yonovitz, walks on an Odessa boulevard and sees his friend Volka Wolfman—a man with a "Russian look," who is active in revolutionary circles—sitting in a café eating watermelon together with a security guard and a few other non-Jews. Yitzḥak stops himself from greeting his friend and joining him at the café because he thinks that it is better not to reveal his Jewishness.[67]

The end of the novel comes after several acts of violence against Jews and revolutionaries. At this point, the plot moves from the seaside and the boulevards of central Odessa to the suburb of Moldavanka, which had become infamous for its destitute Jewish residents and for poverty and crime. The narrator describes a humble café, with simple food, that is owned by a Jewish family and frequented by Jews. Yitzḥak and his friends and a Jewish merchant who normally would not be seen around go to this Jewish café and talk about the violent events in Odessa. One of the visitors, an owner of a small hotel, complains that "there is no rest, they destroy the city, the commerce, and everything. And we are Jews."[68] It is unclear if Yitzḥak refers to the revolutionary activists or to the perpetrators of the violent pogrom. But the implication in Rabinovitz's novel is clear: during these turbulent times, Jews of all backgrounds feel more at home and more able to talk about their situation in humble cafés in the Moldavanka or in the Jewish and Zionist self-defense circles than in places such as Cafés Fanconi, Robina, or Libman.

After the devastation of the revolution and the pogroms, Odessa seemed to calm down and return to normal. However, social, religious, ethnic, and especially economic tensions were always simmering just beneath the surface. Odessa became full of anarchist movements, Jewish self-defense groups, and ordinary criminal gangs, with gangster leaders such as the Jewish Mishka Yaponchik. Before the Russian-Jewish writer Isaac Babel wrote his famous "Odessa Stories" in the 1920s and captured these tensions and the contraband activity that took place in the city after 1905, Sholem Aleichem described them in a Yiddish short story, "Dray lukhes" (Three calendars, 1913). The story is a monologue of an unnamed Odessan Jew, a married man with children, who makes a living by selling contraband, namely, smutty "interesting postcards from Paris."[69] The historical context for this monologue, and for the narrator's unusual occupation, is the tenure of Ivan Nikolaevich Tolmachev as a governor of Odessa between 1907 and 1911, which brought some order to the streets of Odessa but was also heavily repressive. Many Jews considered Tolmachev to be not only counterrevolutionary but also anti-Jewish.

The narrator explains that the fact that he sells smutty postcards has something to do with his interaction with Tolmachev before 1905, when "a Jew could roam around as free as a bird" and sell his Jewish books near Café Fanconi, because "you could always run into Jews there, for that was the area where speculators, agents, and various other Jews hung around waiting for a miracle." The narrator tries to sell a few calendars that were left in his stock a few weeks after the High Holidays. Looking at the habitués of Café Fanconi, he realizes that he knows "every single one of them even blindfolded." Then he sees a decorated army general sitting by the front table in the open veranda of the café, accompanied by an assistant, whom he is in the process of sending to his wife at home with an important message. When the general catches a glimpse of the narrator standing in front of him, the narrator asks him in his broken Russian, "Your Excellency, how would you like to buy a calendar?" The general actually buys one from him, apparently to get rid of him.[70]

The narrator, desperate to sell the last calendars in his stock, remembers Tolmachev's home address and goes there, selling another calendar to his young, beautiful wife. After this success, the narrator hurries back to Café Fanconi in an attempt to get rid of the very last calendar. He sees what appears to him to be another army general, but then he realizes that he is "just one of the waiters from Café Fanconi, running with a napkin tucked under his arm and wiping the sweat from his face." When the waiter tells the narrator that the general asks to see him again, he is sure that "his general" likes the Jewish calendar so much that he has sent the waiter to fetch him another one, and he begins to negotiate the price. The story then cuts off abruptly, but we know the end was not good: "We don't dare show our faces on the streets selling a Yiddish or Hebrew book or a paper. We have to hide it inside our coats like contraband or stolen goods. . . . So I have to have a sideline business—'interesting postcards from Paris.'"[71] Sholem Aleichem's satire is directed in this story toward the narrator, a simple Jew, a family man, who tries and fails to adjust to the new times. But the bitingly ironic story is multidirectional. It demonstrates that in the years before World War I, Odessa cafés were the sites of political and economic change and also of tense negotiations. The negotiations in the thirdspace of the café occurred between Jews and gentiles, unwanted migrants and the authorities, the poor and the rich. All of these elements represented different versions of Odessa's cultural identity and of what it meant to be an Odessit in the café.

Middle-Class Respectability, Gender, and Jewish Gangsters

In Sholem Aleichem's "Three Calendars," the poor Jewish man who used to sell Jewish calendars around Café Fanconi turns into a dealer in smutty postcards from Paris; other Jews become swindlers and gangsters in and around Odessa cafés. According to Jarrod Tanny, the years before World War I were critical to the development of the Odessa mythography, as writers, journalists, and other myth makers depicted "the thieves and other deviant characters who shaped and were shaped by Odessa."[72] A good example of this mythography is the work of the Jewish-Russian writer Semyon Yushkevich and especially his three-volume novel *Leon Drei* (1908–1919). The main protagonist, Leon—whose last name derives from the Yiddish word *dreyen*: to spin or to swindle—likes to create an image of himself as a financially and romantically successful person. He is engaged to Bertha, and both of them think about opening a store. Leon is happy to deposit the dowry he received from his future father-in-law. As he leaves the bank, Leon contemplates, "It's time to have a snack! I want to drink a shot of vodka and eat a sandwich with sardines."[73] But then, Leon changes his mind: "He felt that instead of vodka, he would happily drink a good, fragrant cup of coffee with cream, and he directed his steps toward the French Dupont Café. He chose Dupont because this café was considered to be the best in town. Many distinguished citizens gathered here: dealers, bankers, merchants, frivolous music stars, high-society ladies, cardsharpers, and other no less respected and respectable people. Leon had his day schedule planned when he entered the rotunda, where the habitués of the café sat at tiny marble tables."[74]

This is a good example of how Odessa and its cafés became tied, together with the fictional Leon Drei, with swindlers who make appearances in cafés. In the popular and literary imagination, Odessa in the 1910s became a "city of rogues and gangsters," and this depiction was linked to Jewishness and to Jewish culture and to café culture, implicitly or explicitly. As in Prohibition-era Chicago, crime was central to the city's identity. William E. Curtis, a traveler from North America, wrote that Odessa was "one of the most immoral communities in Europe," where the locals are "given to gambling and dissipation of all kinds." He noted the many cafés in Odessa, where "all night the air is filled with music and laughter, and pleasure-seekers turn night into day," and he wondered when the people in the cafés "attend to their business."[75]

The American journalist Sydney Adamson, in his profile of Odessa in 1912, also perceived the cafés as an essential part of the cultural identity of the city and its citizens.[76] He wrote that "everybody in Odessa goes, at some time or other, to Robina['s], or to Fanconi['s] across the way." He noted especially the presence of "ladies," which was a growing phenomenon in the cafés, and of men of "commercial and official monde." His impression of Café Fanconi's "comfortable atmosphere of tea and cakes" reminded him of "Parisian shops in the Place Vendome or Rue de la Paix" and "might even belong to Fifth Avenue" in New York City.[77] Apparently, both gangsters and respectability could exist in Odessa cafés side by side in an elusive and potent harmony.

These impressions of Odessa's famous cafés and their habitués and visitors raise the issue of what the historian Roshanna Sylvester has called "respectability," which was of utmost importance to many journalists and others who attempted to safeguard Odessa's reputation and its public space.[78] Moreover, the comparisons of Odessa and its cafés to other cities, made by visitors and locals alike, seem to be part of an anxiety about Odessa's identity and in particular the notion that Odessa was a pale imitation of other, more "authentic" and much larger urban centers. This anxiety can also be seen in a 1913 guide to the city, in which Grigory Moskvich, who composed a series of guides to cities in the Russian Empire, wrote that the dream of the "essential Odessit" was to "transform himself into an impeccable British gentleman or blue-blooded Viennese aristocrat." Then, "immaculately dressed, with an expensive cigar in his teeth," the Odessit was ready to meet his public. Whether "getting into a carriage or sitting down in one of the better cafés," the Odessit was "out to impress by his appearance, aware of his own worth, looking down on everyone and everything below."[79]

Not only Russian and American travelers to Odessa were worried about the issue of middle-class respectability and paid much attention to life in its urban cafés. Sylvester has analyzed how Odessa's Russian newspapers, especially the progressive *Odesski listok* and the more lurid publication *Odesskaia pochta*, covered the city and its cafés in their feuilletons and stories. Many of the journalists who wrote in these papers were Jewish, and the dominant culture of the city was marked as Jewish because lower-middle-class Jews were "more responsible than any others for giving texture to the Odessan form of modernity."[80] One of the most prolific and popular journalists who covered Odessa's urban scene was the Jewish Iakov Osipovich Sirkis, who used the pseudonym Faust. Faust wrote in *Odesskaia pochta* many feuilletons about the city's social and cultural landscape and claimed that when Odessa infants start to talk, "the first word they pronounce is [Café] Robina! Especially clever ones utter the phrase, Robina and Fanconi!" he proclaimed. The father rejoices, Faust continued, "As I live and breathe, the baby will be a big merchant!"[81]

Another feuilletonist in the same paper, with the name Satana (Satan), expressed similar feelings about the importance of the city's two most prominent cafés: "Every Odessan, regardless of social position, considers it necessary to go to the Robina or Fanconi at least once in their lives," Satana declared, but especially to the Robina. "To live in Odessa and not go to the Robina is like being in Rome and not seeing the pope." In a feuilleton penned by Leri, one of *Odesski listok*'s journalists, in June 1913, the journalist wrote about Odessa's popular cafés: "It is always the way in Odessa. First, the tasteless smoke-filled mansions of Robina, Libman. . . . a cup of coffee, and business conversation; then, an assault and battery, breach of the public peace; then, the bleak chamber of the justice of the peace. And the next day small synopses printed in the newspapers. Such are our ways, a kind of Odessan fun-house mirror."[82]

Café Robina, mentioned in so many of these feuilletons, was founded in the 1890s, across the way from Café Fanconi on Deribasovskaya Street. The two cafés were competitors but also formed a kind of symbiotic relationship, as visitors used to move from one to the other. In the early 1910s, the local newspapers reported that Café Robina became Odessa's most fashionable haunt, a main hub of middle-class social life. Among its denizens were some of the city's most high-profile personalities: politicians, financiers, high-ranking officers, distinguished professionals, and "stars" from the world of entertainment, as well as many journalists and writers, who no doubt made the place more famous and desirable by writing about it. Part of the reason for Café Robina's popularity was that it served so many purposes. Businessmen and politicians came there to work, negotiating deals or conducting meetings over coffee and sweets. Others came in search of work, hoping to strike up profitable acquaintances with successful entrepreneurs, exporters, merchants, or brokers. Many others, including women, came simply to relax, enjoy the company of friends, and catch up on the news of the day.

Odessa's middle-class women were a growing public presence on the streets of the city. They were known to "take tea" in the "ladies' sections"—it is unclear whether these sections were completely segregated or were created more ad hoc with certain tables of the café—that presumably existed in Café Fanconi, Café Robina, and other Odessa cafés. But there was much male anxiety about the growing phenomenon of the modern, independent women sitting in cafés. An *Odesski listok* piece titled "Ladies Chatter" tried to give readers some insight into what these women do in the café and the content of their half-Russian,

Figure 1.2. Postcard of Café Robina, early twentieth century

half-French conversation: "Yesterday evening we intended to go to the
Café Robina. . . . We got in the carriage and arrived—where do you
think—at Ditman's! . . . Imaginez vous! . . . I, of course, was astounded."[83]
It was not only the presence of "unrefined" women in the cafés that worried the journalists and writers. Journalists also reported on the fact that
Café Robina charged astronomical prices for their food and drink in
spite of not-so-perfect sanitary conditions. Odessa's journalists mounted
a critique of the visitors, especially young people who were drawn to
the Robina's "fairy-tale atmosphere." The columnist Faust declared that
when "a bashful youth" wanted to "fix a meeting with a girl," he would
exclaim, "To Robina!" When a "proper" lady wanted to talk with a
"proper" gentleman, she would whisper, "To Robina!"[84]

The journalists in Odessa's local press began to speak about a type:
the Robinist, the habitué of Café Robina. The most typical Robinist was
presumably a young man, son of the middle class, well bred and well
educated, who should have been the pride of polite society but was its
nemesis. According to journalists, Robinisti were always immaculately
dressed, giving every appearance of gentility, but in fact were devious,

cynical men. The journalist Satana pointedly unmasked the young men as social frauds: "Look at them. They have chic visiting cards, collars brilliant and elegant, ties that are something delicious. All signs stamp them as higher gentlemen. But if you probe one, you will find a rogue, a thorough rogue."[85]

Eliezer Steinman, a modernist Hebrew writer who lived in Odessa during much of the 1910s, before he moved to Warsaw's and Tel Aviv's cafés, gets at the gender and socioeconomic hierarchies in Odessa's cafés, as well as their implicit middle-class respectability and Jewishness, in his novel *Esther Ḥayot* (1922).[86] At the center of the novel is Esther, a young, married, Jewish woman from a small town in the Pale of Settlement. Locked in an unhappy married life, she decides one day to leave her home and family and to follow her younger sister, Hanna (Anna Avramova in Russian), to Odessa. In the big city, Esther lives in a room of a hotel and meets various men, who show interest in Esther or in her sister. One of them is the young Russian Adolf Grigorovich, "a native Odessit and the loyal, loving son of the city."[87]

Adolf takes Esther and her sister Hanna for a walk in the boulevards of Odessa, and in no time, they arrive at Café Fanconi. Seen through the eyes of the poor migrant Esther, from whom the author keeps an ironic distance, the café, as the city itself, is a complex thirdspace of appearances and mirrors that needs to be deciphered: "When the doormen opened the doors of the café, it seemed to Esther for a moment that the doors of new life had opened." Esther recognizes that "all the smiles, politeness and gentility were, of course, a matter of transaction, and yet the sham was not too jarring to her heart," for "in the café the deceit was elevated here to the level of truth." Unused to café life, for Esther, "the mundane is transformed and elevated into a holy day." This passage highlights the considerable currency of bourgeois appearance in Odessa and its cafés. Fashionable clothing, traveling in a carriage, shopping at an expensive boutique, and going out to a chic café were part and parcel of the city's "respectable" lifestyle. And yet, as Esther notices, the café was also a place of social transactions: "Surely there was some order here, but the hierarchies were fluid. Each person here was a guest but also owner. Everything was different."[88] As a Jewish woman in Odessa, Esther learns that in the mirror house of the café, the social order can be, to some degree, suspended, though it is unlikely to be completely upended.

The second part of the novel, in which the two sisters, Hanna and Esther, wander through the streets of Odessa, suggests how the fluidity of social order in the café may enable, at least on the imaginary level, an indeterminacy of gender identities and hierarchies. The sisters, having become wary of the men they know, imagine themselves to be "Cavalier" and "Dame": "Let's walk around Deribasovskaya Blvd. without any men; leave them alone. Later we'll walk to Café Fanconi and catch a table. I will smoke a cigarette . . . and invite 'the dame of my heart,' feed her with pastry and chocolate . . . just like a man." As female flâneuses, the two sisters, who imagine themselves as a couple, make their way to Café Fanconi, drink hot chocolate, and read the newspapers, which are full of sensational stories about strange events and adventures in Odessa. But when they leave the café, the potential narrative energy of their imaginative release is immediately restituted when they meet a new man, a medical student, who invites them to his "regular table" in the more fashionable and more "exclusive" Café Robina.[89]

On the one hand, Steinman seems to articulate a critique—very common in the journalistic and literary writings of Odessa in this period—of the "ladies' chatter" that ridicules their attempts to appear "cultured." On the other hand, the femininity and the provincial Jewishness of Esther and her sister, which the narrator never lets the protagonists or the readers forget, also act as a double-edged sword. If the café is chiefly a masculine, bourgeois domain, to which urban men can chivalrously invite their "ladies," it also enables the two sisters to enact a performance of gender that exposes its social conventions. The space of the café becomes, by the 1910s, a site in which the identity of the "New Jewish Woman" is enacted and examined. It is a mirror that reflects and sometime distorts her social, personal, and gender identity, her passions and desires, which are both real and imaginary, public and private.

World War I, Sovietization, and the Cafés of "Good Old Odessa"

When World War I was declared in 1914, Odessa was far away from the major battlefields. There was an attempt by the Ottoman Empire, which joined forces with Germany, to attack Odessa's port, but it was not successful. During the war, the city lay near the geographical intersection of the Russian, Ottoman, and Austro-Hungarian Empires, and business was continually interrupted; but the city itself was unperturbed. Ya'akov Fichman, a Hebrew poet who lived in Odessa during the first years of the 1900s, came back to the city in 1915 and observed that Odessa during the Great War was "calmer and quieter than the day it was established": "The deserted port seemed as if it stretched to the eastern horizon. . . . The city itself was full of life. The cafés were full of people. . . . The War years—I am afraid to say—were the most carefree years in our life."[90]

Even amid the war and during the 1917 revolution and the civil war that erupted in Russia, Odessa did not experience the widespread violence that convulsed much of Ukraine and the Russian Empire more generally. However, the city passed back and forth nine times between Russian "Whites," Ukrainian nationalists, the French, and the Communists. Soviet control was consolidated in 1920. Between 1917 and 1919, it seemed like a Jewish renaissance was about to take place in Soviet Russia; Odessa, which, as we have seen, was always a stronghold of Hebraists, produced 60 percent of all Hebrew books published in Russia. However, the situation changed rapidly. Soon Jewish schools, synagogues, and other religious groups, including nearly all non-Bolshevik cultural institutions, were closed. The Evsektsiya (Jewish section of the Communist Party of the Soviet Union) waged campaigns against persistent ritual customs such as circumcision, as well as against Hebraists. Almost all Hebrew and some Yiddish writers left Odessa in 1921, after Hebrew was declared a "reactionary" Zionist language in the Soviet Union. Many of them found new homes in Berlin, New York, and Tel Aviv.[91]

However, Jewish creativity in Russian and Yiddish did not come to a halt, nor did the world of the Jewish café culture disappear immediately. During these tumultuous years, an extraordinary group of Jewish Odessan writers and cultural figures who wrote in Russian appeared on the horizon. They became, for the first time, a dominant force in the Russian literary and cultural sphere. Many of these young Russian writers, Jews and gentiles, created the *Kollektiv poetov* (Poets' collective), an informal club that met in the cafés, as well as in private apartments. Among its members were Lev Slavin, Eduard Bagritsky, Valentin Kataev, Yuri Olesha, Semyon Gekht, Ilya Ilf, and Evgeny Petrov. The young Isaac Babel, who was associated with the group, boldly declared in his 1916 sketch "Odessa" that "this town has the material conditions needed to nurture, say, a Maupassant talent."[92] Babel and his friends fulfilled the promise. The important Russian critic Victor Shklovsky called this group of writers "the Southwestern School" of Russian literature. Some of them were Jewish by birth and upbringing, and some were not; some lived in Odessa, and others left it for Moscow or St. Petersburg (renamed Petrograd). But they all absorbed a common Odessan atmosphere, which included strong Jewish undertones.[93]

The most prominent articulations of Odessa's café culture during the chaos of war and revolution are found in the writings of Babel, who was doubtless Odessa's most important Russian modernist writer. Babel was born in the Moldavanka in 1894, but soon after his birth, the family moved to the nearby town of Nikolayev. In 1905, they returned to live in the center of Odessa. Much of Babel's writings, including the famous "Odessa Stories," are based on his experience of the city between 1905 and 1915. Babel lovingly evoked the city and its cafés in an Odessan-Jewish style that constantly made use of Yiddish and Hebrew expressions and "types," such as the *luftmensh*, the rabbi, and the good-hearted swindler.[94] Babel wrote about the humor of Odessa that developed in the city's cafés, as well as the characters he saw and met in them—from Benya Krik, the Jewish gangster, to middle-class merchants, aspiring writers, fashionable women, and such people as cross-dressers—who constantly traversed the social and cultural borders.

In 1918, Babel published in Petrograd's newspaper two feuilletons with the title *Listki ob Odesse* (Odessa dispatches), in which he describes Odessa in the period of the 1917 revolution and civil war.[95] In spite of the chaos of these years, and Babel's living away from his city, his feuilletons manage to capture something of Odessa cafés in times of turbulence. In one of the sketches, Babel longs for the speedy revival of the city's port and wishes to see its cafés filled with music again. In another feuilleton, Babel takes his readers, without much of an introduction, directly into an unnamed café, where he introduces S., a "female impersonator," who sits alongside retired Russian cavalry officers content to gamble with Jewish youths, the fat wives of theater owners, and thin cash-register girls. All these people are ultimately bound together by Odessa's Café Paraskeva, one of the Greek cafés in the port that remained open in spite of wars and revolutions. Babel describes the "aroma" of Odessa as a strange one, which can be best noticed in the cafés and in Odessa's newspapers and magazines such as the *Divertissement* (published 1907–1918). "In every issue of *Divertissement*," writes Babel, "there are jokes about Odessa Jews, about Café Fanconi, about brokers taking dance classes and Jewesses riding trams." Babel evokes the Odessan humor, which is tied to the cafés, to the local press, and to its sense of Jewishness. With a sly humor, Babel ends the sketch with the declaration, "Odessa stands strong; she hasn't lost her astonishing knack for assimilating people." As an example of this strength of Odessa, Babel tells us about "a proud, cunning Polish Jew" who comes to Odessa, and "before long we've turned him into a loud, gesticulating fellow who is as quick to flare up or calm down as the best of us."[96]

In the story "The End of the Almshouse" (1932), Babel writes about the days of the famine during the period of the civil war, in a mixture of biting humor and compassion: "In the days of the famine, no one lived better in all Odessa than the almsfolk of the Second Jewish Cemetery. Kofman, the cloth merchant, had built an almshouse for old people by the wall of the cemetery in memory of his wife Isabella, a fact that became the butt of many a joke at Café Fanconi."[97] The joke at Café Fanconi is the foundation of the story, which focuses on a band of elderly poorhouse Jews working in a cemetery amid the general euphoria, confusion, poverty, and wretchedness of the years 1918–1920. The Jews of the almshouse, though, make a pretty good living renting out a single coffin, using it and reusing it for all the funerals.

Babel's most famous Odessan character is the gangster Benya Krik, the self-proclaimed "king of Odessa." Benya Krik was based on the real figure of Mishka Yaponchik (Moisey Volfovich Vinnitsky), who operated mostly in the Moldavanka and whom Babel knew well. As is evident from Babel's play *Sunset* and the screenplay that Babel wrote for the *Benya Krik* silent film, the fictional Jewish gangster used to visit Café Fanconi on a regular basis. In *Sunset*, which takes place in Odessa before the revolution, the conversation in the Krik's household is about Fanconi, which is "packed like a synagogue on Yom Kippur," when everybody is "worrying like crazy. One fellow worries because his business is bad, the next worries because business is good for his neighbor."[98] With a typical Odessan speech, inflected with Yiddish, Benya Krik addressed his fellow city dwellers, speaking like Moses and complaining to God about the conditions of the Jews in Russia.[99]

Leonid Utesov, the Jewish musician from Odessa who invented and popularized "Russian jazz," also knew Mishka Yaponchik, the Jewish gangster, and used to meet him at Café Fanconi. During the time of the civil war, artists from Petrograd, Moscow, Kiev, Kharkov, and other Russian cities came to Odessa because it was one of the few places in which they could still perform. Still, many actors went hungry. And so Utesov and other popular artists decided to help their colleagues by organizing a gala concert with proceeds going to the starving performers. However, ticket sales were sluggish because the public was afraid to walk through the city at night, when Yaponchik's bandits were roaming. So in order for the concert to take place, Utesov met Yaponchik at Café Fanconi and asked him to "not touch anyone" the night of the gala, and "The King" agreed. The posters advertising the event had an unusual postscript: "Free movement through the city until 6 a.m." Odessans apparently understood the implicit text, and the theater was full.[100]

By the 1920s, the period of the post-revolution New Economic Plan, Odessa's fame and the stories about its cafés and Jewish gangsters were spread mostly by people who grew up in the city but had moved elsewhere. Most of the famous Odessan writers and artists of the Soviet period abandoned their beloved city for Moscow or Petrograd, which promised more opportunities, or to other cities around the world.[101] In this period, one after another, the cafés closed their doors, and some of their owners emigrated from the city. Some cafés still operated, but they were converted into clubs for navy sailors or soldiers. Now, the city itself was declared "Old Odessa" and represented as "Odessa Mama." "If you want to feel the soul of old Odessa, which is already dying," a journalist declared in 1924, "visit its old cafés and ancient cemeteries." Semyon Kirsanov wrote about the folk figure of the "Odessa Mama" who has been chased out of the cafés and trampled to death.[102]

In the interwar Soviet period, the most prominent "Odessan" writers and cultural figures—Isaac Babel, Leonid Utesov, Ilya Ilf, Evgeny Petrov, and Lev Slavin—who had experienced the heyday of café culture in Odessa, found ways to remember and commemorate that culture in their writings. They were happy to perpetuate the days of "Old Odessa" and write about the city and its cafés, but they also showed, explicitly or implicitly, the radical changes that were taking place. In Babel's screenplay *Benya Krik*, rewritten for the silent film that was produced in 1927,

Café Fanconi becomes a space identified with the anti-Bolsheviks: "businesswomen with large handbags" and "stockbrokers." The café is also full of invalid veterans, "wounded war heroes" who are victims of "imperialist war." Benya Krik, the Jewish gangster, now has some compassion for the soldiers. However, the real hero of Babel's screenplay (and film) is not Benya but the baker Sobkov, who tries to convince the patrons in Café Fanconi to instigate a proletarian revolution. By the time the film was released in 1927, Fanconi had long been converted into a club for sailors of the Soviet navy, and Odessa's collective past was under Soviet ideological control.

The Jewish gangster of the café of bygone days was still very much alive and well, revived in the character of Ostap Bender, the hero of the great satirical novel *Zolotoy telyonok* (*The Golden Calf*, 1931), written by the duo Ilya Ilf and Evgeny Petrov. In this Soviet masterpiece, they describe Odessa as "Chernomorsk" (literally, "the Black Sea") and Café Fanconi as "Café Florida," which becomes, in the Soviet era, "City Diner No. 68." Ilf and Petrov describe "a crowd of respectable-looking old men, babbling away in front of the covered porch of the City Diner No. 68." These old men are "odd people, preposterous in this day and age. Nearly all of them wore white pique vests and straw boater hats. Some even sported panamas that had darkened with age. And, of course, they all have yellowed starched collars around their hairy chicken necks."[103] Like many other Odessan writers, poets, journalists, and musicians, Ilf and Petrov describe in their 1931 novel a space of absence, filled with the memory of what existed before: "This spot near Diner No. 68, formerly the fabled Florida Café, was the gathering place for the remnants of long-gone commercial Chernomorsk." We are told that in the old days, "these people used to gather" in the café to meet each other and "to cut deals." Now, they come to the same place, compelled by a "long-time habit, combined with a need to exercise their old tongues, that kept bringing them to this sunny street corner. . . . The legend of *porto franco* still shone its golden light on the sunny street corner near the Florida Café."[104]

On the one hand, it is clear that Ilf and Petrov describe in their satiric novel a handful of antiquated and decrepit old-timers who linger lethargically in a place that does not exist anymore. On the other hand, these fictional characters express a genuine longing for an era of Odessa cafés that was still very much alive and well, albeit in their memories and their cultural imagination.

The longing for the cafés of bygone days was expressed, however, with the wit and humor with which the city was associated and with the literary and cultural imagination of so many former Jewish Odessans, a generation of many who were compelled or forced to leave the city and migrate to other cities. It was a generation of migrants who often tried to re-create the richness and vibrancy of Odessa cafés in the various cities to which they migrated, whether in the Soviet Union or elsewhere in Europe and beyond. Odessa's cafés were part of an urban modernity that flourished between the mid-nineteenth and early twentieth centuries and was an essential part of the history and the myth of the city and of the network of diasporic modern Jewish culture. The fact that the poet Leon Feinberg and the painter Yefim Ladyzhensky (figure 1.3) remembered these cafés and made them part of their artistic representation of Odessa, even as late as the 1960s and 1970s, when they lived in America

Figure 1.3. Yefim Ladyzhensky, *Ex Café Fanconi*, from the series "Odessa of My Youth" (Courtesy of Gregory Vinitsky)

or Israel, is a testament to their lasting cultural significance as part of a network of modern Jewish culture.

Most of Odessa's cafés were spaces with a confounding mix of business, pleasure, commodity spectacle, and cultural activities, as well as exchange between different languages, nationalities, and ethnicities. One way or another, Jews were central in Odessa café culture. While many people saw Odessa cafés as both a blessing and a curse, it is hard to imagine modern Jewish culture created in the city in this period without them. Thus, Odessa and its cafés became part of a network of transnational, diasporic Jewish culture. Migrant Jews, both common folks and prominent artists and writers such as Gordin, Smolenskin, Babel, Jabotinsky, Steinman, and Bialik, who moved to other European, American, or Middle Eastern counties, carried the memory of Odessa's cafés to new cities and new cafés.

2

Warsaw

Between Kotik's Café and the Ziemiańska

Sitting in a café like at a cloudlike height,
I could sit like this till evening crawls in.
Beyond the windows the bustling rank-and-file,
Though I don't know and I can't hear,
As silent in my autumnal smile,
By distant gazing rockingly I disappear.
—Julian Tuwim, "Melodia" (1928)

Before the Nazis invaded Warsaw in 1939, the Jewish community of the city, with a population of 375,000, was the largest and most diverse in all of Europe. During the first decades of the twentieth century, Warsaw, the capital of Poland, was a "Jewish metropolis." Like in Odessa but on a larger scale, Jews made up a full one-third of the city's population, and aspects of Jewish culture could be found throughout the city.[1] At that point in time, numerous cafés in Warsaw became part of an interconnected network, the silk road of modern Jewish culture. However, the creation of this "Jewish metropolis" did not happen overnight and was a relatively late phenomenon in the long history of Warsaw. Unlike the new city of Odessa, the history of Warsaw goes back to the fifteenth century. The early days of a small town named Warszawa coincided with the first significant wave of Jewish migration to Poland. Warsaw became the capital of the Polish-Lithuanian Commonwealth in 1569, when King Sigismund III Vasa moved the court from Kraków. At that time, a small number of Jews lived in the city under severe restrictions. Over the centuries, despite a series of expulsions, the Jewish population grew, but Warsaw's Jewish community became large and gained importance only in the nineteenth century. This occurred mainly after the partition of Poland, which was confirmed at the Congress of Vienna in 1815; there,

Warsaw became the capital of "Congress Poland," the truncated state of Poland ruled by the Russian tsar.[2]

Despite this shaky political situation, in the nineteenth century, the city evolved into a major administrative and cultural center, the focus of Polish political and economic life. Its population grew rapidly, from 81,250 in 1816 to 223,000 in 1864, and the number of Jews living in the city rose from 15,600 to 72,800. Jews in Poland were not granted the status of citizenship, and most were still banned from living on certain streets in the center of Warsaw. Nevertheless, during the second half of the nineteenth century, Jewish migration from small towns in Congress Poland and the Pale of Settlement to Warsaw increased. The migrants were mostly traditional Jews—Hasidim and their opponents, the *mitnagdim*—but a growing circle of acculturated Jews and *maskilim* also evolved and made Warsaw an important Jewish center.[3]

Geographically, politically, and culturally, Warsaw is located between eastern and central Europe. Its proximity to the capital cities of Vienna and Berlin, as well as to the cities of the Russian Empire, exerted various influences on the city. Like other European cities in the modern period, the taste for drinking coffee and tea, and for the urban institution of the coffeehouse, developed slowly, parallel to the growth of "Jewish Warsaw." In 1724, the first coffeehouse (*kawiarnia* in Polish) in the kingdom was established in Warsaw by one of King Augustus II's courtiers. It was located within the perimeter of the king's Saxon Palace and the royal garden and was mainly attended by men who were part of the king's court. The next café opened in 1763 in the Market Square and was more accessible to the town's residents. During the end of the eighteenth and early nineteenth centuries, a number of institutions selling coffee, tea, and pastries were established in Warsaw. As in Odessa and in other European cities in this period, they were run mostly by foreigners: Italians, Swiss, French, and Germans.[4]

Throughout the nineteenth century, as the Jewish community in Warsaw grew and matured, so too did spending time in cafés, eating, drinking, and socializing, become more common. Early-nineteenth-century cafés such as Kawiarnia Honoratka, established in 1826, became places of meeting for romantic writers, artists, and musicians such as Frédéric Chopin. They were also the setting for some significant historical and political events, such as the Polish national uprisings against the

Russian Empire in 1830–1831 and 1863–1864.[5] Some activities in these revolts were planned in Warsaw cafés, beyond the watchful eye of tsarist policemen and officials, as when young Polish officers from the local "Army of Congress" revolted against the Russian Empire. As we have seen in Smolenskin's novella about the *maskil* who ran away to Odessa from Warsaw, these officers were soon joined by large segments of Polish society, including some Jews. They not only supported the revolt but also joined the "National Guard" or founded a "Civil Guard." While both uprisings were eventually crushed by the Imperial Russian Army, cafés, as thirdspaces that were open, at least in theory, to everyone, were utilized for organizing and radicalizing by anti-Russian activists.[6]

The presence of Jewish writers and intellectuals in Warsaw cafés became more common and more pronounced in the last decades of the nineteenth century. At the same time, the city was gradually becoming a destination of Jewish migration and a major center of Jewish journalism, literature, and culture in three languages: Polish, Hebrew, and Yiddish. In 1862, Ḥayim Zelig Słonimski, a *maskil* who settled in Warsaw, established and edited the first Hebrew newspaper in Poland, *Ha-tsfirah*, mainly as a way to disseminate articles of popular science to the "Jewish masses." Słonimski was inspired by previous Hebrew papers and journals of *maskilim* in central and eastern Europe. *Ha-tsfirah* matured and developed into a major Hebrew paper in the 1880s, published weekly and then daily. At that point, it competed with *Izraelita*, the first Polish-Jewish weekly journal, established in 1866 by Jewish reformers. It took more time, and the approval of Russian censors, to establish Yiddish weeklies and dailies, but they were created and served as an outlet for aspiring young Yiddish writers as well. Y. L. Peretz, Naḥum Sokolow, and David Frishman, major Hebrew and Yiddish writers and cultural figures, migrated to Warsaw, and they joined the acculturated Jewish writers who were active in Polish. In the last decades of the nineteenth century, a number of Hebrew and Yiddish publishing houses were established in Warsaw, and the city attracted both more Jewish writers and also literary and cultural entrepreneurs, who hoped to find in Warsaw a market for modern Jewish literature.[7]

Around the same time, Warsaw became dotted with many cafés; some attracted writers, journalists, and intellectuals as habitués. One such café was Kawiarnia Udziałowa, established in 1884. It was located in one of the most central points of Warsaw, on the corner of Nowy Świat and Aleje Jerozolimskie. Kawiarnia Udziałowa's waiters were dressed in long, dark-red frock coats, and the café organized concerts and had pool tables, something that was quite common in other European cities as well. But it was also important to the Młoda Polska (Young Poland) literary movement. Among the people who congregated there was Leo Belmont (Leopold Blumental), a Polish-Jewish poet, writer, translator, journalist, and lawyer who wrote for the Polish press and contributed to the weekly *Izraelita*. Belmont was a founder of the Polish Esperanto Society, and he translated extensively into that language and strove to popularize it. Another habitué of Udziałowa was Jerzy Wasercug (Wasowski), the last editor in chief of *Izraelita* before it closed down in 1915.[8]

If cafés such as the Udziałowa attracted Jewish writers and intellectuals who wrote mostly in Polish and aspired to be part of mainstream Polish culture, those who were active in Jewish languages—Hebrew and Yiddish—went primarily, though not exclusively, to cafés that were located in the Jewish quarter. Although Jews at the turn of the twentieth century were not restricted anymore to one area of the city, the center of Jewish Warsaw was in the Muranów and Grzybów areas. This large Jewish district occupied around one-fifth of the municipal area, and its heart was a complex of densely populated streets around Nalewki Street, the commercial main artery of Jewish Warsaw.[9] In this large Jewish district, there was an active street life with markets and peddlers, as well as a number of little cafés; some of them were known as *mleczarnie*—dairy restaurants that served kosher food. These cafés attracted Jews from all walks of life, as well as many writers, intellectuals, and political activists. As we will see, the appearance and the atmosphere of these cafés were very different from Odessa's most famous spots, Cafés Fanconi and Robina.

Cafés in the Nalewki area, as well as in other parts of Warsaw during the last decades of the nineteenth century, became important for the emergence of Jewish literature and culture in fin-de-siècle Warsaw. Dovid Pinski was a Yiddish writer and playwright who migrated to Warsaw in 1892 and was immediately involved in a flurry of literary and cultural projects, which he undertook together with two other new arrivals in Warsaw: the writers Mordkhe Spector and Y. L. Peretz. Peretz, who quickly emerged as the most important Jewish literary and cultural figure, moved to Warsaw from the Polish town of Zamość in 1888. Pinski tells us in his memoir about the time he met with Peretz and Spector in a small café on Nalewki Street sometime in February 1894 and how the three of them first came up with the idea to publish *Yontev bletlekh* (Holiday issues), one of the important Yiddish literary and political publications in this period. In the café, the three men decided to edit and publish the periodical in Warsaw, despite limited funding and the Russian Empire's restriction on such publications. Their plan was to issue the journal irregularly on Jewish holidays, camouflaging its literary and social reformist intentions as "reading material for the holiday."[10] In this case, the café was a place of sociability and exchange, an incubator of transnational Jewish press culture and new literary projects, as well as a site of "clandestine" activity, which was necessary in Congress Poland, given the tight censorship of the Russian tsarist regime.

The plan of Pinski, Peretz, and Spector was one of several that launched publications in Yiddish and Hebrew. In 1891, a few years after the establishment of *Ha-tsfirah* as a daily paper, Avraham Leib Shalkovich—known better by his pen name, Ben Avigdor—moved to Warsaw and began to produce a series of inexpensive and accessible volumes of Hebrew fiction with the name *Sifrei agorah* (Penny books). Ben Avigdor's plan was to sell "thousands and ten thousands books" and to gradually "create a [Jewish] reading public with good literary taste."[11] The number of Hebrew readers in this period never reached such high numbers. Nevertheless, Ben Avigdor and other competitors and collaborators created, in the last decade of the nineteenth century, a Hebrew book market in Warsaw. Ben Avigdor's relative success enabled him to open Tushiyah, the first privately owned, modern Hebrew press, and to be involved in the yearly almanac *Luaḥ aḥiasaf*.

Some of these Hebrew literary and publishing projects took place in cafés in or around the Jewish district, further positioning Warsaw and its cafés as an anchor on the map of modern Jewish culture. This placement can be best seen in a story written by David Frishman, a Hebrew and Yiddish writer, critic, and translator who migrated to the city in the 1880s and was instrumental to the growth of Jewish culture in Warsaw. Frishman's story "Be-veyt ha-redaktsya" (In the editorial house, 1892) gives readers a glimpse into Jewish literary life and the centrality of cafés in them.[12] The first-person narrator begins the story with a scene in a café near the gate of the Saxon Garden—directly next to the Jewish district—owned by an Italian named Skartazini, where Jewish writers and journalists gather daily to talk, smoke, and play chess, with some staying in the café "from morning to evening." The narrator tells us about certain characters in the café known by their nicknames—"the professor," the "Rabbi," and the "accountant," as well as a mysterious man nicknamed "the editor," whom no one really knows and with whom the narrator converses and plays chess occasionally. The narrator's interest in this man grows when he walks to his place on Pańska Street and finds much in common with him, as both are involved in Hebrew literature. When "the editor" invites the narrator to enter his apartment, he finds a weekly Hebrew magazine with the title *Reshut ha-yaḥid* (A private domain), whose sole writer and reader is "the editor" himself. To the narrator's great surprise, he finds that "the editor" has written many Hebrew plays and stories, which remained unpublished. The narrator thinks the editor to be mad but quickly comes to realize that he simply could not find his place in the new "market" of late-nineteenth-century Jewish literature.

Frishman's story presents some of the complexity of Jewish cultural life in Warsaw of the last decades of the nineteenth century. The café in his story is presented as a thirdspace—not just as a place of sociability but as a new institution in Warsaw, intimately related to the emerging Jewish press culture of newspapers and publishing houses that connected the city to a network of modern Jewish culture. At the same time, Frishman's story highlights the fact that the café could also be a space of loneliness, alienation, and eccentricity, in which some of the new active players in the creation of modern Jewish culture in Warsaw could thrive and occasionally also be forsaken.

Litvaks and Polacks, Writers and Revolutionaries

At the turn of the twentieth century, Warsaw's industrial growth stimulated a rapid increase in the city's population, which reached 625,000 in 1897, as well as a substantial increase in the Jewish population, which rose to 210,500 in 1897 and 337,000 in 1914. This resulted not only from natural growth and migration from the small towns of Congress Kingdom but also from the movement of Jews from the Russian Pale of Settlement to Warsaw. The migration was mainly due to secularization and the decline of the economic opportunities in the shtetls. In all, by the outbreak of World War I, around 150,000 Litvaks, as Jews from these areas were called, had moved to Warsaw. Jews played a major role in the burgeoning industries of Warsaw and were particularly dominant in the textile, clothing, and tobacco trades. The years down to 1914 also saw a significant increase in the number of Jews who declared their main language as Polish, as well as the number of Jews in business and in the liberal professions. A major catalyst for the cultural and political renaissance of Jewish Warsaw was the attempted Russian revolution of 1905, which resonated especially in the capital of Congress Poland and its Jewish community.[13]

Cafés with Jewish owners in the Nalewki area became an integral part of Jewish urban culture and served important social, literary, and political roles. Warsaw became a major center of Jewish commerce, which only increased the importance and volume of its newspaper and book publishing. Writers, journalists, and political activists, as well as the growing class of businessmen, gathered around the tables of these cafés. The cold climate of Warsaw, the cramped space in the middle of a commercial center, and the political tensions that characterized Warsaw were all quite different from the situation in Odessa. This difference was reflected in the cafés themselves, which tended to be small, simple, and without much decoration or amenities. The cafés were built inside and were designed to accommodate Warsaw's harsh winter weather. They were sometimes hidden within courtyards, but they were nevertheless teeming with life.

It is not hard to understand why many Jewish writers who came of age in the first decade of the twentieth century—those young people who were born in the 1880s in the small towns of the Pale of Settlement, Congress Poland, and Galicia, whose mother tongue was Yiddish, and who received traditional education that included immersion in Hebrew texts—were engrossed by Warsaw, an emerging metropolis with the largest Jewish population in Europe. It was in the first years of the 1900s that young writers such as Sholem Asch, Avrom Reyzen, Hersh Dovid Nomberg, Y. Ḥ. Brenner, Gershon Shofman, Uri Nissan Gnessin, Hillel Zeitlin, Pinchas Lachower, Zalman Shneour, Ya'akov Fichman, Y. D. Berkowitz, and Ya'akov Shteinberg moved to Warsaw. In this period, Warsaw became the most significant publishing market for literature and journalism in the two Jewish languages, created by bilingual (or tri-lingual) writers, with a readership that extended far and beyond into the rest of Europe and the world.[14] The young people who came to Warsaw aspired to leave behind the traditional, and often despised, occupation of many *maskilim*, that of tutoring the sons or daughters of rich Jew-ish families. Instead, they hoped to find, not always successfully, steady work in Warsaw's literary market as editors or writers in a publishing house, a newspaper, or a journal.

To be sure, just as in Odessa with its "sages," turn-of-the-century Warsaw was also home to esteemed figures with widespread reputations. Some of them established "salons," private spaces in which Jewish writ-ers and intellectuals gathered on a regular basis. The most famous and well attended was located in Peretz's house at 1 Ceglana Street in the Grzybów district.[15] There were also such gatherings in Sokolow's house until 1905 and later also in Zeitlin's house.[16] However, much activity—less restricted, more open and uncontrolled—took place in the many cafés that dotted the Jewish district. This becomes clear in the writings of the figures who arrived in Warsaw in the early years of twentieth cen-tury. Fichman, who moved from Odessa to Warsaw in 1903, remem-bered that he did not know where he would go: "Peretz, Frishman and Sokolow were simultaneously dear to our heart and remote." Fichman was not focused on specific personalities but rather on the city itself, with its intense cultural activity and its "bohemian life": "On the very first day, I met Ya'akov Shteinberg and Zalman Shneour, who like me came from the south, attracted to the boisterous literary center. In a few days, I became a habitué in the tiny and smoky café of Kotik. There we sat with a cup of coffee with Asch and Reyzen. The bohemian life at-tracted all of us to the Polish metropolis."[17]

The existence of cafés and their importance was not just the subjective experience of Fichman but was attested by many others; nor were they only sites of literary exchange. The newly established Hebrew newspaper *Ha-tsofeh* noted, in an article written by the editor A. A. Friedman in 1904, that "the number of cafés in our city has grown at an alarming rate of late." The reason Friedman gave for the rise and popularity of cafés in Jewish Warsaw was "the growing number of people living in our city on their own without their families."[18] These were young single people, who often left their parents and extended family behind in the small town.

As new migrants to the big city, they found a home in such places as the "Zionist café" on Dzielna Street, Glotser's café on Dzika Street, and Sholem's café on Gęsia Street, all in the crowded Jewish district. As Scott Ury has claimed in his study of the transformation of Warsaw Jewry in the period leading to and around the aborted 1905 revolution, cafés were sites of intense cultural and political exchange.[19] These cafés were vital thirdspaces that fostered debate and the exchange of ideas and were crucial in making Warsaw part of a network of transnational Jewish culture during these stormy years.

The activist Abraham Teitelbaum remembered how he became radicalized and intoxicated with revolutionary politics in Sholem's café:

> Our secret group used to gather for enlightenment, education, conversations and lessons in Sholem's café on 29 Gęsia St. . . . One ascended a few steps to enter the not too big room with tables, which were always packed with young men and women, who would lose their temper and discuss, laugh and be loudly angry. The place always smelled of coffee with cheesecake. The same was also in the further smaller rooms. But the very last room was given to our group, when we used to . . . listen to the talks of our leader, comrade Lampert, or to the leaders of other groups that would come to us.[20]

Sholem's café—built of multiple, and ever-smaller, rooms and similar to other cafés in the Nalewki area of this period—was later depicted in Sholem Asch's Yiddish novel *Varshe* (Warsaw, 1929). In the novel, the café is the center of the Jewish socialist party, where the members of the "Central Committee," who keep their identity hidden at any price, meet inside the kitchen of the bustling café. In this café, the protagonist of the novel, Zachary Mirkin, the alienated son of a Russian-Jewish industrialist, has been recruited to socialist circles. This was accomplished with the thought that he could help by preying on the stronghold of "capitalist" industry in Łódź, using his family connections.[21]

Reyzen, who lived in Warsaw between 1900 and 1911, before migrating to New York City, remembered another place in the Jewish district of the city as an important space of politics and culture: "the Zionist café" on Dzielna Street. This café, which was owned by a man known simply as "the quiet Jew," was, like Sholem's café, "hidden deep in a courtyard, on the first floor." According to Reyzen, it was good that this "Zionist café"—which, despite its nickname, nevertheless attracted socialist revolutionaries who were not part of the Zionist movement, like Reyzen himself—was hidden because "voices and screams could always be heard from there." Reyzen wrote that in a café facing the street, it would certainly be impossible to conduct "the warring arguments so freely and undisturbed," since "people who pass by would interrupt because of curiosity, or the police would have to get involved."[22] Reyzen also wrote about Glotser's café on 45 Dzika Street, a place that attracted mostly *maskilim* and Hebrew tutors and teachers. Among the teachers there were some young Hebrew writers who belonged to the literary movement ushered in by Ben Avigdor, the editor and publisher. According to Reyzen, the owner, Mr. Glotser, was a *maskil* and "could not bear to see how one of the young Hebrew teachers and writers 'wickedly' tore off the crowns of the 'old' *maskilim* writers." Thus, Reyzen claimed, in Glotser's café, the poetic war between old and new in Hebrew literature took place, with people such as the bilingual Hebrew-Yiddish writer Hersh Dovid Nomberg leading the call for modernist literature in the two languages.[23]

The most important and famous Jewish café during the first decade of the twentieth century was Kotik's café. It was located at the very heart of Jewish Warsaw, in a courtyard on 31 Nalewki Street. Established by the activist Yehezkel (Khatskl) Kotik in the 1890s, the café quickly became a regular meeting point for Jewish writers, intellectuals, and activists from a variety of political and ideological backgrounds.[24] The Yiddish journalist and folklorist A. Litvin (Shmuel Leib Hurwitz) wrote that in the early 1900s, "[Kotik's] café was the most remarkable Jewish café in the entire world."[25]

The Jewish publisher Shlomo Shrebrek, who came to Warsaw from Vilna, confirmed in his memoirs that during these years, much of the literary activity of the young writers was done in Kotik's: "During this time, Reyzen and Nomberg were active, and around them was a happy gang in the café; they started to create a new culture in Yiddish."[26] In Kotik's café, writes Shrebrek, "people always read new stories and poems before they were published." Shrebrek's description highlights the experience of the café: in its cramped and smoky space, "everybody took off their mundane clothes and donned literary and artistic attire." Yet Kotik's café was not only a place for writers. Shrebrek writes that many visitors were actually "modest businessmen, mediators and agents, clerks and sometimes the occasional teacher." Apart from the fact that it was inexpensive, the attraction of Kotik's café was the existence of free newspapers in various languages. Because papers were readily available, "people would sit there for hours and hours; they would read the paper, get to know one another, and converse." Even those who met there for the first time, claimed Shrebrek, "would speak to each other like old friends, . . . about new literary works, recent newspaper articles, and the lives of the writers themselves, . . . about Zionism, local and general affairs."[27]

Litvin remembered how when he first came to Kotik's café, the owner gave him a Yiddish pamphlet he had written. When Kotik learned that Litvin could read Hebrew, he gave him a pamphlet written in Hebrew as well. According to Litvin, Kotik had an uncanny sense of his customers, and he knew which reading materials he should give to whom.[28] Reyzen also remembered that Kotik's café was frequented by "salespeople and clerks, budding writers and Hebrew teachers, Zionists and Bundists, PPS [Polish Socialist Party] members and the unaffiliated. This mixture of habitués naturally sparked off debates."[29] According to Reyzen, Mrs. Kotik, who ran the operation together with her husband, did not enjoy the arguments and angrily rushed to hush the contestants, fearful that the noise would draw unwanted attention from the police. Kotik sometimes neglected the business of the café, devoting himself instead to the publication of his pamphlets at his own expense.[30]

Litvin claimed that Kotik's café was especially important for Litvaks such as Kotik himself, that is, for the Jews who relocated from small towns in Lithuania and the Pale of Settlement to the big city. The majority of the Hebrew and Yiddish writers in Warsaw were Litvaks, who had to adjust to life in the Polish metropolis. Litvin, like many others, took notice of the fact that Kotik was not merely a café owner but a devoted member of the community, forming mutual aid societies for the needy migrants who felt lost in Warsaw. Kotik, writes Litvin, could have used his personal connections and become a successful merchant, but instead he opened a café. Although he did not enjoy great profits, Litvin commented, neither did he run up large expenditures: "and there was food there at least, and he would thus not die of starvation."[31] There was a telephone in the café—a rare commodity in early-twentieth-century Warsaw—utilized by Kotik in the service of the public matters in which he took an interest. Kotik's organizational activity revolved around his café. He published communal and political brochures, distributed for free to all those who frequented his café. Reyzen claimed that Kotik took pride in these publications and engaged in preaching the same principles of proper moral behavior about which he wrote.

Kotik's café appeared, by its name or otherwise, in literary texts as well. One notable example is a text by Sholem Aleichem, who visited Warsaw many times in the first decade of the twentieth century and became friends with Kotik.[32] Sholem Aleichem transferred his antihero Menakhem-Mendl from Odessa and Kiev to Warsaw in the last series of letters to his wife, Sheyne-Sheyndl, which was serialized in the Yiddish newspaper *Haynt* in 1913.[33] Now Menakhem-Mendl was not an aspiring stock-exchange merchant but was employed as a journalist, writing on current events and Jewish and international politics. As soon as Menakhem-Mendl finds work as a journalist, he looks for a café in which he can "enjoy a coffee with a friend, along with everything else which a human being requires." Not surprisingly, Menakhem-Mendl's first stop is Kotik's: "I take my walking stick and go to my café to drink coffee and to chat with people. My café is on Nalewki, Kotik's place. Why Khatskl Kotik's place, you ask? To spite the Polacks [the Polish Jews]!" According to Menakhem-Mendl's letter, some Poles decided to boycott Jewish businesses such as Kotik's café, and while some "assimilated" Polish Jews avoided these places, he and other Litvaks went to Kotik's place as an act of resistance. "We sit and sit, Khatskl Kotik and me, over a cup of coffee and discuss our Jewish brethren."[34] The conversations between Menakhem-Mendl and Kotik, which always take place in the café, range from politics and wars to imaginary "projects" and "schemes" suggested by Menakhem-Mendl. Despite the fact that Sholem Aleichem was not a Warsaw resident, the letters of his Menakhem-Mendl about Kotik's café give us a good glimpse into the conversations and movements that took place in this urban space during the first decade of the twentieth century and its importance to the creation of transnational modern Jewish culture.

Gender, Class, Sociability, and Loneliness in the Café

Looking at Kotik's political undertakings around his café and some of the writings about it, it is tempting to describe the café as a remarkable example of "a Jewish public sphere." While this is true to some extent, Kotik's café should also be understood as a thirdspace. It did function as a space in which individuals from a variety of political and intellectual camps could gather to debate and create the affairs of the day, but this does not mean that Kotik's café and others like it were truly open to all or free of economic, social, and cultural tensions.[35] Sholem Aleichem's Menakhem-Mendl alluded to some of these tensions when he wrote about boycotts of some Jewish cafés, but we can see other conflicts when we read both the fictional stories and some of the memoirs written by other Hebrew and Yiddish writers. One of the tensions had to do with gender and with the presence of women, which is especially vivid in one of Sholem Asch's early short stories.

When Asch arrived in Warsaw in 1900, he wrote and published in both Hebrew and Yiddish. The Hebrew story "Mi-ḥaye ha-yehudim be polin-rusya" (From the life of Jews in Russia-Poland, 1901) takes place mostly in Warsaw, recounting the travails of Neta Woolf, who turns to God in search of relief from financial hardships and familial problems.[36] Reb Neta's young and beloved daughter, Rokhele, is a modern Jewish woman, educated and independent in spirit. With knowledge of Yiddish, Russian, and Polish, she relocates to Warsaw and finds work in a local café on Twarda Street, and tensions quickly arise. Women were often employed as café waitresses in Warsaw, and as a server in such a café, Rokhele is exposed to the lusting eyes of the young, single, Jewish men, the habitués of the café who gather around its tables and chat in a mixture of Yiddish, Polish, and German. Rokhele's father, who comes every evening to visit the café alone, is pained to see his daughter as the target of so much sexual attention. The short story reaches its open-ended conclusion with this double perspective—that of the older father and the young daughter—who view the same events in different ways. However, both the father and the daughter cannot participate in the conversation and the exchange that takes place in the café: Reb Neta because of his age and traditional background and the fact that the café is the realm of young Jewish men; Rokhele because of her gender and the fact that the café is very much a masculine homosocial space, in which women such as Rokhele can only be an object of men's gazes and desires.

The gender aspect of the Warsaw Jewish cafés can also be seen in an impressionistic Yiddish story by Lamed Shapiro, who lived and worked in Warsaw in the first decade of the twentieth century, before he migrated to New York City. Shapiro's story "Berte" ("Bertha," 1906) takes place in a "Litvak café" in Warsaw. Bertha is a young waitress who catches the attention of Mr. Riegel, a habitué of the café. Bertha is described by Shapiro's narrator as someone with an "almost childish figure that was slender yet very well proportioned, small dainty hands, and a slim, finely chiseled face."[37] Riegel is attracted to Bertha "on his very first visit to the café" and was "haunted ever since by her soft voice, her way of talking, . . . and especially her smile."[38] Riegel, who comes daily to the café, becomes more and more smitten with Bertha, and eventually, she seems to him a mystery to be deciphered: "Her smile vexed him. . . . It appeared to him unnatural, even distasteful." He does not know whether she is "a beautiful, modest Jewish maiden, or a courtesan with a certain chic." This ambiguity about Bertha drives him crazy: "I must find the truth once and for all. I will put her to the test." At the end of the story, Riegel does indeed "put her to the test"—by seizing her hand and arms—but it comes too late, after he finds out that she is engaged to a young Jewish man who works in a Łódź clothing store.[39] Shapiro's story highlights the place of young women in Warsaw's Jewish cafés. These cafés were spaces of homosociality and at the same time fueled sexual desire and tensions. As a server who did not participate in social and cultural masculine exchange, a woman was often an object of male desire and could easily be seen as a sexually available courtesan.

Sometimes, however, the young women who served as waitresses in Warsaw cafés provided the male protagonists with a sense of comfort, which many of the male figures in the café required badly as strangers in the big city. In Eliezer Steinman's Hebrew novel *Seḥor seḥor* (Around and around, 1917–1918) the protagonist, the writer Shalit, puts on his clothes and makes his way to a café on Nalewki Street, where a blond waitress serves him a cup of tea with a graceful smile:

At once, like a bolt of lightning, joy overcame Shalit, and he felt his entire body intoxicated. The cup of bitterness of yesterday, which was awaiting him when he woke up, was now gone. The dark mask that covered his face since he settled down in Warsaw suddenly dissolved like breaking cobwebs, and he could not understand in any way the nature of the élan, the spleen that took hold of him like a pincer. The sense of melancholy moved away from him, and he called the waitress softly as a sister, and all the other café habitués were like his brothers. . . . Shalit left the café into the street, and everybody walked toward him in pairs or groups, and he saw himself as a member of a densely populated family.[40]

Other literary texts that take place in Warsaw cafés of this period emphasize the economic difficulties of living in the metropolis. Although these cafés were very different from the spectacle of commodities and respectability that were typical of Odessa's more upscale cafés, they still highlighted the gaps between those who could afford to pay for them and those who could not. This disparity can be seen in a feuilleton by the Hebrew and Yiddish writer Zalman Shneour, who arrived in Warsaw in 1902: "Beit ha-kahava shel ha-sofrim, Grontzel" (The writers' café, Grontzel, 1903). The story tells us about a certain café, in which "many writers visit each evening, conversing and arguing among themselves."[41] According to the narrator, this café is especially smoky and steamy, similar in appearance and ambiance to a *shvitz*—a traditional Jewish steam bath, very common in eastern European towns—in which men used to gather before Shabbat to sweat and to chat. The comparison of the café to the site of male social life, familiar from much of Jewish literature in eastern Europe, is evocative but hardly surprising. However, the narrator focuses on the fact that some of the writers who frequent the café can afford the price of admission to this modern *shvitz* by buying a cup of coffee or tea and something to eat, but other writers, or aspiring writers, must resort to *shnorring*—to borrowing a few pennies in order to stay in the café and not to raise the wrath of the owner. Whenever an unfamiliar person appears in the café, the habitués investigate his "talent," code for his ability to pay. The narrator himself gains such a reputation and thus is asked for loans, especially by a man known as Grontzel, who came to Warsaw from a small town in the Russian province of Podolia. The reality that Shneour's sketch reveals is one of poor, hungry young Jewish men, hoping to make money by teaching and publishing, finding refuge in the café with the reluctant support of more successful writers.[42]

Even more poignant is Reyzen's Yiddish story "Fermashkent zikh aleyn" (To pawn yourself, 1905). This dark story is told through the point of view of Velvl Klinger, a young, single, and penniless Jewish teacher who shares a cold apartment in Warsaw with two other teachers like him. He dreams about being a poet but has been unable to publish any of his poems in the Warsaw press. One sunny morning in the early spring, he walks around the streets of Warsaw hungry and thirsty, and then he passes by "the famous café," where "teachers, poets, critics, and readers he knew could be found whenever they had a few *groshn* [pennies] in their pockets."[43] Velvl goes in the café, but he cannot find any friends to borrow money from. He knows he must order something to quiet his gnawing hunger and to avoid the suspicion of the young waitress. The café gradually becomes for Velvl a self-imposed prison, where he feels as if he "pawns his own body and soul." Even the ending of the story, in which someone finally lends Velvl twenty kopeks, does not bring real relief to the anxious protagonist. The Warsaw café in this story is not a place of gathering and exchange but a claustrophobic space of desperation, alienation, loneliness, and the miserable economic condition of a young, educated Jewish man who cannot find an anchor in the city. The female waitress and the unfamiliar visitors are dreaded because they cannot provide the protagonist any help.

The ethnic, sexual, and socioeconomic tensions and conflicts around Warsaw cafés, which are so pronounced in the stories of the writers who presumably were their most faithful habitués, find echoes in a memoir written by Ephraim Kaganowski, one of the very few Yiddish writers born and raised in Warsaw. He told about an incident involving Sholem Asch, when he had started to rise in fame in Poland and abroad and became a well-paid writer. At that point, Asch, Nomberg, and Reyzen sat in Kotik's café, and Asch took out a hundred-ruble note, which provoked much excitement. According to Kaganowski, everyone in the café inspected the note. Reyzen said that he saw such a large sum of money for the first time in his life, while Kotik did not even have enough to give change for such a large note.[44]

Kaganowski also wrote about the significant changes that happened in Jewish Warsaw during the years after 1905. "The Jewish sons and daughters who wanted to merge with the Polish world," he claimed, "unwillingly joined the streaming march to a new realm, which was only steps away from the Nalewki area."[45] According to Kaganowski, the young Yiddish and Hebrew writers discovered that on the main streets of the city, one could see the Polish writers and artists, whom they secretly admired: "One can see them as living people in a café, at a table in Marszałkowska Street."[46] Kaganowski remembered that another young Yiddish writer and journalist, Moyshe-Yosef Dikshteyn, known to everybody by the pseudonym Kawa ("Coffee" in Polish and many languages), discovered one day that "in the big, bright Café Ostrowski, on the corner of Marszałkowska and Złota, Nomberg and Reyzen, and sometimes Asch, sit at a table every evening, and even the revered Y. L. Peretz likes to go there from time to time." And at this, remarked Kaganowski, "the big divide between the young and the known and recognized arose again."[47] The fact that Jewish writers and intellectuals during the years leading to World War I went to Café Ostrowski was also noted by A. Litvin. In 1914, he wrote, "Today there are Jewish literati, for whom it is beneath their dignity to drink coffee at Kotik's. They find their way to the refined cafés 'Bristol' and 'Ostrowski.'"[48]

The lure of the Polish cafés to Jewish literati in this period might explain one of Menakhem-Mendl's more enigmatic letters, written in 1913. Menakhem-Mendl writes to his wife, "Our writers, they write and write and in the end they take themselves to a Polish café to drink tea, in spite of the people who look at them as if they were dogs eating *shalakh manos* [a traditional gift that one sends on Purim]." He claimed to have

Figure 2.1. Postcard of Café Ostrowski

pleaded with them, " 'Brothers, how is it possible to do such a thing? It's a shame, an embarrassment before the whole world! . . .' They said: 'What can we do that there is no choice? There's no proper Jewish café in Warsaw.' " When Menakhem-Mendl heard this pronouncement, he immediately came up with a new scheme:

> "If there isn't one, we should see to it that there is one." They said, "You are a man with schemes, Menakhem-Mendl himself, why don't you come up with a scheme for one?" And I said: "Give me one week." . . . So off I went and planned a project . . . of a Jewish café [financed] by stocks. The café will be for writers and also for nonwriters, and there one could get not only a cup of coffee, tea, chocolate, bread with butter, and so forth but also at cost food and drink, a glass of beer, cigarettes, a hat if you need it. . . . With the profit left after the stockholders' dividends, we could support all the Jewish writers in Warsaw."[49]

Always attuned to Jewish urban modernity, Sholem Aleichem gives us, through the seemingly outrageous plans of Menakhem-Mendl, a good rundown of the various tensions in Jewish café life. He also points at the exact moment when Yiddish and Hebrew writers would venture into Polish cafés because they wanted to move beyond the confines of the Jewish quarter and shed their association with the impoverished Jewish community and cafés such as Kotik's. As we shall see, Sholem Aleichem also gave an almost prophetic glimpse of what was to come next in Warsaw Jewish cultural life and its cafés in the interwar period.

"This Is How Jewish Culture Is Created": The Writers' Club in Tłomackie 13

The outbreak of World War I brought a deterioration of the economic and political position of Warsaw Jews. Both the tsarist authorities and the Polish nationalists saw Jews as supporting the German war effort. It is not surprising that many welcomed the defeats of the Imperial Russian Army in the spring of 1915 and the brief German rule during the war years. After the war, on November 1918, Warsaw became the capital of an independent Polish state freed from Russian rule. A large civil service now made its home in the city, and Warsaw was the focus of the country's political and cultural life. After the Bolshevik revolution, as some forms of Jewish culture in Soviet Russia were suppressed, Warsaw's importance for the cultivation of Jewish cultural life increased even more. At the same time, the migration out of eastern Europe to such cities as New York, Berlin, and Tel Aviv attracted many figures central to Jewish culture. The migration to and from Warsaw during the early 1920s, in addition to sharpening of political, ideological, and literary alliances, created a dynamic but also very tense atmosphere in the city. The young Yiddish writer Isaac Bashevis Singer, who settled in Warsaw in 1923, wrote that "the Zionist, socialist, and communist movements snatched most of the young people. Organizations, clubs, and libraries sprouted like mushrooms after a rain. Jewish Poland, in these first years after the war, experienced a spiritual revolution."[50]

In terms of urban space, the heart of Jewish Warsaw still revolved around Nalewki and the nearby Grzybów district, but Jews could now be found in significant numbers throughout the city. The interwar period ushered in a cultural and political struggle over the nature of the newly independent Polish state, as well as over what it meant to be Polish and Jewish. Increasing numbers of educated and acculturated Jews used Polish as their primary language of communication, and some of them became highly prominent in Polish literary and cultural life. At the same time, Polish nationalism and anti-Semitism became stronger and more vocal. A large part of Warsaw Jewry strongly identified with Jewish nationalism, religious orthodoxy, socialism, communism, and "folkism." Literary and cultural movements also became highly politicized, and the choice to write in Yiddish, Polish, or Hebrew was more aligned along political lines.

These deep divisions within Jewish culture, as well as some points of contact between different people and groups, were centered in this period around several cafés. The interwar period was, in fact, the golden age of café culture in Warsaw, and Jews were absolutely central to this culture. But the deep divisions made particular cafés strongholds of certain figures, who became their habitués, but were almost a forbidden zone to others. Establishments in the center of Warsaw, such as Pod Picadorem, IPS (Instytut Propagandy Sztuki: "Institute of Art Propaganda"), and especially Café Ziemiańska, were associated with Polish modernist movements of poetry and literature, as well as with Polish cabaret, hugely popular in this period. Some of the most famous habitués, Julian Tuwim, Antoni Słonimski, Marian Hemar, and Aleksander Wat, were writers of Jewish origin. On the other hand, the robust interwar Yiddish cultural life and the more feeble Hebrew life were focused around the Farayn fun yidishe literatn un zhurnalistn (Association of Jewish writers and journalists) in Tłomackie 13, which was close to both the Nalewki and Grzybów districts and next door to one of Warsaw's largest synagogues.[51]

For twenty years between 1918 and 1938, Tłomackie 13 was the address of the association. On the map of Jewish literature and culture during the interwar period, Tłomackie 13 was one of the most important locations. The association was established on March 24, 1916, shortly after Y. L. Peretz's death in 1915, and was meant to preserve his legacy, as well as to unite and support Yiddish and Jewish writers in Poland. This effort seemed to echo Menakhem-Mendl's 1913 fictional "scheme" to open such a café for all Jewish writers that would also provide them financial support and protection. To some extent, Menakhem-Mendl's plan was implemented in Tłomackie 13.[52] When activities in Tłomackie 13 began to take place, it served as the address not just of a professional association but of literary and cultural movements that attracted many people. There were drinks, coffee, and simple food on the premises. A number of rooms were furnished with tables and chairs, works of art, and many newspapers, as well as chess and other games and a gramophone with music. The premises functioned as a social meeting place not only for members (i.e., journalists and writers) but also for actors, artists, teachers, guests from abroad, and others who were interested in Jewish culture. In addition, the association offered a large variety of literary readings and parties both for its members and for the general public.[53]

As we have seen, in the years prior to World War I, many young Jewish writers and journalists were attracted to the cafés in the center of Warsaw, away from the Jewish district. After the war, the attraction did not stop. However, for a variety of reasons, including the fact that the most prominent Polish cafés in interwar Warsaw were associated with "assimilated" or even "converted" Jews, Tłomackie 13 came to fulfill the function of a "literary café." This happened despite the fact that it was not a privately owned business. This was something that became evident to many people who knew the place, spent much time there, and wrote about it. Thus, Eliyahu Shulman wrote that "Tłomackie 13 was a real literary café, a literary gathering place in the European manner, . . . the nerve center of Jewish literature and life."[54] Photographs of Tłomackie 13 in the Yiddish press also depict it as a renowned literary café, or *kibitzernya*, a Yiddish term that was brought to Warsaw from New York City's cafés (figure 2.2).

Isaac Bashevis Singer, who as a young man made his first foray into Yiddish literature in Tłomackie 13, called the place "Der shrayber klub" (the writers' club), which was the title of his first autobiographical novel, serialized in 1956.[55] Bashevis Singer claimed that "the entire modern Polish Jewry gathered in the writers' club," which was also a second home for him and for many others like him.[56] He described the first time he went into Tłomackie 13 in 1923 as a young aspiring writer, following the

Figure 2.2. Photograph of Tłomackie 13, published in *Illustrirte vokh* (Warsaw), August 17, 1928

footsteps of his older brother, Israel Joshua. He was in awe of the revered figures, about whom he had heard and read so much before:

> Before I opened the door . . . I tried for some time to summon courage. Why am I trembling like this?—I asked myself—after all they are only flesh and blood. . . . They also don't live forever. . . . I opened the door, and I saw a hall. Opposite, on the other side of the hall, there was a buffet, like in a restaurant. The writers sat by the tables. Some of them ate, others played chess, and some chatted. All of them seemed terribly important to me, full of wisdom and higher knowledge of the kind that elevates man above worldly troubles. . . . I expected someone to ask me who I am, what do I want, but no one approached me. I stood there with wide-open mouth.[57]

Bashevis Singer's retrospective look at Tłomackie 13 beautifully captures his perception of the place as a "literary café," a place of lofty cultural aspirations, which was nevertheless a space of "flesh and blood," where people not only wrote, conversed, and debated but also ate, drank, chatted, played games, and gossiped. He also compared, with a mixture of wit and reverence, the space of Tłomackie 13 to a Hasidic synagogue. When Hasidim, he wrote, wanted to have a synagogue of their own, they rented a room and installed shelves full of books, an ark filled with scrolls of Torah, a table, and a few benches. When writers, journalists, and activists wanted to create a space of modern secular Jewish culture, they did the same: they rented a hall and put in some tables and a kitchen, and everything needed was there, as long as people showed up.

Food and drink were central to the place. According to Kaganowski, the owner of the kitchen that served the simple meals, coffee, and tea in Tłomackie 13 was a waiter in one of the city's many cafés prior to World War I. He was known to everyone as Max, and he ran a café that catered to the "aristocracy of the Jewish underworld." After an accident and a heart attack, Max could no longer serve these "big guests," but he wanted to re-create that café feeling in Tłomackie 13, together with his wife, who cooked the food. He never understood, according to Kaganowski, what kind of a place it was and what all those people were doing in such a place, a mixture of café, restaurant, lecture hall, and a space for other activities.[58]

The vexing mixture of cultural activities, both "high" and "low," is evident also in a caricature published in the Yiddish press, with the title *Oyfn Olimp* (On the Olympus; figure 2.3). The cartoon describes revered luminaries—Jewish and non-Jewish, from the ancient and from the recent past—looking from heaven above at Tłomackie 13 below, where there is music and dancing. The caption describes Y. L. Peretz asking, "What kind of literature is it?" Sholem Aleichem, who presumably knows better about such matters, answers, "This is how 'Jewish Culture' is created." The cartoon captured Tłomackie 13 as a space of sociability, with food and drink and people listening to music and dancing but also at the heart of poetic revolutions and literature.

Many of the younger writers who migrated to Warsaw in the years after World War I were not happy with the state of Yiddish literature and sought a change. The modernist Yiddish poets, writers, and artists Melech Ravich, Uri Tzvi Greenberg, Peretz Markish, and Israel Joshua Singer (Isaac's older brother) used Tłomackie 13 as a platform to launch their new, revolutionary style of Yiddish literature. They articulated their poetics, as well as their frustration over the attitude of the older Yiddish literary establishment toward them, and established modernist groups and small magazines such as *Khaliyastre* (Gang), which brought the expressionist mode into Yiddish literature.

Stormy debates over the current and future character of modern Yiddish literature took place in Tłomackie 13. Isaac Bashevis Singer called Tłomackie 13 "the temple of Yiddish literature" and "the bourse," the stock exchange of Yiddish literature in Poland.[59] This was not a place like Café Fanconi in Odessa, where presumably business activity also took place, but a place of literary and cultural "business." Thus, writes Bashevis Singer, it was "always filled with young talents who came from every corner of the country . . . with the will to make a revolution in literature. They strolled in provincial fur coats and boots. In the little magazines they published . . . they used a difficult archaic Yiddish, thickened with provincialism."[60] The poet Melech Ravitch, who moved to Warsaw in 1921 from Vienna, remembered how lively and full of contradictions this thirdspace was. In the same building of Tłomackie 13, he wrote, the office of the youth movement of Mizrahi (Orthodox Zionist Jewry) was also located.[61] The wide stairs of the building were full of Jews in traditional garb and visitors who came to Tłomackie 13. Every evening, music

Figure 2.3. Yiddish caricature depicting Tłomackie 13 as a literary café, published in Ber Isaac Rozen, *Tlomatske 13* (Buenos Aires: Tsentral-Farband fun poylishe yidn in Argenṭine, 1950)

was pouring down from the building, mixing with the hustle and bustle of carts, the shops, the buses, and trams. Inside this noisy atmosphere, the space was used as a social meeting place and as a club for debates that sometimes reached a fever pitch.

Tłomackie 13 was the gathering place for writers, poets, and journalists from different shades of the Jewish political spectrum, and somehow the space accepted them all. Ravitch wrote that there were four to five hundred members of the professional association, who were paying dues, but the place was always full of people, whether they were members or not, whether they paid or not.[62] Zusman Segalovitsh remembered the place as the *bude* (den). "Without it," he wrote, "we could not live. Its door was always open. We felt free there."[63] Kadya Molodowsky was one of the very few women who, while teaching children in Jewish schools in Warsaw, made a name for herself as a Yiddish writer and journalist. She used to visit Tłomackie 13 but felt marginal in what was experienced as mostly a homosocial, masculine space. In her memoir of Warsaw in the 1920s, Molodowsky wrote that from her perspective, "it was always dark" in Tłomackie 13. There was, she wrote, "a medley of different 'institutions' in one place. By day, there was a café-restaurant. . . . People would eat, talk, and some played chess." However, it was difficult for Molodowski to understand "how Yiddish writers could sit over chess boards with furrowed brows . . . when there was so much poverty [in Jewish Warsaw]."[64] Molodowsky made it clear that Tłomackie 13 might have fulfilled the role of café, but it was hard for her to find a place there as a woman writer who was mostly concerned about children and the poverty and desperation of Jewish life in interwar Warsaw.

Ephraim Kaganowski wrote that Tłomackie 13 became a professional institution only for the newspaper guild, and writers of poetry and fiction were merely "tolerated" there. He claimed that the publishers of the daily newspapers opened the door for the "unfortunate writers, who nevertheless gave the place a particular charm."[65] Kaganowski might have been correct about the real source of money and power within Tłomackie 13. However, the place was also significant to the development of all highbrow Yiddish literature. The best example of this development was *Literarishe bleter* (Literary pages, 1924–1939); the most important literary and cultural Yiddish weekly journal in interwar Poland and around the world was located, physically and symbolically, within the walls of Tłomackie 13. Initially, Ravitch, Markish, I. J. Singer, and Nakhmen Mayzl edited and published the new periodical at their own expense. Later it was part of the Boris Kletskin publishing house, and Mayzl became its editor in chief. *Literarishe bleter* was highly influenced by a similar Warsaw literary magazine, *Wiadomości literackie* (Literary news), which was published in exactly the same years, between 1924 and 1939, and was the most important journal of Polish literature and culture in the interwar period. Mayzl wrote in his memoir, "We read *Wiadomości literackie* with great enthusiasm; we were impressed by its large canvas, and we were jealous."[66]

Mayzl and his friends, who closely followed the developments in Polish literature and culture, decided to do something similar in Yiddish, and their efforts saw much success with *Literarishe bleter*. The similarity between these "twin weeklies," as Aleksandra Geller has called them, is closely related to Warsaw cafés, because both the Yiddish and the Polish journal were rooted in café life.[67] Significantly, this was one of the few points of contact between the Jews who were active in Polish and those who were active in Yiddish, at the same time that two groups experienced an ever-growing chasm.

Jewishness and Polishness in Interwar Warsaw Cafés and Cabarets

Wiadomości literackie was created and edited by Mieczysław Grydzewski, who came from an acculturated Jewish family and even converted to Protestantism but never denied or tried to hide his Jewishness. According to Grydzewski, the very idea of the journal was "born between two tables at Café Ziemiańska on Mazowiecka Street."[68] Grydzewski often criticized the separatism and "backwardness" of Jews who did not acculturate into Polish culture. Grydzewski and *Wiadomości literackie* were closely related to Skamander, the most important and active modernist Polish literary group in the interwar period.[69] The prominent members of Skamander were Tuwim, Słonimski, Jarosław Iwaszkiewicz, Kazimierz Wierzyński, and Jan Lechoń. Of the group, which was described by the Jewish-Polish poet and writer Aleksander Wat as a constellation of talent "one encounters once in a hundred years,"[70] the most gifted and versatile were Tuwim and Słonimski. Słonimski was the son of a Jewish father and a Catholic mother. His grandfather Ḥayim Zelig Słonimski was, we might recall, a *maskil*, the founder and editor of the journal *Ha-tsfirah*. His good friend Julian Tuwim was born into a middle-class Jewish family in Łódź and had a remarkable gift for verse, writing not only modernist poetry but also for cabarets and for children with much success.[71]

The friendship between Tuwim and Słonimski, and their poetic activities, took place mostly in the aforementioned Café Ziemiańska. However, the group was created on November 29, 1918, in another café, a small establishment called Pod Picadorem on 57 Nowy Świat. The poster advertising the founding of the café exuded a mix of artistic and political exuberance: "Countrymen! Workers, soldiers, children, seniors, people, women, and dramatic writers! . . . A great tournament of poets, musicians, and painters, daily from 9 to 11 p.m. Young Varsovian artists, unite!!!"[72] The opening night of the café was a great success. Słonimski recalled that Pod Picadorem was arranged to resemble the newly created modernist clubs and cafés in Russia. The great Russian poet Vladimir Mayakovsky, who was involved in such a café, was admired by the Skamander group.

Słonimski wrote that everyone "could enter Pod Picadorem Café for as little as five marks. They were selling neither vodka nor meat there." According to his account, it was a small café where "sober poets used to read their poems aloud in front of random audiences." Words such as "liberty, independence, Poland, communism, and revolution did not have the sound . . . of disappointment; we were full of strength and hope. In the evening, on the day of the opening of the café, all the elite of contemporary Warsaw came."[73] In December 1918, the newspaper *Świat* reported that "Café Pod Picadorem has nothing to do with Parisian Chat Noir or Lapin Agile. Quite different in its character, it is something between an ordinary Parisian café, and even a Berlin café, and a Warsaw cabaret. It was established for the public, . . . which should support not only the café itself, with its electricity, heating, and the servers dressed as Dutchmen, but also the poets associated with [it]."[74] The poet Kazimierz Wierzyński described the interior of Pod Picadorem as making an "odd impression." This is because futurist artists painted the room "in a manner full of fantasy and humor. It took a while to get used to the overwhelming chaos of their work. Waitresses dressed in some kind of costumes with Bretonne bonnets moved in these 'futurist frames.' . . . A flier on the table announced the dictatorship of the proletariat."[75] Thus, Café Pod Picadorem functioned as both a café and a poetry cabaret, where poets "performed" their poetry, something that was quite new in Poland but became more widespread in the 1920s and 1930s.

In the electric atmosphere of the café, the poets established the group Skamander and its journal. In the first issue of the journal, they articulated their poetics: "We want to be poets of the present, and this is our faith and our whole 'program.' . . . We know that the greatness of art does not appear in subjects but in the forms through which it is expressed, . . . of words transforming a rough experience into a work of art. We want to be honest workers in that game, through our efforts hidden under frivolous shapes."[76] However, in early 1919, just a few months after the "grand opening," Pod Picadorem had to move to the basement of the Europejski Hotel, and it closed down soon after, in April 1919, due to lack of funding. The success of the café, which enabled the creation of the most important Polish poetic movement in the first half of the twentieth century, could not sustain it economically. After less than a year, the Skamander poets settled, together with others, into a more permanent and more financially stable home at Café Ziemiańska. Mała Ziemiańska—"little Ziemiańska," because there were other branches of Ziemiańska in Warsaw—at Mazowiecka Street 12, was established on April 14, 1918, and became the most important literary and cultural café in interwar Warsaw.

In the mid 1920s, the Skamander poets and their publisher, Grydzewski, eventually had a special table reserved for themselves and their guests on the mezzanine of Café Ziemiańska.[77] This spatial arrangement had no doubt evolved with their rising reputation and success, as the owner of the café wanted to build on the appeal of these literati who were adored by Polish readers. The admiration of Skamander by the public was the result not only of their poetry and journalism but also of their participation in the world of the Polish cabaret. The 1920s and 1930s constituted the golden age not only of Polish modernism and café culture but also of cabaret, when little theaters (*teatrzyk* in Polish, *kleynkunst revi-teatr* in Yiddish) proliferated in Warsaw. Café culture, cabaret, poetry, and satire were closely related in Warsaw, and there was a strong Jewish presence in all of them.[78] The most famous cabaret venue and company was Qui Pro Quo (1919–1932), which assembled the creative talents of the Polish-Jewish writers Julian Tuwim and Marian Hemar. Hemar, whose real name was Jan Maria Hescheles, was born in Lemberg/Lwów when it was still part of the Habsburg Empire to well-to-do Jewish parents and began to write and publish poems and songs for cabaret when he was a student at the local university. He moved to Warsaw in 1924 and was recruited to Qui Pro Quo by the manager, Jerzy Boczkowski.

The stellar writing from Hemar, Tuwim, and Słonimski played a significant role in the artistic success of Qui Pro Quo over twelve years and even after its demise, when successive writers and performers managed to revive its model of literary cabaret in different incarnations—until 1939. The ever-changing constellation of artists at Qui Pro Quo, which featured Jews and gentiles alike, worked closely together in ensemble and socialized in Café Ziemiańska and IPS (established in 1930).[79] Sometimes the shows themselves were given in cafés, including *Małe Qui Pro Quo*, which operated on the top floor of Café Ziemiańska as a dedicated space for performance.[80] The cabaret *Cyrulik Warszawski* (The barber of Warsaw) gave its name also to a Polish satirical weekly published in Warsaw from 1926 to 1934. Hemar, Tuwim, and Słonimski were among its main contributors, and cafés appeared often in their work, sometimes with whimsical references to Jews and Jewishness.[81]

Thus, it is evident why the Skamander table on the mezzanine of Café Ziemiańska acquired the meaning of an "elevated space" for revered poets and cultural figures. Writers from various parts of Poland's literary scene paid visits to this table, including Adam Ważyk, the futurist Jewish poet Aleksander Wat, and the older poet Stefan Żeromski, as well as the young modernist prose writer Witold Gombrowicz.[82] Gombrowicz wrote in his memoirs about visiting Ziemiańska every single evening around nine. He sat at a table, ordered a "small black coffee," and waited until his café companions gathered. "A café," wrote Gombrowicz, "can become an addiction. . . . For a real habitué, not to go to the café at the designated time is simply to fall ill. In a short time, I became such a fanatic that I set aside all my other evening activities." Gombrowicz claimed that one entered Café Ziemiańska "from the street into darkness, a fearful haze of smoke and stale air, from which abyss there loomed astonishing faces striving to communicate by shouts and

Figure 2.4. Photograph of a literary group in a Warsaw café, 1933 (Courtesy of Narodowe Archiwum Cyfrowe, Warsaw)

gestures in the ever-present din." Like many other observers, Gombrowicz noted that Café Ziemiańska had its own hierarchy: "in the intellectual sense it was a multistoried edifice, and it wasn't so easy to transplant oneself from a lower floor to a higher one."[83]

The "elevated space" of the Skamander poets highlighted their Jewishness and their highly contentious status as both "Jews" and "Poles." Gombrowicz, who was raised Catholic but defined himself as a "secular humanist," wrote about the poetic alliances he had at Café Ziemiańska, which was, according to him, marked as a Polish-Jewish space: "my friendship with Jews began to blossom, and in the end in the Ziemiańska I became known as 'the King of the Jews,' since it was enough for me to sit down at a table to be surrounded by hordes of Semites; at the time they were my most gracious listeners."[84] The elusive sense of "Jewishness" of Ziemiańska's habitués had conflicting meanings to different people. As the historian Marci Shore has claimed, those among the Polish intelligentsia who were of Jewish origin (Tuwim, Słonimski, Wat, and Grydzewski) were "first- or second-generation assimilated Jews, Polish

Figure 2.5. Władysław Daszewski, caricature showing Jan Lechoń, Julian Tuwim, and Antoni Słonimski sitting at their table at Café Ziemiańska with Colonel Bolesław and Wieniawa-Długoszowski, *Wiadomości literackie* 36 (1928)

patriots and cosmopolitans, their families often split apart by differing responses to modernity."[85]

Aleksander Wat, the poet and prose writer who was close to Skamander but was mostly associated with the futurist movement, is a good example of Shore's assertion. Wat's father's spoken language was Yiddish, and he was steeped in the study of Jewish mysticism and kabbalah, as well as Russian and Polish culture. Still, Wat had a memory of traditional Jews "in gabardines, dirty, merchants, money," at the same time that he acknowledged that he "perceived himself through categories of guilt and punishment," which was his "burden as a Jew."[86] Wat was highly aware of the link that was created, for better or worse, between Polish Jewishness and the Warsaw café: "I grew up in the cafés—that's my weakness. And so when I'm in that atmosphere, I'm capable of kibitzing with my worst enemies." He writes that "sitting in that imaginary or real literary café, I was so disarmed that I immediately felt friendly towards them, a great rush of genuine affection."[87]

Tuwim and Słonimski had to defend themselves very often against the attacks of Polish right-wing nationalists. Tuwim, who grew up in an acculturated Jewish family in Łódź and made many references to Jews and Jewishness in his poems, feuilletons, and cabaret pieces, wrote in 1934 about his aversion toward those Jews who are "uniformed men in beards" and toward Yiddish, which he called "Hebraic-German garble," as well as the "traditional mutilation of Polish speech."[88] Słonimski admired what he perceived as the rebellious spirit of his Jewish *maskil* grandfather: "I don't know if my grandfather was a good Jew or a bad Jew, . . . but he was a magnificent person."[89] But this admiration of his grandfather, as well as his sympathetic visit to Palestine in 1922, did not stop Słonimski from writing in 1924 one of his most notorious feuilletons in *Wiadomości literacki*, devoted to the "oversensitivity [or irritability] of the Jews" in Poland. He claimed that "Jews disdain everything: they butcher the language they speak, they ignore the purity of speech, body and heart, while attaching an irrational value to money."[90]

Even with such virulent attacks against traditional Jews and against Yiddish (which seem to be examples of "Jewish self-hatred"), all these figures never denied or tried to hide their Jewishness. In fact, Słonimski wrote, "Some gents from Jewish newspapers bemoan my becoming an 'anti-Semite' because I have once written a few negative words about the Jews. 'A grandson of [Ḥ. Z.] Słonimski attacks Jews!' No, my dear sirs, I am not an anti-Semite. But nobody can forbid me to talk about what is evil among Jews." Słonimski asked in another of his feuilletons, "How are the Jews hated in Poland—and why? These are complex issues. Only one thing seems doubtful to me: can the word 'Jew' be an argument in the discussion? Here it is mostly the Jews who are useful [for Poland] who end up being fought against, while those who are harmful are defended." When thinking about Polish-Jewish poets such as himself, he asked, "Who are we? Are we the blossoming flowers of Polish poetry? Or are we 'Skamander' Jews? Are we the brothers of Slavs, Germans, Jews, and Ukrainians? All depends on the good or bad humor of he who would write about us."[91]

The proud and witty Słonimski and Tuwim frequently became targets of anti-Semitic attacks. Sometimes, the very existence of their "elevated space" brought anti-Semitic attacks into Café Ziemiańska. Słonimski remembered that he was attacked in Café Ziemiańska because of his ironic poem "Dwie ojczyzny" (Two fatherlands, 1933), which included the following lines:

> When you flash, the morning star,
> Heaven, earth, and heart are quiet.
> You are my snowy Lebanon, dark-haired girl.
> I would leave the sad lands of the North and the fertile soil
> For one kiss I'll give two fatherlands.[92]

This complex and sensitive poem was oversimplified by Polish nationalists, who did not like what they perceived as the overtaking of Polish culture by Jews. Słonimski related how one day in Café Ziemiańska, a group of young people sat by the table next to the door. One of them approached and hit him while shouting loudly, "It's a punishment for 'Two Fatherlands.'"[93]

It is hardly surprising that the Jews who wrote in Yiddish and Hebrew identified with the goal of autonomous Jewish culture in Poland, from Zionism to the socialist Bund, and rejected the idea of total assimilation into Polish culture and society, detested the prominence of such figures as Słonimski and Tuwim in Polish literature. To be sure, in the interwar period, the overwhelming majority of Jewish writers, journalists, and intellectuals in Warsaw, and much of their audience, knew and read Polish well. Many of them wrote in Polish as well, especially in the Zionist-leaning newspaper *Nasz przegląd*, published between 1923 and 1939, with circulation between twenty and fifty thousand. They followed the writings of Skamander, and some of them admired the group and journal and even translated Polish texts into Yiddish and Hebrew. However, there was little real contact between these groups of producers of Jewish culture, one situated physically and symbolically at Tłomackie 13 and the other in Café Ziemiańska. The disdain, which was probably mixed with envy, can be seen sharply in the few but significant examples in which Yiddish and Hebrew writers ventured into Ziemiańska and had a chance to see the activity that took place there and encounter the famous Polish-Jewish writers and poets who were their most loyal and revered habitués.

The Yiddish actors and comedians Shimen (Szymon) Dzigan and his friend Yisroel Shumacher were the most popular performers of Yiddish theater and cabaret in Łódź and in Warsaw during the interwar period. Dzigan remembered Antoni Słonimski as a "distinguished personality on the Polish street" who "quite often told off, sharply and harshly, the Polish reactionaries and anti-Semites," while they "did not forget that he is the grandson of H. Z. Słonimski, and in order to underscore his Polishness to them, he used to periodically tell off the Jews as well and to give them advice on how they should 'Europeanize' themselves."[94]

Dzigan, who like Julian Tuwim came from Łódź to Warsaw, spent much time in local cafés. He recalled sitting not in Café Ziemiańska but in its new competitor, the IPS, when he read one of Słonimski's columns about Jews in Poland in *Wiadomości literackie*. In Dzigan's recollection, the feuilleton declared that "the Polish Jews with their strange garb shouldn't be intruding on Polish cafés and in general on places where 'Pollacks' come . . . and make fun of Jewish clothes, of Jewish posture, and so on." Dzigan wrote that Słonimski's feuilleton vexed and infuriated him and his friends, and they wanted to do something.[95]

Being actors, Dzigan and his friends decided to put on makeup and dress in traditional Hasidic garb, and with this outfit, they entered the IPS Café one after the other. When the manager of the café noticed that a Jew in a traditional caftan wanted to come inside the café, he rushed to the hallway. "Excuse me," he said to Dzigan, "this café is not for you. It's better if you go to the Jewish neighborhood; you'll feel better there." When he saw more people who looked like traditional Jews, the owner thought to himself that there was "a Jewish invasion" and asked his workers not to let Dzigan's actor friends come into the café. Later, the actors went back to the studio, changed their clothes, and took off their makeup to appear like their modern European selves. Of course, this time they could get into the café without much of a problem, and some of the guests even told them that they should have seen the scene that unfolded just before their arrival. Finally, Dzigan and his friends revealed that these traditional-looking Jews were themselves in disguise: "The Jews with the robes and beards don't aspire to come into your café. . . . [We] just wanted to test your courtesy."[96] Dzigan concluded his recounting of the events by observing that he was upset not so much by the treatment by the non-Jews but by the attitude of the Jews who were present in the café. "I saw how they lowered their heads and looked at the floor, and I could swear that they were angrier at me for my boldness than some of the non-Jewish guests."[97] Dzigan's seemingly humorous account indicates that notions of Polishness and Jewishness in Warsaw cafés during the interwar period were difficult to experience. However, these tensions were also productive, an essential aspect of Jewish culture: high and popular, in Polish, Yiddish, and Hebrew.

Yitzhak Katzenelson was a Hebrew and Yiddish poet and playwright who resided primarily in Łódź but worked and spent much time in Warsaw. In 1936, he published a Hebrew poem with the title "Varsha" (Warsaw). The poem begins with the speaker, identified with Katzenelson himself, sitting in a café in the center of Warsaw. Although the name of the café is not specified, it is quite clear that it is Ziemiańska:

> One day, Sunday, the first day of the Jewish week, I sit in a café
> Between a withered crowd, there is the convert Antoni Słonimski,
> At every table a woman adorns herself and a man clings to the counter,
> Everybody tweets and chats in a prettified but not pretty language.[98]

Clearly, for Katzenelson's speaker, the Polish café is not a pleasant place but a place of degeneration and artificiality, in which sexuality and language are being mutilated and where people like Słonimski the *meshumad*—a traditional Hebrew and Yiddish word for convert that literally means "destroyed one"—might be adorned but in reality are "withered." The speaker is revolted to see in the Warsaw café not only Słonimski but many Jews who frequent the place, which makes him feel that these Jews—including himself and those around him—are small-minded and despicable. Then, full of revulsion, he leaves the café and walks to Dzika and Gęsia Streets, at the heart of the Jewish district, where he sees "Jews, real Jews . . . who are broken and meager, but the *shekhina* [the feminine image of God] is bestowed on their parchment-faces." In this poem, Katzenelson highlighted not only the cultural aversion that he felt toward Ziemiańska and toward Polish poets of Jewish origin such as Słonimski but also the economic difference between the posh and expensive Warsaw cafés and the poor Jewish streets. This is significant because many Jews who were active in Yiddish and Hebrew culture in Warsaw avoided places such as Café Ziemiańska not only because of the tangled complexity of "Polishness" and "Jewishness" and because of the fact that they did not feel comfortable there because of anti-Semitism but also because of economic reasons. Most Jews in Warsaw—like those whom Katzenelson's poem describes—could not afford to pay for food and drinks in the famous cafés, nor did they have the clothes that one had to put on in order to go there.

This situation becomes clear in the writing of one of the few Yiddish writers and intellectuals who actually used to visit Café Ziemiańska: Y. Y. Trunk. Trunk was born to a respected and wealthy Hasidic family. His father inherited a fortune from his own father-in-law, and Trunk himself married a grandchild of Y. Prywes, the "iron king" of Poland from one of the country's richest Jewish families. Trunk moved to Warsaw in 1925, and as a writer and critic of distinction, he was involved in many Yiddish literary projects and activities in Tłomackie 13. However, he also ventured beyond and visited famous cafés in the center of Warsaw. In his memoir, written with the narrative force and style of a powerful novel, Trunk wrote about how he used to go from time to time to Café Ziemiańska together with his dog, an "aristocratic poodle" whose name was Nik. With a mixture of sardonic irony and the poise of someone who knew he was a wealthy man, Trunk wrote,

> Besides going for walks with me in God's great outdoors and to ponder the world and its dear creatures, one of Nik's greatest pastimes was to go with me to Café Ziemiańska. This was the artists' café of Warsaw. In Ziemiańska gathered both Jewish and Polish writers and artists. Nik simply felt like he was in seventh heaven when he could lie under a table around which gathered—according to his grasp—the greatest gods of the words. Once, Nik even stole a lick of the black nectar. It felt like a wild bitterness and a nasty taste to him. But he maintained that a mortal like him could not really enjoy that divine drink. From then on, he was content to lie under the table between the feet of an author, to take a nap and to think the loveliest thoughts that only a dog can dream.[99]

Trunk observed about Nik, "[He] knew precisely the time when I was about to go . . . in Café Ziemiańska. . . . He waited quietly by the door of my office, so I should not, Heaven forbid, forget to bring him with me to the worlds of pleasures."[100] Using the point of view of Nik the poodle and telling us about his dog's perceptions and dreams enabled Trunk to poke fun at both the presumptuousness of Café Ziemiańska's habitués and how people who came to be close to the Polish writers and artists thought, like Nik the dog, that they were "the greatest gods" and that coffee was the "nectar of gods." But Trunk also poked fun at himself, at how his financial well-being and his curiosity led him to visit Café Ziemiańska, which seemed to him and to his dog as the "worlds of pleasures." There is hardly a doubt that Trunk, like so many other Jews, was very curious and eager to follow the actions and the writing of Polish figures from the Skamander group and other Poles of Jewish origin who were at the forefront of Polish culture.

A different perspective on the relations between different kinds of Jews and café culture in Warsaw of the 1930s can be found in the writing of the aforementioned Yiddish writer Kaganowski:

> The Jewish walk is a short one, a few streets that are crowded with Jews, and then back home. A few cafés crowded with Jews, where one waits for a table, for half a chair, to drink the half black coffee. This is "Ziemiańska." The avant-garde of the Polish-Jewish cultural world comes here. Writers, poets, and painters come—a special family that complains, at every opportunity, about the "Jewish mob." They are not yet secure with their own Polishness and suddenly realize that they spend their time among Jews.[101]

From Kaganowski's point of view, it is ironic that Słonimski and Tuwim, who tried so much to remove themselves from Jewish nationalism, Yiddish, and traditional Judaism, frequented Café Ziemiańska, which continued to be seen as a "Jewish space." The reality that Kaganowski described is of Warsaw in 1937, a couple of years before the Nazis invaded and when anti-Semitism, Polish nationalism, and economic crisis converged to make the situation of Warsaw's Jewry dire. In this period, the Association for Jewish Writers and Journalists was in decline, and it eventually moved out of its famous location in Tłomackie 13 to the third floor of a building on Graniczna 11. Even before the change of location, many Jewish journalists, writers, and actors abandoned it. Bashevis Singer, Ravitch, and Molodowsky migrated to other parts of the world; others found alternative places to visit and to socialize in Warsaw. Zusman Segalovitsh claimed that "there was an elegant Café Europa, Ziemiańska, the café of Polish artists, and the Jewish restaurant Piccadilly. . . . One started to avoid Tłomackie 13, with a reason, or without. The 'den' lost its prestige among strangers and our own. More and more chairs remained empty."[102] After the place was destroyed together with most of Warsaw's Jewry in World War II, Melech Ravitch wrote that Tłomackie 13 was a space in which "history was not made" but "a place of refuge to which people escaped from history."[103]

Cafés and Cabarets, Entertainment and Survival in the Warsaw Ghetto

Soon after the Nazi invasion of Poland in September 1939, Jews were segregated into ghettos. The Warsaw Ghetto was sealed in November 1940. In order to create it, the Nazis compelled 113,000 Poles and 138,000 Jews to leave their homes. In the ghetto, almost half a million Jews from Warsaw and from nearby towns and cities were incarcerated in what was effectively a combination of the largest Jewish "prison city" in Europe and a forced labor camp. Astonishingly, despite the harsh conditions, the ghetto and its institutions seemed to achieve a modicum of stability, and cultural life began to proliferate.

Many Jewish writers, artists, actors, and musicians who did not manage to escape Poland before the war broke out soon found themselves closed off in the Warsaw Ghetto. The Association of Jewish Journalists and Writers had an emergency meeting. One of its decisions was to create a soup kitchen for writers. Such a soup kitchen was established at 40 Leszno Street, and it provided hot meals until the mass deportations of Jews from the ghetto to Treblinka in 1942. At first, writers and intellectuals tried to create there a social, literary space, but because of the huge crowds of hungry people, they were compelled to look for a smaller and quieter location. There were a few such institutions: a small "café" on 5 Karmelicka Street, Y. M. Appleboym's home on 13 Graniszna, and 13 Leszno Street, a space that functioned as a cultural club, with "literary dinner" on Sabbath afternoons.[104] Another soup kitchen that was used as a club was Gospoda literaracka (Literary kitchen) on 6 Orla Street, which was especially popular as a meeting place for visual artists.[105]

In contrast to these soup kitchens, which tried to foster highbrow literary and artistic activities, there was a strong demand in the ghetto for musical and theatrical productions, both in Yiddish and in Polish. Many of these activities took place in cafés. Some of the cafés had lavish food and drink, and others were no more than meager soup kitchens. At the beginning of 1940, the Nazis granted permission to open some establishments that sold drink and food and provided entertainment. Residents of the ghetto who could afford to pay liked these cafés, and their financial success promoted the establishment of many other cafés that were operated by members of the Judenrat (the council of Jewish elders appointed by the Nazis) and Germans who used their influence to secure license. The Yiddish and Polish actor and director Jonas Turkow—who spent most of World War II with his wife, the singer and actress Diana Blumenfeld, organizing theater performances and working with the underground resistance in the Warsaw Ghetto—wrote in his memoir, "During the year 1940, many halls were opened, most of which were 'cafés' with artistic performances. This was so successful that every second house became a café or restaurant with an artistic presentation. In the summertime, there was a flood of 'summer gardens' where musicians and actors performed."[106]

Turkow remembered that in the same building where the famous Tłomackie 13 operated, there was a café with a German woman owner, Café Gertner, which played a new role in the ghetto. Early in 1940, the owner received permission to arrange entertainment, for which she engaged Yiddish artists. Turkow contended that these Yiddish shows had such success that on Saturdays and Sundays there were also matinees, with performances by Yiddish and Polish artists. What kind of audience came to the shows in Café Gertner? According to Turkow, it consisted of young men who used to make trips over the border to Russia, smuggling people and goods and gaining a fortune in this way. "They squandered their money lavishly," he wrote, "and after returning to Warsaw from such a trip, they became steady customers of Gertner, where they also took their 'girlfriends.' Their bills there ran to thousands of złotys. After the program was over, the dancing began."[107] The Jewish historian, politician, and social worker Emanuel Ringelblum wrote in his diary on November 29, 1940, that at certain hours, "the cafés are full of people, the streets are empty."[108] This situation became very strange when the

Jewish Cultural Organization applied for permission to organize cultural performances on its premises, but permission was granted only on condition that it would be organized as a café; and thus many of the soup kitchens in the ghetto were turned into "cafés" so they could get a license to perform.[109]

There were many controversies about these cafés and the activities that took place there, as well as about the moral aspects of their existence and popularity. Many of the cafés opened with the help of Gestapo or Judenrat members and could continue to operate only through high-ranking connections. Most of the owners exploited the thirst of ghetto dwellers for entertainment and culture, charging high prices for food and drink and for shows. Most of the people in the ghetto could not even dream about visiting there. The historian Shirli Gilbert has shown that for most people in the ghetto, the only musical sounds were those of beggars singing for money on the streets or the occasional free concerts in the soup kitchens. Only a small upper stratum of the ghetto had access to the cafés.[110]

Mary Berg (Miriam Wattenberg) was a Polish-Jewish teenager when the war broke out. Her mother was an American citizen, and thus she had a privileged position within the ghetto, as she could possibly be exchanged for German prisoners of war. Berg wrote in her diary about her life in the ghetto: "new cafés . . . have appeared where everything can be had."[111] An entry in the *Łódź Ghetto Chronicle* in May 1941 recorded a speech by the Judenrat chairman, Ḥayim Rumkowski, in which he shared his impressions from a recent trip to Warsaw:

> There is a striking contrast in the Warsaw ghetto between the tragic poverty of the enormous majority of the people and the prosperity of the small handful who still remain wealthy and have access to every sort of restaurant, pastry shop, and store, where the prices are, of course, dizzyingly high. Aside from that "frippery" and the small number of fortunate people who are dressed in the latest fashion and perfectly well fed, one sees immense crowds of unemployed people whose appearance is simply frightening.[112]

Michel Mazor wrote in his memoir about young girls and women from various social strata who offered their services as waitresses, so that the owners had an ample choice. He claimed that "no city in the world had as many beautiful and elegant women serving in cafés as did the short lived ghetto."[113] When the demand for different types of performers increased, cafés owners would take young pretty girls and youngsters who knew how to dance a step or two or sing a song. Suddenly, there was a flood of new musical and dance "performers," and they were subject to the whims of the café owners and proprietors.

Café Sztuka (Art) on 2 Leszno Street became the most popular establishment in the ghetto. Mary Berg remembered that "at elegantly set tables, to the sound of a brilliant orchestra, the high society of the ghetto disports itself."[114] The singer Vera Gran performed there, and the pianist Władysław Szpilman played piano at Café Sztuka as well as the Café Pod Fontanną (Under the fountain). For many people who were Yiddish speakers and did not belong to the economic elite of the Jewish ghetto, these activities in Café Sztuka were infuriating. Jonas Turkow claimed that Yiddish was practically banned in Café Sztuka because the audience would find the sound of Yiddish grating to the ears.[115]

Ya'akov Tselemensky wrote that when he ventured to Sztuka, his companion suddenly said to him, "Be careful not to step on a corpse." In contrast to the grim reality outside, inside the café,

> every table was covered by a white tablecloth. Fat characters sat at them eating chicken, duck, or fowl. All of these foods would be drowned in wine and liquor. The orchestra, in the middle of the nightclub, sat on a small platform. Next to it a singer performed. These were people who once played before Polish crowds. Now they were reminded of their Jewish heritage. . . . The audience crowding the tables was made up of the aristocracy of the ghetto—big-time smugglers, high Polish officers and all sorts of big shots. Germans who had business dealings with the Jews also came here, dressed in civilian clothes. Within the walls of the cabaret, one could not sense the tragedy taking place a few yards away. The audience ate, drank, and laughed as if it had no worries.[116]

The pianist Władysław Szpilman wrote that when he performed at Café Sztuka, he lost two illusions: "my beliefs in our general solidarity and in the musicality of the Jews."[117] As Szpilman's case illustrates, it is important to remember that many of the writers, actors, musicians, and others who struggled to earn a livelihood sought employment in these places in order to supplement their meager incomes. Mary Berg wrote that one of the cafés ran a contest for young talent, in which she participated, with a prize of a week's contract as a performer in the café.[118] Szpilman's work at the cafés enabled him to support his family of six.

In terms of the content of the theater, cabaret, and music performed in the cafés, it was essentially a continuation of the prewar cultural life in Warsaw; some of it was decidedly lowbrow, but some was of very high quality. In Café Sztuka, the biggest attraction soon became the satirical cabaret show called *Żywy dziennik* (The live journal), created by the artists who performed there. Performed every week, this spoken chronicle of the ghetto was extremely popular, largely due to the poems written by the Polish-Jewish poet Władysław Szlengel, who wrote for Warsaw cabarets before the war. Using lively and colorful language and witty monologues, the show was successful based on references to everyday life in the ghetto and the sharp satire used to comment on current events.[119]

Thus, cafés were some of the very few places where there could be satirical expression of the conditions of ghetto life.[120] When Mary Berg visited Café Sztuka and saw the performance with "songs and satires on the police, the ambulance service, the rickshaws, and even the Gestapo, in a veiled fashion," she concluded, "It is a laughter through tears, but it is laughter. This is our only weapon in the ghetto—our people laugh at death and at the Nazi decrees. Humor is the only thing the Nazis cannot understand."[121] Similarly, Michel Mazor rhetorically asked about the cafés' "continuous existence in a city which the Germans regarded as a cemetery—was it not, in a certain sense, the ghetto's protest, its affirmation of the right to live?"[122] It seems that nothing could stop these cafés, at least until the liquidation of the ghetto that began on the eve of Passover, April 19, 1943, when the Nazis sent the remaining Jews to death in Treblinka.

The very existence of cafés and cabarets in the Warsaw Ghetto was astonishing and highly controversial. There is no doubt that there were elements of corruption and collaboration with the Nazis in the cafés, but these cafés also enabled the survival of Jewish writers, musicians, and artists. Even in a time of an extreme rupture in Warsaw's Jewish life, ghetto cafés were among the few places where modern Jewish culture, in Polish and Yiddish, could still be created under the most devastating circumstances. The ghetto café was thus a complex site of collaboration, cultural survival, commercialism, and elitism. It shows that even at some of the most horrible sites of Nazi destruction in World War II, Jewish cultural creativity continued to develop in strange ways. As such, the ghetto café both continues and disrupts our understanding of the café and its role as a space of Jewish culture in Warsaw as part of a cultural nexus of urban cafés that created the silk road of transnational, diasporic modern Jewish culture.

3

Vienna

The "Matzo Island" and the Functioning Myths of the Viennese Café

Perhaps nothing has contributed to the intellectual mobility and the international orientation of the Austrian as much as that he could keep abreast of all world events in the coffeehouse and at the same time discuss them in a circle of his friends.
—Stefan Zweig, *The World of Yesterday*, 1944

In 2011, UNESCO (United Nations Educational, Scientific, and Cultural Organization) added "Viennese Coffeehouse Culture" as a new item to its list of "protected intangible cultural heritage sites" in Austria. UNESCO declared that "the tradition of the Viennese Kaffeehaus culture goes back to the end of the seventeenth century, and is given distinction by a very specific atmosphere. Typical for Viennese coffeehouses are marble tables, on which coffee is served. . . . The coffeehouses are a place where time and space are consumed, but only the coffee is found on the bill."[1] UNESCO's recognition of *das Wiener Kaffeehaus* (the Viennese coffeehouse) as an Austrian site of cultural significance is unprecedented. No other city in the world had its café culture "protected."[2]

This success in preserving the heritage of Viennese coffeehouse culture surely helps the business prospects of Vienna's contemporary coffee shops, which are now threatened by global chains. The UNESCO decision is also a source of local and national pride and ensures the status of the Viennese café as a museum-like tourist attraction. But is the decision justified? It creates an impression of the continuity of a distinctive "cultural heritage site," unique to the city of Vienna and, by extension, to Austria. It also opens many questions: Are Viennese cafés today similar to cafés at the end of the seventeenth or the end of the nineteenth century? Is (was) Viennese café culture so unique? Furthermore, what does the narrative about the uniqueness and the historical continuity of Vienna reveal, and what does it conceal? Does it not obscure the transnational aspect of the café, the fact that its early history is tied to Turkish and Armenian coffee and coffeehouses and that Jews were so essential to Viennese café culture in its most emblematic period, from the 1880s to the 1930s?

When pondering these questions, we might turn to a different text about Vienna café culture. The text is "Traktat über das Wiener Kaffeehaus" (Treatise on the Vienna coffeehouse), written by the Jewish writer Friedrich Torberg—whose original name was Kantor-Berg—in 1959, after he returned to Vienna from New York City. In the feuilleton, Torberg called Vienna "the city of functioning myths." Recognizing that the interplay between myth and reality is something that all cities, in fact, are built on, Torberg sardonically wrote that what is "typical of Vienna, and only Vienna, is that here legends still work and will continue to function as long as realities are guided by them." After giving a few examples of "functioning myths," Torberg wrote that the Viennese café is "by far the most complicated of these legends."[3]

Indeed, the history of Vienna cafés, as of other cities, is full of legends, and sometimes, as Torberg writes, realities are even guided by them. This can be seen, for example, in the famous legend about the first coffeehouse in Vienna, which—the story goes—was opened by Georg Franz Kolschitzky (originally, Kulczycki). The story is that this translator, imperial messenger, and businessman, who worked in the service of the Habsburg monarchy but was born in Galicia to a Polish family, established the first Viennese coffeehouse called Zur blauen Flasche (To the blue bottle), soon after the end of the Turkish siege of Vienna in 1683. The story goes that Kolschitzky, clad in Turkish dress, managed to penetrate enemy lines, and in reward for his excellent service and courage, he was awarded sacks of coffee beans left behind by the Turkish army and was granted permission to open his coffeehouse in Vienna.

This is a very good story, but the historical reality was quite different. The first coffeehouses to operate in Vienna were opened by two Armenians: Johannes Diodato in 1686 and Isaak de Luca in 1693.[4] Armenia was on the fringe of the Ottoman Empire, and like coffeehouses all over Europe, Vienna cafés were established and operated by foreigners who were involved in coffee trading and coffeehouses in the vast Ottoman territories.[5] The narrative and its staying power is, however, a good example of Torberg's claim about the efficacy of the myth in Vienna. The narrative about the smart translator who saved the Habsburg Empire from the Turkish enemy became an emblem of the Viennese *Kaffeehaus* that began to flourish in the early nineteenth century. References to Kolschitzky and his café became part of the urban space, with streets named after him and his statue part of the public domain, and the name is still widely known and used today.[6]

The turn of the nineteenth century, in which cafés began to be part of Vienna's urban space and culture, was also the period of growth of the capital of the Habsburg Empire, as well as the development of the still-small Jewish community in the city. There is evidence of a Jewish presence in Vienna that goes back to the twelfth century, but the community's growth and well-being were constantly interrupted by restrictions on residence rights, religious intolerance, persecution, violence, and a series of expulsions. In January 1782, this situation started to change, when Emperor Joseph II promulgated the Toleranzpatent, the Edict of Tolerance for the Jews of Vienna and Lower Austria, which intended to make the Jews "more useful . . . and more usable to the State."[7] This document, which enabled a small number of Jews to be legally "tolerated" in Vienna, paved the way for the emancipation that took place in the middle of the nineteenth century. But already toward the end of the eighteenth century, several Jews had achieved considerable recognition, and the process of acculturation into German language and Habsburg cultural norms began to be felt. Vienna also became, following Berlin and Lemberg, a small but important center of Haskalah. This happened when, after the partition of Poland, Galicia was annexed to the Habsburg Empire, and *maskilim* flocked to Vienna and were active in the city. The Hebrew journals *Bikkurei ha-'itim* and *Kerem ḥemded* were published in Vienna between 1820 and 1843 and made Vienna a center of Hebrew publishing.[8]

By 1779, the city had only eleven cafés, but this changed quickly as cafés began to proliferate in Vienna of the nineteenth century.[9] In 1824, Ignaz Neuner opened a café, nicknamed the silbernes Kaffeehaus (Silver café) because of its interior design, which included luxurious details such as silver tableware, silver pots, and silver coat hangers and door

Central Islip Public Library
33 Hawthorne Avenue
Central Islip, NY 11722

handles. The unabashed luxury of the café continued also in its billiard room, which was a popular feature of a number of Viennese cafés in this period.[10] The silbernes Kaffeehaus, which operated until 1848, became known also as a place of literature and high culture. Some of the habitués of the café were part of Vienna's cultural elite.[11] As in other cities in the eighteenth and nineteenth centuries, there was also the rival urban space to the café: the salon. In Vienna, salon life, unlike café life, was dominated by Jewish women as hostesses. Fanny von Arnstein, a patroness of music, arts, and literature, was the outstanding *salonnière* of Vienna in the late eighteenth and early nineteenth centuries. The tradition of the salon continued well into the mid-nineteenth century with Arnstein's sister Caecilie Wulff and her daughter, Henriette von Pereira-Arnste.[12] But the salons were very different spaces compared to the café. They were modeled on the French aristocratic institution of the salon and were very exclusive, though they enabled Christian nobility and Jewish high society to socialize. As urban thirdspace, open, at least in theory, to everybody, the café attracted a more varied mixture of habitués and visitors, Jews and non-Jews.

According to Sigmund Mayer, a Jewish textile manufacturer who migrated with his parents to Vienna and later became one of the leaders of the community, there were a few Jewish writers and artists such as Ludwig August Frankl who used to frequent the silbernes Kaffeehaus and Café Geringer at the Bauernmarkt.[13] Mayer, a businessman, was more familiar with cafés in the Leopoldstadt, a district across the Danube Canal from the main city that used to be the Jewish ghetto and continued to attract many Jews and was nicknamed the "Mazzesinsel" (The matzo island). Mayer wrote about Café Friedrich, Café Mehringer, and Café Fetzer as places with a strong Jewish presence; business was the dominant topic of conversation, as these cafés became the informal centers of commodity exchange of textiles, wheat, and spirits.[14]

John Strang, a British traveler to Vienna in the 1830s, confirmed the presence of Jews, among others, in Vienna cafés: "the Turke, the Greek, the Armenian, the Jew, and the Gentile, are constantly to be seen amusing themselves, and realising, in respect to the variety of tongues spoken, no imperfect idea of Babel."[15] In spite of this lively impression of a multiethnic, multilingual Tower of Babel, the cultural activity in Vienna cafés was still limited until the revolutions of 1848. Part of the reason was the severe restrictions of the regime on all forms of expression, journalism and literature included.[16] There is evidence that reading of foreign newspapers in cafés was monitored by the head waiter, who was sometimes a police informer.[17] Furthermore, even in the silbernes Kaffeehaus, many habitués were known less as writers and more for their skills at billiards.[18]

The Jewish partaking in café culture, as well as the growth of the city and its Jewish community, was quite stagnant until 1848, the year that ushered in an era of political unrest and revolutions that had immense impact on Vienna. The widespread revolutions of 1848 against the monarchies brought many people across the European continent into political life, and on March 13, crowds of mostly students and members of liberal clubs demonstrated in Vienna for basic freedoms and a liberalization of the regime.[19] Jewish intellectuals were part of the revolution of 1848. The physician Adolf Fischhof pleaded for freedom of the press, and Ludwig August Frankl, Moritz Hartmann, and Ignaz Kuranda published poems and articles calling for the emancipation of Jews as part of the general call for freedom.[20] A period of revolutions and counterrevolutions ensued, but a new constitution emerged, which promised freedom of press and expression and eventually lifted most restrictions on Jews, ushering in an era of Jewish emancipation that culminated in 1867. In that year, in which the Habsburg monarchy became the dual Austro-Hungarian Empire, it granted male Jews and all male residents equal civic, political, and religious rights.[21]

During the second half of the nineteenth century, the Jewish population of Vienna dramatically increased because of migration from other regions of the Habsburg Empire, particularly from Hungary, Moravia, Bohemia, and Galicia. There was also a smaller migration of people from Russia and Poland. Some of the migrants were *maskilim*, such as Peretz Smolenskin, who, we should recall, moved to Vienna from Odessa in 1868, and the itinerant Velvl Zbarzher, who settled in Vienna by 1878. The large-scale migration from small towns into the city was made by people in search of the freedom and opportunities for education, economic advancement, and culture that came in the wake of emancipation. In 1857, there were no more than 6,217 Jews in the city of Vienna. By 1900, that number swelled to almost 147,000, around 10 percent of the total population.[22] This Jewish migration to Vienna coincided with a period of modernization and urban and economic expansion, known as the Gründerzeit, in which the city became, for the first time, a metropolis. The capital of the Austro-Hungarian Empire not only doubled in size but also attracted a striking array of talents in all areas of human endeavor.

Most Jews who lived in Vienna at the end of the nineteenth century were migrants or the children of migrants. The term "assimilation" is often used to describe what happened to Vienna's Jews in this period, although it is far from clear what this term means, as it encompasses a range of distinct changes in Jewish behavior. Historians Marsha Rozenblit and Steven Beller have demonstrated that Viennese Jews were overwhelmingly acculturated into German language and cultural norms, which they admired as the embodiment of *Kultur* and *Bildung*—as exemplified in the high culture of Goethe, Lessing, and Schiller—and the ideals of the Enlightenment. At the same time, their acculturation made them not just "German Jews" but specifically Viennese Jews.[23] Significantly, this meant that Jews were acculturated mostly in the company of other Jews. Thus, they kept a distinctly Jewish ethnic, social, and cultural identity and to some degree a Jewish religious identity as well. This process occurred mainly due to patterns of Jewish residence in certain districts and neighborhoods of the city, such as Leopoldstadt and Alsergrund, through gymnasium and university education, and through typical "Jewish professions" and networks that kept them connected to each other.[24]

"The Jew Belongs in the Coffeehouse"?

The unprecedented emancipation and acculturation in Vienna in the late nineteenth century was linked to the extraordinary role of Jews in literary and artistic modernism in the metropolis and in Viennese cafés. The last decades of the nineteenth century signaled the beginning of Vienna as a hotbed for modernism, as well as for café culture; both reached their peak at the fin de siècle. Vienna around the year 1900 is considered by many scholars to be "the focal point of European modernism," in various fields.[25] In 1900, there were no less than a thousand cafés throughout the city of Vienna, probably more than any other city covered in this book.[26] Of course, this huge number included all kinds of cafés. There were large entertainment cafés in Vienna, such as the ones in the Prater park, which presented musical comedies, operettas, and other stage acts, similar to the *café-chantants* in Odessa. Other cafés in the city center, as well as in the middle-class and working-class neighborhoods of the metropolis, provided a space for informal socialization and leisure.[27] Only a handful of cafés were also spaces of significant literary, artistic, and political activities. New or second-generation immigrant Jews were dominant in all these cafés.

The most well-known cafés in Vienna of this period were Café Griensteidl and Café Central, located at the very center of Vienna. Café Griensteidl on Michaelerplatz at the corner of Herrengasse and Schauflergasse was already an "old" establishment in the 1890s, when it was celebrated as a "literary café." It was established in 1847 and promptly became the headquarters of democrats, nicknamed "Café National" as a reflection of the political sympathies of its patrons. In the 1850s and 1860s, conservative circles met in the Café Daum, while the Café Griensteidl was a center for "malcontents and raisonneurs."[28] The socialists were a noticeable presence within the fluctuating political trends since the 1870s, but the café's "political" role had been superseded in the 1870s and 1880s, when it became a focal point for the actors and directors from the nearby Burgtheater.

In the 1890s, the Griensteidl became known as a "literary café." It was especially noted as the gathering place for the modernist Jung Wien (Young Vienna) group, whose members included Hermann Bahr, Arthur Schnitzler, Richard Beer-Hofmann, and Hugo von Hofmannsthal.[29] It was in the 1890s that the Griensteidl earned the nickname "Café Größenwahn" (Café megalomania), which pointed to the importance and narcissism of this space. As we shall see, it is quite common that well-known cafés were immortalized just when they closed their doors. This happened with Café Griensteidl in Karl Kraus's satire *Die demolirte Literatur* (The demolished literature, 1897), in which he mock lamented both the closure of Café Griensteidl and the Jung Wien group.

The nearby rival Café Central, also on the Herrengasse, was established in 1876. It was a grand space with domes and arches and a central hall, described in Franz Werfel's novel *Barbara oder die Frömmigkeit* as "Säulensaal" (pillar hall), as well as a few smaller rooms that provided quieter spaces of retreat.[30] Café Central attracted, almost from

Figure 3.1. Reinhold Völkel (1873–1938), painting of Café Griensteidl, 1896

the beginning, people from all walks of life, politicians and clerks and in particular writers and journalists. The Jewish writer and journalist Anton Kuh wrote that "Café Central had its roots in the 1890s," and indeed it was only in the late 1890s that Café Central began to be identified as a "literary café," with habitués such as Peter Altenberg, who listed his address as "Vienna, First District, Café Central," as well as Alfred Polgar, Egon Friedell, and the younger Anton Kuh, Franz Werfel, and Franz Blei. Most of these figures were Jewish or of Jewish origins.[31] After the demolition of the Café Griensteidl, members of Jung Wien, as well as their critic Kraus, joined the crowds in Café Central. In spite of the opening of more modern cafés—notably, Café Museum, built by the architect Alfred Loos in 1899—Café Central dominated the cultural and literary scene until the end of World War I.[32] Café Central was also a place of politics, both for people from the Habsburg Empire in its final years and for people who traveled to Vienna from elsewhere in Europe. Leon Trotsky (Lev D. Bronshtein), the Russian-Jewish Marxist who lived in Vienna from 1907 for a number of years, was a habitué of Café Central.[33] There is a well-known anecdote about Leopold Berchtold, the foreign minister of Austria-Hungary, who was warned that World War

I might provoke a revolution in Russia and beyond, to which he replied, "And who will lead this revolution? Perhaps Mr. Bronshtein [Trotsky] sitting at the Café Central?"[34]

Apart from Griensteidl and Central, there were other culturally significant places such as Café Imperial, Café de l'Europe, and Café Landtmann on the Ringstrasse that attracted many of Vienna's writers, journalists, musicians (Mahler, Schoenberg), artists (Klimt, Kokoschka), architects (Loos, Wagner), and philosophers (Wittgenstein). Sigmund Freud used to meet his friends in Café Landtmann, so it was important to the emerging field of Viennese psychoanalysis. It is not necessarily that a certain café was the exclusive domain in one field of activity. This is evident from Edward Timms's influential mapping of the widespread cross-fertilization of several "circles" and groups with intersecting membership within Viennese modernism.[35] As Timms claimed, virtually all these circles were connected to a network of cafés, and thus the institution of the coffeehouse was located as the center of the public sphere of Vienna.[36]

In retrospective memoirs, many people wrote about the inimitable nature of the Viennese café in this period. Especially well known is Stefan Zweig's description of the Viennese café of the "world of yesterday" as "a particular institution which is not comparable to any other in the world, . . . a democratic club to which admission cost the small price of a cup of coffee."[37] The link between cafés and modern literature and culture might have been especially intense in Vienna, but it was not singular. Rather, it was part of the silk road of transnational modern Jewish culture created in urban cafés in Europe and beyond. One unique feature to which Zweig alluded is the fact that the cafés were very hospitable to people who wanted to linger. The Viennese ritual of serving a glass of water with any order of drink signaled that the patron—whether an occasional visitor or a habitué—was welcome to stay as long as he wanted, including the pleasure of being alone to write and think. This tradition was different from Café Fanconi in Odessa, for example, where it was not common for people to sit alone in cafés for a very long time.

A good illustration of the modernist network and the possibilities that were opened to people in cafés, as well as the relatively hospitable nature of Viennese cafés in this period, can be found in the figure of the aforementioned Peter Altenberg. Altenberg's real name was Richard Engländer. He was born in Vienna in 1859 to a well-to-do Jewish merchant family. Engländer was drawn to cafés since he was a student at the University of Vienna in the late 1870s, although he never graduated. During the 1890s, Engländer became estranged from his family and adopted a bohemian lifestyle, as well as the name Peter Altenberg. He slept in hotel rooms and spent a significant part of his time in cafés, socializing, reading the local and international newspapers available in the café, and eventually writing. Like others, he adopted the form of the feuilleton and made his special mark, writing brilliant urban miniatures. According to his own account, perhaps a "functioning myth," he was completely unknown as a writer. In a sketch called "Wie ich Schriftsteller wurde" (How I came to be a writer, 1913), he claimed that he was sitting in Café Central reading a newspaper story that caught his attention. He wrote the feuilleton "Local Chronicle" as an elaborate response to it. While he was writing at the table, Bahr, Schnitzler, Hofmannsthal, Beer-Hofmann, and Felix Salten came in and noticed him writing. Apparently until that point, they were not aware of any distinction of Altenberg apart from being a bohemian, occasionally asking for money for his coffee and food. Because Altenberg was sitting at the café writing, others became curious, read his piece, and were impressed by it, thus launching his literary career.[38]

Altenberg's account might already contain an echo of another well-known anecdote about Hugo von Hofmannsthal, who entered the literary scene at age of seventeen with the publication of his first poems and essays under the pseudonym Loris. Apparently, after reading one of his poems, Hermann Bahr wrote that he summoned Loris to Café Griensteidl. To his surprise, a high-school student appeared, with "a soft caressing hand, the tender hand of a woman very much in love," and to Bahr's astonishment, the student announced, "Ich bin nämlich Loris" (I am Loris).[39] These telling anecdotes go a long way to explain the allure of the café and the pivotal role that it played in the life of Altenberg and Hofmannsthal. But when we realize that, with the exception of Bahr, virtually all of these figures were Jews, the question emerges: How and when was the link formed between Jews, Jewishness, modernism, and these cafés, and, more importantly, what did it mean in the context of fin-de-siècle Vienna? This is an especially tangled web to unravel.

First, there is the association of Jews and turn-of-the-century Vienna modernism. Carl Schorske wrote in his seminal study that "the failure to acquire a monopoly of power left the bourgeois always something of an outsider, seeking integration with the aristocracy. The numerous and prosperous Jewish element in Vienna, with its strong assimilationist thrust, only strengthened this trend."[40] While for Schorske "Jewishness" was incidental to the literature and culture that so many people of Jewish origin produced in Vienna, other scholars developed the insider/outsider paradigm articulated by Schorske in order to equate Viennese modernism with Jewishness or Jewish culture. The architectural historian Peter Hall has written, "the Viennese golden age in its ultimate florescence was peculiarly a creation of that Jewish society: a society of outsiders, who, for all too brief a time, had become insiders."[41] Steven Beller emphasizes Vienna's highly acculturated Jewish population, which had attained unprecedented cultural prominence by the turn of the century, especially in literary circles of Viennese modernism.[42] Jacques Le Rider claims, "The historical circumstances of the Jewish intellectuals who settled in Vienna help us to understand why they in particular were predestined to experience the modern crisis of identity" that is the heart of Viennese modernism.[43]

Since much of fin-de-siècle Vienna modernism was centered in cafés, it was impossible to ignore the huge presence of acculturated Jews in these Viennese literary and artistic cafés. Beller claims that "the two institutions which provided the main milieu for liberal cultural life in Vienna at the turn of the century were the salon and the coffeehouse, . . . and both of them had very high Jewish presence."[44] Harold Segel maintains that what distinguished the fin-de-siècle Viennese literary café from similar institutions in Europe was "its heavily Jewish character."[45] Edward Timms declares that "the Jewish contribution to this exchange of wit constituted an additional enrichment."[46] What was, then, the "Jewish character" of the Viennese café of this period? Is it possible to define and identify its Jewishness? As in other cities discussed in this book, the answer to these questions depends on who wrote about these cafés, when, and where. Perhaps not surprisingly, there is a huge difference between real-time accounts of these urban spaces and reminiscences from between the wars or, even more noticeably, from after World War II. There are also significant differences between accounts of people who used to be habitués and those who looked from the outside, between Jews and non-Jews observing and writing about the café, and between acculturated Jews who wrote in German and those, while no less acculturated to European culture, who wrote in Yiddish and Hebrew.

To be sure, the link between Viennese cafés and Jewish culture began in the years leading to the 1890s and the efflorescence of modernism in Vienna. Arthur Schnitzler, born in Vienna in 1862 to Jewish migrants from Hungary, became a physician, playwright, and writer of fiction and was one of the members of Vienna's famed Jung Wien. He wrote in his autobiography about the time he was a medical student in the early 1880s, when he preferred to meet his friends outside the University of Vienna "on a more neutral ground, in a more congenial atmosphere." The "neutral ground" for Schnitzler was "usually some coffeehouse, like Café Central, where [he] would spend hours reading the papers, playing billiard and dominoes, and . . . chess, with a gray-bearded Polish [i.e., eastern European] Jewish man." Schnitzler wrote that in spite of being a medical student, he felt "altogether so much more at home" in the atmosphere of the café, "especially when there was a bohemian air about it."[47]

Theodor Herzl, who was born in Budapest in 1860 and moved to Vienna with his family in 1878, became best known as the founder of the political Zionist movement in 1897. As a young man, he studied law at the University of Vienna, but like Schnitzler, he was attracted to the world of literature, theater, and journalism, in which he excelled for over twenty years, mainly as a writer of feuilletons.[48] In the 1880s, the young Herzl was a *Stammgast* of several cafés in Vienna, including Café Griensteidl, and he wrote about it in one of his feuilletons: "Das Kaffeehaus der neuen Richtung" (Coffeehouse of the new movement, 1887). In this text, Herzl depicts a group of young people in the café who "boldly identified themselves with the idea of bringing about a radical change in all social, political, literary, and artistic affairs, gasping for fresh air, for new directions in defiance of the outdated systems and senescent authorities."[49]

Peretz Smolenskin moved from Odessa to Vienna in 1868 when he was twenty-five years old. His aim was to study philosophy at the very same University of Vienna, but being penniless, he never managed to do so. To support himself, he worked at a Jewish publishing house that established, in 1869, the Hebrew *maskilic* journal *Ha-shahar* (The dawn), edited in Vienna until Smolenskin's death in 1884. Smolenskin used to visit Vienna cafés in the 1870s and early 1880s and became a habitué of Café National, located at 18 Taborstrasse in the Leopoldstadt. According to Reuven Brainin, "in Café National Smolenskin became Viennese." The waiters knew him and reserved a table for him, where he used to meet both locals and Jews who migrated or visited the city from Galicia and from Poland and Russia.[50] Smolenskin was also instrumental at the founding meeting of the new Jewish Students Association in December 1882, headed by Nathan Birnbaum; the meeting took place in Café Gross at Obere Donaustrasse by the canal. Smolenskin even provided the Hebrew name, Kadimah (Forward), for the association.[51] Being familiar with the cafés and with the press of Vienna, Smolenskin began to experiment with writing Hebrew feuilletons and sketches. In 1878, he established a new, short-lived Hebrew weekly journal with the name *Hamabit* (The spectator), inspired by London's coffeehouse newspaper the *Spectator* of the 1710s and its many adaptations. Smolenskin had hoped that his weekly would sell well and be read by a wide audience. He published many feuilletons, some set in Viennese cafés. One such feuilleton, "Mishpatei bnei-adam" (The trials of men), describes the crash of the Viennese stock exchange in 1873, when many merchants became unemployed and the "question of workers" suddenly became a topic of conversation in the cafés.[52]

Thus, what attracted young, acculturated Jewish men to these cafés in the 1870s and 1880s was the cultural, social, and political movements that presented an alternative to what they found elsewhere in Vienna, even in the university: a "neutral ground," which also facilitated the establishment of new ideas and genres. This can be seen in the case of one of the pioneers of Yiddish theater and poetry in the nineteenth century. The son of well-to-do parents, Benjamin Wolf Ehrenkranz, known as Velvel Zbarazher, was a *maskil* from the town of Zbaraż in Galicia who became a poet and "folk bard," writing his own songs and performing them in Yiddish in cafés and wine cellars. Zbarzher lived in Vienna from 1878 to 1889 and performed at the Café Hackel on Taborstrasse in the Leopoldstadt. His audience there consisted mainly of newcomers, Galician merchants, Jews from established Viennese families, and *maskilim* who flocked to the city from throughout the Habsburg Empire.[53]

In order to better understand the experiences of Schnitzler, Herzl, Smolenskin, and Zbarazher in Vienna's cafés, it is important to remember that during this period, Jewish migration and acculturation occurred in the context of conflicting ideologies and political movements that merged in the cafés of Vienna. At the same time, cafés became identified as "Jewish spaces," as well as breeding grounds for literary and artistic modernism. Thus, side by side with these Jewish students, budding writers, and *maskilim*, one could find in Vienna's cafés such people as Georg Ritter von Schönerer.[54] Schönerer, the founder of the Pan-German Party in 1885, was the best-known spokesman for popular antidemocratic sentiments in the empire and anti-Semitic ideology.[55] Karl Lueger, a Viennese politician who at first tended toward liberalism, founded the Christian Socialist Party in 1893. The party regarded itself as serving the interests of the lower middle classes and attempted to address their needs and fears during a period of rapid social change by using slogans that were anticapitalist, antiliberal, and explicitly anti-Semitic. Eventually, Lueger led his party to gaining the majority in the 1895 municipal elections, and he ended up being the mayor of Vienna from 1897 until his death in 1910.[56]

The *Neue Freie Presse*, a Viennese newspaper and a bastion of the liberal press, reported on December 1896 about a meeting of "Christian Social Women": "In the Praterstrasse noisy and disgusting riots took place. Many women from the respectable middle classes, for whom such kinds of behavior would not have been thought possible, took part."[57] The newspaper reported that the meeting was dissolved by the police, but in its aftermath, many protesters marched through the Leopoldstadt, invading shops and blaming Jews for engineering the dissolution of the meeting. "At Café Licht," the newspaper reported, "the crowd comes to a halt again: several Jewish guests are sitting at the windows, which enrages the mob, and several . . . women tear open the doors of the establishment . . . shouting: 'Down with the Jews! Invade the café.'"[58] As Steven Beller has claimed, both the newspaper report and the often-used proverbial phrase "the Jew belongs in the coffeehouse" point to the strong connection that developed in this period between Viennese cafés and Jews.[59] As the attack on the café shows, this link between Jews and Viennese cafés could be a negative, anti-Semitic claim: if Jews "belong" in the café, they do not belong elsewhere in Vienna, and thus the very institution of the Viennese café becomes "tainted," from an anti-Semitic point of view, with Jewish presence. On the other hand, it also became obvious to everybody, to the point that there was no need to articulate or emphasize it, that Griensteidl and Central, the spaces of modernist literature and art, were perceived as a Jewish realm in the cultural landscape of fin-de-siècle Vienna. This is in spite of the fact that they were not exclusively Jewish. Besides, many Jews in Café Licht and in the famous "literary cafés" of Vienna were acculturated, German-speaking Viennese, whose relationship to Jewishness was complex.

From this perspective, it seems to make sense that young Jewish writers and intellectuals, faced with the rise of anti-Semitism in Viennese politics and society in the 1880s and 1890s, would seek a "neutral ground," or a place to retreat into the café. But the Viennese café, not unlike cafés in Odessa, Warsaw, and other cities, was hardly just a place of refuge. These Jewish writers and intellectuals brought into the space of the Viennese café, which was a space of urban modernism, much of their brilliance and talent, as well as their internal debates, their concerns and fears, their lack of security, and their sense of alienation.

Jewishness, Masculinity, and Modernism in the Fin-de-Siècle Café

All of the foregoing elements can be seen in literary texts in various genres and forms written by Jewish and non-Jewish writers in Vienna. Real or fictional cafés became prominent in stories, plays, novellas, and novels written by many of Vienna's foremost modernist Jewish writers. The genre that was mostly associated with the café was the feuilleton: the hybrid literary-journalistic form of the sketch that mixed cultural criticism with storytelling. The feuilleton originated in Paris's newspapers in 1800 but became popular all over Europe, including in Vienna, in the second half of the nineteenth century, when the master feuilletonist was the Jewish writer Daniel Spitzer. By the turn of the twentieth century, the feuilleton began to function as a modernist literary "snapshot" of the metropolis, with texts that blur the lines between short stories, sketches, journalistic essays, and even the cabaret.[60] As we have seen, the feuilleton also became central in Jewish culture not just in Vienna but all over

Europe and beyond, in German, Russian, Hebrew, Yiddish, and Polish languages, and it was linked with café culture in all these cities. Thus, it is not accidental that the feuilleton was sometimes attacked as being a "Jewish form" by anti-Semites such as Richard Wagner, Heinrich von Treitschke, and Adolf Bartels, as well as the satirist Karl Kraus.[61]

Kraus, born in Jičín, Bohemia, in 1874 to a well-to-do Jewish family which soon migrated to Vienna, became one of the most influential cultural figures. Kraus published his widely read satirical journal, *Die Fackel* (The torch), from 1899 until he died in 1936. Kraus was also a habitué of Café Griensteidl, Café Central, and others.[62] He was initially close to writers associated with Jung Wien. However, what had gained Kraus early notoriety was the pamphlet *Die demolirte Literatur*, in which Kraus wrote about Café Griensteidl when it was about to be torn down in 1879:

> Vienna is now being demolished into a metropolis. Together with the old houses the last pillars of our memories are falling, and soon an irreverent spade will have also leveled the venerable Café Griensteidl to the ground. This was the decision of its proprietors, the consequences of which cannot be foreseen. Our literature is bracing itself for a period of homelessness; the threads of artistic creativity are being cruelly severed. . . . That coffeehouse, . . . like no other, appeared suited to represent the true center of literary activity . . . Who does not remember the almost crushing profusion of newspapers and journals that made the visit to our coffeehouse a virtual necessity for those writers who had no craving for coffee?[63]

To a reader not perfectly attuned to the irony of Kraus, this might sound very much like a celebration of the café, a lament about its demise. But as one continues, the intention and the target of the satire become clearer: the Jung Wien group, "the new literary movement" and its "coffeehouse life."[64] The thrust of Kraus's criticism was that these "modernist iconoclasts" formed, in fact, a coffeehouse clique whose members have the same sensitivities, moods, and opinions, about which they write in similar and faulty ways. In his opinion, they lacked the very radical energy for which they were celebrated.[65] Kraus did not emphasize in the text the fact that most of these writers were Jewish. Rather, he underlined the frivolity of their café existence and their linguistic and literary shortcomings. However, the way in which he wrote and the terms he used make it clear that the criticism is also a reflection of the subtle and complex relation between Viennese modernism, the café, and Jewishness.

Kraus's satire employed an original literary technique, as he emphasized the hierarchical succession from the central figure in the café down to the more marginal ones, adopting the vantage point of the waiter in order to perform a transition between tables.[66] When the text focuses on the central figure, Hermann Bahr, he is repeatedly described as "der Herr aus Linz" (the gentleman from Linz), while the young "Schar von Anhängern" (band of followers) are around him. Kraus's phrasing indicates that the originality and personality, which he attacks no less, belong to Bahr, the Catholic man from the Austrian province widely associated with anti-Semitism. This was true especially of the 1882 "Linz Program," a political platform that called for the complete Germanization of the Austrian state.[67] On the other hand, for Kraus, the largely Jewish and urban followers of Bahr in the café, the writers of Jung Wien, are mere imitators: they follow Bahr in the same way in which Hasidim follow their Rebbe at his table. While this is highly implicit in the text, toward the end of the pamphlet, Kraus's narrator follows the waiter's gaze and arrives at one of the marginal tables. Over there, there is one, writes Kraus, "who over a period of years, and through the changes of direction to which this café was subject, held steadfast to his point of view; the one comment you read from him even today is 'Jew!' "[68] Kraus parodied the anti-Semitic fixation with Jews and indicated that one critic remained steadfast in this fixation, which manifested itself in his attempts to identify others as being "Jewish." Thus, even with only one explicit reference to Jews, Kraus's satire underlines the perceived "Jewishness" of the Vienna café as a highly contentious thirdspace, in which anti-Semitism and liberalism, conservatism and urban modernism, productivity and frivolity are entangled.

In another pamphlet by Kraus, *Eine Krone für Zion* (A crown for Zion, 1898), Jewishness and "the Jewish Question" play an explicit role. The pamphlet was essentially a critique of the new movement of Zionism after the first Congress in Basel, 1897. But Kraus continued to target the same object of criticism in "The Demolished Literature." In this text, he coupled the issue of Vienna's café life and its modernist writers

and journalists with a new theme: the bad consequence of Jewish assimilation and the Zionist attempt to escape it by driving the Jews to a
"new Ghetto" elsewhere.[69] Here Kraus writes that the Jewish sons of the
wealthy bourgeoisie "have perfected a moral emptiness and an aristocracy of the fingertips, . . . a special type of the feudal Jew." As an example
of the modern type of false "Jewish nobility," Kraus describes a certain
man, perhaps Herzl himself, "who only appears in his *Stamm* ["regular"
but also "inherited," "race"] café, wearing his steel-tipped shoes because
he wants to summon a suggestion of the equestrian. The matching horse
is no doubt stuck somewhere in the Middle-Ages."[70]

This new "Jewish knight," riding on an imaginary medieval horse in
search of integration and assimilation by seeking a way out, can only
enact such fantastical performance in his *Stammtisch*, his regular table,
already inherited from a previous generation in the Viennese café. Thus,
both literary-bohemian and bourgeois-Zionist culture, with their partly
overlapping circles, from which Kraus wanted to distance himself, are
manifested in particular Vienna cafés that took on a certain "Jewish"
character. The fact that Kraus was Jewish and went to the same cafés is
at the heart of the profound paradox he created. As Paul Reitter claims,
Kraus never ascribed the shortcomings of Vienna's Jewish modernists or
Zionists to an inherited cognitive flaw or to an unbridgeable cultural al-
terity, as in anti-Semitic discourse. Nevertheless, he constantly asserted
his opposition to Jewish anti-Semitism, as well as Zionism, modernism, and the bourgeoisie, in anti-Semitic terms as part of his rhetorical
strategy.[71]

Kraus was far from being the only person to do that. The main objects of Kraus's satire in *Eine Krone für Zion*, Theodor Herzl and Max
Nordau, did something quite similar in their writing. In 1891, Herzl,
the talented feuilleton writer and playwright, became the Paris correspondent for the *Neue Freie Presse*. By the time Herzl left the Paris position in 1895 in order to become the feuilleton editor of the newspaper
back in Vienna, he gradually came to a realization that Der Judenstaat
("The Jewish State," which would become the name of his famous 1896
pamphlet) was the only possible solution to the "Jewish question" and
to the modern anti-Semitism that vexed him. Herzl enlisted Max Nordau, a physician, antimodernist intellectual, and author of the book
Entartung (Degeneration, 1892), to help him, and both of them were

instrumental in establishing Zionism as a political movement and convening its first Congress in Basel, 1897.[72]

The "Jewishness" of the Viennese cafés has been described as something very negative by the founding fathers of Zionism, despite, or perhaps because of, the fact that they were themselves café habitués. In Max Nordau's oft-quoted address to the Second Zionist Congress in 1898, "Muskeljudentum" (Muscular Judaism), he called for Jews to become "men of muscle" instead of remaining "slaves to their nerves." Unlike the "coffeehouse Jews" of the Diaspora, the "New Jews," said Nordau, should "rise early . . . and not be weary before sunset, . . . have clear heads, solid stomachs and hard muscles."[73] When Nordau's colleague Theodor Herzl wanted to portray what seemed to him to be the dire situation of Viennese Jews—and Jews in western and central Europe in general—he used the space of the café as an illustration of his new ideology. This is in spite of his 1887 text about Café Griensteidl and the allure of the new movements there. In 1902, when Herzl published his major literary work, the Zionist utopian novel *Altneuland*, he chose Dr. Friedrich Löwenberg, a quintessential "coffeehouse Jew," to be one of the main protagonists. In fact, the scene that opens this novel takes place in a fin-de-siècle Viennese *Kaffeehaus*:

> Sunk in deep melancholy, Dr. Friedrich Löwenberg sat at a round marble table in his café on the Alsergrund. It was one of the most charming of Viennese cafés. Ever since his student days he had been coming there, appearing every afternoon at five o'clock with bureaucratic punctuality. The sickly, pale waiter greeted him submissively, and he would bow with formality to the equally pale girl cashier to whom he never spoke. After that, he would seat himself at the round reading table, drink his coffee, and read the papers with which the waiter plied him. And when he had finished with the dailies and the weeklies, the comic sheets and the professional magazines . . . there were chats with friends or solitary musings.[74]

Café Birkenreis in Herzl's novel is located in the Alsergrund, a district that had a large percentage of Jews, most of them middle class and professional. The café, although *gemütlich* (charming or cozy), represents, in fact, the stagnation of "old Europe" in its decline, which is parallel to what is seen as a dead end for emancipated, acculturated Jews. Herzl's narrator emphasizes the "sickly, pale waiter" and the "equally pale girl cashier" as a sign of "degeneration," which is in turn mirrored in the character of Dr. Friedrich Löwenberg—a desperate, overeducated young Jewish man who can do nothing but endlessly read newspapers in the café. Interestingly, some of the very same reasons that made the Viennese café so attractive to Jews from across the empire are depicted as reasons for the Jews to leave Vienna, and Europe altogether, in search of modern Jewish nationalism that is "rooted in the soil" of their ancient home in Palestine, where most of Herzl's utopian novel takes place. As Steven Beller claims, it is quite clear that for most Jews, both the attraction of and the repulsion from the café were exactly in the fact that it was not "rooted in the soil." As much as the café was or became a famed Viennese institution, it was an urban establishment found in many other cities and urban centers all over Europe and beyond.[75]

The café scene in Herzl's novel represented not only a quintessential "Viennese-Jewish" locale but also a gendered, homosocial space. Löwenberg is gazing at "several young men" who "stood about the billiard table, making bold strokes with their long poles." These men, Herzl's narrator emphasizes, are mostly "budding physicians, newly baked jurists, freshly graduated engineers," Jews who completed their professional schooling and now had nothing to do but to play billiards at the café. In spite of the fact that Löwenberg is very similar to these men, he also envies their ability to play billiards and make "bold strokes" with their "long poles"— the phallic imagery is quite explicit. As the novel moves away from the Viennese café and away from Europe into a future Palestine, Löwenberg is transformed from a "green, hollow-chested Jewboy" into a "strong like an oak" man, who might even be "dangerous to women" and thus closer to the ideal of masculinity that Herzl had in mind.[76] Gender and the crisis of masculinity are central to the experience of Jewish café culture in the novel.

For Herzl, Nordau, Kraus, and others, the café is not just a Jewish space but also a gendered space, one that is associated mostly with a "degenerated" masculinity of melancholic, pale, bookish Jewish men.[77] Perhaps the most complex examples of dealing with all three interrelated elements are found within the writings of Arthur Schnitzler, from his breakthrough novella *Lieutenant Gustl* (1901) to the major novel *Der Weg ins Freie* (The way to the open, 1908).[78] The main protagonist in the novel is Georg von Wergenthin, a young Catholic aristocrat and an aspiring composer. However, the faltering Georg befriends several Jewish individuals and unwittingly steps into their heated discussions and their world, which is dominated by cafés:

> [Georg] considered whether or not to go to the coffeehouse. He wasn't particularly in the mood. Bermann stayed at the Ehrenbergs' today; one couldn't count on Leo Golowski coming, and the other young people, mostly Jewish literati that Georg had recently come to know casually. . . . On the whole, he found the tone of these young people among themselves sometimes too familiar, sometimes too strange, sometimes too witty, sometimes too solemn.[79]

For Georg, the café is the domain of "mostly Jewish literati," and this causes his hesitation and a range of reactions, which the narrator follows minutely. But the novel is also full of scenes of Jewish writers and intellectuals inside a café—probably modeled after the Griensteidl— arguing and exposing their vanities, illusions, and fears. In one of these café scenes, the sensitive and constantly probing Jewish writer Heinrich Bermann criticizes Herr Winternitz, another aspiring young Jewish poet, for his use of the German language. Winternitz's poem has four stanzas, each of which ends with a line that begins not with "Ich" (I), but with the "lyrical, subjective Hei" form of German. The scene recounts a discussion over the merit and authenticity of using such a poetic German word. After some deliberations, Winternitz declares that "he hoped sometime to fight his way through to that inner freedom from which it would be allowed to cry out 'Hei,' in a poem." Bermann ends the discussion proclaiming, "this time will never come. . . . You may perhaps get some time to the epic or the dramatic Hei, but the lyrical or subjective hei remains for you, remains for all like us . . . denied for all eternity."[80] A few minutes later, Heinrich and Georg continue the conversation in the café, and Bermann, looking at the Jews talking at a nearby table, contrasts the "lyrical, subjective" German *hei* with the Yiddish *ä-soi* (*azoy*)—a familiar phrase with many different meanings, used as an exclamation—that "is floating on the lips" of many people Bermann knows. When Georg expresses his misunderstanding, Bermann tells him a story about a "Polish Jew who sat with a stranger in a railroad car, very politely—until he realized from a remark of the other that he was a Jew too, whereupon, with a sigh of ä-soi, he immediately put his legs up on the seat across from him"[81]

These scenes in Schnitzler's novel point to a number of significant tensions around the Jewishness of the Viennese café. Chief among these tensions was the anxiety about using the German language, in which many of the young acculturated Jewish writers excelled but never felt that they could be, or were allowed to be, completely at home and perhaps never would be, as Bermann contends. At the same time, the little joke or anecdote that Bermann told Georg about the Polish Jew who is very polite and proper until he finds out that his neighbor is a Jew points to a related anxiety of the acculturated Viennese Jews, namely, that behind their integration and acculturation, even attempts of radical assimilation, lurks the "old" Jew, who is almost always connected to eastern Europe and Yiddish. The anxiety was related, of course, to the fact that many of the Jews in Vienna were themselves migrants or children of immigrants who came from families that not too long before were Yiddish-speaking "Polish Jews." This also explains much of the disdain that the Jewish bourgeoisie and the Jewish artists—bohemian as they might have been—felt toward more recent migrants from Galicia, Russia, and Poland, the *Ostjuden* who were increasingly drawn to Vienna toward the turn of the twentieth century, and their anxiety that this kind of migration would add fuel to the already explosive anti-Semitism in a city whose mayor was Karl Lueger. All these elements played a major role in Viennese café culture and the perception of its Jewishness. The fact that all of these tensions and anxieties are recorded through the viewpoint of the aristocratic gentile Georg, who needs people like Bermann to decipher them, adds to the complexity and subtlety of Schnitzler's novel and its depiction of the culture of the café as a Jewish and homosocial space.

In this context, it is useful to contemplate Friedrich Torberg's retrospective account of Viennese café culture in *Die Tante Jolesch, oder der Untergang des Abendlandes in Anekdoten* (Aunt Jolesch; or, the decline of the West in anecdotes). In spite of the title, in this series of feuilletons, Torberg goes beyond nostalgic anecdotes. He claimed that the café "was the fertile soil from which the dramatis personae extracted their secret life-giving juices, . . . a protection and sounding board, in short, a spiritual home." What is most surprising about Torberg's description of the Viennese café is his understanding of the institution as a spiritual home with links to traditional Jewish culture:

> The coffeehouse had its share of Tante Jolesch, that she is the "missing link" between the Talmudic tradition of the ghetto and emancipated café culture, that she was, as it were, the ancestral mother of all those people who found in the coffeehouse the catalyst and focal point of their existence, and she was their primal mother whether they knew it or not, whether they liked it or not.[82]

The link that Torberg makes—between the "Talmudic tradition" of what he calls the traditional "Jewish ghetto" and the secularized, emancipated, acculturated Viennese world of the café—is oblique but fascinating. Torberg seems to suggest that there was a missing, hidden link—embodied, interestingly, in the female figure of the old aunt from the Jewish shtetl who actually "never set foot in the café"—between the traditional Jewish "house of study," where Jews studied Talmud for centuries, and Vienna's café culture. We have seen such a link made by secularized eastern European Jews who received traditional Jewish educations, but Torberg is not one of them.

Perhaps what Torberg had in mind is the intriguing idea that there is a strong link between the café as "the focal point of their existence" and the Talmudic culture of intellectual debate and homosocial camaraderie that characterized the traditional Jewish "house of study."[83] This makes Torberg's link less oblique, because the café, although far from being an exclusively "Jewish space," functions in a similar way, enabling and fostering bonding, debate, and creativity, at least to the male and highly educated participants in the two institutions. Torberg seemed to suggest that the other side of the equation between the Jewish "house of study" and the café is the idleness and the insularity of the institution that comes along with the camaraderie and argumentativeness, as well as the productivity, creativity, and wit it also generates.

These aspects of the café as a Jewish space are also captured by Alfred Polgar's sardonic feuilleton "Theorie des Café Central" (Theory of Café Central, 1926). Polgar, born in 1873 as Alfred Polak to a Jewish immigrant family that owned a piano school in the Leopoldstadt, was a master feuilletonist and writer of fiction and cabaret, as well as a Viennese café habitué until his move to Berlin in 1925. Polgar used the Café Central to sketch what we might call a "physiology" of a Viennese "literary café."[84] "The Café Central," he declared in an obvious display of wit, "is indeed a coffeehouse unlike any other coffeehouse":

> [It is] a worldview and one, to be sure, whose innermost essence is not to observe the world at all. . . . So much is experientially certain, that there is nobody in the Café Central who isn't a piece of the Central: that is to say, on whose ego-spectrum the Central color, a mixture of ash-gray and ultra-seasick-green, doesn't appear. . . . The Café Central lies on the Viennese latitude at the meridian of loneliness. Its inhabitants are, for the most part, people whose hatred of their fellow human beings is as fierce as their longing for people, who want to be alone but need companionship for it. . . . There are writers, for example, who are unable to carry out their literary chores anywhere but at the Café Central. Only there, only at the tables of idleness, is the worktable laid for them, only there, enveloped by the air of indolence, will their inertia become fecundity.[85]

Polgar did not mention Jews or Jewishness in this feuilleton, yet in his text—as in those of Schnitzler, Herzl, Kraus, Torberg, and other Jewish Viennese writers—the café is marked covertly as "Jewish" and as a third-space with distinctively contradictory features: it is a place of leisure and sociability, as well as a place of production, a literary market and information source exempt from the pressure to consume. At the same time, it is a place of consumption and of noncommitment, of time-killing and gossip, a refuge for dropouts and failures who can find their place only in the café. Polgar depicts the coffeehouse as a "surrogate totality" for uprooted individuals, people "who want to be alone but need companionship for it."[86] The "Jewish space" of the Viennese café has been a space of exchange of literature, criticism, and conversation that mediates the pressures of the alienating outside and the excesses and insularity of the inside.

Ostjuden, Westjuden, Café Arkaden, and the Herrenhof

The justified fascination with fin-de-siècle Vienna produced a perception that modernist creativity in the metropolis consisted of a brief

WIENER CAFE: DER LITTERAT.

Figure 3.2. Moriz Jung, *Viennese Café: The Man of Letters*, 1911
(Wiener Werkstätte)

period during which writers, artists, and thinkers, most of them Jewish, functioned as the primary producers and promoters of modernism.
The world of the Viennese café has been described in the writings of
these acculturated Jews, who quickly became well-known figures in
international modernism. Thus, we tend to ignore the fact that around
World War I, Vienna was also an important site of a different, and more

marginal, Jewish modernist creativity in Hebrew and Yiddish, as well as the fact that Vienna in the interwar period was the arena of new and intensified forms of expression in areas in which Jews played significant roles.[87]

During the first two decades of the twentieth century, there was a new wave of migration of eastern European Jews from small towns in Galicia and the Russian Pale of Settlement to Vienna. With the growth of the Jewish population from 99,000 in 1890 to 175,000 in 1910, Vienna became the second-largest Jewish community in Europe after Warsaw. A large portion of this population growth was due to migration from the east. Most of the Jewish migrants were poor, and after arriving at the Nordbahnhof train station, they settled not far from it, in the Leopold-stadt.[88] Even during this period of intense migration, the Leopoldstadt was not dominated by the Jewish population, but Jewishness was more visible there. With its many synagogues, Jewish shops, markets, and crowded apartment buildings, the area looked and felt to many people like a Jewish shtetl, but the presence of many cafés made it impossible to forget that it was very much part of Vienna.[89] The author Joseph Roth, who was born in Brody, Galicia, and moved from Lemberg to study at the University of Vienna, lived in the city between 1913 and 1923. He wrote in a feuilleton about cafés in Leopoldstadt, where he resided: "The two principal streets of Leopoldstadt are Taborstrasse and the Prater-strasse. The Praterstrasse is almost elegant, . . . peopled by Jews and Christians. There are lots of cafés on it, . . . on the Taborstrasse too. They are Jewish cafés." Roth remarks that "Jews like to go to cafés to read the paper, to play tarocks and chess, to do deals."[90]

Before World War I and during the war years, Vienna became a crossroads for western and eastern European Judaism, and among the migrants, there was a small but extraordinary group of Yiddish and Hebrew writers, journalists, intellectuals, and political activists who were attracted to the city. The list includes the Hebrew writers Gershon Shofman, David Vogel (Fogel), Avraham Ben-Yitzhak (known as "Dr. Sonne"), Zvi Diesendruk, Ya'akov Horovitz, and the Yiddish writers Me-lech Ravitch, Melech Chmelnitzki, Meir Wiener, Avrom Moyshe Fuchs, Moyshe Lifshits, S. Y. Imber, Moyshe Zilberg, and Michael Weichert. It was a diverse group: some of them wrote in both Jewish languages, and some were involved in socialist or Zionist activities, while others

Figure 3.3. Photograph of Türkischer Tempel and a Café in Leopoldstadt, 1900

remained uncommitted. Vienna attracted them because of its relative proximity, as well as its university and its renowned cultural life.

The Yiddish poet Melech Ravitch, who was born in Radymno, East Galicia, and moved to Vienna from Lemberg in 1912, wrote about his "dream of Vienna," a dream that he first had a long time before his actual arrival:

My dream was interwoven with the great and world-famous Viennese literature: Schnitzler, Altenberg, Richard Beer-Hofmann, Stefan Zweig, Hugo von Hofmannsthal, with Viennese art and Viennese beauty. . . . It was bubbling, filled with hopeful youth that knows not even exactly what it wants. How it came about that I combined all my Viennese dreams and hopes with an unshaken determination to be and to remain a Yiddish writer? That I cannot remember today.[91]

Ravitch makes clear that the magnetism of Vienna had to do with the cultural modernist activity of acculturated Jews, but he also emphasizes the commitments of migrants to writing Yiddish or Hebrew. Once Yiddish and Hebrew writers and activists arrived in Vienna, they launched literary periodicals, publishing houses, and newspapers; founded local branches of Zionist and national-diasporic movements; and revived the Yiddish theater in the city.[92] For many of them, the Viennese *Kaffeehaus* was a place to find a substitute of community, a space of connection to other cities, in which they could meet, write, and create and that brought migrant writers, artists, and intellectuals together and sometimes opened new paths for them. Cafés were also places where they experienced the shocks of the metropolis and the upheavals of the period. Vienna fostered close collaboration and exchange between Hebrew and Yiddish writers at a time when these two literatures were gradually separating from each other for political reasons, as well as between the eastern European migrants and the more established Viennese writers and intellectuals who wrote in German. Migrant writers were attracted to cafés in recognizably "Jewish areas" of the city, Leopoldstadt and Alsergrund, as well as to well-known "literary cafés" in the center of the city and to Café Reklame and Café Astoria on the Praterstrasse, where Yiddish theatrical performances took place.

However, in the years before and during World War I, it was Café Arkaden (or Arcaden)—located on the Reichsratsstrasse, near the University of Vienna—that emerged as the most important site for eastern European Jewish writers and intellectuals in the city. Café Arkaden was not as famed as Central or the old Griensteidl, but it was patronized by Ludwig Wittgenstein, Kurt Gödel, and members of the philosophical Vienna Circle, as well as by many students and musicians.[93] Yiddish and Hebrew writers, journalists, and political activists portrayed Café Arkaden as the meeting place of "students, writers, journalists, publishers, artists and bohemians from Austria and from all around the world," but they especially emphasized that it was a place in which Jewish migrants from Galicia, Poland, and Russia felt at home.[94]

Figure 3.4. Photograph of Café Arkaden, circa 1880s

Daniel Charney wrote that in Café Arkaden he would meet the Socialist Zionist leader Ber Borochov, who lived in Vienna between 1912 and 1914, and Nathan Birnbaum, who turned from a Zionist into a fervent Yiddishist, as well as representatives of several Jewish socialist parties of Russia, who regularly held their meetings there. All these Jewish political and cultural activists mingled with those who "at ten in the evening just began their bohemian life" in the café.[95] The journalist Meir Henisch noted that apart from newspapers from the German-speaking world, Hebrew and Yiddish newspapers were available in the Arkaden, which was a huge attraction that set it apart from other well-known Viennese cafés.[96]

World War I was a major break in the life of Vienna and its Jewish population, as it was for all people of the Austro-Hungarian Empire.[97] At first, Jewish loyalty, the "wall-to-wall Jewish patriotism" to the multiethnic empire that emancipated the Jews and to the aging emperor, was prevalent.[98] However, soon after the war began, the frame of mind of many of Vienna's Jews changed, as the situation in Vienna itself deteriorated and as the war in the eastern front intensified with no end in sight and with many Jewish refugees. The breakout of World War I partly suspended the intense Jewish cultural activities of writers, journalists, and activists—both locals and migrants—who had gathered in Vienna cafés. Correspondents of foreign newspapers, especially Jewish journalists with Russian citizenship, had to leave Vienna. Many citizens of the Habsburg Empire were enlisted. At the same time, distressed Galician Jews streamed into Vienna, fleeing the devastations in the war zone, including Yiddish and Hebrew writers, journalists, and actors. The presence of refugees became a constant and pervasive theme of wartime Jewish debate in Vienna, and their influence was felt in many areas. Their visible presence in the city served to highlight the "Jewish Question" in Vienna for Jews and non-Jews alike, precipitating an eruption of virulent anti-Semitism that initially targeted the refugees but was later directed at Viennese Jews in general.[99] Some Jewish habitués of the cafés, such as Joseph Roth and Melech Ravitch, served in the Habsburg army; the Hebrew writers Gershon Shofman and David Vogel, born in the Russian Empire, found themselves "behind enemy lines."

Roth offered a sharp portrait of Viennese cafés around World War I, with the character of the antihero of the novella *Zipper und sein Vater* (*Zipper and His Father*, 1928).[100] The novella is set in Vienna of the 1910s and early 1920s, with Arnold Zipper and his father seen through the eyes of their friend the narrator. Although the Zippers are never explicitly referred to as Jewish, the identification is implicit. The Zipper family welcomes the arrival of their son's fatherless friend, and the boy is attracted to what seems to him to be their cozy middle-class life. Zipper Senior is determined that his children will attain the success that was denied to him. In the years before World War I, Zipper Senior visits a local café daily. The narrator emphasizes that inside the café, "time has ceased to exist": the old clock that hung over the cash desk was still ticking, and the hours were still passing, but nobody knew what the time was—a symbol of the aging Habsburg Empire, which was moving, unknowingly, toward an apocalypse, when "one Sunday, a hot summer's day. The Crown Prince was shot in Sarajevo,"[101] and World War I broke out. At first, Zipper Senior is elated, but it is Arnold Zipper and the narrator who are sent to the front. When the war ends, the economic situation in Vienna turns grim, but Zipper Senior helps his son to get a position as a civil servant in the Finance Ministry of the new Austrian Republic. However, Arnold Zipper cannot bear his job, and his evening visits to the café "became a passion rather than habit."[102] The narrator observes that Arnold

> had found it difficult to spend an evening alone, he was now possessed by a real horror of solitude. Not that he wished to be part of a community. He just wanted to sit in a coffeehouse, nowhere else but his coffeehouse. . . . Only on entering this coffeehouse was Arnold free of his day. Here began his freedom, for although the revolving doors never ceased moving, Arnold could be certain that inside this coffeehouse he would never encounter anyone who reminded him of his work or indeed any work whatsoever.[103]

For Arnold, who "could no longer live without the sight of the small, round white tables," the café is less of a place of sociability, debate, and creativity and more a place of freedom from the oppression of bureaucratic work in the Austrian government, as well as from the double horror of solitude on the one hand and of a stifling community on the other. He is described as a "listener" and a "spectator . . . among the writers" but one that all the habitués liked to have as a receptive audience.[104] Thus, Arnold Zipper is a good representative of the generation of young Jewish men whose lives were shattered following the war and the economic and political upheaval. His strange presence as a habitué in the Viennese "literary café"—like that of his father in the waning years of the empire—was very much a sign of the changing times and the crisis of the crumbling Habsburg Empire, the new Austrian Republic, Vienna, and its Jews.

The same period that is in the heart of Roth's German novel is captured in a very different way in Gershon Shofman's Hebrew story "Bamatsor u va-matsok" (In siege and distress, 1922). The story is set in

Vienna during and after the war; the Viennese café is the space where a group of eastern European Jewish writers, artists, and intellectuals can look for some sense of social belonging and where they try to assimilate into the local and international bohemian and intellectual life. The advent of the war, however, shakes Vienna and reveals the café as a space that could be especially dangerous for émigrés and exiles from eastern Europe. The café reveals a more sinister face. With its elusive promise of social engagement and sense of belonging, the wartime café actually comes to prevent real human connection and communication. Thick cigarette smoke masks people's faces, at once linking people and alienating them within a shared miasma. Nor does the café provide protection against policemen searching for army defectors. The young protagonists quickly realize that the urban space of Vienna comprises many locations that fuse the private and the public and that the desired "outside" can actually become a series of closed and restricting spaces: the café, the army prison, the soup kitchen, the sanatorium. At the same time, the closed space in which they try to create a protective, homey environment is itself permeated by the "outside." Thus, two contradictory desires intersect in the café: the desire for the outside, for Viennese, central European society, and the desire for an intimate, protective place. The conflicted yearning is so strong in the story that the poet David Gol (modeled after David Vogel) is indifferent to the prospects of sitting in an army prison, and a painter gives himself to the police and ends up in a sanatorium.

The literary texts of Roth and Shofman cannot be understood without the historical context of the transformation of Vienna following the Great War. After the collapse of the Habsburg Empire in 1918, the newly established "Republic of German-Austria" was rocked from the very beginning by financial and political crisis. The devastating inflation in the early 1920s brought it close to economic collapse. Vienna's celebrated status as the cosmopolitan, cultural center of a vast monarchy was reduced to that of an overblown capital city of a small nation-state that was in a desperate need to redefine itself, as well as its Jews, as "Austrian." At the same time, the interwar period led to new and intensified forms of Jewish expression in Vienna. The relatively stable, if not unproblematic, self-understandings of Vienna Jews as one minority among many in the vast territory of Austria-Hungary was thrown into disarray by a war, the establishment of the republic, and new forms of Austrian anti-Semitism.

Jews responded to the state of affairs in the reconfigured boundaries of the new Austrian Republic mostly by strengthening their allegiance to Vienna and its cultural reputation as cosmopolitan metropolis.[105]

The interwar period was also a time of growth and demographic transformation in the Jewish community of Vienna. In 1923, the Jewish population reached a peak of 201,513 out of 1,865,780 inhabitants (10.8 percent), including the large influx of war refugees from Galicia and elsewhere. The city became also known in the 1920s as "Red Vienna," when the Social Democrats had the majority and the city was democratically governed for the first time. As Lisa Silverman notes, for the rest of the Austrian Republic, especially the provinces, "Red Vienna" represented a socialist and "Jewish" metropolis. At the same time, within the bounds of the city, a complex coding of "Jewish space" affected how all residents established, used, and described their city. These physical and symbolic spatial distinctions mirrored the country's larger city/province divide.[106] The persistence of the Leopoldstadt as a "Jewish district," as well as a number of cafés that were seen or imagined as "Jewish spaces," served a purpose for both Jews and non-Jews: it enabled them to envision other urban spaces they wished to design or inhabit as "non-Jewish" or even empty of Jews.

One of the most emblematic literary texts of interwar Jewish Vienna was the satirical novel *Die Stadt ohne Juden* (*The City without Jews*, 1922), written by the Jewish-born writer Hugo Bettauer. It was an attempt to imagine what would happen if Vienna were emptied of its two hundred thousand Jews. At the beginning of the novel, the leader of the party, who becomes the mayor of Vienna, declares, "Let's look at Austria of today. Who has the press and therefore the public Opinion in his hand? The Jew! Who has since the calamitous year of 1914 heaped billions upon billions? The Jew! . . . Who owns our theaters? The Jew! . . . Who fills the coffeehouses . . . ? The Jew!"[107] The narrator captures the absurdity of the situation when he describes anti-Semitic demonstrations in Vienna, in which people with "hooked nose or conspicuously black-hair were given a thorough beating" and when "the banks and the cafés closed down their doors and pulled down their shades."[108] Thus, it is clear that even if the cafés do not exhibit anything "visibly Jewish," they are coded as Jewish spaces. Later in the novel, when the Jews are indeed being expelled, Viennese culture dries up, newspapers become boring, cafés empty out, and intellectual life comes to halt. Furthermore, the cafés are replaced by lowbrow taverns whose customers seek drunken revelry rather than conversation and exchange of ideas. Bettauer's novel was very controversial when it was published in 1922, but its power was in making explicit and unequivocal what was implicit and unspoken: the prominence of Jews in Vienna, in Viennese culture, and in its cafés.

The attachment of Viennese Jews to the institution of the café continued in the interwar period, as did the dominance of Jewish habitués in the famous "literary café" of the day. Although there were many people who declared and lamented the "death" of Viennese café culture in the 1920s, together with the demise of the empire,[109] in fact, café culture in Vienna was not dying, but it was changing. The interwar period saw the transition from the dominance of Café Central to Café Herrenhof, which was established by the Jewish owners Bela Waldmann and Markus Klug in 1918, just when Vienna was transformed into the capital of the new Austrian Republic. It was located on the same street, the Herrengasse, as the Central. Compared to Café Central and the old Griensteidl Café, Herrenhof was spacious and modern. It was decorated in *Jugendstil* pattern. It consisted of a large, light-filled central room with glass roof and had a smaller back room that became especially popular among writers and journalists.[110] Anton Kuh, the Jewish Viennese writer and café habitué who was a master of the witty feuilleton genre in the interwar period, wrote that until 1918, "there existed far and wide just a single literary café, the central"; but then one by one the writers withdrew from it, and it "died." The new café was Herrenhof, a "spacious, light, sumptuous, impersonal, bourgeois family coffeehouse," which for Kuh indicated "emancipation from the blasé smell of bohemia," with an air that was of the new "Red Vienna." Kuh also noted the increasing presence of women, to the point that he contrasted the old Café Central as "an asylum for masculine resignation" with the new Café Herrenhof as "a coach house for waiting Ladies."[111]

When reading Kuh's feuilleton, one gets the sense that Café Herrenhof was well suited to interwar Vienna, with the increased political involvement in these tumultuous years, with changing gender roles, and with a new set of habitués that included the younger generation of Kuh, Joseph Roth, Robert Musil, Franz Werfel, Elias Canetti, Hermann Broch, Egon Erwin Kisch, and Friedrich Torberg. Café Herrenhof also attracted, for

Figure 3.5. Photograph of Café Herrenhof, 1930s (Courtesy of Stefan L. Popper)

the first time, a number of women writers such as Veza Canetti, Hilde Spiel, Gina Kaus, and Vicki Baum. As in the cafés of fin-de-siècle Vienna, the overwhelming majority of these writers—men and women—were Jewish. The journalist Milan Dubrovic, who came to Vienna from the provinces, claimed that 80 percent of the habitués of Café Herrenhof were Jewish and that he felt that as a young, aspiring non-Jewish writer in Vienna, he had to create his own space in a "Jewish literary café."[112]

The Hebrew and Yiddish modernist writers in Vienna were equally attracted to Café Herrenhof during the 1920s. This was a time of brief but significant artistic blossoming and intensification of literary activities for many of them.[113] Gershon Shofman and Zvi Disendrook edited and published a short-lived but highly important journal titled *Gevulot* (Borders, 1918–1920) and later *Peret* (1922–1924) that published innovative modernist Hebrew works. This activity in Hebrew publishing coincided with the peak of Yiddish publishing with the journal *Kritik*, edited by Moyshe Zilberg, and the publishing house Kval.[114]

Gender and the Multilingual (Jewish) Literary Space in Interwar Vienna

All these developments were part of a renewed encounter of German-speaking Viennese Jewish writers with Yiddish and Hebrew, which occurred during these years at different levels. During the First World War, many of them saw Jewish life in the Russian Empire for the first time. After the war, they encountered masses of emigrants and refugees from eastern Europe. They also had access to German translations from modern Yiddish and Hebrew literature and were exposed to artistic Yiddish theater from eastern Europe.[115] During the early 1920s, many Hebrew and Yiddish writers and modernist figures working in German and other languages first encountered one another in cafés. Thus, Gershon Shofman met Peter Altenberg in Café Central during the war and ended up translating Altenberg's short stories into Hebrew.[116] This close relationship left a strong impact on Shofman's modernist style, which became even more inclined to the Viennese feuilleton. Elias Canetti met Avraham Ben-Yitzḥak ("Dr. Sonne") in Café Herrenhof and Café Museum, and he admired the modernist Hebrew poet.[117] Canetti recorded in his memoir the connections between Dr. Sonne and Robert Musil, Arnold Schoenberg, Hofmannsthal, Beer-Hofmann, Broch, and James Joyce. Canetti wrote, "I knew nothing about Sonne; he consisted entirely of his statements, so much so that the prospect of discovering anything else about him would have frightened me. . . . He was ideas, so much so that one noticed nothing else."[118] The Hebrew and Yiddish writers David Vogel and Meir Wiener were also acquainted with Viennese modernists whom they met in Café Herrenhof, and these connections are clearly demonstrated in their poetry and fiction.[119]

This rich literary and cultural cross-fertilization occurred both in spite of and because of the marginality of Hebrew and Yiddish in Vienna, a marginality that was not only linguistic but also spatial. Like most eastern European Jewish migrants, Hebrew and Yiddish writers lived and worked on the visible and invisible borderlines between Vienna's cultural centers of modernism and the geographically bounded sections of the city. Even in the 1920s and early 1930s, when Meir Wiener, David Vogel, Avraham Ben-Yitzḥak, and other Hebrew and Yiddish writers spent much time with intellectual friends in Café Herrenhof and Café Museum, Leopoldstadt—with its own cafés—remained their tentative and provisional "home," the base from which the writers and their fictional protagonists explored the city. Hebrew and Yiddish writers David Vogel, A. M. Fuchs, and Melech Chmelnitzki produced literary representations of the cityscape and its cafés, which can be examined side by side with literary texts written by German-speaking Jews. These literary texts—novels, shorts stories, and poems—were clearly written in a mixture of expressionist and impressionist modes with *Neue Sachlichkeit* forms of visual art, mass-produced photography, and cinema. They highlight the changing nature of the metropolis and of gender roles and identities, the changes in Vienna's Jewish geography, socioeconomic tensions, and new kinds of anti-Semitic pressures.

A. M. Fuchs's powerful novella *Unter der brik* (Under the bridge, 1924) is a narrative that breaks the lines between the real and imagined Jewish underworld of Leopoldstadt. "Under the bridge" is the uncharted gray area between the Nordbanhof train station—the point of entry for most eastern European Jews to Vienna—and the nearby Prater, with its famous amusement park and gardens. The protagonist of the novel is Maxl, a Jewish pimp who shares the space "under the bridge" with impoverished prostitutes and disabled homeless men with wooden legs and glass eyes. Maxl imagines himself as a kind of Benya Krik of Vienna, the "king of the Jewish underworld," and he marries one of the "ladies," Mizzi. The novel is full of grim scenes, which in part actualizes in narrative form the fears of many Viennese, Jewish and non-Jewish, when they looked at poor masses of eastern European Jewish migrants who "flooded" the Leopoldstadt after World War I.

Much of the narrative of the novella takes place in the small and smoky Café Glazer, a metonymic space, which is "under the bridge" in miniature. Maxl, Mizzi, and the other "ladies" and pimps are habitués of Café Glazer and feel at home in it. Fuchs's narrator describes a dire picture of post–World War I Vienna, in which "the former 'ladies' under the bridge" no longer hung around there. Some went to work in the gunpowder factories, or became conductors of streetcars. Those with decaying noses, as if moldy, sat like idlers with tired, starving eyes and without socks on their feet, at Café Glazer."[120] Glazer is also the setting for the showdown between Maxl and his rival, Karl, a slim "goy," gentile, who was once engaged to Mizzi. Karl fought in the Great War, and he returned as a "hero" to Vienna and to Café Glazer, where he tells the crowd of impoverished Jews of his adventures, such as cutting off the finger of a dead solider, which he carries with him and shows to the café dwellers and to Mizzi, who seems to be enamored of him. Maxl's Jewish masculinity is being threatened, and in fact, Karl and Mizzi are symbolically reenacting their engagement in the café. Café Glazer, like the entire space "under the bridge," is a "heterotopia," a space of otherness, whose social meaning is out of place and unsettling.[121] Café Glazer is the exact opposite of the image of the cozy Viennese café, or the literary café as a Jewish space of openness and exchange. In Fuch's novel, both Viennese Jewish culture and café culture are grotesquely inverted.[122]

Perhaps the most surprising example of mapping interwar Viennese cafés and probing the ways in which the thirdspace of the café is related to Jewishness and gender can be found in David Vogel's Hebrew novels. Vogel's *Ḥaye nisuim* (*Married Life*, 1929) did not attract much attention (or attracted negative attention) when it was published, but it has been recognized since as one of the most important modernist Hebrew novels of the first half of the twentieth century. The plot of *Married Life* takes place in Vienna of the early 1920s and recounts the troubled, sadomasochistic relations between the young Jewish intellectual Rudolf Gurdweill and his wife, the Austrian "baroness" Thea von Takow, from the day of their first meeting in a Viennese café. The novel makes a self-conscious, subversive use of anti-Semitic and gender stereotypes. Throughout the period of destructive "married life," Thea abuses Gurdweill physically and emotionally. She sleeps with his friends, and after she gives birth to a baby boy, she tells him that the baby is not his. In spite of Gurdweill's attempts to take care of the baby, the boy survives only a year and dies from neglect and a fatal illness. Throughout this period, Gurdweill seems completely unaware that he is the object of desire of one of his closest friends, a Jewish woman named Loti Budenheim. After Gurdweill fails to respond to her love, Loti commits suicide, which brings about Gurdweill's emotional and psychological disintegration toward the end of the novel, when he finally kills his wife.

Married Life is the European modernist Hebrew urban novel par excellence. Gurdweill, a migrant from Podolia (like Vogel himself) and an aspiring Hebrew writer who lives in the Leopoldstadt, becomes an eastern European Jewish flâneur, a man who wanders the streets and boulevards of Vienna. Gurdweill and his friends spend much time in Café Herrenhof, which serves as a metonym of Vienna: a substitute for a "real" home, a space that interfuses the public and the private, the inside and the outside, the culture of bohemia and the bourgeoisie. The café brings the city inside, but it also shields its regulars from the "crowd" and the "masses." One of the many times Gurdweill and his friends meet at the Herrenhof, a woman asks the group, "How long can you people go on sitting in cafés? Don't you ever get tired of it?" To which Gurdweill's friend Ulrich responds, "Sitting in cafés is a barrier against the enforced activity which makes our lives miserable. . . . People like us always have the mistaken feeling that they are wasting time, missing something irretrievable."[123] Vogel's narrator idealizes the café much less than Ulrich does. If camaraderie is presented as a key element of Viennese *Kaffeehäuser*, the other side of the coin is the acrimony that is born of the too-close, at times alienating experience of the social space of the café. As in Wiener's novel, the patrons of Vogel's *Kaffeehaus* demonstrate ambivalence toward the café that captures much of the quality of urban experience in *Married Life*.

In spite of the centrality of Café Herrenhof in Vogel's novel, it must be noted that much narrative activity takes place in small and simple local cafés in Leopoldstadt and in Alsergrund. Here is how the narrator describes one of these small cafés:

> It was nine at night. One by one the Stammgäste of the little café near the university assembled: students and minor officials who sat in the same chairs night after night, and ordered their "Turkish" coffee as if they were finishing off their evening meal at home. These customers were as much a part of the café and its particular atmosphere as the ragged, threadbare velvet sofas around the walls and the dark, dirty, marble tables. It was rare for a "stranger" to appear here.[124]

In this café, Gurdweill meets Thea von Takow for the first time. Of course, it is exactly the fact that Thea, whom Gurdweill believes to be from a fallen Viennese nobility, is actually a "stranger" who rarely appears in the café that catches Gurdweill's initial attention and constitutes his uncontrollable desire for the "other," the gentile woman whom Gurdweill is unable to "take his eyes off."[125] This charged encounter between Gurdweill and Thea sets in motion the entire sadomasochist plot of the novel. But much of the power of this scene, and the novel in general, stems from this position of Gurdweill. Gurdweill is an insider and an outsider, a *Stammgast* and a "stranger" in the café and in Vienna. The same is true of Vogel and other Hebrew and Yiddish modernist writers who lived in Vienna for the most productive periods of their lives.

Vogel wrote another interwar Viennese novel that he never published in his lifetime.[126] The novel, recently published under the title *Roman Vina'y* (*Viennese Romance*), focuses on the life of Michael Rost, a young male protagonist from eastern Europe, but one very different from Rudolf Gurdweill.[127] Rost's original destination was Palestine, but he ended up in Vienna and found "no reason . . . to continue his journey."[128] The randomness of Rost's journey, without a clear destination or goal, is the starting point of a provisional life in the city: "He regarded the carriages, the automobiles, the people passing with magnanimity. How good it was that all this existed, free for the taking; existed for him, for his benefit, for his enjoyment."[129] The main plot of *Viennese Romance* presents a fantasy of a young man, celebrating urban life and the sexual exploration it offers. Indeed, Rost forms passing relationships with many people who cross his path and is involved in a double love affair with his older landlady, Gertrud Shtift, and her teenage daughter, Erna.

Much of the narrative of *Viennese Romance* occurs between cafés in the city center and Reb Ḥayim Stock's strictly kosher and cheap café with the name Aḥdut (Unity) in the Leopoldstadt, which caters to eastern European Jewish migrants.[130] These "shouts and arguments," heated discussions of the plight of Jews in time of crisis and the possible routes of Jewish migration, are an essential part of the Jewish Viennese café, although this society of migrants forms a linguistic and cultural minority. These ideological, political, and economic discussions about the Jewish predicament—reminiscent of Meir Wiener's café scenes—form the backdrop to Rost's adventures and inner life. Rost is more focused on finding a place to spend the night and on taking advantage of the possibilities that the urban space of Vienna has to offer. After all, "the terraces of the cafés were full of fashionably dressed idlers, whose time was their own," and he yearns to join them.[131] Rost's adventures and wanderings in Vienna are enabled by his encounter with a rich businessman named Peter Dean. Rost and Dean meet in the luxurious Viennese café, and it is there that Dean offers the young Rost a generous stipend. This scene closely resembles the opening of Herzl's aforementioned utopian novel *Altneuland* (1902), which makes the contrast between them more pronounced. In Herzl's novel, the relationship is between a well-to-do Dr. Friedrich Löwenberg and the poor eastern European migrant David Litwak, whom he encounters as a beggar outside the café. The money that Löwenberg gives Litwak enables him to exploit the possibilities of education in Vienna and then to transform into a respectable, educated man who migrates to Palestine and becomes a leader in the Jewish "new society." Löwenberg reads in the café the strange proposal by a mysterious man called Kingscourt, who takes him for a trip to an isolated island. After staying on the island for twenty years, they make their way to Palestine, where Löwenberg is being transformed from an "over-educated young man" into a productive man when he marries Litwak's sister, Miriam.

Vogel was drawing on Herzl's novel but took it in the opposite direction. Instead of serving as the point of departure for a journey that eventually leads from Vienna to Palestine and to a "solution" of the Jewish problem and a cure to the "malady" of Jewish masculinity, in Vogel's novel, Vienna becomes the place in which Rost settles. The encounter with Peter Dean in the café is what enables him to become a flâneur in the city and to experience its erotic and social possibilities and boundaries fully. However, the fulfillment of Rost's male fantasy becomes dark when he encounters female sexuality. This becomes clear in the casual meetings of Rost and his Viennese friend Fritz Ankor with the city's prostitutes, as well as between Rost, Erna Shtift, and Friedel Kobler in elegant Viennese cafés. Vogel's narrator examines the changing contours of gender, with figures of young "new women" such as Erna and her friend Freidel, who declares, "I like sitting in cafés. . . . Mother forbids it. 'Young girls have nothing to look for in cafés,' she says. She's probably afraid I'll be seduced, ha, ha, but I'm not a little girl anymore."[132] In spite of noticing that Freidel is attractive, Rost seduces her good friend Erna at the same time that his erotic relations with her mother come to an end. However, the sexual fantasy and the fleeting moments of erotic intimacy in the café cannot bridge the gap between Rost, Erna, and the others. All of them live their lives as if they are part of a performance or a film, foreshadowed by the girl in the opening scene of the novel, who meets Rost in a café after she left the cinema watching "a boring film."[133]

In Vogel's and Fuchs's novels, it is quite clear that gender became an important element of Jewish café culture in interwar Vienna in a way that is quite different from the fin-de-siècle focus on masculinity and closed homosociality. The presence of so many women in the cafés—both well-known "literary cafés" and local cafés in this period—is well documented and is described in literary texts by mostly male Jewish writers. This can be seen also in Melech Chmelnitzki's Yiddish poem "Shene, fremde froy in royshingn kafehoyz" (Beautiful, strange woman in a noisy café, 1921). In the poem, the male speaker looks with bewilderment at the "beautiful, strange woman" who sits in the café. He is attracted to the woman whom he observes but is left with his own subjective fantasy. He can only imagine her "yearning glance" and how "overflowing with joy" is the cup of coffee that her hand holds, but the marble table of the café keeps him apart from this "unfamiliar and foreign" woman. It is only in his imagination that they are both "stormily wailing," until the final realization of how "silly" and unreal all of this is.[134]

Unlike these erotic fantasies about women in cafés written by male Jewish writers, the interwar period also saw the first time in which a few Jewish women writers became part of café culture in Café Herrenhof. Still, it is far from clear how much these women were accepted in the café as writers and artists. More commonly women were seen as "muses" for men, such as the unnamed woman in Chmelnitzki's poem or the character Hedda Ascherman, described as a "radiant, gaily dressed young lady," in Franz Werfel's novel *Barbara oder die Frömmigkeit*.[135] The Jewish journalist and writer Vicki Baum, who began her successful literary career in Vienna in the early 1920s and was part of the literary circle at Café Herrenhof, remarked sarcastically in her memoir, "I don't remember a ladies' room in the Kaffeehaus."[136]

One of the Jewish Viennese women writers active in interwar Vienna was Veza Canetti, who was born in Vienna and was part of the modernist circles in Cafés Herrenhof and Museum in the 1920s, where she met her future husband, the writer Elias Canetti. Her book *Die gelbe Straße* (*The Yellow Street*) consists of five interconnected short stories that were published only posthumously by her husband.[137] These stories take place in the fictional "Yellow Street" that was based, in an oblique way, on the author's own Ferdinandstrasse in the Leopoldstadt. The street was the location of mostly Jewish leather merchants and residents, including a small Jewish Sephardi community, like Veza's family. The stories, clearly influenced by *Neue Sachlichkeit*, are marked by poverty and injustice and focus on the experience of Jewish women, despite the fact that most of them are not identified as Jews.

"Der Tiger" (The tiger) follows Frau Andrea, who marries her husband, Herr Sundoval, in order to escape a life of poverty, but when the modest fortunes of the family have vanished, Andrea is compelled to answer a newspaper ad for a "lady" who wishes to "put her services as a piano-accompanist at the disposal of a singer."[138] Andrea ends up spending every afternoon at Café Planet in Yellow Street, where musical performance is part of the entertainment provided to the visitors. She plays in order to earn some money for herself and her daughter, Diana, who dreams about being a sculptor and tries in vain to get commissions. Only a certain "Mr. Tiger" is ready to have his bust sculpted by Diana. Mr. Tiger is the owner of Café Planet and four other cafés: "The coffeehouse belonged to him, but his function was more of a spectator than anything else. . . . Those who frequented the café in Yellow Street, they were all on the hunt for female conquest. Herr Tiger more than anyone."[139]

Mr. Tiger is attracted to both Andrea and Diana, and one day he takes Andrea to an establishment outside the town. He gives Andrea one hundred shillings as a fee for the bust, which her daughter is to prepare for him, and runs with her back in a private room. The story ends when Andrea refuses Mr. Tiger's sexual advances, to his utter astonishment: "This is an insult; you play the piano in my coffeehouse! I don't want any kind of a scandal; I just wanted to put some easy money your way! You could be more reasonable."[140] As it turned out, for a woman to be a robust presence in a Viennese café, even if she is an artist, writer, or piano player, was perceived as a form of sexual exposure that made her vulnerable to the gaze of the male owner and his guests. The story should be read also as a comment on the position of Jewish women in interwar Vienna and its cafés and even on the place of Canetti herself as a Jewish woman writer. That Andrea and the other figures are not identified in any explicit way as Jewish makes the story a universal one. At the same time, the fact that the story takes place in Leopoldstadt marks the fictional Yellow Street and Café Planet as "Jewish" in ways that highlight the complex identification of the Viennese café as a thirdspace, an imagined Jewish and gendered space.[141]

Vogel, Fuchs, and Canetti had to rely more than ever on their power of imagination. Most of these texts were written and published after their authors left Vienna to other places. Those who remained in the city left it as refugees after 1933 or right before the Anschluss (the annexation of Austria into Nazi Germany in 1938). The Nazi takeover of Vienna signaled the end of Jewish Viennese café culture. Bela Waldmann and Markus Klug, the owners of Café Herrenhof, were imprisoned on the day of the Anschluss, and the café itself was declared a Nazi property. Although some Jewish writers and intellectuals such as Friedrich Torberg and Hilde Spiel returned to Vienna after World War II, most left Vienna to other cities, where they tried to replicate its café culture.[142]

In one of the most memorable feuilletons, Friedrich Torberg wrote about a Jewish refugee who spent the years of the Second World War in the far-flung city of Nairobi, writing to a fellow refugee in Shanghai: "Of course, they have no coffeehouses here, but the emigrants who live here meet on the main square every afternoon, on a street corner where a coffeehouse should be, and exchange news."[143] Torberg was the one who recognized that the café was the most powerful of the "functioning myths," a thirdspace in which the complex interplay between myth and reality, public and private, men and women, Jews and gentiles took place. As such, the Viennese café was indispensable in the production of modern Jewish culture, not only in Vienna but as part of a transnational silk road that stretched to other cities that emulated, as well as influenced, the city's café culture. After all, both Jews and cafés were migrating from one city to another a full century before 1939. In spite of the claims for the uniqueness of the Viennese café—articulated in the UNESCO decision to protect it as "heritage site"—modern café culture and Jewish culture were migrating, mobile cultures. For this reason, they were not lost with the advent of the Anschluss and World War II. Instead, they were transformed and preserved, at least in memory, in various locations after Jews had to flee Vienna in the face of the devastation of the Nazi era.

Berlin

From the Gelehrtes Kaffeehaus to the Romanisches Café

Secretly we all think of the café as the devil, but what would
life be without the devil?
—Else Lasker-Schüler, 1912

The Romanisches Café is a place where one has his own
table and he must come here every day, just as one has to
pray every day.
—Israel Rubin, 1930

In October 1930, the Hebrew poet and prose writer Leah Goldberg traveled from Kovno (Kaunas) in Lithuania to Berlin in order to pursue
advanced studies at the Friedrich-Wilhelms-Universität. As much as
the young Jewish student was interested in ancient Semitic philology,
in which she eventually earned a PhD degree, she was fascinated by the
vibrant metropolis of Berlin in what were to be the last years of the Weimar Republic. A few years after, Goldberg began to write *Mikhtavim
mi-nesi'a meduma* (Letters from an imaginary journey, 1937), an epistolary novel in Hebrew, in which Ruth, the autobiographical narrator of
the novel, describes her wanderings in the streets of Berlin. Soon after
arriving in the city, Ruth explores its cafés. She explains,

> Because those who now sit at the Romanisches Café are Jews looking for
> sensational news in foreign press, and because Café Lunte doesn't exist
> anymore, and because the disciples of Jesus who worshipped Else Lasker-
> Schüler left the temple of Café des Westens a long time ago and found
> their Mt. of Olives in Café Le Dome and La Coupole in Paris, . . . and
> because Menzel, who used to sit in Café Josty had died before I was even

born, . . . because of this and other reasons, I'm sitting in "Kwik," a small café which our Jewish "brothers" still frequent.[1]

Ruth is clearly aware of her belatedness. She writes about the fact that the 1930s are years of "twilight" and that the "golden age" of Berlin's cafés had already passed: "They say that the lions of art and literature used to sit in the Romanisches Café. . . . I didn't see these lions. . . . But for anyone interested in Jewish literature, there was a rare opportunity to encounter some of their wild manes in this café."[2] At first glance, the detailed attention given to these coffeehouses might seem strange and rather esoteric. But Goldberg was capturing something very significant—the long and profound link between Jewish culture and café culture in Berlin, as well as the importance of these cafés in the silk road of modern Jewish culture writ large.

Berlin could never be considered "a Jewish city," and its Jewish population never reached the size or the proportion of the general population in such European cities as Odessa, Warsaw, or Vienna. Yet the city occupies a distinguished place in Jewish culture over a long period from the eighteenth century to the rise of the Nazis. Records show Jews in old Berlin as early as the thirteenth century. Between 1244 and 1671, Jews settled in Berlin repeatedly, but these years were punctuated by periodic expulsions as the larger community blamed Jews for the plague and other ills. Berlin did not play much of a role in Jewish history until the dawn of modernity. In 1671, the Great Elector Friedrich Wilhelm of Brandenburg allowed fifty prominent Jewish Viennese families to relocate to Berlin, hoping that their wealth and enterprise would stimulate greater prosperity. These Jewish families came as *Schutzjuden*—protected or "tolerated" Jews who paid for a residence permit allowing them to engage in certain businesses and to worship in private homes. Over the next century, *Schutzjuden* paid heavily for their privileges and had to deal with the consequences of an influx of poorer Jews who lacked permits and jobs. Nevertheless, a small community rose in Berlin during the eighteenth century.[3]

Around the same time, the *Kaffeehaus* slowly arrived. Because of opposition from the crown, Berlin, the capital of the Kingdom of Prussia since 1701, was the last major German city to establish a coffeehouse.[4]

In 1721, Frederick William I granted a foreigner, probably from Italy, the privilege of conducting a coffeehouse in Berlin free of all rental charges. It was located in the Lustgarten (Pleasure garden), which was part of the palace, and was intended for a small circle of officials and Prussian royalty.[5] Eighteenth-century Berlin was no metropolis but was a fast-growing town of over one hundred thousand, including soldiers, bureaucrats, and tradespeople, many of them settlers, and a smattering of Jews. At the same time, despite the fact that Berlin did not have a university in the eighteenth century, around 1740, it had become a center of Aufklärung, the German Enlightenment. The Haskalah, the Jewish Enlightenment movement, gained force in Berlin during the last decades of the eighteenth century and from there spread to other cities in central and eastern Europe and beyond.

Moses Mendelssohn, the father figure of the Haskalah movement, made his first significant entry into German Enlightenment circles in a "learned coffeehouse." Mendelssohn, who was born in Dessau, 1729, arrived in Berlin in 1743 together with his rabbi and studied Talmud in the city's yeshiva. Seven years later, he decided not to receive rabbinic ordination but rather to become a tutor for the sons of a wealthy Jewish silk merchant in Berlin, who in turn made Mendelssohn a clerk in his factory. During these years, he taught himself several European languages, voraciously read philosophy and literature, and made the acquaintance of "enlightened" figures, a broadening of his social circle made possible in part by the emerging café culture. The writer Friedrich Nicolai explained, "Towards the end of the year 1755, a coffeehouse . . . was established in Berlin. . . . Jacobi, like Moses and myself, was a member. Every four weeks a paper was read by one of the members, the rest standing around a billiards table. I remember that Johann Albrecht Euler . . . read a thoughtful paper on billiards entitled: 'On the Motion of Two Balls on Horizontal Plane.'"[6]

Nicolai wrote that Johann A. Euler, Aaron Gumpertz, and Friedrich P. Jacobi played a game of tarot cards in the coffeehouse, and when they had an argument, Mendelssohn exclaimed, "How marvelous! Three mathematicians cannot properly count to twenty-one."[7] This was the Gelehrtes Kaffeehaus (Learned coffeehouse), which existed between 1755 and 1759, not as a commercial café but as a rented space in a building known as the Englisches Haus on Mohrenstrasse, where like-minded people could meet to socialize, drink coffee, and play billiards and tarot cards.[8] The educator, journalist, and translator Johann Georg Müchler was the initiator of the Gelehrtes Kaffeehaus. In a letter from April 1756, Müchler wrote,

> I must inform you of a new establishment that I founded here in Berlin. I created a society of forty people, mostly men of learning, but artists too, who have rented two large rooms; in one we placed a billiards table, where the society can make money. Members can go there every day. Coffee and whatever one wants is to be had at a cheap price, and one meets a pleasant company. Once a week all members assemble. One talks, jokes, and reads something to others. One finds there all kinds of learned newspapers, journals. . . . Each member pays an entrance fee of only two thalers. The remaining costs are covered by billiards.[9]

Gelehrtes Kaffeehaus should be understood in the context of the coffeehouses, clubs, and debating societies that began to flourish in mid-eighteenth-century Europe. In Berlin, there was only one such club, Der Montagsklub (Monday club), established in 1749; its membership was limited to twenty-four people, who met for dinner and conversation every Monday.[10] Some of Mendelssohn's new friends were part of this club, and apparently, he was invited to participate but declined because the food was not kosher. The Gelehrtes Kaffeehaus was a good alternative for Mendelssohn, because it both served only coffee and was, perhaps, less intimidating to the young man. The friendly atmosphere of Gelehrtes Kaffeehaus was not only pleasant to Mendelssohn but also stimulating. It furnished the inspiration and the setting for the delivery of one of his first important philosophical treatises, "Thoughts on Probability."[11]

Mendelssohn's participation in Gelehrtes Kaffeehaus became instrumental to his writing. At the same time that Müchler came up with the coffeehouse initiative, he established a new journal, *Der Chamäleon* (The chameleon) and invited his new friend Mendelssohn to co-edit and contribute to it.[12] *Der Chamäleon* was published in eighteen volumes, part of a genre of publication known as *moralische Wochenschriften* (moral weeklies). The moral weekly originated in London with the *Tatler* (1709–1711) and the *Spectator* (1711–1712), with a primary focus on manners, morals, and letters.[13] The goal was "to enliven morality with wit, and temper wit with morality." The genre was essential in disseminating Enlightenment sensibilities and developing a new understanding of "virtue"; the spectrum of subjects addressed in it included questions of upbringing and education, social conduct, aesthetics, literature, and language.[14] Moral weeklies were intimately related to the coffeehouse from the very beginning, and these two institutions went hand in hand first in English and French cities and later in German-speaking cities as well.[15] The papers attracted avid subscribers and were read in coffeehouses that catered to readers. It is estimated that each issue of the English *Spectator* reached sixty to eighty thousand readers. The essential activities of the coffeehouse—newspaper reading, political discussion, and socializing— were all objects of discussion in these publications, further evidence of the symbiotic relationship between these institutions.[16]

Der Chamäleon was an extension of the Gelehrtes Kaffeehaus. One of the most important traits of the moral weekly was the introduction of fictional authors and editors. Relying on masked, anonymous writers and editors allowed these journals to achieve a high degree of aesthetic appeal and to communicate moral arguments and observations. This is exactly what Müchler and Mendelssohn did in the eighteen issues of *Der Chamäleon* they wrote, edited, and published. Compared to Mendelssohn's philosophical writings,[17] his investment, together with his co-editor Müchler, in bringing the journal to Berlin's readers is clearly related to his active participation in Gelehrtes Kaffeehaus and influenced his creation of an unprecedented Hebrew moral weekly, *Kohelet musar* (Moral preacher).[18] This short-lived journal, Mendelssohn's first journal in Hebrew, was published sometime in the second half of the 1750s. The publication signaled a major new consciousness in Jewish thought and culture.[19] As the journal's name indicates, Mendelssohn's aim in writing and publishing this journal was to introduce the new European medium of the moral weekly into Jewish culture. In this journal, ideas of Enlightenment were conveyed, for the first time, via Hebrew, a language familiar only to the learned elite and associated with the world of biblical and rabbinic scholars. The style of the moral weekly, however, presupposed an ability to address readers in direct colloquial prose, a style that did not exist in Hebrew at that time. Mendelssohn had to invent something that might have read like colloquial language by exploiting the Bible, reassembling a pastiche of biblical quotations. By using biblical language in innovative ways—including staples of the moral weekly, such as fictive editors and letters to the editor—this journal introduced a new sense of playfulness, taste, and morality.[20]

However, as pioneering and important as Mendelssohn's *Kohelet musar* was, only two issues of the journal were published, each containing just a few chapters. While early scholars believed the censorship of Berlin's rabbis forced Mendelssohn to close it down, it is more likely that the journal simply did not achieve the goal that the author set for himself, since it attracted very few readers. The reasons for this can be seen in the gap between the world represented in the text and the reality of Jews in Berlin. Mendelssohn tried to communicate in his journal what was "the art of living": enjoying and appreciating, in moderation, the physical and social delights that life affords, but with emphasis on socializing in a learned fraternity.[21] The allusion to Mendelssohn's own experience is clear: Gelehrtes Kaffeehaus and its delights were different from both the strictures of traditional Jewish law and the revelry and hedonist indulgence typical of taverns and wine houses. However, the beguiling social structure that Mendelssohn created was quite alien to Jewish society in Berlin of the eighteenth century. In the 1750s, there were virtually no coffeehouses in Berlin in which most Jews could enjoy a fellowship of men such as that of Mendelssohn and his learned friends. There was also no coffeehouse in Berlin of the 1750s in which *Kohelet musar* could be disseminated, read, and discussed; it was half a century before this situation changed.

Part of the reason for the lack of coffeehouses, especially cafés that were open to all, was a Prussian legislation that limited coffee consumption.[22] This started to change in the following decades. In 1779, the publisher Friedrich Nicolai, Mendelssohn's friend and a fellow Gelehrtes Kaffeehaus habitué, wrote a guidebook to the city of Berlin. In the book, he listed about a dozen cafés where one could drink, eat, and also play billiards. The list included "Philipp Falk's Kaffeehaus" on Spandauerstrasse, a "Jewish coffeehouse" that was also a *Speisehaus* (restaurant).[23] We do not know much about Falk's kosher coffeehouse or what kind of activity took place there, but it was located on the same street in which Mendelssohn lived with his family from 1762 until his death in 1786.[24] In this period, some acculturated Berlin Jews might have consumed nonkosher food in cafés in Berlin. This is evident from Isaac Euchel's Yiddish *maskilic* play *Reb Henoch* (1793), in which the young Jewish Hedwig dines with gentiles in a café. When her father finds out, he faints.[25]

By that time, a new institution was taking over Berlin: the salon. During the quarter century between 1780 and 1806, when the number of Jews in Berlin was thirty-five hundred, some of Berlin's best-known salons were hosted by Jewish women. Henriette Herz, Rahel Levin-Varhangen, and Dorothea Mendelssohn-Schlegl (Moses Mendelssohn's daughter) were educated Jewish women from well-to-do families who were searching for a new role in life outside the patriarchal structures of their families, and they found that role by establishing salons.[26] The designation of "salon," which came from French society of the seventeenth century, was attached to these gatherings much later. At the time, these institutions were called *ein offenes Haus* (an open house), *Teegesellschaft* (tea society), *Theetisch* (tea table), *ästhetischer Tee* (aesthetic tea), or *Kränzchen* (social circle). The guests—mostly gentiles and some Jews, mostly noblemen and some commoners, mostly men and a few women—were referred to by the term *Hausfreunde* (friends of the house).[27]

Despite fostering interaction and intellectual exchange, these "Jewish salons" were quite limited and controlled. Different from cafés, they were, in fact, a social one-way street with clear rules. The hostess's gender provided her with a special tradition: the tea table was the woman's realm. Moreover, the Jewishness of the salon hostess meant that her outsider status was guaranteed, as both a woman and a Jew. The only way to break out of this status was to convert and to marry a Christian aristocrat, which many of these Jewish women did. The institution of the salon continued to exist in some ways in Berlin through the nineteenth century, but what became known as the Jewish women's salon was both a short-lived and quite limited phenomenon.[28] But the shortness of that life was, as we will see, in part because of the explosive growth of the café.

Humor amid the Censors in Berlin *Café-Konditoreien*

Berlin in the first half of the nineteenth century attracted a number of migrants of Jewish origin who came to play leading roles in German and European culture. These were primarily young men who came to the city following the establishment in 1810 of the Universität zu Berlin—where 7 percent of the students were Jewish—and the 1812 Prussian "Edict of Toleration." The edict promised to abolish the system that required all Jews to apply for "protection" from the state and brought hope for many. In the coming years, following the French Revolution and the chaos of the war against Napoleon, which ended in 1815, came a period known as "restoration" in central Europe. This "age of restoration" meant increasing conservatism and repression of freedoms in Prussia. Especially notorious were the Carlsbad Decrees of 1819, a series of harsh laws mandating censorship, surveillance, and other limitations designed to suppress dissent.[29]

These political and social developments in the early decades of the nineteenth century coincided with the appearance of a new, increasingly popular institution in Berlin: the *Café-Konditorei*, a term that approximates to "café-confectionery." Between the 1810s and the 1840s, a startling number of these—Josty, Stehely, Kranzler, Spargnapani, Fuchs, Royal, Court, and Koblank—were opened in Berlin, mostly by Swiss migrants.[30] Those *Konditoreien* attracted Jewish residents of Berlin from different backgrounds and orientations. A link between cafés and Jews was evident in the 1820s and 1830s and could be interpreted in different ways. When the writer and army officer Adolph von Schaden from Bavaria wrote about "Berlin's lights and shadows" in 1922, he mentioned two familiar *Kaffeehäuser*. However, he claimed that in both, the "People of Israel" are up to their tricks and "show their true nature." Thus, he found these cafés repellent and advised anyone with a "fine nose and sensitive ear" to avoid them.[31] In the early 1840s, A. F. Thiele published a book with accounts of "Jewish crooks and organized crime," based on his experience as a high-ranking official in the Royal Prussian criminal office in 1830s Berlin. In his book, he reported on a gang of Jews, headed by Marcus Joel, who executed a robbery of Konditorei Kranzler, which opened in 1834 on the corner of Friedrichstrasse and Unter der Linden, at the center of Berlin. He commented on the sophistication of the robbery, performed with a chisel and duplicate key, and mentioned that the café and its owner were thoroughly familiar to the Jewish robbers.[32]

The commercial *Café-Konditoreien* were not just associated with alleged organized crime and infused with the era's typical prejudices against "the People of Israel" but were also marked by the growing circles of *Bürgertum* (urban bourgeoisie) and the press. Restoration-era Berlin, especially after the restrictive 1819 rules, offered limited possibilities to gather in public places or to express and publish anything that was not in line with the Prussian regime. *Café-Konditoreien*, although far from being free of government surveillance, emerged as places for exchanging and expressing ideas, especially for those who were not part of the aristocracy. A number of these cafés were known for their good selection of newspapers and journals, which made such culture accessible to people who could not afford to buy a subscription.[33]

In an 1834 handbook of Berlin, Leopold von Zedlitz writes about the new reading rooms adjacent to *Café-Konditoreien*. In Josty, patrons found "a wide selection of the popular journals."[34] In Stehely, in addition to the "recognized quality of its pastry, its reading room is the most abundant of all such establishments."[35] Moreover, people did not only read journals and newspapers in these cafés. In the period between the Carlsbad Decrees and the revolution of 1848, citizens of Berlin made a link between the *Café-Konditorei*, new modes of public discourse, and the press, especially the recent genre of urban journals, which featured wit and humor. This linkage was recorded by Adolf Glassbrenner in the 1830s:

> The sun is setting, it is evening. From the *Konditoreien* of Stehely, Spargnapani, Giavanoli, Josty, Courtin (and however else the free Swiss gentlemen who have brought cake instead of freedom to us like to call themselves), emerge the celebrated political correspondents of Berlin. Their faces are lit up; they have just confected so much news to be able to assemble an article containing diplomatically veiled attacks.[36]

Glassbrenner, a humorist and journalist and Berlin native, was not Jewish, but his mentors, like many people associated with the local press, were acculturated Jews who had migrated to Berlin. One of those who enjoyed, for a short time, Berlin's newfangled café culture and its link to print and student life was the poet and prose writer Heinrich Heine. He was born as Harry into a Jewish family in the city of Düsseldorf in 1797. After brief attempts to study law at the Universities of Bonn and Göttingen, Heine arrived in Berlin in March 1821 and attended the local university. Berlin, which at this point was a sizable city of approximately two hundred thousand citizens, gave the young Heine access to philosopher Georg Wilhelm Friedrich Hegel, with whom he studied. In Berlin, Heine published a slim book of poetry, *Gedichte* (*Poems*, 1822), which was the first step in his becoming one of the most celebrated German poets of the nineteenth century.[37] Heine met Rahel Levin-Varhangen, in whose house he acquainted himself with many important figures, but he also spent much time in *Café-Konditoreien*.

These cafés played an important role in Heine's first piece of prose writing, *Briefe aus Berlin* (Letters from Berlin). It was published, anonymously, between January and June 1822 in the newspaper *Rheinisch-Westfälischer Anzeiger*, issued in Hamm but read in Berlin and all over Prussia.[38] These "letters" were the first part of what Heine later called *Reisebilder* (Travel pictures), in which he mixed impressions from various places in which he lived and traveled with narrative episodes, musings on the narrator's inner life, fictional elements, and poetry. Significantly, *Briefe aus Berlin* constitutes the first example in German of a feuilleton, the genre that had flourished in Paris since 1800. Thus, Heine is thought of as the "father of the feuilleton" in Germany. The link between Heine, the feuilleton, urban cafés, and Jewishness became evident, if not always explicit to many commentators since then, especially in the late nineteenth and early twentieth century. It was made famous in 1910 Vienna, when Karl Kraus pronounced, "Ohne Heine kein Feuilleton" (no feuilleton without Heine), and charged Heine of "loosening the corset of the German language."[39] Employing the device of fictional "letters to the editor" is one of the striking similarities between Heine's feuilletons and Mendelssohn's earlier moral weeklies. But Heine's text was also characteristic of nineteenth-century Berlin. It is composed of a mosaic of urban spaces and cultural scenes, impressions of the city as seen from its threshold. Heine took the role of a flâneur, the wanderer in the city armed with wit and the power of observation and cultural critique.

The narrator takes the imagined reader of *Briefe aus Berlin* on a "textual tour" of Berlin, which includes a number of cafés. It starts in the Königstrasse and its endless crowd of people and moves to the Stechbahn, which is the place where one finds the *Café-Konditorei* Josty: "You gods of Olympus," exclaims the narrator, "I shall spoil your Ambrosia if I describe the sweets which are displayed here! Oh, Aphrodite, had you emerged from such foam you'd have been sweeter still!" After such rhetorical conceit, the narrator finds it necessary to deflate the tone:

"The premises are narrow, it is true, and decorated like a tavern. But the good always wins over the beautiful; here, packed together like herrings, are the grandchildren of the 'Brennen' comfortably seated, while they lap cream and smack their lips with enjoyment and lick their fingers."[40] This *Konditorei*, established by the Swiss brothers Daniel und Johann Josty in 1812, was one of the places where Heine went to drink, eat, and meet people. In the witty text, his narrator contrasted the narrow and dingy tavern-like place with the godly ambrosia of the coffee and Swiss pastry, and the liberal students and journalists with the officers, bankers, and government officials, the "grandchildren" of the old Berlin aristocracy.

At this point, Heine's narrator does not mention Jews in Josty. However, Jewishness appears shortly after, when he arrives at the nearby Berlin University. The narrator reports on a duel between two medical students, Liebschütz and Febus, who fell into a quarrel because both of them laid claim to what they thought was the same seat in the lecture hall. A duel ensued, and Liebschütz was hurt and died. "Since he was a Jew," the narrator remarks, "some of his student friends took him to the Jewish cemetery. Febus, also a Jew, took flight, and . . ."[41] The narrative abruptly ends here and moves back to the streets and the cafés. The subtext of this strange story is missing from Heine's feuilleton but was meant to be clear. The duel reveals the bind that Jewish students, like Heine himself, were in. They could either take the manners and codes of German nationalist students or fight them.[42] Heine draws attention to the restrictive Carlsbad Decrees of 1819, as well as the ban on Jews entering academic professions, which was reenacted in 1822. All these restrictions were key in the establishment of the short-lived "Verein für Kultur und Wissenschaft der Juden" (The society for culture and science of the Jews) in 1822 under the guidance of Heine's good friend Eduard Gans, a law student like himself. Heine joined the group and belonged to it until he left Berlin.[43]

The narrator guides the reader from Berlin University into the famed Unter den Linden. But here it is the narrator's own attention that is interrupted by the sight of a building on the corner of Charlottenstrasse: "This is the Café Royal! Let us turn in there, I beg; I cannot pass without a glance inside." Heine's narrator describes Café Royal as what we have called a thirdspace, a space that requires deciphering, one between the inside and the outside, the real and the imaginary, the Jew and the gentile: "Outside, it is the handsomest café in Berlin; inside, it is the prettiest restaurant. It is a meeting place of the educated fashionable world. Interesting men are often to be seen here." These "interesting men" consist of both real and imaginary figures. "Notice over there that big broadshouldered man in the black overcoat? Here is the celebrated Cosme'li, who today is in London, tomorrow in Ispahan. Thus I picture to myself Chamisso's Peter Schlemihl. He has a paradox at the moment, on the tip of his tongue." Heine refers not to the writer Adelbert von Chamisso but to the protagonist of his 1814 novella *Peter Schlemihl,* about the man who sold his shadow. Peter Schlemihl was modeled after the assimilated Berlin Jew that Chamisso found in the figure of Julius Eduard Hitzig. Mentioning the fictional figure of Peter Schlemihl in Café Royal draws attention to Berlin's Jews and to perceptions of Jewishness, conversion, and assimilation. Heine's wandering narrator mockingly admonishes his reader, who is purportedly not interested in literature and asks only "for the petty news of the town." The narrator finds in the café a friend and turns to him: "My dear Herr Gans, what is the news?" But Gans "shakes his gray reverent head and shrugs his shoulders." Heine refers to his friend the aforementioned student Eduard Gans, the cofounder of Verein für Kultur und Wissenschaft der Juden, as someone who is part of Café Royal but cannot—perhaps because of restrictions and censorship—supply the news that is of real interest. Instead of Gans, the narrator then turns to a "little red-cheeked" man who is full of safe news from the musical world but also casually reports on the censorship of literary texts.[44]

Jews and coffeehouses appear again in the second letter, as the narrator links two new and significant events: the opening of Berlin's stock exchange and the "old but newly revived project of the conversion of the Jews." The narrator, who never identifies as a Jew, claims sardonically that he cannot say too much about these two related events because he has not yet been inside the new stock exchange, and "the Jews are too sad a subject" to touch.[45] Part of the reason that the Jews are such a "sad subject" is the establishment of a new organization in April 1822: the Berlin Society for the Promotion of Christianity among the Jews. The aim of the organization was to make religious conversion a necessary condition to full civic emancipation, reflecting a prevalent view that Jews could never really become Prussian citizens if they clung to their Jewish religious identity. The comment was especially poignant because many of Berlin's acculturated Jews chose to convert to Christianity in order to advance in the worlds of business, academia, and literature. In fact, just a few years after Heine wrote *Briefe aus Berlin*, he felt that in order to get a chance of making a living as a writer and intellectual, he had to be baptized, a choice that he famously described as an "admission ticket to European culture."[46] After his oblique comments on conversion, he refers to some "obscure books" that have been subject to police supervision. Among them are the "books of Adolph von Schaden, who recently published 'Lights and Shadows in Berlin,' which contained many false assertions."[47] In that book, von Schaden made the anti-Jewish claim that Jews reveal their "true nature" in the coffeehouses. Throughout the text of *Briefe aus Berlin*, Heine subtly links Berlin's cafés with the presence of Jews and with anti-Jewish sentiments as well as with restrictions on Jews, free speech, students' organizations, the press, and literature, without making his cultural and political criticism explicit in a text that was itself subject to the censorship he was subtly referencing.

Heine's intense but brief participation in Berlin's intellectual life and café culture was not singular but was shared by other Jewish figures. One of the most controversial of these figures was Moritz Gottlieb Saphir. Born as Moses Saphir in 1795 to an observant, Yiddish-speaking family near Budapest, he studied in a yeshiva in Prague but was more attracted to German culture and in his twenties began composing German verse and Yiddish comic stories. In 1825, just after Heine left Berlin, Saphir moved to the city, where he stayed for the next four years. His great achievement was to establish two publications: *Berliner Schnellpost* and *Berliner Courier*. Saphir's publications are essential to what became known as *Berliner Witz*, a journalistic display of biting wit that was very popular with the reading public. Unlike Heine's work, Saphir's humor was not of high literary quality, yet his newspaper functioned as "an alternative political forum," especially amid the strict censorship of this period.[48] Largely because of the dominance of Saphir and his protégé Eduard Maria Oettinger, people understood this "Berlin humor" of this period as specifically *Judenwitz* (Jewish humor). Nineteenth-century critics viewed its practitioners as mean-spirited and "un-Germanic," an unsubtle nod to the enduring outsider status of Jews. While highly popular, *Judenwitz* was also a pejorative concept that questioned the ability of Jews to master German, the quality of their journalistic and literary pursuits, and their intentions.[49] Saphir was at the center of this roiling controversy about this brand of satiric humor and its "Jewishness," much of which unfolded in the press and in Berlin's *Café-Konditoreien*, where both Saphir and his enemies were habitués.

That centrality of the café can be seen in a telling anecdote about Saphir in Café Royal in May 1826. Much of Saphir's witty criticism was directed at the rivalry between the two popular theaters in Berlin: the Königliche Bühne and the Königstädter Theater. Saphir constantly ridiculed the Königstädter Theater and especially its prima donna, the singer Henriette Sontag, who was particularly adored by the group of journalists and critics who met at Café Royal. Saphir decided to write a satirical poem about Sontag and revealed his plan in the café; within moments, he was challenged to a duel by the publisher and theater critic Carl Schall, a large and imposing man. Apparently, the eruption was so volcanic that all the guests in the café stopped to listen.[50] The anecdote became famous due to the fact that the person who came to the rescue of the Jewish satirist was none other than the great philosopher Hegel, himself a frequent café-goer. Everybody could see how ridiculous the idea of a duel between Saphir and Schall was, and the antagonism was diffused; but the symbolism of the moment lingered. Both the satire and the Jewishness of Saphir flamed many passions in the city and its press, and places such as Café Royal were at the center of the controversies.

Like many others, Saphir not only wrote in cafés but also wrote about cafés. One of his journalistic pieces, collected in a volume called *Conditorei des Jokus* (Konditorei of Jokus/Jokes) is a satiric plan to establish a *Café-Konditorei* for female artists. In explaining the "logic" for such a plan, Saphir wrote,

How happy are the learned men and male artists! They go to wine taverns and *Café-Konditoreien*. They have learned societies because one always needs to eat and to drink! Green beans and green manuscripts, whipped-cream and whipped punchlines, cold soup and cold lectures, long asparagus and long speeches. But the female artists, scholars, poets, translators, critics, readers, singers, dancers, and all "insider" women (with more outside than inside) have no public meeting place. How great it would be if Lady Stehely established a *Konditorei* for female artists.[51]

Saphir referred in this text to Café Stehely, which was established in 1820 and emerged as a leading *Café-Konditorei*, known for its "reading room" and as a meeting place for journalists and writers. The fact that all habitués of Stehely were men is evident in Saphir's text. He mocked the self-importance of the "learned men" and "male artists," who indulge in eating and drinking while producing cold and boring work, but he also ridiculed the idea that there should be a café for female intellectuals. He suggested that such a place would have no mirrors because "artists regard one another already as a mirror before which they can view themselves."[52] Saphir's wit might seem a bit stale and very misogynist today, but the audacity of his writings took Berlin by storm; according to rumor, even the king read his pieces. This acclaim did not last long, as the Prussian censors did not appreciate a writer who poked fun at them. In 1829, Saphir lost his residence permit in Berlin after defending Oettinger, his fellow humorist who was more political and more vocal and who demanded the freedom of the press in Prussia.[53]

Oettinger's more politically daring humor can be seen in "Berlin Sketches," a satire written in 1848 and centered on Cafés Kranzler and Josty; he describes Prussian lieutenants spending a lazy morning at the cafés, reading newspapers, preparing for a parade that only a few shoe-makers and farmers attend, and cursing their difficult service.[54] This kind of political humor, challenging the army and the Prussian regime, grew more prevalent in the 1830s and 1840s, along with the growth of the city of Berlin, the diversification of its economy, and the emergence of a more self-conscious working class, including politically radical intellectuals and students. The café was essential for this political blossoming. *Konditoreien* provided official and unofficial newspapers, as well as debating forums, as evident in the description of the journalist Ernst Dronke:

> Cafés-[*Konditoreien*] are the meeting place of the like-minded who speak out about their interests; they are a kind of club. The merchant who wants to consider his affairs and the status of his stocks with someone;

the journalist who must hear the latest and must catch up on the day's events from the newspaper; the man of private means who does nothing and yet wishes to appear as something; officers, students, in short, everyone who has any kind of interest at all in public life turns out in the *Café-Konditoreien.*[55]

Of Berlin's expanding number of cafés, the one that became most identified with "anyone who is interested in public life" was Stehely and its adjunct reading room, with its hundred journals and papers. Stehely was described as "the Eldorado of Berlin's idlers" but also "the grandest, most often visited educational institution," frequented by those who want "to quench their thirst for knowledge, to end the starvation of their minds, and to satisfy the tickling of their aesthetic palate."[56] Dronke claimed that in the morning, secret administration agents gathered at the Stehely to discuss the latest news, followed by university staff, teachers, and the intelligentsia. Though these groups had diametrically opposed politics, what they shared was the necessity of the café—it was the place where life happened.[57]

Figure 4.1. Illustration of Café Stehely

Berlin's *Café-Konditoreien*, and Stehely in particular, aided the political and ideological foment that led to the March Revolution of 1848 in Berlin and Prussia. For nearly twenty years prior to the revolt, Café Stehely was viewed with terror by some people as a hotbed of revolutionary ideas and dismissed by others as ineffective. The Rote Stube (red room), one of the café's rooms, named for the color of the wallpaper, was the venue for daily gathering of liberal and radical journalists, professors, and students, who met to read and discuss the many newspapers. The gathering in the red room became especially known for the group that called itself the Junghegelianer (Young Hegelians), greatly influenced by the philosophy of Hegel, who had died in 1831.[58] The group included Bruno Bauer, Max Stirner, and David Strauss and debated issues of philosophy, religion, politics, and ideology. Between 1837 and 1841, the young Karl Marx was part of the group and a habitué of Café Stehely.[59] Marx, whose Jewish father converted to Christianity when he was six years old, came to Berlin in 1836 in order to study law at the university. The Jewish socialist thinker Moses Hess, who was associated with the Young Hegelians, wrote to a friend coming to Berlin in 1841: "You can prepare yourself to meet the greatest, perhaps the only true living philosopher . . . Marx."[60] That same year, the poet and prose writer Robert Prutz described the "red room": "Every afternoon over a cup of coffee innocent conversations and discussions take place, stimulated by the perusing of newspapers and the events of the day. . . . Their politics consist of loud chatter and eating meringues at Stehely."[61]

In 1841, Prutz could have not known that "the innocent conversation and discussions" in Stehely would have long-lasting influence not only in Berlin but all over Europe. Marx and Engels, who participated in the Stehely discussions, soon moved from Berlin to less restrictive cities, but they contributed to the revolutionary spirit that swept much of Europe in 1848 and came finally to Berlin. Though the flourishing of radicalism in the capital city was belated and incomplete, it was inextricably linked to the presence in the city of both a small but vocal Jewish population and an increasingly important café culture. In 1848, there were an estimated ninety-six hundred Jews in Berlin, around 2.3 percent of the population. The participation of Berlin's Jews in the revolution of 1848 was proportionally much greater than that of the general population.

On March 18, crowds of people gathered in Berlin to present their demands in an "address to the king." Ultimately, the March Revolution faltered and was considered by many people to be a failure. It shook the system but left the power of government largely in the hands of the old structures of bureaucracy and army, which remained almost untouched. The revolution was significant for Jews in Berlin not so much because of actual changes that were implemented but in the hope that accompanied these events. A victory for German liberalism would have brought with it a liberalization of policies toward the Jews. As the revolution vacillated, so did the hopes of German Jews. Still, 1848 initiated a change in Berlin for Jews and non-Jews alike. Jewish politicians appeared for the first time at the state level, some gaining unprecedented prominence. From a negative perspective, the events of 1848 brought to the surface the public resistance to granting equal rights to the Jewish minority. As in so many other moments in Europe's history, the crisis of 1848 also manifested itself in anti-Jewish sentiments and even acts of violence.[62]

Fin-de-Siècle Berlin Cafés and Jewish Culture

The Jewish population of Berlin grew significantly during the second half of the nineteenth century, as did the city itself, especially in the century's last three decades. In June 1871, after the conclusion of the Franco-Prussian War, Berlin became the capital of a unified imperial Germany and the seat of the government of the Kaiserreich. For the first time in its history, Berlin began to emerge as a metropolis, a European capital to rival London, Vienna, and Paris. The physical transformation of the city after unification was decisive. With its new status as the center of German communication, transportation, business, and learning and the emerging electrical and chemical industries, Berlin expanded at a dizzying rate. An enormous amount of new infrastructure was built, and surrounding towns were incorporated as city suburbs and neighborhoods. Berlin's population reached a million by the 1880s and two million by 1910.[63] Between 1871 and 1910, the Jewish population of Berlin also increased at an accelerated rate, from a little over 36,000 to over 144,000. Most newcomers emigrated from surrounding Prussia but also from Galicia, Poland, and the Russian Pale of Settlement. In both class and culture, the Jewish community was overwhelmingly bourgeois and educated. Jews tended to live in Berlin-Mitte, the old city center, as well as in new western neighborhoods such as Charlottenburg.[64]

Though civic and social equality were tenuous for many people in imperial Germany, Jews were legally equal to all other citizens under the new constitution. This was considered a major feat, and most Jews embraced German citizenship and *Bildung*—the pursuit of German culture and learning—with enthusiasm and loyalty. At the same time, though equality existed on paper, there were important areas of public life—the court, the army, the government and state bureaucracy, and most of academia—to which Jews were denied access. This probably caused many Jews to turn to, and find success in, the less organized realms of the public sphere.[65] Another major change in Jewish life was the Austrittsgesetz, the Secession Law of 1876, which meant that German Jews could choose to remain members of the Jewish community or leave it but had to be registered as Jews. Instead of converting to Christianity, which many Jews did early in the nineteenth century, the emergence of a voluntary community placed the burden of belonging on the individual. All these new developments caused Jews in Berlin to search for spaces where their Jewish and German belonging was expressed, and chief among these spaces were Berlin cafés, both the established *Konditoreien* and the new coffeehouses that opened after 1871. Berlin Jews went to certain cafés and, through them, gained access to—and helped to create—what became distinctly German-Jewish spaces.[66]

The expression of both Jewish and German belonging manifested itself in various ways in Berlin's turn-of-the-century cafés. In some cases, it was through consumption, business, and trade, which was done in Berlin cafés in similar ways to cafés in Odessa, Warsaw, and Vienna in the same period. Henry Vizetelly, an English journalist, author, and publisher who lived in Berlin in the 1870s, documented the transformations of "Berlin under the New Empire": "Years ago," Vizetelly claimed, the "leading conditorei . . . was Kranzler's, . . . long the chosen resort of the dandies, military and civil." However, Vizetelly complained that recently, "it has fallen from its high estate into the hands . . . of the Jews, who have converted it into a kind of minor Börse."[67] Vizetelly commented on the fact that while Berlin's stock exchange was closed on Sunday and Christian holidays, "the bulk of the great speculators are Jews, who are thus driven" on Sunday to Café Kranzler.[68]

These remarks show how for many people, Jews and cafés became associated with wealth and speculation, but the tone of these observations also shows how this association became tied with a new kind of "racial anti-Semitism" that swept Berlin and Germany in the imperial period and led to fierce debates on the "Jewish Question."[69] On New Year's Eve 1880, a mob marched through Berlin's city center shouting "Juden raus" (Jews out) at what they assumed were Jewish customers in two different cafés. As some papers reported large student participation from the Berlin University, the rector made inquiries and was told by the police that there had been many students among the thousands of rioters. During this riot, Jews were turned out of Café National and Café Bauer, and a brick was thrown, smashing the large window of Café Bauer.[70]

Café Bauer was a new landmark in imperial Berlin when it opened in October 1878. It was the first "Viennese-style" café in Berlin and a bold attempt to create a new breed that would eventually replace the old *Konditorei*. The Jewish journalist, dramatist, and critic Paul Lindau wrote that huge Café Bauer "has attained a fame that reaches far beyond the precincts of the city."[71] The opening of the café was noted as a news item, and papers reported on the opening and the luxurious interior, which was unprecedented in Berlin. Its location on the corner of Unter den Linden and Friedrichstrasse (opposite the old Kranzler) afforded it a particular prominence. Café Bauer was also the first to be illuminated by electricity.[72] Café Bauer replaced the "red room" of bygone Stehely, as "all the daily, weekly, and monthly periodicals of the old and new worlds were brought together there." According to Lindau, Berliners were at first "allured by curiosity to inspect what was to them a new species of public-house," but soon it became the customary resort of all those who had formerly frequented the *Konditoreien* and of the great number of strangers and newcomers to the city.[73] In 1884, the *New York Times* reported on Café Bauer and called it "Berlin's Tower of Babel" due to the "cosmopolitan visitors," who are "representatives of nearly every nationality on the globe," as well as the newspapers and journals "in eighteen different languages."[74]

The presence of Jews in this cosmopolitan café was taken for granted. Many Jews in Berlin came to enjoy the huge selection of papers and journals and to socialize with others, Jews and non-Jews alike. Hirsch Hildesheimer, an Orthodox journalist and the son of Berlin's Orthodox community rabbi, was among the many visitors. He used to go to Café Bauer daily, even on Sabbath afternoon, in order to read and select items for publication in *Die jüdische Presse*, which he edited.[75] The example of Hildesheimer shows the extent to which Jewish culture in Berlin was transformed. At the turn of the twentieth century, Jewish journalists, writers, and artists in Berlin worked not in order to promote the cause of emancipation and equal rights but to establish new forms of Jewish-German culture. Through cafés such as Bauer, turn-of-the-century Berlin became a magnet for the avant-garde. The emerging modernist art and literature established itself in the city's changing landscape of cafés. In 1905, Hans Ostwald, the avid and perceptive chronicler of Berlin, observed,

> Life in the coffeehouses of Berlin, which used to be rather meager and a little restricted, has become noticeably richer over the last ten to fifteen years. Not only that the coffeehouses have multiplied as fast as the population of Berlin, maybe even faster, but at the same time the Berliners themselves have become increasingly accustomed to the coffeehouse. And so a whole range of different types of such establishments have emerged.[76]

The first place associated with the modernist avant-garde in Berlin was Zum schwarzen Ferkel ("The Black Piglet"), which flourished in the 1890s.[77] Soon there would be other places favored by artists, writers, journalists, and theater people: Café Kaiserhof, Café Austria, Café Sezession, Café Monopol, Café Casino Nollendorfplatz, and even the old Konditorei Josty, which reinvented itself as a new café when it moved to Potsdamer Platz between the old center and West Berlin. However, from the turn of the century until World War I, the most important café associated with Berlin modernism, especially the emerging movement of expressionism, was Café des Westens, which opened in 1893 as the first coffeehouse on the Kurfürstendamm, a fashionable boulevard and a new center of commerce and entertainment in the western part of Berlin.[78]

Initially called Das kleine Café (The little café), it was renamed Café des Westens in 1898. Hans Ostwald declared in 1905 that "Bohemian life . . . in Berlin is gathered almost exclusively in the Café des Westens."[79] Unlike the fashionable Café Bauer, it was not the elegance of Café des Westens that attracted the artists and writers, who were by now deemed "bohemians." Apparently, the interior of the café looked more like an apartment that had its walls removed. It was adorned with cheap tapestries and stuccos that became brown from cigarette fumes. However, the drinks and the homely food there were reasonably priced, and waiters were willing to extend credit. On the second floor of the café were free billiard tables and chess boards. In 1904, the new café owner, Ernst Pauly, employed a special waiter—known as "Red Richard"—whose specialty was serving newspapers and journals to habitués. Pauly also installed a telephone booth, a novelty used eagerly by those same regulars. These features were quite important to the mostly young habitués who made the café their home.[80]

Yet these amenities—which, after all, were becoming increasingly common in the city—were not what made Café des Westens so attractive to the *Stammgäste*. Rather, it was the intensive activity that took place there. In its first years, it was a gathering place for painters and artists. In 1900, Ernst von Wolzogen established the first Berlin cabaret, *Die bunte Bühne*, in the café. A year after, the Jewish director and playwright Max Reinhardt initiated—on the café's tables—his avant-garde literary cabaret *Schall und Rauch* (Sound and smoke).[81] In the following years, it seemed that the bohemia of Berlin invaded and dominated the café. In 1904, the Jewish artist and critic Herwarth Walden established in Café des Westens his Verein für Kunst, an association for the arts that included artists, critics, and others interested especially in expressionist art. Walden's original name was Georg Levin, and he was the son of a bourgeois Jewish physician in Berlin. Levin met the Jewish poet Else Lasker-Schüler, who moved to Berlin from the provinces in 1894 and married the physician Jonathan Lasker. Walden and Lasker-Schüler fell in love in the café and got married after Else got divorced in 1903. Lasker-Schüler gave Herwarth Walden his new name, as well as the name for the expressionist journal *Der Sturm* (The storm), which he started publishing in 1910.[82] *Der Sturm* was followed in 1911 by another expressionist journal, *Die Aktion*, edited by Franz Pfemfert. Both journals were edited in Café des Westens. By then, the café was also the launching pad of a heady combination of poetry readings, performance, and music. The origin of such activity was in Der neue Club (The new club), an association of mostly Jewish students including Kurt Hiller, Ernst Blass, and Erwin Loewenson that began as a liberal fraternity and went on to organize "public evenings" that introduced expressionist poetry and art. In 1910, the club had changed its name to the Neopathetisches Cabaret. Café des Westens was quickly becoming not only the chief gathering place for expressionist circles centered in Berlin but also a magnetic pole for modernist writers and artists from all over Europe. It earned the nickname Café Größenwahn (Café Megalomania), used also for Café Griensteidl and Central in Vienna, and became notorious for the extravagant dress and eccentric behavior of its *Stammgäste*.[83]

The ubiquity of Jewish figures in Café des Westens before World War I was noticeable. Regulars included Reinhardt, Walden, and Lasker-Schüler, as well as the poet Ernst Blass, the poet and anarchist Erich Mühsam, the novelists Gustav Meyrink and Alfred Döblin, the painters Ludwig Meindner and John Höxter, and the art collector and editor Paul Cassirer.[84] At this point, the pervasiveness of Jews, which was no doubt associated with the café's "bohemianism," attracted both positive and negative attention. In 1911, a conservative paper compared Café des Westens to a "swamp" and asked whether this kind of place was to be permitted. This critique followed a court case in which the café was

Figure 4.2. Photograph of Café des Westens and its habitués, *Berliner Tageblatt und Handels-Zeitung*, May 21, 1905

accused by some citizens of its fashionable, upper-middle-class West Berlin neighborhood of being a magnet that attracted "the vermin of Berlin's arts crowd," who turn it into a "swamp."[85] Walden published in *Der Sturm* a passionate and witty feuilleton in defense of the "undesirable elements" in the café, imagining how the habitués of the café would look to an unassuming bourgeois from West Berlin, who hurries past this "pit of hell" and sees "men with long hair, rippled ringed curls, wild fluttering suits, and secessionist socks." Walden wrote that each time he goes to this "harmless place," he "looks around in astonishment." He ended the feuilleton by describing the Café des Westens at midnight, when the "bourgeoisie of Berlin is asleep" and secret rituals of mutual adulation among the habitués take place.[86]

Jewishness and anti-Semitism were hardly explicit in the attack on Café des Westens but rather were embedded.[87] The first decade of the twentieth century was the first time in Berlin's history that Jews had an enormous impact on the creation and dissemination of modern art, literature, theater, and film. They felt at home with non-Jewish poets and artists such as Peter Hille, Gottfried Benn, George Heym, and Jakob van Hoddis. That evolution was very much due to the break with bourgeois convention that became the norm for many young writers, artists, and intellectuals, Jewish and non-Jewish, during these years.[88] Those who came from Jewish families were essentially fighting against what their parents' generation aspired to: upward mobility, social status, and the prosperity that opened to them with emancipation. As Ernst Blass suggested in his memoir of Café des Westens, these younger Jews were "not bohemians in the usual sense" but "had a sharply defined feeling of responsibility." They were engaged in a "battle against the soullessness, the deadness, laziness, and meanness of the philistine world." In the café, by contrast, "soul was still worth something."[89] Many young Jews in these years felt that the Judaism of their parents, whether liberal or Orthodox, was superficial. The way to escape this was through the various new artistic directions that floated in the air of the metropolis. That art—particularly the rise of what became known as "expressionism"—was a crucial aspect of Berlin's modernism but also had a special meaning as part of modern, secular Jewish culture.[90]

This is when Martin Buber called for a "Jewish renaissance," not through organized religion but through culture. Buber became interested in the cultural aspects of the new movement of Zionism and promoted Jewish renewal through his study and publication of Hasidism, as well as in his new conception of modern Jewish art and literature. Buber wrote about his vision of renaissance in 1901, in the new Berlin-based magazine *Ost und West* (East and West).[91] The very existence of such a magazine and its name indicated the new tendency in German Jewish culture away from religious strictures and toward pan-Judaism. Buber's essay, and the journal itself, assumed that the renewal of Judaism must come by looking at the "authentic" *Ostjuden*, the eastern European Jew who was seen by many German Jews as backward and unmodern. In the first decade of the twentieth century, German Jewish intellectuals and writers suddenly fixed their gaze on eastern Europe or, more vaguely, on "Oriental" Jewry, a term that enabled them to stress their distance from tradition, while still claiming a spiritual as well as genetic connection. They regarded the eastern Jews as exotic, and yet they saw in the *Ostjuden* a vision of their origins, a vestige of an authenticity they were trying to regain.[92]

This new cultural orientation can explain why the expressionist poet Else Lasker-Schüler turned to "Oriental" motifs and spent nearly a decade writing her *Hebräische Balladen* (*Hebrew Ballads*, 1913). This book was in line with the expressionist principle of self-making but also was a very particular version of the new Jewish culture growing in Berlin. In spite of the fact that Lasker-Schüler had hardly left Berlin since 1903, in her poetry, she projected herself back into the Middle East of biblical times and associated herself with the figure of Joseph. She signed her letters, and some of her literary texts, as "Prince Jussuf of Thebes," dressed in Oriental clothes, and constructed her own biography as an "Oriental" Jew. In her myth-making expressionist way, Lasker-Schüler claimed that her poetry was actually a translation, originally written in the fictive biblical and "Asiatic" language of the *Wildjuden* (wild Jews). She, like so many others in Berlin, was determined both to explore new avenues and to distance herself from the bourgeois, assimilated German Jew.[93]

The sudden fascination with eastern European Jews and with cultural Zionism was aided by the fact that around the turn of the century a number of important Hebrew and Yiddish writers flocked to Berlin, and its cafés, from the Pale of Settlement. Micha Yosef Berdichevsky, an original thinker, scholar, and pioneer of modernist Hebrew fiction, lived in Germany from 1890 to 1921. Berdichevsky studied at the universities of Berlin, Breslau, and Bern in the last decade of the nineteenth century and continued to work and write in Germany for the rest of his life. Shay Ish-Hurwitz, Reuven Brainin, Shmuel Horodetsky, Marcus Ehrenpreis, Ya'acov Kahan, and other migrants turned Berlin into a small but important Hebraist center.[94] Many of these figures lived in and around the Scheunenviertel (the barn quarter), a district in the center of Berlin that emerged as a center of migration for eastern European Jews before, during, and after World War I.[95]

The fiercest proponent of this group was Itamar Ben Avi, the oldest son of Eliezer Ben Yehuda, by then known as the "reviver of Hebrew" in Palestine. Itamar, born in Jerusalem and eventually mythologized as "the first Hebrew child," went to study in Europe at the age of seventeen, first in Paris and then, between 1904 and 1908, at Berlin University. Like many others, young Itamar was attracted to the culture and politics abundant in Berlin's cafés. In his memoir, he wrote about Café Monopol, "to which thousands of Jews flocked, and in which the Zionists created a 'center' to spend their evenings."[96] Ben Avi recalled that "you could read the best newspapers from Germany and all over the world" and meet "all of German Jewry, with its guests from Moscow, Warsaw, Odessa, Vilna, Lemberg, Prague. . . . You merely had to order a cup of coffee with a single pastry on the side, and this enabled you to spend many hours there." In Café Monopol, which was opposite the train station of Friedrichstrasse, not far from the Scheunenviertel, Ben Avi claimed, "together with Aharon Hermoni . . . we created our own corner, our own table—the first Eretz Israeli corner," where they "met every evening" and "edited Sokolow's Ha-olam."[97] *Ha-'olam*, the Hebrew counterpart of *Die Welt*—the official German-language organ of the Zionist Organization—was created in 1907 with Sokolow in charge, but in fact it was edited by Aharon Hermoni (Ginsburg) for a couple of years before it moved to Vilna, Odessa, and other cities. Hermoni, who also spent time in Berlin as a student and journalist, wrote that during this time,

> Café Monopol was considered the Zionist center in Berlin. Every Zionist activist from Russia-Poland who passed through Berlin knew that in the café . . . he could meet at any time colleagues from east and west and friends from the Zionist congresses. . . . In this café, we, the few Hebraists

in Berlin, created a "Hebrew corner." . . . The language spoken at this table in the café was Hebrew, and this was a novelty, almost a miracle: the Berlin Zionists were visiting this table from time to time, to hear how modern, cultured people converse in the language of the prophets. Even the gentile waiters—among them the head waiter, Eduard the magnificent—were welcoming us with "Shalom."[98]

These memoirs all highlight the "Hebrew corner" and the Zionist activity at Café Monopol, but this place in the heart of Berlin was a multilingual, transnational hub of communication and modern Jewish culture. In June 1902, Reuven Brainin published a feuilleton in the Yiddish newspaper *Der Yud*, in which he takes the readers on "a tour of Berlin," consciously following the example of Heine. Brainin wrote that "if you are interested in seeing where the Jews in Berlin gather, you need to leave the restaurants and taverns . . . and go into Café Monopol,"

Figure 4.3. Postcard of Café Monopol, Berlin

which was one of the few places where German Jews and Jews from Russia, Poland, and Romania can and do meet. There, wrote Brainin, "sit the journalists and writers, and many literary creations and plans are taking place."[99] The author Z. Drulitsh wrote in the Warsaw Yiddish newspaper *Der Moment* that "in every national Jewish enterprise . . . Café Monopol plays some role." Drulitsh reported that, apart from German, "in one corner you can hear Hebrew, in another, Yiddish, in another Russian."[100]

Yet most German observers associated Café Monopol not with Russian, Yiddish, or Hebrew cultural activity, which they hardly noticed, but with German culture. The presence of Max Reinhardt, one of the major figures of the twentieth-century theater, was especially important. During meetings in Café Monopol, Reinhardt gathered together a group of actors and dramatists and developed an agenda for a revolutionary symbolist theater. The café was also the favorite place of the anarchist writers Gustav Landauer and Erich Mühsam and of the critic and journalist Alfred Kerr. The heady mix of German theater directors, actors, critics, journalists, and writers, many of them Jews, was what attracted both well-known and up-and-coming Jewish writers, including Yiddish writers, to the café. This is what brought Sholem Asch, a rising star of Yiddish literature who, we should recall, was a habitué of cafés in Warsaw, to Berlin. Asch met Max Reinhardt and the famed actor Rudolph Schildkraut (originally from Romania) in 1907 at Café Monopol. Apparently, Reinhardt fell in love with Asch's daring play *Got fun nekome* (*God of Vengeance*) and decided to stage a production with Schildkraut in the leading role. Reinhardt's production of the play, depicting a brothel keeper's attempt to strike a bargain with God to keep his daughter pure, was a great success.[101]

Shortly after, the more established but cash-hungry Sholem Aleichem came back to Europe after a failed attempt at a breakthrough in New York's Yiddish theater scene. Sholem Aleichem, a habitué of cafés in Odessa and Warsaw, came to Berlin and to Café Monopol with the idea that, like Asch, he could meet Schildkraut and Reinhardt and interest them in his recent play, *Di goldgreber* (*The Gold Diggers*). Reinhardt rejected it, but that did not stop Sholem Aleichem from staying in Berlin and frequenting Monopol. In Y. D. Berkovitz's biography of Sholem Aleichem and his generation, he writes that people who just met each other in one of Warsaw's cafés could meet again a few days later in Café Monopol.[102]

Much of this literary and theatrical activity, which was conducted mainly in Yiddish and German, can actually be gleaned from Hebrew accounts of Café Monopol, not so much in the memoirs but in a fascinating piece of publishing, a satirical supplement to *Ha-ʿolam* published during Purim in 1908 with the title "Ha'azpan." In it, there is a satirical drama called "'Osey ha-dramot" (The makers of the dramas). Its first act takes place in Café Monopol, with "rows of round tables. Huge noise. By each and every table sit groups of Berlin's writers and scholars. Out of the noise, one can hear some fragments of the conversation: 'Hassidism . . . Haskalah, Eretz Israel, The Gaon of Vilna, Koln, Usishkin and the Beshet." The play presents the owner of the café exclaiming that "those damn Russians" are "strange people." The entire evening they sit on one cup of coffee, speak noisily, make strange facial expressions."[103]

One of the protagonists of the play is a "great writer" (the image does not leave any doubt that this is Sholem Aleichem) who arrives

Figure 4.4. Illustration of Sholem Aleichem and Sholem Asch in Café Monopol, *Ha-ʿolam*, March 18, 1908

in the café and asks, "This is the famous Monopol? This is the awe-inspiring place of the great dramaturges? . . . I have written a new drama from the life of the real Jews, and I want to stage it in the German Theater."[104] The text gives us a real-time glimpse into the intellectual and social life of this Berlin café in which Jewish modernism was created. Discussions about "neo-Hasidism" and its place in Hebrew and Yiddish literature are mixed with political debates, the life of the German theater, and the aspiring writers in Jewish languages who want to succeed in Berlin.

Café Monopol was not the only place in Berlin where eastern European Hebrew and Yiddish writers went; the bohemian Café de Westens became for them a literary destination. Berdichevsky, Shay Ish Hurtivz, David Shimonovitz, and other Hebrew, Yiddish, and German writers and intellectuals used to meet every Thursday evening for what Berdichevsky called "literary table," first at the Monopol and then at Café des Westens. Shmuel Yosef Agnon, who arrived in Berlin in 1912, spent some time there while he became acquainted with many German Jewish writers and intellectuals.[105] Notably, the overwhelming majority of Jewish café habitués in Café Monopol and Café des Westens, as in other cities explored in this book, were men. This was in spite of the fact that cafés were opened to everybody and that there were certainly women who visited there, but hardly any woman was noted as a writer, artist, or intellectual. The only exception to this was the aforementioned Else Lasker-Schüler, who was one of the few women to frequent Café des Westens and the only one associated with the expressionist movement who received wide recognition and notoriety. Walter Benjamin wrote that before World War I, women in Berlin cafés were mostly "coquettes." He mentioned Lasker-Schüler as a women who was the exception to the rule, a "privilege" due to her status as an artist, which set her apart from other "ordinary" women.[106] Thus, it is not surprising that her appearance and behavior in the café, like her poetry and literature, created controversy and unease. In her poem "Heimweh," she wrote that she "does not speak the language of the land." Her friend the Jewish anarchist Gustav Landauer wrote that "she doesn't fit anywhere and certainly not in the milieu in which you see her."[107] Lasker-Schüler's play with reinventing herself and crossing borders was extended to her gender identity. She dressed up as her literary characters, such as Prince Jussuf of Thebes, who is sometimes masculine, sometimes an androgynous youth. Her performance thus thrived on playing with gendered identities.

In the fictitious "Briefe nach Norwegen" (Letters to Norway), first published in installments in *Der Sturm* and later as the novel *Mein Herz* (*My Heart*, 1912), Lasker-Schüler portrayed herself among the Berlin café habitués. The work is both a vivid picture of the artistic and bohemian culture of Berlin cafés around 1910 and at the same time a very personal testimony of a woman poet and writer. The epistolary novel was inspired by Walden's brief trip to Sweden in 1911, when Else and Walden were drifting apart. In one of the letters, she wrote, "For two evenings now, I have not been in the café, my heart has been bothering me." Referring to the expressionist writer Alfred Döblin as "Doctor Döblin von Urban," she wrote, "[He] came to offer a diagnosis. He thinks that I am suffering from a thyroid condition, but actually I have a longing for the café."[108] She described this "longing for the café" in erotic terms, like a lover without whom she cannot live, though aware of the destructive nature of this desire.

The expression "our café" soon acquired a new and different meaning; around 1913, the Café des Westens "closed for remodeling" so that it could reopen in a new location, a few houses down the Kurfurstendamm road, as a more "respected" bourgeois establishment. Although the new café existed until 1921, the new location signaled the banishing of the writers and bohemians.[109] In 1913, Lasker-Schüler published a public letter titled "Unser Café" (Our café), addressed to Paul Block, the feuilleton editor of the newspaper *Berliner Tageblatt*. In this letter, she wrote, "Sir, you want to know about our café, but since around Pentecost, our café is no longer our café."[110] In the letter, Lasker-Schüler pretends that she has received from her sister in Chicago a newspaper clipping stating that the owner of the café prohibits her from coming to the café because she has not ordered or consumed enough. She declares this an outrageous insult, a humiliating dismissal of her authenticity as a poet: "Think! Is a poet who orders a lot even a poet?" "Others felt the same," she announced, "so they left the café in indignation." Their rage seems strange, but it was real: "We artists brought Café des Westens into the world, for all intents and purposes. We artists gave it its first raiment. We artists elevated it to the King of all cafés! . . . Our rage now hangs over Café des Westens as though it were a lost paradise, where we had not sinned but rather were sinned against."[111]

When Lasker-Schüler wrote about the "lost paradise" of Café des Westens, she did not know that a few months later, Berlin, the Kaiserreich, and all of Europe would be consumed by the fighting of the first World War, which brought dramatic and unforeseen changes.

World War I, Weimar Berlin, and the Romanisches Café

When World War I erupted, the Kaiser hoped that it would unite his subjects. On the morning of August 4, 1914, he announced, "from this day, I recognize no political divisions or parties, only Germans." In response to this call for unity, the leading institutions of the German Jewish community endorsed the patriotic cause. A Berlin Orthodox synagogue introduced a special prayer imploring God, "Help our king . . . our people . . . our fatherland." Soon after, one hundred thousand German Jews enlisted in the army. But that optimism dissipated as the chaos grew and the body count increased. As conditions deteriorated, anti-Semitism thrived; Jews were accused of profiteering, of avoiding military service, even of spying. In October 1916, War Minister Adolf Wild von Hohenborn commissioned a census of Jewish soldiers to ascertain how many were actually serving at the front.[112] By then, most Jews in Germany, and especially in Berlin, had grown disillusioned with the idea that the war would make Jews more integrated with larger German society.

A number of writers and artists died while on active duty. Others, such as the Jewish artists Ludwig Meidner and Jakob Steindhardt, returned from the front, but their wartime experience left an indelible scar. For many German Jewish soldiers who served on the eastern front, the war brought an encounter with *Ostjuden*, especially in small towns. Some Jewish writers, artists, and intellectuals—those who used to gather in the "old Café des Westens," as well as a new generation of young Berlin Jews that included Walter Benjamin and Gershom Scholem—were strongly opposed to the war from the very beginning. These young students, journalists, and writers, like all Germans, could be enlisted to serve in the war at any point. Scholem, whose experience of World War I led him to Zionism and the historical study of kabbalah, wrote about meeting Benjamin at the "new" Café des Westens on the night of October 20, 1914, preceding his friend's reexamination for military service. Benjamin consumed vast quantities of black coffee, a practice followed by many young men prior to their military physicals, in the hopes of being declared unfit for service.[113] Benjamin himself wrote later about 1914, when "Berlin cafés played a part in our lives."[114] Although much more gloomy and less bohemian than in the period before 1914, cafés were a refuge of a kind, however temporary.

When the Hebrew writer Agnon came to Berlin in 1912, he grew close to the circle of intellectuals opposed to the war and suffered from it. Agnon's Hebrew novel 'Ad hena (To This Day) is loosely based on his experience of World War I in Berlin.[115] The novel is marked by its preoccupation, even obsession, with pensions, hotels, and cafés, as well as with injured soldiers and the despair that gripped Berlin. The first-person narrator in the novel, a Jew from Galicia who is stranded in Berlin by the war, tries to find and maintain a new room in the city after he lost his old pension room when he left for a visit to Leipzig. In the course of his wandering, the narrator describes a number of grotesque scenes in unnamed Berlin cafés. When he goes to one of these, he notes, "The café was packed. All through the war the cafés were crowded with people. The men came to be with other men, and the women came because their husbands had gone out and they didn't want to be left behind. New cafés opened daily and still there wasn't enough. You had to push your way into them, and others pushed from behind while you were pushing."[116]

Agnon's highly ironic narrator articulates the terrible sadness that abounds in the café, showing Berlin as a place full of men and women who are afraid of being alone and being "left behind." In this description, the café is full of cripples and ersatz substitutes, and yet it is the place that everybody is attracted to. As much as the narrator complains about "what passes as coffee," the crowds, and the oppressive atmosphere, he himself clings to his seat in the café and will not let go. Agnon did not start writing this novel until the 1930s, and thus it both embodied the feel of wartime Berlin and was also influenced by his experience of Berlin in the 1920s. This intense period of the Weimar Republic—between Germany's defeat in World War I in 1918 and the fall of the Kaiser, and Hitler's rise to power in 1933—saw Berlin as the hectic center of Weimar culture, a fertile ground for intellectuals, artists, and innovators from many fields, in which the social, political, and economic situation was chaotic. After the Holocaust, it is nearly impossible not to read this moment as a precursor to the Nazi's eventual efforts at extermination, yet Weimar Berlin was the epicenter of what the historian Michael Brenner has called "the renaissance of Jewish culture."[117] The poet Gottfried Benn observed that "the overflowing abundance of stimuli, of artistic, scholarly, and commercial improvisations, that brought Berlin into line with Paris during the years 1918–1933," was largely because of the city's Jews.[118]

The Jewish population in Berlin reached its high point during the Weimar period, with 173,000 in 1925, among them 44,000 *Ostjuden*, who fled the upheavals of the Great War and the pogroms and revolutions that swept Russia and the rest of eastern Europe. The poor among these migrants lived in the Scheunenviertel, around Alexanderplatz in Berlin Mitte, or (like Agnon's protagonist) in pensions and rented rooms in West Berlin. Among the migrants who made Berlin a temporary home, some for days and some for years, were many Hebrew and Yiddish writers. H. N. Bialik and Shaul Tschernichovsky from Odessa, David Frishman and D. H. Nomberg from Warsaw, Zalman Shneour and Moyshe Kulbak from Vilna, Dovid Bergelson and Der Nister from Kiev, Uri Zvi Greenberg from Lemberg, and Ya'akov Shteinberg from Warsaw and Tel Aviv were among those who joined Berdichevsky, Agnon, and others who were already living in Berlin during the war.[119]

One of the places that these eastern European migrants in Berlin frequented was the Romanisches Café, established in 1916 by the businessman Karl Fiering, across from the Kaiser-Wilhelm-Gedächtniskirche. It was named after the large building in which it was located in West Berlin, built in Neo-Romanesque style. From around 1918, it became the preferred Berlin meeting spot for writers and artists. Berlin of the 1920s had approximately 550 cafés; among them, several were owned by Jews, such as Café Dobrin, with a number of branches in the city owned by the brothers Moritz and Isidor Dobrin, and Café Lunte on Eislebener Strasse, owned by Frieda Ehmann, who was nicknamed "Die Lunte." However, the Romanisches Café was an undisputed center of Weimar Berlin.[120] It became a new headquarters of the expressionists, as well as the so-called *Neue Sachlichkeit* (new objectivity) movement and, ultimately, of most writers, artists, intellectuals, and bohemians—German and non-German alike—in Berlin.[121] The Romanisches Café performed many of the functions of Café des Westens before World War I, and it also inherited the dubious name "Café Megalomania." Among many well-known figures who frequented the café were Else Lasker-Schüler, Franz Werfel, Kurt Tucholsky, Stefan Zweig, Alfred Döblin, Erich Kästner, Ludwig Meydner, Gottfried Benn, Joseph Roth, Bertolt Brecht, Walter Benjamin, Egon Erwin Kisch, Otto Dix, and Billy Wilder. Many of them wrote in and about the café and depicted it in their artwork.[122]

But the Romanisches Café was indicative of Weimar culture in many ways, including that this very large café was far from the exclusive location of a small group.[123] On the one hand, the owner quickly recognized that the encroachment of the artist community would help his business. At the same time, he also employed a manager, Herr Nietz, who controlled the flow of visitors. Jewish and non-Jewish writers and critics who frequented the café noted how heterogeneous the crowd was. Joseph Roth, who moved to Berlin from Vienna in 1920, wrote a feuilleton about "Richard the Red," the "newspaper waiter." In Roth's text, Richard becomes a metonym for many of the writers and artists to whom he used to deliver newspapers personally and to whom he used to "look like a king in exile."[124] Walter Benjamin, in his *Berliner Chronik*, describes the function of the café in this period as an "elementary and indispensable diversion of the citizen of a great metropolis," which offered entrance "into another world, the more exotic the better." From Benjamin's perspective, in the Romanisches Café, "the artists withdrew into the background, to become more and more a part of the furniture, while the bourgeois . . . began to occupy it, as a place of relaxation."[125]

After Erich Mühsam had been granted amnesty following five years of imprisonment for his role in the Munich revolt of 1924, he wrote, "The bohème that I remember no longer lives." He claimed emphatically, "No one will seriously see the exchange of opinions in the Romanisches Café as the meeting place of free spirits, of the protest-driven uprooted, and of the voluntary outcasts who knew the old Café des Westens. . . . Today, it seems to me that the foyer has become a scene, the café a hotbed of catechized radicalism, which lacks any creative radicality."[126] The Jewish journalist and critic Paul E. Marcus described Romanisches Café as "another bohème . . . of praxis and not of the ideal. Business, the buzzword of the day, has even them in its grasp."[127] Ilya Ehrenburg, a Russian

Jewish author who lived in Berlin from 1921 to 1924, composed a set of travel sketches and feuilletons. One of those is titled "Pis'ma iz kafe" (Letters from a café), in which Erehnburg outlines his perception of Berlin: "You can listen to Europe's heart only in Berlin"; but this heart does not work as it should. "I am writing this letter," Ehrenberg informed his readers, "from the Romanisches Café. . . . It resembles a headquarters for fanatical vagabonds, everyday folk, and the educated crooks who have been entirely cured of narrow-minded nationalism. . . . I'm afraid you won't believe me—it obviously sounds paradoxical: I have grown fond of Berlin."[128]

By the mid-1920s, the large café seemed to have been separated into different rooms according to an unwritten hierarchy. It was compared by Matheo Quinz to a huge public bath, divided into a "large pool for swimmers and a smaller pool for nonswimmers." When one walked

Figure 4.5. O. Ang, *Personen im Romanischen Café sitzend beim Rauchen, Lesen und Unterhalten*, 1930/1933 (Bundesarchiv Bild 183-R25288)

Figure 4.6. H. Hoffman, interior view of the Romanisches Café in Berlin, 1925 (© Ullstein)

through the almost constantly rotating revolving door, past Herr Nietz, to the left was the larger room, the "pool for swimmers," which was reserved for the already-known habitués, mostly impresarios and people who worked in the film and advertising industry. The "players' tables" were reserved for chess and parties of women. To the right of the entrance was a large rectangular room, the "pool for nonswimmers." Here many young hopeful writers and artists gathered; among them were "scholars of Talmud."[129]

Those who seemed to Quinz as "scholars of Talmud"—his only reference to Jewishness—were most likely the Hebrew and Yiddish writers and artists who migrated to Berlin after World War I and throughout the Weimar period and flocked to the Romanisches Café.[130] In fact, some accounts create the false impression that Romanisches Café was a kind of a pan-Jewish urban space. Thus, Naḥum Goldman writes that "each [Jewish] group had its own table; there were the 'Yiddishists,' 'Zionists,' 'Bundists' and so on, all arguing among themselves from table to table."[131] The Yiddish poet A. N. Stencel describes the scene of the Romanisches Café from the angle of those who were "fleeing the pogroms in Ukrainian shtetls . . . and the Revolution": "A kind of Jewish colony formed itself in the west of Berlin, and the Romanisches Café was its parliament. It was buzzing with famous Jewish intellectuals and activists, well-known Jewish lawyers from Moscow and Petersburg, Yiddish writers from Kiev and Odessa. . . . It buzzed like a beehive."[132]

Lev Bergelson wrote that his father, Dovid Bergelson, used to "spend many evenings in the Romanisches Café, which at that time was the favorite haunt of Berlin bohemians. Sitting around the café's marble tables, people would drink coffee, smoke and chat, but they would also read and write poems, create script for new films, and play chess."[133] Daniel Charney attested, "In the Romanisches Café of Berlin . . . I met again good old friends and colleagues who occupied the East Wall of the so-called 'Rakhmones Café' [Pity Café]: Bergelson and Numberg, Hirshkan and Onokhi, Der Nister and Kvitko, Latski-Bartoldi and Leschinski. . . . I was simply drunk with joy."[134] When a Canadian Yiddish writer visited the café, he found there an assorted group of Jewish intellectuals, such as the philosopher and Zionist Jacob Klatzkin, the actor Alexander Granach, the folklorist Immanuel Olsvanger, the popular Yiddish novelist I. J. Singer (who had just arrived straight from Warsaw), and finally Daniel Charney and David Bergelson, coming together around eleven p.m. When the editor of the New York Yiddish newspaper *Forverts*, Abraham Cahan, came to Berlin, he knew he had to go to the Romanisches Café in order to recruit the best Yiddish writers who could write for his paper.[135]

In a sketch called "A briv fun Berlin" (A letter from Berlin), Daniel Charney wrote about the Romanisches Café "through which came almost the entirety of Yiddish literature and almost the entirety of Jewish society from all corners of the world during the years 1920–1935!" In the Romanisches Café, claimed Charney, "the good idea to found the Yiddish Scientific Institute [YIVO] came about . . . and the Jewish encyclopedia. . . . The Romanisches Café was, one can say, the transit hub of the entire Yiddishland." The idea that almost all of "Yiddish literature" could pass through one specific café in Berlin of the Weimar period seems outlandish, even ludicrous. However, we begin to apprehend the profound experience of the café when Charney writes,

> Nomberg, of blessed memory, often used to say . . . the air here is so thick and smoky that viruses are dying off. . . . Moyshe Litvakov . . . wrote in "Emes" that Bergelson "graduated from the Romanisches," as one graduates, for example, from a university or a college. For me, the Romanisches Café was actually both a "sanitarium" and a "college" for a good decade. I healed my lungs with nicotine and caffeine, and I learned the most important rules of writing in the Romanisches.[136]

The intense presence of eastern European Jewish writers in the Romanisches Café attracted much interest outside Germany, praised by some and derided by others. The Yiddish educator and journalist Israel Rubin wrote, "At the tables of the Yiddish writers in the Romanisches Café all possible topics have already been exhausted. . . . Everyone has been denigrated and slandered. . . . All literary and social dialogues and prognoses have been outlined, and matters are now approaching the point of repetition." He noted that writers would congregate every evening in the café to "pray a Romanisches evening service [*ma'ariv*]."[137] In a feuilleton titled "Silhuetn fun romanishes kafe," the writer and socialist critic Nokhum Shtif, under the pseudonym Bal Dimyon, satirizes the hot-house atmosphere of the café with its noisy, smoke-filled rooms and its pretentious clientele. The implication is that the literati and bohemians to be found there were idlers and dreamers, even if they were Yiddish artists and intellectuals. To Shtif, who wrote for a Yiddish socialist journal, a gathering place such as the Romanisches Café was far removed from reality and the needs of the "masses."[138]

When Melech Ravitch, a habitué of cafés in Lemberg, Vienna, and Warsaw, wanted to criticize the Yiddish writers who made Berlin home, he wrote, "Somewhere in Berlin, in the smoky atmosphere of the Romanisches Café, some of the best creators of Yiddish culture are hanging around, pretending to create a Yiddish culture. But those who are sitting in the Romanisches Café and looking at us from afar, as we are pulling the carriage of our culture, are simply deserters."[139] The Yiddish writer Peretz Markish similarly attacked what he called "the new Golus [exile] of the Romanisches Café, which is becoming a new Jerusalem," and mocked this "third temple."[140] However, just a few months after he published this scathing criticism, Markish himself visited Berlin and rushed to the Romanisches Café to meet Uri Zvi Greenberg and Vladimir Mayakovsky, who were in Berlin at the time.

These conflicting images of the Romanisches Café—as "The Café of Pity," a new Jerusalem or Yanve, and a place of *kibetz goluyos* (the ingathering of the exiles)—are a testimony to the tensions inherent in the thirdspace. For some people, the café became a symbol of the detachment of Yiddish and Hebrew writers from their readers and from the Jewish masses more broadly; yet it is clear that the café was also a place of unprecedented creativity.[141] The café quickly became a metonym for Berlin's modernity. The Yiddish and Hebrew writers Bergelson, Stencel, Greenberg, and Shteinberg encountered many important figures of Berlin modernism in the Romanisches Café, and these experiences left strong marks on their literary and intellectual development. During these years, many important Jewish émigré artists from eastern Europe lived and worked in Berlin, including Marc Chagall, Natan Altman, El Lissitzky, Issachar Ber Ryback, Ya'acov Adler, Henryk Berlewi, Mark Schwartz, and Mordekhay Ardon. Many of them found in the Romanisches Café a space that opened their horizons to new developments in German and Russian modernism.[142] Chagall, who arrived in Berlin in 1922, wrote, "never in my life have I met so many miraculous Hassidic rabbis as in inflationary Berlin, nor such crowds of constructivist artists as at the Romanisches Café."[143]

There are many literary and artistic representations of the Romanisches Café in Jewish literature. In an essay on Else Lasker-Schüler (1926), the Hebrew and Yiddish modernist Uri Zvi Greenberg wrote in his characteristically fragmentary expressionist style, with its expansive grammar and outrageous images, "We drank together dark coffee in the Romanisches Café, and until midnight this bitter drink was dripping in our hearts, and seeping through even deeper to the 'inner existence,' around the heart and beyond it like dark blood."[144] One of the most interesting modernist texts that were inspired by and devoted to the Romanisches Café is a cycle of Hebrew poems—*Sonetot mi beit ha-kafe*

(Sonnets from the coffeehouse, 1922)—written by the Hebrew and Yid-dish writer Ya'akov Shteinberg. As the writer and critic Ya'acov Kopelo-vitz (Yeshurun Keshet), who was Shteinberg's good friend in Berlin, attested, Shteinberg came to understand the Romanisches Café both as a kind of "imaginary Jewish space" and as a place in which "regulars" are the "cultural elite full of decadence, smoke and the syncopated rhythm of the metropolis."[145] The cycle creates a tightly knit narrative that oc-curs solely in the space of the café, which itself becomes an object of ob-servation and introspection. It presents a speaker who sits and "watches in front of the lampshade," before disappearing again, "in a screen of smoke."[146]

Each of the sonnets in the cycle tells us a short and concentrated "story" with a character and with a specific event or narrative situation in the café—the waiter, a couple indulging in "a desire that has been revealed," a woman who sits alone and one does not know if she is a "queen" or a "prostitute," the abandoned newspapers after the café's clos-ing. The large but enclosed space of the café, with its ever-changing vistas and moods, contains everything because it can be full or empty, bright and dark, airy and smoky, friendly and hostile, familiar and anon-ymous. All these different aspects of the café serve as a way to decipher the urban experience of Berlin and the experience of Western modernity in general from the point of view of the Jewish migrant. The café is de-scribed both as a place of "happiness and chatter" and a place to which people can flock in order to avoid the "deep sadness" that lurks every-where in the metropolis. This duality is captured in the metaphor of the "newspapers that are rolled up like idle hieroglyphic scrolls,"[147] which require, and resist, deciphering, as well as with the Hebrew expression *beit-moed*, which is both a space in which people congregate and a space that houses people who are in fact dead in life. The café is thus both a space that is a refuge from oblivion and a space that embodies the void and abyss of contemporary life.

In Leah Goldberg's novel *Avedot* (Losses)—written in the 1930s but not published during her lifetime—the emphasis is on the ethnic and gendered nature of the space and the fluid, sometimes deceptive sexual-ity that marks it. Toward the end of the novel, the narrator recounts a visit of the protagonist Elhanan Kron, a poet and a scholar, to a Berlin café. At this point in the plot, Kron meets Elvina Shaydman, a bohemian young woman, a divorcee, and an actress from a German Jewish family who lost her work in the theater because of the rise of the Nazis. Together with Elvina, Kron enters

> an expansive café hall lit by a large chandelier, in the style of the large restaurants before the [First World] War. By the round tables were soft, heavy armchairs, upholstered with ruby red fabric. The café was cozy, unmodern, and it reminded one of a Jewish bourgeois house in the "old west" of Berlin. . . . The red curtains on the windows separated between them and the night of the big city. The German night of the year 1933.[148]

It is precisely because the café resembles a comforting, bourgeois Jewish house and because it seems to Kron that the curtain shields him and his companion from the city and its cultural and political tumult that nothing prepares him for what he witnesses inside the café. Kron stares at a violin player of the orchestra that plays the tango in the café. Suddenly, he notices that the violin player has the "face of a girl; his lips are painted and his eyebrows are done with a pencil. The painter did not harmonize with the petit-bourgeois appearance of the café, with its soft armchairs and the solid, heavy fabric of the curtains."[149] At that point, the musician smiles at Kron "an indulgent and promising smile," but Kron turns his head with fear. In this case, the bourgeois-looking café underlines the sexual openness and experimentalism, as well as gender identity confusion. It also highlights the political, ethnic, and religious tensions in the city at this point in time. Kron discovers that in the thirdspace of the café, the inside and the outside, the private and the public, the male and the female meet and cannot be, after all, separated.

These literary descriptions of the Romanisches Café suggest the essence of the encounter of multilingual Jewish writers with the urban space of Berlin. These writers encountered Berlin modernism within the walls of the Romanisches Café, and their endless hours there left strong marks on their literary and intellectual development. Their experience of the café as a kind of "hieroglyphic" spatial image of Berlin emphasizes their participation in modernist Berlin culture and their simultaneous marginality; the commodity spectacle of "surface" and sexuality and the potential for artistic creativity inherent within; and the undeniable energy of the metropolis as well as its decadence, corruption, and sense of deep despair. The sense of decadence and despair became very evident to those Jewish figures who remained in Berlin and its cafés in the 1930s. Even before Hitler came to power in 1933, Romanisches Café was known and targeted by the Nazis as a hub for Jewish intellectuals. On September 12, 1931—Rosh Hashanah, the Jewish New Year—Hitlerist thugs were stationed at strategic points through the city in which Jews would have to pass. One spot was outside the synagogue in West Berlin. Tellingly, another was near the Romanisches Café; as these troops attacked and harassed Jews, they also erected a megaphone, and the thugs took turns keeping up a constant shout: "Death to the Jews" and "Germany, awaken!" and "Die Judas!"[150] For these Nazis, the Romanisches Café was an indelibly "Jewish space," akin to a synagogue.

Wolfgang Koeppen wrote about the Romanisches Café after 1933: "We saw the terrace and the café disappear, . . . dissolve into nothing." The habitués of the café "were scattered all over the world or were captured or killed; others sat still in the café . . . ashamed."[151] It is highly significant that Koeppen, like Leah Goldberg and many others, understood that with the rise of Nazis, the Romanisches Café—the symbolic embodiment of Berlin café culture that developed in the nineteenth and early twentieth centuries—dissolved, and its role in history ended. This is despite the fact that the café was *not* shut down until it was destroyed in a bombing raid in 1943. While it physically continued to exist, this Berlin institution clearly lost its importance as a center of culture after the Nazi takeover, when most of its Jewish habitués migrated to other cities in Europe, America, or Mandatory Palestine. Some of them killed themselves; others frequented cafés in whatever city they fled to. Lasker-Schüler made it to Jerusalem, where she was admired by young Hebrew poets, but most of the patrons in her new café did not even recognize the prematurely old woman.[152] Wolf Ze'ev Joffe, after moving to Tel Aviv, wrote an entire unpublished manuscript—"Ein Jahr im Romanischen Café" (One year in Romanisches Café)—which portrayed the Berlin café at the end of the 1920s.

One of the Jewish migrants who had to flee Berlin was the writer and journalist Egon Erwin Kisch. In 1933, Kisch was one of many prominent opponents of Nazism to be arrested. He was jailed and then expelled from Germany. In the late 1930s and until his death in 1948, he traveled to Spain, France, Mexico, and the United States, unable to find a place to call home. A couple of years before his expulsion from Berlin, Kisch tried to answer the question that is at the heart of this book: Why the café? What is the reason for going to the café? Kisch saw the café as a European institution. "Of course," he claimed, "we in Europe can answer this question with ease, because we have the beloved *Kaffeehaus*, without which, in my opinion, one cannot live." The second-person plural that Kisch employs here is never explicit, and yet it is quite clear that he is speaking in particular about European Jews such as himself. As such, he declared about the *Kaffeehaus*, "It is what we Europeans . . . miss so much when we go over to America."[153] Was the café, and its role in Jewish culture, a European phenomenon? To Kisch, the answer is quite clear, but as we will see, for the Jewish migrants who fled Europe and found new homes in New York and Tel Aviv, the café was just as central there to their experience of Jewishness and to the continued creation of modern Jewish culture in spite of the devastation of the war and Nazi fascism.

5

New York City

Kibitzing in the Cafés of the New World

My New York remains the New York of the cafeterias, the
salesmen, the evening session students, the countermen,
the kibitzers.
—Alfred Kazin, 1951

New York nights, multicolored and aflame,
White, loud, impertinent.
Broadway. Nights full of café to café.
—Aaron Glantz Leyeles, 1963

In 1940, Alfred Polgar, the Jewish writer, feuilletonist, and café habitué, arrived in America after fleeing Nazi-occupied Vienna. Nearly a
decade later, Polgar wrote a short story called "Sein letzter Irrtum" (His
last error). In the story, an exiled Austrian editor declares, "In America,
there are no coffeehouses where one could sit for hours at a time, and
if there were, they would not be at all congenial; and if they were, they
would long have gone out of business."[1] The quote encapsulates a truism
held by many people that European cafés cannot really exist in ultra-
capitalist America. However, the fictional editor, and perhaps Polgar too,
was unaware that New York City had a long history of coffeehouses and
café culture that intersected with the history of the city's Jews, especially
in the period between the 1880s and the 1960s. New York cafés were
imported from Europe along with the many migrants who arrived in the
New World. These cafés fascinated non-Jewish writers and intellectuals,
who tried to make sense of them. They were experienced by immigrant
Jews as both similar to and different from cafés in eastern and central
Europe. Eventually, New York cafés became important points in the

constantly evolving and increasingly mobile network of modern Jewish culture that stretched from Europe to America and beyond.

Both the history of Jews and of coffeehouses in New York began in the colonial, revolutionary, and early republic periods, and both were linked, perhaps not surprisingly, with capitalism and commerce. On September 1654, twenty-three Sephardi Jewish refugees from Brazil arrived at New Amsterdam, as it was then called, and were granted asylum. After the surrender of the Dutch to the British in 1674, the city was named New York, and English manners and customs were rapidly introduced, including the English coffeehouse. A number of New York coffeehouses—the Exchange Coffee-House, the Merchants' Coffee-House, Tontine Coffee-House—achieved renown as sites of commerce and exchange, including the early New York Stock Exchange.[2] Jewish merchants visited these coffeehouses, and the first synagogue building of Congregation B'nai Jeshurun was purchased in 1826, at an auction in the Tontine Coffee-House on the corner of Wall Street and Water Street.[3]

In the 1830s and 1840s, migration from German-speaking countries into the U.S. was on the rise. Many of the immigrants lived in a dense five-block stretch between Canal Street and Rivington Street known as Kleindeutschland (Little Germany). A group of German Jewish migrants, including Henry Kling, Isaac Dittenhoefer, and Henry Jones, began meeting every Sunday morning at a café owned by Aaron Sinsheimer on Essex Street. These gatherings culminated in 1843 in the formation of B'nai B'rith (Sons of the covenant), a secular fraternal organization combining the traditions of Judaism and the Free Masons.[4] The founders of B'nai B'rith met in Sinsheimer Café, which was a saloon as much as a café, serving not only coffee and food but also beer and other alcoholic drinks.

In the 1850s and 1860s, saloons, taverns, and clubs replaced English-style coffeehouses in New York. A beer cellar on Broadway near Bleecker Street owned by Charles Ignatius Pfaff earned a reputation among journalists, critics, writers, and artists as New York's first and only "bohemian" nightspot. The idea of bohemia, which came to New York via Paris and London, involved a new understanding of the relationship of social class to artistic respectability and of both to urban life. It incorporated cultural outsiders and dissenters and made them, and their work, visible and commercially appealing to urban audiences. The great American poet Walt Whitman and Henry Clapp, the editor of the *Saturday Press*, were Pfaff's most famous habitués.[5] As far as we know, Jews were not part of the new bohemian circles at Pfaff's, with the exception of the actress Adah Isaacs Menken, who was one of a handful of female artists welcomed there. It is unclear whether Menken was born Jewish or converted when she married her husband, but she identified herself as Jewish for the rest of her life. At the same time that she achieved international notoriety as the star of the melodrama *Mazeppa*—in which she appeared onstage clad in only a flesh-colored body stocking, on the back of the "wild horse of Tartary"—she also contributed many poems to the *Israelite* and the *Jewish Messenger*.[6]

While Pfaff's was a haven for talented and eccentric bohemians—perhaps the only place in New York where someone like Menken could interact with Walt Whitman—mid-nineteenth-century New York's social clubs represented an entirely different world of bourgeois social mobility. New York's first was the Union Club, founded in 1836 by and for "gentlemen of social distinction."[7] In 1852, six German Jewish immigrants who were excluded from the Union Club established Harmonie Gesellschaft (Harmonie Club). After convening at Broome Street, the Harmonie Club rented a succession of modest quarters in and around Kleindeutschland. In 1867, it moved up to Forty-Second Street. Membership in the Harmonie Club was limited in number and was accorded only to those men able to pay its high initiation fee and annual dues, usually prosperous bankers, businessmen, and professionals. It soon came to have much in common with the clubs of the Protestant upper class that excluded Jews.[8]

By the early 1880s, beer cellars, saloons, and clubs dominated New York's social and cultural realm, and they both upheld and occasionally blurred divisions of class, religion, and ethnicity. In the period between 1850 and 1880, it was difficult to find a coffeehouse in the United States, even in New York City. In 1881, the New Yorker, businessman, and writer Francis B. Thurber wrote, "The coffeehouse . . . no longer exists among us." In spite of the fact that "Americans are the greatest coffee consumers in the world," they "take the beverage mostly at meals, either at home or at the restaurant." The reason for this, Thurber explained, is that "we are perhaps too busy a people to support cafés like those of Europe."[9]

Thurber doubted whether capitalist America could sustain a European café culture. However, when he wrote these words, he did not recognize that New York was being transformed by mass migration on a scale never seen before, out of which a new, robust café scene would reemerge, much of it associated with immigrant Jews. In the next four decades, millions of immigrants, among them countless Jews from eastern Europe, flowed through New York's Castle Garden and Ellis Island, fleeing poverty and violence. Most stayed in New York, their port of entry, joining abundant immigrant populations from Ireland, Italy, Germany, England, and the Russian and Austro-Hungarian Empires. By 1920, there were over a million and a half Jews in New York City. If in the early and mid-nineteenth century most Jewish immigrants came from central Europe, by the last decades of the century, Yiddish-speaking, mostly poor eastern European Jews predominated. They settled en masse in the East Side, the area we now refer to as the Lower East Side.[10]

When the first large wave of eastern European Jewish migrants arrived in New York, many were attracted to politics and to Schwab's and Sach's. The Frankfurt-born Justus Schwab migrated to New York in 1869. He became embroiled in radical politics during the Panic of 1873, the economic depression that lasted several years and marked the maturity of the American labor movement. Schwab was arrested during the Tompkins Square Park Riot in 1874, turned to socialism and later anarchism, and in the early 1880s opened his establishment at 50 First Street, near Tompkins Square. Schwab's quickly became "the gathering place for all bold, joyful, and freedom-loving spirits," including a number of eastern European Jewish immigrants involved in radical socialist and anarchist politics, including Shoel (Saul) Yanovsky, Dovid Edelshtat, and Abraham (Abe) Cahan, who migrated in the early 1880s and became important figures in Yiddish journalism and literature.[11]

These Jewish intellectuals found an additional home, just a few blocks down from Schwab's, on Norfolk Street. This was at Sachs' Café, where "Mrs. Sachs served fine coffee and cheese cake, and where the 'cream' of the *radikalen* gathered nightly."[12] The critic James Huneker, who moved to New York from Philadelphia in 1886 after living in Paris, was impressed with the city's small, but slowly growing, café culture. "It should not be forgotten," he wrote, "that in New York as in Paris, the café is the poor man's club. . . . It is the best stomping ground for men of talent."[13]

Indeed, there was a strong link between the working-class and cafés in New York, and most of the radicals and intellectuals at that time were "*men* of talent," with very few women. Emma Goldman, who migrated from Kovno, Lithuania, was the prominent exception. In her autobiography, Goldman wrote about her first day in New York, August 15, 1889. She knew very few people in the city, but one of them was Hillel Solotaroff, a Russian-born Jewish anarchist who lectured and wrote in Yiddish. Solotaroff took the twenty-year-old Goldman to Sachs' Café, which, as he informed her, was "the headquarters of the East Side radicals, socialists, and anarchists, as well as of the young Yiddish writers and poets." Goldman recalled how for one who had just come from the provincial town of Rochester, New York, the noise and turmoil at Sachs' Café was intimidating: "The place consisted of two rooms and was packed. Everybody talked, gesticulated, and argued, in Yiddish and Russian, each competing with the other."[14] Goldman saw her initiation into Sachs' Café as establishing her lifelong intellectual and political engagement, first as a Yiddish lecturer and writer and later as a writer in English, as "red Emma" or "the most dangerous woman in America." Although Goldman distanced herself later from the Jewish East Side, by the 1890s, a number of cafés attracted other European Jews involved in politics, the press, literature, and theater, fostering a rich culture that emerged within the poor, densely packed district of tenements, factories, and docklands. Small and simple cafés with Jewish owners—places like Zeitlin's, Schreiber's, and Herrick's—began to dot the district.[15]

Amid the radical politics of the East Side, Yiddish theater in New York developed and matured in these cafés. Between 1887 and 1891, the pioneers of Yiddish theater, Abraham Goldfaden, Jacob Adler, and Jacob Gordin, traveled from Odessa and its robust café life to New York's East Side. They joined Boris Tomashevsky, David Kessler, and Sigmund Mogulesco, who arrived in New York earlier. The migration of so many figures from eastern Europe to New York was partly motivated by the Russian regime's ban on the Yiddish theater in 1883, one of many attempts to suppress the disorder that had been unleashed by the assassination of Alexander II. The story of Jacob Gordin exemplifies the growth and the influence of New York as a center of Yiddish theater, as well as the role of cafés in making this American city a major new anchor in the silk road of modern Jewish culture. While in Odessa, Gordin was a *maskil* journalist and short story writer in Russian, drawing inspiration from Tolstoy and Turgenev. In New York in 1891, Gordin met at an East Side café with the actors Adler, Kessler, and Mogulesco. He came out of the meeting thinking, "If Yiddish actors are men like other actors of the world theatre, why should the Yiddish theatre not be like other theatres?"[16] This meeting in the café led Gordin to try his hand at writing his first Yiddish play, *Sibirya* (Siberia), produced and performed in November 1891 at the Union Theatre. This first effort, which was met initially with misunderstanding, was followed by plays such as *Di yidisher kenig lir* (The Jewish King Lear), *Mirele Efros*, and the aforementioned *Safo*, which revolutionized Yiddish theater in New York and ushered it into artistic maturity.

Gordin and younger playwrights and actors became habitués of Zeitlin's Café at 126 Canal Street, owned by Gordin's good friend Philip Zeitlin. Leon Kobrin remembered how Gordin used to sit in Zeitlin's Café surrounded by habitués who looked up to him with reverence.[17] Zeitlin's Café seemed to have also been Gordin's classroom and workshop for theater. He watched the actors to match them to the roles he was writing, and he gave them acting notes, pushing them to be more realistic in their work. If an actor was angry or joyful in the café, Gordin would say, "Now, why can't you act like that onstage?" In stage rehearsals, Gordin would tell his actors to pretend they were with him in the café.[18] In 1908, around the same time that Gordin died, Zeitlin's Café closed down to make room for the new Williamsburg Bridge.[19] By that time, Schreiber's Café on 33 Canal Street had become the preferred meeting place of Yiddish theater. A staunch supporter of the Yiddish theater, Schreiber had a reputation for generosity. His simple and cheap lunches fed the Yiddish stage.[20]

On Division Street, not far from Canal Street and its cafés and theaters, was Herrick's Café, owned by two Jewish brothers. It advertised itself as "a café, saloon, and restaurant."[21] Herrick's Café was especially significant as a gathering place at the time when New York became home to the world's first mass-circulation Yiddish newspaper market. While many immigrant intellectuals read and wrote in Russian, German, and—after their arrival in America—English, Jewish intelligentsia took shape as a socially and culturally significant community through its use of Yiddish, which enabled these intellectuals to become opinion shapers within the immigrant Jewish population. The first commercially successful Yiddish daily was the conservative *Yidishe tageblat* (Jewish daily news), but much of the Yiddish press at the turn of the century was heavily involved in socialist and anarchist politics. It ranged from the weekly *Di fraye arbeter shtime* (The free voice of labor, established in 1890) to the monthly *Di tsukunft* (The future, established in 1892) and the daily *Forverts* (Forward, established in 1897).[22] During the 1890s and early 1900s, Herrick's Café was "the gathering place of the East Side intelligentsia" and especially Yiddish writers and journalists. There "the various factions, . . . and the fractions of factions, met nightly at the round tables with their red and black checkered cloths, smoked Russian cigarettes, downed oceans of tea, and consumed pounds of Hungarian strudel."[23]

Figure 5.1. Yiddish advertisement for Herrick's Café, *Forverts*, April 22, 1898

The Yiddish press and intelligentsia did not emerge in isolation from its surroundings. Immigrant Jews who composed this sphere had contacts with American journalists, writers, and intellectuals.[24] The critic Van Wyck Brooks was among those American-born intellectuals who discovered on the East Side a world that seemed to him more vital than the sedate environment in which he and many of his contemporaries had been raised and educated. Brooks recalled spending his Sundays in a café on East Houston Street, reading and writing on one of the marble-topped tables: "I was surrounded there by the real mysteries of the ghetto and by Yiddish actors and newspapermen playing chess and drinking tea, like figures from the Russian novels I was greedily absorbing."[25]

Abraham Cahan was at home in the two partially overlapping worlds of Yiddish and English journalism and literature in this period. In 1897, he became a full-time reporter for the *New York Commercial Advertiser*. It was there that Cahan turned into a trailblazing investigative journalist. He made good use of his new expertise when he assumed the editorship of the Yiddish *Forverts* in 1902 after it fell into troubles, and he turned it into the largest foreign-language daily newspaper in the United States. In his autobiography, Cahan related how when he was working for the *Commercial Advertiser*, he used to meet with friends and colleagues from the Yiddish press at Herrick's Café every evening or for lunch. One telling anecdote about Herrick's Café as a "Jewish space" comes from Cahan during the Dreyfus Affair, the accusations against Alfred Dreyfus of treason that divided France. On September 9, 1899, Alfred Dreyfus's second trial concluded with a sentence of ten years' imprisonment, which made Cahan extremely agitated. Lincoln Steffens, Cahan's editor, said to him, "you probably want to be with your Jewish friends." Cahan felt that Steffens was right. "I left," he wrote, "for Herrick's Café at 141 Division Street, where our comrades gathered."[26]

During less charged times, Cahan would take Steffens to visit the café. Steffens wrote in his own autobiography, "Cahan took us . . . one by one, or in groups to the cafés where the debate was on at every table." Steffens knew he was an outsider in the predominantly Jewish café, and he was impressed: "A remarkable phenomenon it was, a community of thousands of people fighting over an art question as savagely as other people had fought over political or religious questions."[27] Steffens did not know that there were also fights over "religious questions" at Herrick's Café, and sometimes they even turned violent. While the owners and most of the habitués of the café were secular Jews who abandoned religious observance in eastern Europe or when they arrived in America, there were still plenty of observant Jews on the East Side.

In September 1898, the *New York Sun* reported that while other Jewish establishments closed their doors for the Eve of the Day of Atonement, Herrick's Café stayed open. "The Herrick brothers," the *Sun* reported, "are noted on the east side among the Hebrews." Their café is the meeting place of "political spell-binders and labor agitators." These people, according to the paper, could not resist the temptation to eat and drink in the café on the day of fasting. This offended "the gray-bearded orthodox patriarchs," who gathered before the doors and told the owners of the café that they ought to close it, but the owners "merely shrugged their shoulders." The tension grew, and someone threw a stone that broke the windows; and a row began that required the intervention of the police.[28] The *New York Times* reported that the Herrick's brothers, who are "Hebrews and Socialists," announced in the Yiddish *Forverts* that the café would be "open alike to Jew and Gentile." After the night's violence, the café opened in the morning of the holy day, and more violence ensued, with several people arrested by the police, who had to use clubs to control "the riotous mob of several thousand Hebrews."[29]

Outsiders and Insiders in the Jewish Ghetto

By the turn of the twentieth century, cafés on the East Side had become visible "Jewish spaces." Outsiders began to gather there, hoping to decipher and describe them. One of the most prominent was Hutchins Hapgood, a journalist who, between 1892 and 1902, published sympathetic sketches of the Jewish East Side in various magazines, with illustrations by the young immigrant Jewish artist Jacob Epstein (fig. 5.2). These sketches were collected in the volume *The Spirit of the Ghetto* (1902). Hapgood wrote about the "little Russian Jewish cafés" at "the heart of the east side," where Jewish men "get together and talk by the hour . . . about politics and society, poetry and ethics, literature and life." According to Hapgood, in these cafés, "excellent coffee and tea are sold, . . . everything is clean and good," and "the conversation is often of

A GHETTO CAFÉ
(Sketched from life by Jacob Epstein)

Figure 5.2. Jacob Epstein, "A Ghetto Café," *Critic*, March 1900

the best," because "there assemble, in the late afternoon and evening, the chosen crowd of intellectuals."[30]

For Hapgood, these establishments inside the teeming and poor Jewish "ghetto" were a unique creation of "Russian, Jewish, and exile." Hapgood was impressed with the "enthusiastic young men" who became intoxicated not with alcohol but with the "excitement of ideas." Trying to understand this phenomenon, which seemed to him unique in New York (and in America), he ascribed it to the "intense idealism of the combined Jew and Russian—the moral earnestness of the Hebrew united with the . . . mental activity of the modern Muscovite."[31] Hapgood's reaction to, and description of, the East Side Jewish cafés that welcomed him as an outsider evinced a complex mixture of his sense of affinity with the intellectuals and poets among the Jewish immigrants and his search for "American bohemia," as well as his curiosity and occasional condescension toward the "ethnic other." He differed from fellow journalists and social reformers such as Jacob Riis, whose book *How the Other Half Lives* exposed "the slums" of the East Side to the upper and middle classes and who purposely focused on the neighborhood's filth and poverty. Hapgood found in the cafés uncommon cultural vitality.

Hapgood was one of the most sympathetic among the legions of social reformers and journalists who visited and worked with the immigrants and tried to understand them and to improve their lives. This growing group of reformers sought to understand these recent immigrants and to help them to Americanize; in turn, they also fought against the xenophobia of America's growing nativist movement. The anti-immigration movement was aligned with the temperance and prohibition movements. An Anti-Saloon League, which was founded in 1893, characterized New York as an immigrant city, a place full of "unwashed and wild eyed foreigners."[32] Thus, it is not surprising that almost all journalists and social reformers, Jews and non-Jews alike, who visited the East Side cafés emphasized the difference between the alcohol-soaked saloon and the "clean" café, even when they struggled whether to characterize it as "foreign" or "local."

A feature story with photographs published in the Sunday illustrated supplement of the *New York Tribune* on September 30, 1900, is one example of this attempt at deciphering café culture (fig. 5.3). The reporter assured the readers, "These people want no saloons. When they drink liquor, they drink at home." However, he claimed, "their tea they take in public" in the East Side cafés "and over it discuss the questions of the day for hours at a time." In these cafés, "there is much political work done, much earnest and clever talk on the problems of government." Thus, they can be seen as the "intellectual centers" of the East Side. Nevertheless, the article was also condescending in tone and aimed to satiate the thirst of its readers for the exotic: "as one steps into them, he has taken a journey into another world . . . fascinating in the extreme."[33]

East Side cafés received much attention as well in the first book dedicated to the social condition of the Jewish immigrants: *The Russian Jew in the United States* (1905). In a chapter on "health and sanitation," the Jewish physician and medical anthropologist Maurice Fishberg noted, "in the cafés of the Ghetto one may always observe people sitting for

Figure 5.3. Photograph of East Side Café, *New York Tribune*, September 30, 1900

hours and drinking tea." He claimed that this habit had been acquired in Russia, where "excessive tea drinking is common." In a pseudoscientific tone, Fishberg proceeded to explain that Russian Jews are "the most nervous of people." According to him, their nervous system is often "fatigued and exhausted from worry, care and anxiety." While other people use alcohol for such purposes, Jews prefer tea, which "overstimulates their nervous system, and a depression is the result, which requires larger doses of tea to overcome it. A vicious circle is thereby established, which by no means contributes to the health and well-being of the Russian Jew."[34] Abraham H. Fromenson claimed that "as the Jewish population increases, the number of gin mills decreases." Instead of the saloon, the Jewish East Side has cafés or "coffee and cakes parlors," which by 1905, according to Fromenson, numbered between 250 and 300. Here, Fromenson announced, "there is an absolute guarantee of sobriety and a free, democratic foregathering of kindred spirits."[35] In 1906, Louis H. Pink wrote that the "power of the saloon in populous centers is not far to seek," and he asked how to combat it. His answer was the café, which in the East Side is "competing with the saloon and driving it from business." Contemplating the origin of the café, Pink explained that it is "partly of foreign origin, partly a natural outgrowth." While in Europe the café "is part and parcel of the life of all peoples," conditions in America "have not proven happy for its growth."[36] All these established American Jews made clear that New York was the only city in America with cafés because of the presence of so many eastern European migrants.

Around the same time, the celebrated writer Henry James came calling. James, a native of New York City who had lived in England since 1876, traveled through the United States from August 1904 to July 1905. He wrote about his visit at what he called the "Yiddish quarter," the "New Jerusalem on earth" and the "ghetto" of the East Side. His first impression was that of the crowds—"a great swarming . . . that had begun to thicken, infinitely, as soon as we had crossed to the East side."[37] James wanted to visit a space that would be more amenable and less crowded but would still show him some essence of the East Side's immigrant culture. He was quite astonished to encounter the cafés of the East Side, which he both discovered on his own and had "picked" for him by insider hosts. James described what he saw in the East Side and its cafés in a highly ambivalent manner that reflected both an astonishment and a "genteel, high-culture anti-Semitism."[38] On the one hand, he experienced and understood the cafés as a product of a "sweet dream." He explained that he went to half a dozen cafés that had "been selected for its playing off some facet of the jewel, and they wondrously testified, by their range and their individual color, to the spread of that lustre."[39] Visiting these cafés made James realize that "truly the Yiddish world was a vast world, with its own deeps and complexities, and what struck one above all was that it sat [in the café] at its cups . . . with a sublimity of good conscience that took away the breath, a protrusion of elbow never aggressive, but absolutely proof against jostling."[40]

James made here the same distinction as reformers between the "pure and simple" cafés and the saloons and beer bars of the Bowery area.[41] Thus, he viewed cafés as "triumphs of art" and as "tiny temples," produced not in the gilded and guarded "private room" but in the Jewish ghetto. The café, in James's estimation was a "barrier against vulgarity" consisting of a few tables, chairs, and coffee cups.[42] James also probed the mixture of languages, dialects, and cultures. He emphasized the auditory impression of the Jewish cafés: "the East Side cafés—and increasingly as their place in the scale was higher—showed to my inner sense, beneath their bedizenment, as torture-rooms of the living idiom; the piteous gasp of which at the portent of lacerations to come could reach me in any drop of the surrounding Accent of the Future."[43] If the cafés are the "torture-rooms of the living idiom," James is thinking not about Yiddish or Hebrew but rather *his* English being "tortured." Even in this judgment, James refused to condemn what he heard in the cafés. This "accent of the future" was surely strange and unsettling, and yet it was not bereft of some unsuspected beauty.[44] Even in his bias, James's "accent of the future" was prescient; café culture was helping to create a distinct American Jewish culture in English, Yiddish, and Hebrew, epitomized by the new phenomenon of Yiddish literature in America.

In the early years of the twentieth century, a number of Jewish writers wrote for Jewish and non-Jewish audiences in Yiddish and English. One of them was Bernard Gershon Richards, who was born in 1877 in Keidan, Lithuania, and migrated to the United States in 1886. Richards was an activist and journalist. In the first years of the twentieth century, he published a series of feuilletons, the European hybrid genre of literature and journalism that was associated with cafés, Jews, and Jewishness but did not take root in the mainstream American press. In one of these sketches, called "My Vacation on the East Side," the fictional Keidansky had moved from New York City to Boston but missed "his regular haunts, such as the cafés, Jewish book-stores and the debating clubs."[45] Keidansky is not interested in the great open spaces of rural America, so he takes a weeklong "vacation" in the big city, not in "sedate Boston" but in New York City, which is a "refuge of all radicals, revolutionaries, and good people." To begin his urban vacation, Keidansky goes directly to the East Side cafés: "They are all there, the comrades, the radicals, the red ones, and dreamers; people who are free because they own nothing. Poets, philosophers, novelists, dramatists, artists, editors, agitators, and other idle and useless beings, they form a great galaxy in the New York Ghetto." They go to the café because there, "among the East Side Bohemians," they "feel freely, act independently, speak as they think and are not at all ashamed of their feelings." For Keidansky, the cafés are the "universities of the East Side." With gentle humor and self-irony, he claims that in the cafés, all things are determined: "Is there a great world problem that puzzles and vexes all mankind?" He assures us that the opinionated people in the cafés "take it up at their earliest discussion and soon the problem is solved and the way of human progress is clear again."[46]

A decade after Keidansky's vacation, Abraham Cahan, the editor of the Yiddish *Forverts*, wrote *The Rise of David Levinsky*, a major realist novel in English. The origin of the novel, narrated in the first person, was four chapters of "Autobiography of an American Jew" that Cahan produced in response to a request by the editors of *McClure's Magazine* to write about the topic of "Jews in business." In the novel, Cahan fashioned, with much irony, a protagonist, Levinsky, who is a poor eastern European Jewish migrant rising from extreme poverty to great wealth in New York. Levinsky becomes a cloak manufacturer "worth more than two million dollars" and represents the social and economic mobility of the Jewish immigrants in America. One of the important scenes in the novel takes place in "Yampolsky's café, . . . a well-known gathering-place of the East Side Bohème."[47] This is where Levinsky meets the aging Hebrew poet Avraham Tevkin for the first time. It is a fascinating scene precisely because David Levinsky is *not* a poet, journalist, actor, or political activist. He is *not* part of café culture but a "rank outsider." When Levinsky comes to the café, he testifies to feeling "wretchedly ill at ease at first." "I loathed myself," he says, "for being here. I felt like one who had strayed into a disreputable den. In addition, I was in dread of being recognized."[48] The habitués of the café seem to Levinsky both politically threatening and socially repulsive. Nevertheless, after spending some time in the café and speaking to some of its habitués—especially with Tevkin, the father of his love interest—Levinsky begins to reevaluate the café. He hears that "an intellectual-looking Gentile" has appeared on the scene, "either a journalist . . . or simply a man of literary tastes who is drawn to the atmosphere of this place."[49] Suddenly, the café rose in Levinsky's estimation, but it also brings out his ambivalence. It reminds Levinsky of his earlier ambitions to become a Talmud scholar in Russia and to attend college in New York, and he becomes less secure in his own position. Suddenly, this café is not "disreputable," but rather it offers an intellectual status that is perhaps even more valuable than his own enormous wealth.

Levinsky became even more surprised and confused about the café when he heard of a "literary liquor dealer" who "would be a celebrated writer, if he were not worth half a million." The number impresses Levinsky, but the fact that this person is a Jewish writer and wealthy man destabilizes his assumptions about the café and about its habitués. Even more surprising to Levinsky is the fact that the poet Tevkin produces a business card that shows him to be also a small real-estate agent. Tevkin tells Levinsky with bitterness, "this is the kind of poetry that goes in America," but he also declares, "Business is business and poetry is poetry. I hate to confound the two. One must make a living."[50] Levinsky himself puts on a performance of a sort in the café. He tells Tevkin, "I am just a prosaic businessman," but at the same time, he tries to show that he is more than this and "veered the conversation back to" poetry. Levinsky tries to impress Tevkin with a sense of "deep and critical appreciation of what I had read in his three volumes."[51]

Through the conflicted, unreliable observations and pronouncements of both Tevkin and Levinsky, the East Side café is revealed as a place of contradictions, where literary and intellectual pursuits are in fact inseparable from business. Writers and poets are evaluated, by insiders and outsiders, as if they are in the marketplace, and it is not easy to tell who is a businessman and who is a poet or writer. Is this situation a result of the corrupting influence of America and especially American capitalism? Is it unique to the Jewish environment of immigrants who aspire to be socially and economically mobile? Is it part of café culture in general? These are questions that Cahan's novel raises, and invites readers to ask, without providing definite answers. Anyone familiar with cafés in Europe knew well that these dilemmas were part and parcel of Jewish urban modernity, which America only made more acute and immediate.

Richards's feuilleton and Cahan's novel are good examples of Jewish literary texts about East Side cafés written in English by Jewish insiders. In the same period, we start to see various literary representations of cafés in Yiddish fiction that matured in New York. In 1909, the playwright and fiction writer Leon Kobrin, who migrated to America in 1892, undertook "the first attempt in Yiddish literature to present a broad picture of American Jewish life in novel form."[52] *Di imigrantn* (The immigrants, 1909) focuses on the Etinger family from Kiev, currently living in an East Side tenement.[53] One chapter follows the young Lyuba Etinger and Dr. Volodya Epstein, who introduces Lyuba to the literary and artistic society of the East Side café. Epstein views the Yiddish writers, the habitués of the café, as losers, but he also enjoys their company. As Lyuba goes to the café with Dr. Epstein and his friend Dr. Raykhman, they identify it as the "*kibitzarnya*":

> You must come in with us, Miss Etinger. . . . Don't be afraid, no one will *kibets* you. . . . Really, you must get to know our *kibitzarnya* if you want to know the Jewish quarter in New York. . . . There world politics are decided. . . . There littérateurs, opera singers and actors give letters of recommendation. . . . Fists often fly there in the name of an idea, proper punches, though with an ideational lining . . . come. Miss Etinger, there you'll meet a lot of people with famous names, and even famous names without people!" . . . When Doctor Raykhman opened the door, he met a commotion of voices and a white steam, like from a steam room.[54]

Epstein's description of the East Side café as a *kibitzarnya* and as a *shvits-bod* (steam room) uses emblematic Jewish spatial images. These were places associated with business and gossip, spaces of masculine sociability that were reminiscent of Jewish life in eastern Europe, but they were also a new American urban creation. The Yiddish words *kibets* (or *kibitz*), to chat, and *kibitzarnya*, a place associated with chatting and sociability, might have come from German and Hebrew, but they were, as Sholem Aleichem recognized when he came to New York in 1906, Yiddish words "born on American soil, in the Jewish press and the Jewish theater."[55] Miss Etinger is impressed with the "lively, heated faces" of the young people, "their shining eyes," and the seriousness of the discussions in the café, which ranges from music to politics and literature, from Nietzsche to Ibsen and Heine.[56] However, she also sees the Yiddish writers as "flesh and blood," people envious of success and bitter about failure. The picture of the Yiddish literary scene is far from being upbeat or ideal. Another character in the novel, Alex Hudkin, claims that Yiddish literature in New York's cafés "suffer[s] both economically and spiritually, without the sympathy and support of an intellectual element. . . . The writers, driven to work under its charge have lost respect both for themselves and for their friends."[57]

In Sholem Aleichem's Yiddish novel *Blonzhende shtern* (*Wandering Stars*, 1909–1911), the narrator claims that New York's Yiddish culture is being created within the confines of the *kibitzarnya*, "a kind of club, or café . . . where a certain class of intelligentsia gathered, involved in literature, theater and politics." These people will "seat themselves at their regular table, surrounded by their devoted followers. . . . They would order something and the kibitzing will begin."[58] The kibitzing at the café, writes Sholem Aleichem, can involve both productive discussion and fellowship, as well as a *gehenam* (hell) of idleness and gossip, a *shvits-bod* (steam room) in which people lash out at each other. For Jewish writers in the early years of the twentieth century, the cafés of the East Side were thirdspaces experienced as located between Europe and America and between productive cultural exchange and lethargic indolence.

Poetic Revolutions, Male Fellowship, and the Lone Woman

When Kobrin and Sholem Aleichem wrote their novels, the migration from eastern Europe to America was at its peak. In the year 1905 alone, with the crisis of the aborted revolution in the Russian Empire, the renewed pogroms, and the aftermath of the Russo-Japanese War, no fewer than 129,000 Jews arrived in the United States. As in the previous years, most of the migrants settled in the East Side; among them were young Yiddish writers including David Ignatov, Isaac Raboy, Mani Leib, Moyshe-Leyb Halpern, Joseph Opatoshu, Zishe Landau, and Reuben Iceland, who arrived in New York during the years 1903–1907. This group of writers, who became known as Di Yunge (The young ones) ushered in a modernist revolution in Yiddish literature. Their aim, declared in a new Yiddish journal, *Di Yunged*, in 1908, was "to create for Yiddish literature in America its own, independent home," without help from any established organs. "Yiddish literature in America," they claimed, "has been boarding out with the press that treats it like an alien, a stepchild," and they described the poetry of their predecessors as "the rhyme department of the Jewish labor movement." Although most of them also worked in factories or as artisans, they eschewed the "sweatshop poetry" of their predecessors and redefined Yiddish literature as "a probing into the self."[59]

The writers of Di Yunge, like their predecessors, also gravitated to the East Side cafés. Around this time, the aforementioned Café Herrick on Division Street closed down, and a new café with the name Sholem's opened in the same location. Yiddish writers and the journalists and editors who worked at the *Forverts* and its new competitors *Die wahrheit* (The truth) and *Der tog* (The day) frequented Sholem's café, which was open twenty-four hours a day, perhaps as an expression of Jewish American capitalism, and advertised itself as "the headquarters of all intelligent people of the East Side."[60]

Melech Epstein wrote that he was brought to Sholem's Café upon his arrival in New York, and he found there under one roof more well-known novelists, poets, journalists, and labor leaders than one could find in many similar cafés in eastern Europe combined.[61] Sholem's Café was also the place where the clash between the older and the younger Yiddish writers first unfolded. While members of Di Yunge called for aestheticism and freedom from the Jewish press and politics, others felt that these writers disregarded their true audiences and "imported" into Yiddish inadequate and outdated models of European literature. As one critic wrote, "When all literary traditions were crumbling, when art for art's sake had expired in Europe and even its heirs, expressionism

Figure 5.4. Advertisements of Sholem's Café in *Der groyser kibitzer*, February 1909

and Dadaism, had vanished, here in America we imported it right to Sholem's Café and enthroned it before a cup of coffee and cream."[62]

Morris Rosenfeld—the older "sweatshop" Yiddish poet and the main target for Di Yunge's critique—struck back by characterizing the young poets as "decadents." He did it by publishing a feuilleton in the *Forverts* with the title "Berl der piskuter vert a decadent" (Berl the foul-mouthed becomes a decadent).[63] Berl used to be a comic rhymer, but under the influence of the "young writers," a clear reference to Di Yunge, he became a "decadent" who wrote "moodish" impressionistic poetry. Rosenfeld wrote that he did not want to step into the café where Berl and his "decadent comrades" gather. In the café, Berl composes a poem that reads, "Down with the Old Poets / Who can stand them today? . . . they are too sober for our taste. / No Smoke and no hint, / And moreover, the audience understands them."[64] Thus, Rosenfeld's feuilleton mocked Di Yunge members for what he perceived as their pretentious rebellion, which manifested itself in their poetry, manifestos, and arguments in the café.

A place like Sholem's Café, where various groups of Yiddish writers clashed, appears in David Ignatov's Yiddish novel *In keslgrub* (In the whirlpool).[65] Its main protagonist is Borukh, a young Yiddish writer and intellectual who tries to combine an elitist aestheticism with a populist plan to settle immigrant Jews in America's rural areas. New York City is presented in the novel as an "iron giant" that dehumanizes its Jewish workers. Borukh himself works in a factory, but when a fire erupts, he becomes "free" to spend more time among the Jewish writers and intellectuals in "Kroyzkop's Café."[66] In the café, Borukh meets Raykher, who attacks him as a representative of the new movement, which consists of "Madmen! Decadents!": people with whom "one can't even speak . . . one word! One should lock you up in a madhouse!"[67] Ignatov's novel presents a darker description of an East Side café, a site of confrontation between different approaches to Yiddish literature. The description of the café in the novel reflects the place of the young Yiddish author in New York. Borukh might have some poetic accomplishments, but he fails to realize his dreams. At the end of the novel, Borukh moves away from the city to a secluded house across the river. On a cold winter day, he pours kerosene on his house and sets it on fire in what seems like an act of suicide.

We find another dark picture of café life in a short story by the Yiddish writer Isaac Raboy. Raboy, who was associated with Di Yunge and later became well known for writing novels about farming and the American prairie, was born in 1882 in Podolia, migrated to New York in 1904, and worked at a hat factory. From Raboy's autobiography, we know that he used to go to cafés at night after work and on weekends. His story "In a kafe-hoyz" (In a coffeehouse) is an impressionistic account that takes place in the city on "one autumn night with its gray-blackish fog."[68] The story is told from the point of view of a young woman, a poor server in a smoky coffeehouse. The café is full of men who are "heavy and bent" and tired from difficult work. It seems to the server that these men had lost their last spark of life. They sit in the café like motionless corpses who do not know that their life is ending. Out of this ghastly scene emerge two Jewish musicians who chat and play a faint tune. Only later in the story do the woman—and the readers—realize that these musicians are trying to collect a few nickels in the café in exchange for their playing. The café in Raboy's story is a dark, morbid place, where all the characters are exhausted from their crushing work. It is also a space of disorientation, because it is hard to tell whether the café is located on the East Side of New York or in a small European town that has lost its vitality.

Such depictions of cafés reflect the modernist poetics of Di Yunge; indeed, we saw similarly bleak portrayals of human existence in the café in literature written around the same time in Vienna, Warsaw, and Berlin. But this literature also expresses deep doubts about the place of writers and artists in New York and its Jewish society. Interestingly, part of their solution was to create a kind of self-segregation. How did that happen on New York's crowded streets? By replacing one café with another. Although initially members of Di Yunge went to Sholem's Café, they later abandoned it and chose instead a small and simple café at East Broadway named after its two owners: Goodman and Levine's.

Reuven Iceland writes in his lively memoirs that the seemingly mundane act of avoiding one café and choosing another was a crucial element in the poetic revolution of Di Yunge.[69] Iceland remembered that "the young writers then in New York" used to stream into Goodman and Levine's Café not because of the food, which was very bad, but because "there you could read or listen to a poem. There, you could always hear and learn something about poetry and stories, because discussions about literature never ceased. There, you could meet the few young writers whom talent or luck had lifted . . . and who were already famous, while others were unknown. And there, one could also expect to hear—with beating heart—how you were currently rated as a writer or a poet."[70] Although Goodman and Levine's Café became the center of Di Yunge in the years before World War I, it was almost unknown outside their circle, while Herrick's and later Sholem's were famous even outside New York City. Why did the young writers and poets choose not to go to Sholem's? Iceland gives two reasons: one is that the café was too expensive for the writers who were either poor workers at the factory or unemployed and could not spare even a quarter. The other reason was that Di Yunge simply considered it beneath them to spend time in the same café with the older writers. In order "not to be under one roof with the older writers," Iceland remembered, "we went to a separate café."[71]

By the time these poetic revolutions took place in the cafés, a number of already established Yiddish writers and poets, both young and old, had migrated to New York. In 1911, the poet and writer Avrom Reyzen and the short story writer Lamed Shapiro both moved from Warsaw and settled in New York. They were followed by a young poet, H. Leyvik (the pen name of Leyvik Halperin), and the Russian and Yiddish writer, playwright, and journalist Osip Dymow in 1913. In 1914, at the beginning of World War I, the established writer Sholem Asch journeyed from Warsaw to New York. These writers were joined by Sholem Aleichem, who came to New York for the second time and lived in the city during the last two years of his life. While World War I devastated Europe, the Jewish population of New York City continued to grow, and by the end of the war, it reached one and a half million. New York became the city with the largest number of Jews in the world. It also rivaled European cities such as Warsaw as the center of Yiddish literature, theater, and the press.[72]

In 1916, a new migrant from Warsaw, Menakhem Boreisho, joined Moyshe-Leyb Halpern in editing a collection of poetry and fiction by writers associated with Di Yunge with the title *Ist Brodvey* (East Broadway). This important collection opened with an extended feuilleton by Menakhem. The entire feuilleton takes place "at the tables of the literary café," where "a whole colorful novel is played out." The speaker declares, "I will lead the novelist to several tables at the café and let him have a look at the people who sit by their cups of coffee." The characters of this imaginary novel are "writers, poets, and various intrigues, movements and slogans; these are simply the occurrences of a developing life, a growing art." All of these elements might seem very simple, even banal, as the narrator recognizes, "but the whole is at once the most interesting thing that can pass before your eyes."[73]

The emphasis on the "literary café" on East Broadway as both a simple fact and "the most interesting thing" shows that by 1916, the writers of Di Yunge and the others who migrated to New York felt self-confident about the city being a center of Yiddish literature and culture. "Here Europe is dethroned. . . . The colony has declared itself independent—and sooner or later it will learn to follow the path of a metropolis." At the same time, the author of the feuilleton recognized that the social and economic base of Yiddish writers was quite precarious. In spite of the declaration of independence from Europe and high aesthetic achievements, these Yiddish writers "longed for a patron," someone with means who "will free the writer from work and allow him to pass idly through the streets." The poet released from financial concerns will gradually begin to find the sought for "I" and will begin to find profound connections with "the ordinary masses" and will be able to produce a literary work that will be at once "social, individual, traditional, and free."[74]

This was a utopian vision. In the meantime, Yiddish writers had to contend with working for the Yiddish press and to find moments of relative freedom in the small Goodman and Levine's or a new café with the name "Central" that the Yiddish writer Lamed Shapiro opened with his wife. The name of the café was likely inspired by the famous Café Central in Vienna, but Shapiro's place on East Broadway was a small, vegetarian café. Shapiro was probably the first Jewish writer who opened a café, and indeed it turned into a small center, at least for a short time. According to Zishe Weinper and Reuven Iceland, Shapiro's café became "a neutral ground, a place where both Di Yunge and older writers could meet and feel at home." Late at night, when other customers would leave, Shapiro announced to his friends, "now I am not a café owner anymore."[75] However, perhaps unsurprisingly, the café failed and closed soon after it opened, mostly because Shapiro would only reluctantly charge his customers, since many of them were his good friends.[76]

The new place that seemed to have replaced both Goodman and Levin's and Shapiro's Café Central in the years following World War I was the small Café Europa, on East Broadway at the corner of Division Street. Konrad Bercovici, who came from Romania to New York, wrote that from the outside, Café Europa looked no different from any other café in the neighborhood, and it required "no particular audacity to go in and inspect it from the inside." Although "strangers are welcome" and come from time to time, Bercovici wrote as a habitué. "Nowhere else am I as comfortable. . . . Each patron of the place has his favorite table, to which he comes to sit in a fixed time."[77] The journalist Berl Botwinik wrote in the *Forverts* about Café Europa with light irony: "now there is a new *Kibitzarnya*. . . . There had to be a rendezvous for Jewish writers, because without it the world could not exist. . . . The little tables are exactly the same as in the old place. . . . As long as the café remains small and the owner is one of them, the breath of Jewish literature will be in the air."[78]

Figure 5.5. Joseph Foshko (1891–1968), *Kibitzing in a Literary Café*, with images of Sholem Asch, Abraham Reyzen, Joseph Opatoshu, Baruch Rivkin, Moyshe-Leyb Halpern, and Moshe Katz, 1910s (From the archive of the YIVO Institute for Jewish Research, New York)

Like Goodman and Levine's and other similar institutions on the East Side, Café Europa was extremely small, very different from large, multi-level European institutions such as Romanisches Café, Café Central, or Café Ziemiańska. Nevertheless, it loomed large in the imagination of Chaver Paver, the pen name of Gershon Einbinder, who arrived in New York in 1923 as a young, aspiring Yiddish writer and journalist. Paver recalled, "the land of Yiddish writers in America was an area the size of the interior of Café Europa, about twenty feet wide and forty feet long. If you pushed open the door and stepped outside, you found yourself on the other side of the border, in an alien country."[79] This remarkable total identification made between "the land of Yiddish writers in America" and the tiny space of one specific café, as well as the assertion that outside it, there is an "alien country," demonstrates that Café Europe was experienced as a thirdspace between the inside and the outside, with an invisible but experiential border between them. The spatial experience was culturally bound in a specific Jewish way. Here is what happened, according to Paver, when the older and well-known Yiddish poet Avrom Reyzen stepped outside the café:

> On the steps, [Reyzen] seemed still gay and exhilarated, like a guest who went to a wedding for the first time, ate cakes, drank liqueur, and danced with the bride. But the further he went, the more disheartened he became. He tried smiling to passersby; perhaps among them were a few who would recognize him, . . . but none of the bystanders knew him. . . . Inside, his *table became a Yeshiva*. There, a poem or a story would be interpreted, discussed, and analyzed in detail. . . . Yes, Reyzen's table was like a Yeshiva, a *besmedresh*, but other tables also served the same purpose. There were many "rabbis" in Café Europa, and every rabbi had his own following.[80]

In this café as a secular house of study, the older and more established writers are like the rabbis of yesteryear; their café table is like the rebbe's *tish*, in which the rabbi sits at the head of the table and the Hasidim who follow him gather around to listen to his words. Instead of Talmud or the weekly portion of the Torah, this secularized rabbi and his followers interpret, discuss, and analyze a poem or a story. The migrant Jewish writers rarely had gone to college or had any formal literary training. "In

Figure 5.6. Raphael Soyer, *In a Jewish Café* (1925),
watercolor and pencil on paper, 21¾ × 19⅜ in.
(Courtesy of the Smithsonian Institution, Washington, DC, Gift of Joseph H. Hirshhorn, 1966)

the café, Gershon learned about the different schools, tendencies, trends,
and moods in literature and other arts."[81] The debates in these cafés "had
the flavor of the yeshivas and houses of study where some of the participants had spent their youth," but the "competitive male camaraderie of
traditional Jewish society stimulated a new kind of culture, at once freed
of religious restraints and yet reminiscent of them."[82]

If the reader of Paver's memoir had any doubts, he makes the gendered nature of the café quite clear: the space Paver described was a
space of men and for men. More than this, the café, like the yeshiva
and house of study, was, or was experienced by Paver and many others
as, a "homosocial space," which is marked by what Eve Kosofsky Sedgwick and Naomi Seidman have called "homosocial desire."[83] In Paver's
text, when Reyzen leaves the café, he is exhilarated like "a guest who
went to a wedding for the first time . . . and danced with the bride."[84]
But who is the bride in this wedding image? If there are no women
habitués in the "literary café," then the bride must be the text, which

is the "glue" that enables the homosocial desire and space of (and for) the men. Just as in traditional Jewish culture, in which the image of the Torah is feminized, in the early twentieth century, what bound these men together was their desire for secular literature and the space of the *kafe-hoyz*.[85]

What Paver expressed in his memoir can be discerned in Iceland's work as well, particularly in an anecdote he related about one Saturday, when he worked only half a day, came home, ate lunch, and went to a barber for a shave. In the barber's chair, he suddenly felt that he could "smell the café" and could hardly wait for the barber to finish his job. It occurred to him that it would be better to go home first and tell his young wife and baby daughter where he was going; but his "feet were already pointing to the direction of Goodman and Levine's on East Broadway," and he was thinking with deep longing about the male colleagues he would find in the café. It turned out that the café was full of members of Di Yunge: "From a sea of faces and clouds of smoke emerged the figure of Mani Leib . . . squinting at the freckled yet vibrant and insolent face of Moyshe Leyb Halpern." There was an almost erotic excitement in the air. Iceland's desire to be in the presence of Leib, Halpern, and the other members of Di Yunge was so strong that he forgot his responsibilities as a married man. These young men were fully immersed in a discussion that went on until early in the morning, fueled by coffee, tea, pancakes, blintzes, cookies, rolls, and cigarettes. When Iceland came back home at dawn, the grocer at the local shop greeted him with the news that his wife was looking for him at the police station.[86]

What would happen, then, when a woman walked through the café door? After all, the East Side cafés were open to everybody, and we have some textual and visual records of women visiting them. In the aforementioned article by Fromenson about East Side cafés, he claimed that one of the defining features of the "politically radical cafés" was women's presence: "where the cigarette smoke is thickest and denunciation of the present forms of government loudest, there you find women!" But here we can also see the fear of men regarding these women. According to Fromenson, "one wishes he could write these women down gently," presumably as frivolous and morally suspicious. He writes that it is hard to "criticize these women" because the house, which is presumably the natural place for women, "is such a dingy, dreary place; the walls so close they seem to crush the unfortunate whose 'home' is within its oppressive limits." On the other hand, the café "is light and cheerful; the noise is only the swelling chorus of spirits." Trying to enter the mind of these "Jewish radical women," the author claims to have known that "they are not the objects of fine courtesies and considerateness, they do not miss them; perhaps they never knew them. The stern realities of life, the terrible disappointment of thwarted ambition, the bruising friction of tradition and emancipation, the struggle for existence, all these have conspired to rob them of the finer attributes of womanhood."[87] Reading this analysis of the female patrons' "womanhood"—or lack thereof—one cannot help but conclude that the "new (Jewish) woman" who frequented the East Side's cafés was seen as profoundly unsettling. The fact that these "new women" were poor Jewish migrants enabled their male observers to sympathize with them at the same time that they put them down and to "explain" their deviancy in social and psychological terms. Yet there is little doubt that women such as these, and their presence in the café, caused much anxiety.[88]

In Hapgood's *The Spirit of the Ghetto*, he describes a scene that begins, characteristically, with four men who sit at a small East Side café "where the Socialists and Anarchists . . . were wont to meet late at night and stay until the small hours." Almost at midnight, a young man enters, accompanied by a young woman known as Sabina, who is "dark and slender, with very large, emotional eyes and a mobile mouth, [and] had just come from her lecture to a crowd of workingmen, to whom she had spoken eloquently of their right to lead a life with greater light and beauty in it. The emotions expressed by her eloquence, and stirred by it, still lay in her deep eyes as she entered the café."[89]

The mysterious Sabina worked in "sweatshops in the daytime" and in the evening "had devoted herself to the cause." Her companion, Levitzky, was a poet, with whom Sabina had fallen in love, though it was not until the evening of the scene in the café that she fully understood that. However, upon entering the café, Levitzky remarks that a "Russian man loves an inaccessible mistress . . . while the despised American wants a legal wife whom he can enjoy and be sure of." In the café, in the presence of Levitzky and four other men, these words cause Sabina to be ashamed of herself, filled with an "irrational emotion" of grief for what she looked on as a betrayed ideal.[90]

A YOUNG MAN AND A YOUNG WOMAN JUST ENTERED THE CAFÉ

Figure 5.7. Jacob Epstein, illustration in *The Spirit of the Ghetto*, 1902

After leaving the café, Sabina walks back home humiliated. She felt like someone who "betrays a governmental trust because of the repeated frenzy of an emotion" and felt like a "sinful creature." The tragic end comes fast, when in the next morning, Sabina is found dead, most likely by committing suicide. A few days later, the discussions between Levitzky and the other men continue, and Hapgood laconically comments that "he had forgotten Sabina."[91] Reading Hapgood's anecdote, it is quite clear that "radical" women, or women with intellectual and political ambitions like Sabina, who ventured into the world of the café and Jewish politics could not ultimately be part of it. In this extreme case, entering the café and its world seems to be what killed Sabina.

Women were rare in the realms of Yiddish literature and journalism and even rarer in the world of its cafés. One of the exceptions was Rosa Lebensboym, best known by the pen name Anna Margolin. In 1913, she settled permanently in New York and joined the staff of the newly established daily *Der tog*, where she wrote a weekly column titled *In der froyen velt* (In the women's world). In 1920, she began to publish exquisite and daring modernist Yiddish poems that appeared under the name Anna Margolin, an unfamiliar name that aroused much curiosity.

In a letter on January 8, 1921, Reuven Iceland, who was Margolin's lover, wrote to her, "I can't help telling you that last night Anna Margolin was the main topic of conversation in the new *kibitzerniya* [café]. A thousand hypotheses were offered about who might be hiding behind the name, and the general opinion is that it must certainly be a man." In another letter, Iceland expanded further:

> Why people want Anna Margolin to be a man is beyond me. The general opinion, however, is that these poems are written by an experienced hand. *And a woman can't write like that.* That these poems are produced by an experienced hand is also the opinion of Mani Leyb. As we were talking in the café Saturday night, he told me how much he liked Anna Margolin's poem . . . and of course, no woman could have written such a poem. Now do you understand?[92]

Margolin's poems elicited heated debates in the cafés, and people could not believe they were written by a woman. Although women were sometimes present in these cafés as companions, servers, or owners, they were almost never habitués who participated in the discussions about poetry and art.[93] In Margolin's case, male Yiddish writers could not believe that a woman could write such mature and artistically accomplished poems.

One of the poems that were a topic of heated discussion in the café was a dense, three-part poem, "In kafe" (In the café), that Anna Margolin published in 1922.[94] Perhaps not surprisingly, the poem begins with a woman sitting by herself, removed from the other tables of poets, writers, and journalists, whose words are reduced to fragments of voices that the speaker can barely hear:

1.
Now alone in the café,
when voices extinguish and fade
when lamps kindle pearly
and float out of the café

like shining swans
over the street—
—Waiter, black coffee, demitasse.

Now alone in the café,
when moments rustle like silk
I raise to the street, to the distance
my black and perfumed wine.
And like a song is the thought
that falls from me in the dark
a white glow.

אין קאפע

‎.1

איצט אליין אין קאַפע,
ווען עס לעשן זיך שטימען און וויאַנען,
ווען פּערלדיק צינדן זיך לאָמפּן
און שווימען ארויס פֿון קאַפע
ווי לויכטנדע שוואַנען
איבער דער גאַס —

— קעלנער, שוואַרצע קאַווע — דעמיטאַס.

איצט אליין אין קאַפע,
ווען עס שאַרכן די רגעם ווי זייד,
הויב איך אויף צו דער גאַס, צו דער ווײַט
מיין שוואַרצן און דופטיקן ווײַן.
און ווי אַ געזאַנג איז דער געדאַנק,
אַז ס'פּאַלט פֿון מיר אין טונקלקייט
אַ ווײַסער שײַן.

Figure 5.8. Part 1 of "In kafe" in Yiddish

In part 2 of the poem, the solitude of the speaker who observes the minute voices and the visual details gives way to an emotional alienation in the café's smoky atmosphere:

2.

And all the faces in smoke like masks.
A joke, a shrug, a bleak glance,
and false words are kindled, pale.
Have I hurt you, my lover?

We all wear here contemptible cold masks.
With clever irony we disguise the fever
and a thousand smiles, and shouts, and grimaces.
Have I hurt you, my lover?

.2

און אַלע פּנימער אין רויך װי מאַסקן.
אַ װיץ, אַן אַקסל-צוק, אַ בליק אַ טריבער,
און פֿאַלשע װערטער צינדן זיך, פֿאַרבלאַסן.
האָב איך דיר װי געטאָן, מײַן ליבער?

מיר טראָגן אַלע דאָ פֿאַראַכטלאַד-קאַלטע מאַסקן.
מיט קלוגער איראָניע פֿאַרשטעלן מיר דעם פֿיבער
און טויזנט שמייכלען, און געשרײען, און גרימאַסן.
האָב איך דיר װי געטאָן מײַן ליבער?

Figure 5.9. Part 2 of "In kafe" in Yiddish

The extinguished voices and kindled lamps merge here in the "false words," which turn out to be not just the words of the café habitués but perhaps also the words of the speaker. She includes herself ("we all") in the company of those who wear "contemptible cold masks" and employ "clever irony," in order to "disguise the fever" that burns inside. The smiles, the shouts, and the grimaces are incomprehensible, just as with the mask-like faces in the smoke. This is perhaps the reason why there is no real communication in the café, including the speaker's question, "Have I hurt you, my lover?" This leads to the third part of the poem, when the speaker's silence is highlighted:

3.
With the frosty glow of lamps
And glances, and voices
In front of you floats my silence—
a covert and luminous sign.
Curls like a summer wind around you.
Speaks trembling to you
About you and me.
Ah, quiet, quiet words
about you and me.
And is silent.
And rocks you with longing hands.
And takes you with white and twitching hands.

.3

מיטן פראָסטיקן שײַן פֿון די לאָמפּן
און בליקן, און שטימען
שווימט דיר אָקעגן מײַן שווײַגן —
אַ געהיימער און ליכטיקער סימן.
קרײַזט ווי אַ זומערווינט אַרום דיר.
רעדט ציטערדיק צו דיר
וועגן דיר און מיר.
אַ, שטילע, שטילע ווערטער
וועגן דיר און מיר.
און שווײַגט.
און וויגט דיך מיט בענקענדע הענט.
און נעמט דיך מיט ווייסע און צוקענדע הענט.

Figure 5.10. Part 3 of "In kafe" in Yiddish

Toward the end of the poem, the speaker seems to retreat, and instead her silence takes over and finds its own language. Her silence in the café paradoxically assumes an agency by becoming a visible and audible active presence. It confronts the lover, embracing and curling around him, and then "speaks" to him with quiet words about "you and me." The speaker seems to find strength only in the silence's "covert" but "luminous" language, and through it, she is able to communicate her physical erotic desire. Margolin's poem thus gives us a representation of the familiar café in the present moment ("now") but one in which the poet-speaker is alone, observing and creating the images that make up her café experience. Her desire, communicated in the silence and in the intricate images of the poem, is not the familiar homosocial desire of male bonding and camaraderie. Instead, Margolin's poem is presented as an experience of an individual woman-speaker who insists on expressing her eroticism and lyrical presence in the Jewish literary world of the New York cafés.

This cycle of poems was part of Margolin's only published book, a crowning achievement that was not—perhaps could not be— perpetuated, a fact that further dramatized the dynamic of language and silence in her poetry and her presence and absence in the masculine environment of New York Jewish café culture. At the same time, the very fact that Margolin has written one of the most powerful and poetically intricate texts about the New York café in Jewish literature disrupts the assumption that the café was, or must have been, a masculine space. Margolin's thematic focus on being alone or together, on appearance, as well as the modernist interrogation of the self and desire, has been central to writings about the café, but in her case, it was done from a singular feminine perspective.

Jewish Multilingualism Moving West (Again)

In 1919, Joseph Opatoshu published the Yiddish novel *Hibru* (Hebrew), which highlights the low social prestige and poverty of Jewish educators, something that he probably experienced when he worked as a teacher in a Hebrew school after his arrival in New York.[95] One of the novel's chapters portrays a bohemian café-restaurant in Greenwich Village called Grine lape (Green paw), which Grin, Fridkin, and a number of their friends from the East Side visit. The café looks to the visitors like "a peasant's hut," with strange-looking guests who are "rarely seen" in other parts of New York: "Sloppily dressed men whose faces look troubled even when they laugh; women, dressed in half-masculine clothes, with cropped haircuts, cigarettes in their mouths, at the first glance made an impression of cross-dressed boys. It seemed as if all these people sleep during the day, and at night, when the law falls asleep together with its law-abiding children, they crawl out of their bedrooms, glide stealthily around the walls of the tenement houses and hurry to 'the village.'"[96] Despite the strange appearance of the habitués, many turn out to be Jewish. In one corner sits the editor of a weekly magazine with the strange name: the *Pagan*. Among the regulars whom Grin introduces to his female friend Bessy are Shloyme Mander, "the greatest Yiddish novelist"; Moyshe Khoyzek, "the greatest humorist"; and Mr. Vays, "the greatest Yiddish critic." When the perplexed Bessy asks Grin, "Is this a Jewish place?" Grin responds, "How else?"[97]

The café and the habitués described in this chapter of Opatoshu's novel seem out of place, detached from the reality of Jewish New York. In fact, Opatoshu's novel portrays a key shift in the city. Around 1910, a company of writers, theater people, political radicals, and artists began to settle in Greenwich Village; they declared their neighborhood a new bohemia, a center of "experimental life." They advocated a revolution in personal morality, as well as in art and politics. They insisted that radicalism, feminism, progressive education, and modern art all shared the same goal: liberating people's capacity for self-expression. These "new bohemians," many of them from bourgeois families and with Ivy League educations, were drawn to the Village, which was cheap, exciting, and full of promise at the time. Greenwich Village, centered in Washington Square, was only a few blocks west of the East Side. "In the bohemian geography of the imagination," the historian Christine Stansell writes, "Greenwich Village was proximate and permeable to the Jewish Lower East Side."[98] The borders between the neighborhoods, and the intellectuals and "bohemians" who inhabited them, were quite porous. Not surprisingly, the neighborhood had its own cafés, tearooms, and saloons where habitués met to eat cheap food and discuss modernism and social problems.[99]

In contrast to much of New York society, the bohemians were open to Jews and found inspiration in Jewish ideas and movements. Randolph Bourne, a central intellectual in this new scene, argued that Jewish ideals promised to bring forth a new kind of cosmopolitan American identity, a "trans-national America."[100] Moreover, a number of Jewish writers and artists were prominent in Greenwich Village during this time; Waldo Frank, Joseph Kling, Walter Lippmann, and James Oppenheim, American-born and affluent, all moved to the neighborhood. Others, such as Ludwig Lewisohn and Konrad Bercovici, came from migrant families. Jews were particularly prominent as writers and as founders and editors of "little magazines," which became central to American modernism.[101] Frank and Oppenheim helped to establish the magazine the *Seven Arts*. Kling was founder and editor of the *Pagan*. Moreover, Kling became close to Yiddish writers such as Moyshe Nadir and published in his magazine English translations of Yiddish texts by Leib, Opatoshu, Reyzen, Asch, and Nadir, who were consistently represented in the *Pagan* between 1916 and 1922, as was Y. L. Peretz, whose work was translated by Kling himself.[102] When Opatoshu wrote in his novel about the fictional Grine lape and how Yiddish writers and humorists met there with the editor of a strange magazine called the *Pagan*, it is because he knew this milieu firsthand.

One of the cafés in Greenwich Village catering to the bohemians was Strunsky's Café, known as "Three Steps Down." It was owned and operated by Mascha and Albert ("Papa") Strunsky, Jewish migrants from Russia, and was located in the basement of 19 West Eighth Street. As in Europe, and on the Lower East Side, Strunsky's Café advertised in the literary magazines of the village as "one of the most popular gathering places for villagers and those who appreciate well-cooked food and a congenial atmosphere" (fig. 5.11). The walls of the café were adorned with paintings by the young Jewish artist A. Walkowitz, one of its habitués. "Three Steps Down" was actually the second café owned by the Jewish Strunsky family. The other café was located on 201 Second Avenue.

Between these cafés, and the people who frequented them, a new, multilingual Jewish American bohemia was created, with much interaction between immigrants (both from Europe and from other places in America) and American-born Jews and non-Jews. In 1918, the Jewish

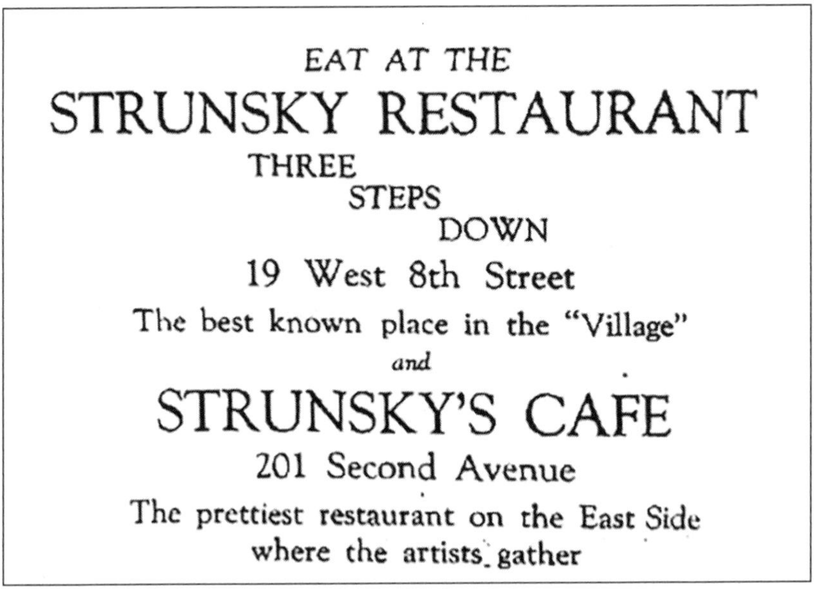

EAT AT THE
STRUNSKY RESTAURANT
THREE
STEPS
DOWN
19 West 8th Street
The best known place in the "Village"
and
STRUNSKY'S CAFE
201 Second Avenue
The prettiest restaurant on the East Side
where the artists gather

Figure 5.11. Advertisement for Strunsky's Café, *Society of Independent Artists*, 1920

journalist Matthias Newman published in the weekly magazine the *American Jewish Chronicle* a feature story called "Jewish Bohemia." Newman makes clear that the new phenomenon of American Jewish bohemia is poorly understood, but both those "who scoff at Jewish Bohemia" and those who accept it "at its own serious valuation" agree that it is a "charming retreat from the haste, hubbub and confusion of New York's East Side." Newman presents the question that his readers probably asked: "Just where is Jewish Bohemia?" He acknowledges that Bohemia is more of an "artistic or spiritual condition" than a fixed location, but he indicates that it has a few living centers in lower Manhattan. Such centers, according to Newman, are cafés on Division Street and on Second Avenue, cafés "such as you find in the Jewish quarter of Warsaw," while other cafés possess a "distinctively American-Jewish atmosphere."[103] One is left to ponder what the differences are between European cafés and those that are distinctively American or American Jewish and how Newman understands Greenwich Village's cafés in this geography of bohemianism in New York. However, it is clear that the multilingualism of these spaces, and the exchange between Europe and

America and between English and Yiddish, was crucial in the construction of bohemia in New York.

The engagement between Yiddish and English in the new bohemian environment had a smaller, but equally important, companion: the relationship between Hebrew and Yiddish. One of the central characters in *Hibru* is Grin, a Yiddish poet who believes that Hebrew schools should be reformed by introducing Yiddish as a link between Americanized children and their eastern European parents. Another chapter in Opatoshu's novel takes place just a few blocks away from Greenwich Village, in the fictional Wexler's Café on Canal Street, where Jewish intellectuals and journalists argue about the "question of languages": Hebrew or Yiddish? The discussion is loud and heated, and ideology is mixed with personal ambition and old feuds. Just as the argument heats up, Mr. Rapsky enters Wexler's Café and tries to sell the latest issue of *Ha-shiloah*, the prestigious Hebrew literary journal published in Odessa. *Ha-shiloah* was edited by Ahad-Ha'am and Bialik, and it both advanced the ideology of Hebraism and exemplified the achievements of modern Hebrew literature. It was seen as a model of Hebraists in America. Grin, the Yiddish poet, likes Mr. Rapsky, but he fails to understand why he dedicates his life to Hebrew or what seems to him to be the strange phenomenon of Hebrew literature in America.[104]

The scene in Wexler's Café is indicative of a real debate and a real Hebraist movement in America. As was clear in Cahan's novel and in Hapgood's sketches, side by side with Yiddish and English writers, there was a group of American Jews who were dedicated to modern Hebrew literature and culture. It was a small group, acutely aware of its own smallness. Side by side with the older writers M. M. Dolitzky and N. H. Imber, a young generation of immigrant Jews was attracted to Hebrew. It included such people as the journalist and essayist Daniel Persky and the poet and prose writer Shimon Halkin, both of whom arrived in New York between 1906 and 1914. Both of them worked as educators and published in the Hebrew newspaper *Ha-do'ar* (The post).[105] In 1926, Halkin published, under a pseudonym in *Ha-do'ar*, a feuilleton with the title "Al beit ha-kafe" (About the café):

> The café is the temple of shadows that alleviates the soul of the artist. In the thick cloud of incense that veils the lights of the sickly lamps, . . . in

the midst of the intoxicating steam that arises both from the cup and the
brain, the awe and trepidation of artistic creation is alleviated. . . . Here
the poet can find freedom from the yoke of prophecy, from the terrible
decree, into which, with pain and joy, he has been consecrated in distant
worlds of spirit.[106]

We have already seen the image of the café as a house of study, but here
we find the image of a *temple*, fused with Hebraic imagery of the poet as
a "creator" and prophet. In Halkin's poetic vision, the café is a modern
Jewish temple, and the smoke of the cigarettes and steam of the coffee or
tea is like a holy, intoxicating "thick cloud of incense," in which the poet-
prophet can find freedom. This is a romantic image of the poet in the
café, now clad in biblical garb. However, Halkin also paid attention to
the social interaction between the group and the individual in the café:
"The shadows quiver, stirring in the dark corners of every noisy, dark-
faced group; they erupt with every entry of a new guest, who always
halts for a minute, hesitant and wondering, as if he stands on the threshold of a new world, exhilarating and scary."[107]

Halkin might have drawn on his own experience as a young Hebrew
poet entering the New York café for the first time and feeling like the
hesitant new guest. In any case, he continued the feuilleton not as a guest
but as a habitué in the café who extols its virtues at night as offering the
writer (or "prophet") a "new sense of vision, the sight of the night."[108]

In the next issue of *Ha-do'ar*, a witty responding feuilleton was published, "Beit kafe 'ivri" (A Hebrew café), by Daniel Persky, known as "the
slave of Hebrew." From his perspective, Persky claims that he is familiar
with such cafés in "the artists' neighborhood" of Greenwich Village, but
he finds it very unlikely that the conversations over there are about Hasidic rabbis. Persky observes, "There is no Hebrew café in New York City
of the kind that the Yiddish writers have. They spend their days in Café
Europa and their nights in Café Royal." Given his ironic tone regarding
Halkin's piece, the readers might have expected that Persky would claim
that there is no need for such a café. However, he asserts that this lack
is a problem: "Without such a café, a *kibitzarnya*, there is no prospect
and no chance for the rise of a literary Hebrew movement in America." Persky emphasizes that there is very little that is common between
Halkin's poetic description of the literary café and the prosaic Yiddish

kibitzarnya, where "there is hustle and bustle," noisy gossip, jealousy, and hate. But all of this, in Persky's view, is essential for the existence of a thriving public literary culture. The café for Persky—like Sholem Aleichem's Café Fanconi in Odessa or Romanisches Café in Berlin—is not a temple but a literary "stock exchange" in which writers, editors, critics, and others are conducting their "literary business." In the café, "movements, trends, journals, publishing houses and literary projects" are being born, and writers can be real people and not merely "spiritual beings"; and this is why the café is so important.[109]

The exchange between Halkin and Persky is instructive because it reveals the various functions of the café in Jewish literature and culture and how it was experienced by individuals with different sensibilities. Thus, the café could be both a spiritual place and a place for literary business. The exchange also highlights the competition between Hebrew and Yiddish in New York, the ideological divisions, and the anxieties about the viability of literature and culture created in Jewish languages in America. At the same time, however, the exchange also reveals, perhaps unwittingly, the multilingual aspect of the café and how Hebrew existed in this thirdspace alongside Yiddish and English. Halkin, who became the most prominent Hebrew poet in America in the 1930s and 1940s, embodied these tensions. Halkin was quite ambivalent about his participation in New York's Jewish bohemian world and about his involvement with Yiddish modernism. Like other Hebrew poets, he tended toward romanticism, describing the awe-inspiring beauty of America's landscape rather than the cityscape of New York. Nevertheless, Halkin was a habitué of various cafés in New York.[110] In 1927–1928, while a master's student at NYU and a Hebrew teacher at the Hebrew Union College, Halkin wrote and published a ten-poem cycle called "Café Royal."[111]

The speaker in these poems observes the urban landscape of New York from the place Persky referred to as a new center of Yiddish literature and culture. He highlights the decadent ambiance of the Jewish café and its habitués against the erotic energies that the speaker finds in the metropolis and its multitude of inhabitants. In the first poem in the cycle, "Omanim" (Artists), Halkin's speaker presents Café Royal as a space full of aging habitués, who are recognizable only by their "bald heads" and the "longing of their vanished forelocks."[112] These artists escape the desolation of their apartments and flee to the café in the evening. Only one person is presented as truly alive in the café: a young woman who comes to see the revered artists as one might come to a holy place. The desire and the admiration of the young woman is, paradoxically, what saves these men from oblivion. In another poem in the cycle, the actors are at the center. They seem to the observing speakers like "hairy, blind bats" who come alive only at night when the screen rises and with the applause from an audience eager to see them as celebrities in the café.[113] In another poem, the speaker casts his gaze at an older immigrant Jew who sits in the café and hides a tear, remembering the corner of his town's house of study, which he now substitutes with the smoke rings of Café Royal.

In another group of poems in the Café Royal cycle, Halkin's speaker looks out from the smoky café into the reflection of urban life. He finds the seductive metropolitan energy in unexpected places, even in an empty office building, when a black woman comes to clean it. The speaker imagines seeing this black woman dancing while she is at work, and himself, a migrant Jew, joining her in an erotic dance. The speaker also recognizes the urban erotic energy when he sits in the café watching the red sunset over the city (the windows of Café Royal faced west), causing him to compose a hymn to the metropolis. As the sun sets, "the light will rise up again for us—a sliver of lamps and window-shops. / . . . Tonight the City will renew its immortality, / tonight its sons will hitch up the horses of eternity / to the chariots of desire."[114] The café in Halkin's poems is thus a place of contradictions that mixes the sublime with the mundane, desire with oblivion, the Jew and other ethnic groups, the artists, poets, and people from all walks of life, the urban decadence and the metropolitan erotic energy. In spite of Halkin's strong commitment to Hebraism and the ideological imperatives of competing movements and languages, the New York café was a multilingual space where Hebrew was mixed with Yiddish and English.

The Jewish Cafés Go "Uptown"

As the Hebrew poet Shimon Halkin sat in Café Royal on Second Avenue and composed his cycle of urban poems, dramatic changes were happening, both in New York City and to its Jewish population. By 1920, the number of Jews in the city reached over 1.6 million. But the great migration from eastern Europe that was the main source of population growth was coming to a halt. The emerging anti-immigrant sentiment in America resulted in the Immigration Acts of 1921 and 1924 that enforced quotas by country of origin and provided visas for only 2 percent of the migrant population based on each group's population in the 1890 census. The cessation of immigration from Europe, which hit the Jews more than any other group, transformed New York's Jews from a largely working-class and migrant community to one with an American-born, middle-class majority.

During the 1920s, Jewish immigrants and their children abandoned the East Side's cramped quarters in favor of more spacious and modern housing in Brooklyn and the Bronx. This process began before World War I and accelerated in the interwar period. The East Side remained the seat of many communal and cultural institutions, synagogues, and the editorial offices of Yiddish newspapers, but only the poorest of the city's Jews resided there. Starting in the 1920s, many of those who had moved away from the East Side began to look back fondly at what they had left behind and returned often to savor the sights, sounds, and products. However, as these people came back to visit, much of Jewish life in the East Side was also "moving up" from what we consider today to be the "Lower East Side" to Second Avenue, between Houston and Fourteenth Street.[115] In these years, Second Avenue became known as "the Jewish Broadway" (or "Jewish Rialto"), in large part because it became the world capital of Yiddish theater, which went through its own process of growth, diversification, and maturity.[116]

Yiddish literature was also experiencing its own modernist surge, with the appearance of the sophisticated introspection of the group known as In Zikh (In the self) and championed by Jacob Glatshtein, A. Glants-Leyeles, and B. Minkoff.[117] At the same time, Yiddish literature and even the press began to lose their audience, as many Jews, especially those in the American-born second generation, found sufficient cultural and spiritual sustenance in English. Thus, during the late 1920s and early 1930s, Jewish and non-Jewish newspapers and journals in America were abuzz with discussions of the "fate" of Yiddish culture in New York and the United States.

All these changes were reflected in the shift of café culture to Second Avenue, and especially to Café Royal, at the corner of Second Avenue and Twelfth Street. The beginning of Café Royal is shrouded in mystery, but we do know that when it was opened in 1908, the café was named after its owner, Mr. Breslau. In 1910, when Breslau sold the business, it was renamed Café Royal, the name of many cafés in Europe. At that point, the café had a shady reputation as a place of gambling and card playing. One of the stories told about this legendary place claims that Oscar Szathmary, a businessman from Prague, became the owner of the café when he won a pinochle game. In a second game, he won the café busboy, the Hungarian Herman Tantzer.[118] Whether this really happened or not is beside the point. It is clear that Oscar, Herman, and many of the habitués in the 1910s and beyond continued to play cards, but their largest prize by far was the fact that the Yiddish theater moved right outside their doors.

Second Avenue was "a wide, clean, prosperous street with no elevated tracks overhead and without the derelicts and saloons of the Bowery."[119] The Second Avenue Theatre, the National Theatre, the Yiddish Art Theatre, and the Public Theatre all opened on Second Avenue in the 1910s and 1920s, and some of them sat more than one thousand people. Thus, Second Avenue became a thriving Jewish entertainment center with both "high" and "low" establishments. Of course, the Royal was not the only café. There was Café Monopol on Second Avenue and Ninth Street and Café Boulevard. Out of these, the Royal was the one that thrived and persisted for decades. By the mid-1920s, the café had become the stomping ground of actors, divas, and the people who adored them. The writers and journalists followed them to the Royal.

The Yiddish writer Chaver Paver wrote about the time when Yiddish writers and journalists made their way "uptown" to Café Royal, where it was very different. As a writer, you could not linger for hours but had to order food, which was tasty but not cheap, and the owners did not extend credit to poor writers. The Yiddish poet Judd Teller wrote that Café Royal's "continental décor, tablecloths, high ceilings, paneled walls, and long windows" daunted "the casual passerby." Guests could not choose their tables at will, as they entered through the revolving door and were subjected to the gaze of Herman, the famous busboy, who was alleged to be a millionaire from tips. The café was divided into sections. Apart from a few tables by the door covered with white tablecloths, there was a large hall divided in half: "to the left . . . sat the writers and to the right the actors. In a rear room, shut off from sight by a curtain and a large credenza, chess players mixed with card experts and horse-race betters."[120] According to Paver, "a Yiddish writer rarely sat next to a Yiddish actor's table."[121] The Café Royal attracted celebrities from near and far. Non-Jewish intellectuals and bohemians from Greenwich Village often showed up there, taking part in the discussions. E. E. Cummings would drop in on occasion for a conversation with the In Zikh Yiddish poets. The Russian poet Sergei Yesenin, with his wife, Isadora Duncan, came there when in New York, and even Charlie Chaplin would visit from time to time.[122]

Café Royal was especially important for the theater. Leo Rosten wrote in the New Yorker, "Everybody who is anybody in the creative Jewish world turns up at the Café Royal at least one night a week. To be seen there is a social duty, a mark of distinction, and an investment in prestige."[123] The actor Herman Yablokoff recalled that upon his arrival in New York in 1924, he was taken from Ellis Island to Café Royal. The Royal, he claimed, was known to come fully awake only at midnight, when the actors and all those connected with the Yiddish theater gathered after their respective shows. "They kept the place buzzing into the wee hours." He was so happy to see for the first time the "world-famed" café, about which he had heard so much in Europe.[124] A caricature from 1935 by Yosl Kotler shows a waiter in the café putting in an order during Passover of "one ham sandwich on matzo—for Maurice Schwartz" (fig. 5.12).

Although most Yiddish writers, both the older and the younger generation, went to Café Royal on a regular basis, they did not always feel at home there, and many of them felt dark clouds gathering around them. This was due to the quick acculturation of most Jews into English, which caused Baruch Glasman to claim that in spite of the high artistic achievements of Yiddish literature, it had no future in America. In Glasman's novella In goldenem zump (In the golden swamp, 1926), we read about the bitter arguments among writers in the café, especially those who make a living at journalism and mock those who are still committed to serious literature. The protagonist of the novella is Moyshe Rambam, a middle-aged man who used to write Yiddish poetry in his youth. He writes translations and adaptations of English news stories or popular serialized novels. One chapter follows Rambam to the "writers' coffeehouse," a café on the East Side very much like Café Royal. Rambam enters the

Figure 5.12. Yossl Kotler, "Passover in Café Royal," *Signal* 56 (June–July 1935): 3

café "with raised head, with provocative attention-grabbing glances. Oh, today *he* was a bit of a winner!"[125] He feels good, about which he wants to tell his colleagues and friends in the café. He goes to a central table in the café, where "the very cream of Yiddish literature" sit, where people discuss some "very important matter" for hours, days, and even months. In fact, the writers in the café keep "negating each other," even if they do so with sophisticated politeness. As Rambam spends more time in the café, as the "rings of smoke swirl and fray," and the central table becomes more crowded by the minute, his self-confidence wears down. He tries to convince himself that unlike the literary publication that is doomed to fail soon, the Yiddish newspaper is different. "The new immigrant needs it," but then he is compelled to admit to himself that even the immigrant will abandon Yiddish "once he has a bit of English." The chapter ends with Rambam's bitterness, as he turns to the other writers in the café and asks them, "Well, tell me something good fellas! Everything alright, eh? Who wants a 'cuppa coffee' on me? My treat."[126]

Isaac Bashevis Singer was one of the few writers who managed, in spite of severe immigration restrictions, to emigrate from Warsaw, where he had frequented its cafés, to New York. Initially he compared New York's cafés unfavorably to those he had left behind. He arrived in 1935 and described in his memoirs coming to the house of his older brother, Israel Joshua Singer, who had emigrated a year before him and lived in Brooklyn. Israel Joshua took Bashevis (as he was known in Yiddish) to Manhattan, to Second Avenue and Café Royal. Bashevis compared American Jewish café habitués to those he knew in Warsaw, remembering that they "made the comments of those who have long since shed every inhibition." The people in Café Royal seemed to Bashevis Singer to be vain and rude, to focus on appearance, and to lack intellectual and artistic merits. He remembered that he could not eat even one bite and felt a "rage against America," an urge to go back to Warsaw as soon as possible. "The door to the café kept swinging to and fro. Men and women who apparently were not part of the literary establishment or the Yiddish theater kept on entering and leaving. They pointed to those occupying the tables."[127]

Besides the reservations that might be typical of someone who comes from Europe to America for the first time, Bashevis's memoir also highlighted the fact that in the 1930s, the Café Royal became more of a place where tourists went to visit—as if it were a museum or as if the Yiddish actors there were acting a play. This is also what the Jewish folklorist Nathan Ausubel felt about Café Royal when he wrote his unpublished manuscript "Hold Up the Sun," a series of vignettes focusing primarily on the East Side, part of the Works Progress Administration (WPA) Federal Writers' Project study of the Jews of New York, which was commissioned in the midst of the Great Depression. In a chapter called "Art with Tea and Lemon," Ausubel writes,

It is all unreal, utterly unreal, like some stage play—a pantomime of quaintly amusing ghosts. For years, the Café Royal on Second Avenue has been Yiddish bohemia's lyrical protest against the Machine Age. For years, those rare souls looking for the conversational warmth of other rare souls . . . have made it their rendezvous, their club. With the same habituation and fervor that their fathers attended their synagogues in the Russian and Polish Ghettos, these intellectuals have been haunting the sacred precincts of the Café, a little island of conviviality in a roaring sea of city loneliness, . . . raising each other's blood pressure with heated arguments.

However, writes Ausubel, the arguments are not about real, burning questions of art and politics but "over . . . whether the Yiddish Theatre on Second Avenue has gone *kaput* or *ausgespiel*." Ausubel felt that the habitués are "like characters in a play," who "have taken their places at the tables, which are reserved for them like the grand tier boxes at the opera for the rich." They are a "strange assortment of museum pieces," who "do not fit well into the present scheme of things." The Yiddish actors are "old troupers, . . . men and women fallen from the past glory and affluence," who are being forgotten as Jewish theatergoers are "drifting away to Broadway and the movies." Many of the actors are unemployed, so they come to Café Royal to "gallantly carry on their pretension at well-being, and order just tea with lemon!" The state of the "Yiddish editors and journalists, the freelancing poets and novelists, feuilletonists and playwrights" was even worse than that of the actors. They were like "characters out of the Yiddish Grub Street, . . . pale, moody hungry young poets," who "fall out of step with the rest of the go-getting world."[128]

Despite the fact that the Café Royal was still a thriving establishment in the 1930s, it was widely seen by observers such as Ausubel as a cultural remnant of a bygone world.[129] Even if Jewish American audiences abandoned Yiddish theater, literature, and press for Broadway and the *New York Times*, visitors continued to come to Café Royal time and again in order to reminisce about their past on the East Side: "And so nowadays, when they come down to the Café Royal and listen to the delectable conversation of the hungry Yiddish poets, . . . they begin to relive vicariously the unhappy days of their youth."[130] For those who wanted to relive their youth or to give their children a glimpse of that youth or to find the exotic Jewish "other," Café Royal still had much to offer in terms of atmosphere, or what Ausubel called the "pantomime of quaintly amusing ghosts."[131]

Many articles about Café Royal appeared in English during the 1930s, and the place was mentioned in seemingly every tourist guide to the city. All these articles mentioned the "characters" or "types," who played their part, and that included almost everybody in the café: the owner (by then the widow of Oscar), the Yiddish actors and divas, and even the poor Yiddish poets. The most important characters were Herman, the millionaire busboy, who collected compulsory high tips just from the visitors, and the strangers who did not understand the conventions of the East Side café.[132] With such publicity, perhaps it was inevitable that someone would write an actual play about the "characters" of Café Royal. Hy (Hyman Solomon) Kraft wrote *Café Crown*, a three-act comedy that premiered on Broadway on January 23, 1942, under the direction of Elia Kazan. The play takes place "in and around the Café Crown at the corner of Second Avenue and 12th Street in New York City" in "the early 1930s."[133] Not surprisingly, the main characters in the play were David Cole, who was a star of the Yiddish theater, and Herman the eccentric busboy of Café Royal, who finances Cole's last attempt to produce a Yiddish play. In other words, the play itself was nostalgic. The Broadway production was not critically acclaimed, but it caused "the latest discovery of Café Royal," in the words of one journalist, who described the audience leaving the Cort Theatre in midtown and asking each other, "Do you mean to tell me that there is actually such a café in New York? If so, then why don't you take me there? The answer is 'That's where we're going right now. Hey, Taxi, Café Royal!'"[134]

Postwar Jewish Café Culture in New York

The "rediscovery" of Café Royal probably helped the establishment to last for another ten years. In the meantime, Jewish refugees from World War II Europe arrived in New York and found a warm place among the aging Yiddish actors and journalists. Not surprisingly, the refugees were attracted to the fading Café Royal. In 1945, the Jewish photographer and photojournalist Arthur Fellig, known widely as Weegee, went to Café Royal, attracted by the mixture of Jewish war refugees and survivors and older Yiddish-speaking Jews. Weegee had immigrated to New York as a child in 1909 and grew up on the East Side. He was known for capturing stark images of the city's outcasts and outlaws. Weegee took a series of powerful black-and-white photographs in which he captured the atmosphere of the café in its last years (figs. 5.13 and 5.14). In one of

Figure 5.13. Weegee, *Tea Break at the Café Royal on Second Avenue,
Meeting Place for Yiddish Theater Actors*, September 30, 1945
(2012.1993) (© Weegee / International Center of Photography)

these photographs, a woman with chipped nail varnish resolutely dips a
teabag into her glass, while around her men are conversing. In the other,
older men, perhaps actors or composers, smoke and eat watermelon.

In Isaac Bashevis's semiautobiographical Yiddish novel *Farloyrene neshomes* (Lost souls; published in English as *Meshugah*), the protagonist,
the writer and journalist Aaron Greidinger, meets his long-lost friend
Max Aberdam, whom he thought to be dead in a concentration camp.
Max enters into the first-person narrator's office and into his life, introducing Aaron to his young mistress, Miriam. In the first chapter of
the novel, Aaron and Max take a walk on Second Avenue, where "every

Figure 5.14. Weegee, *Café Royal, Meeting Place for Yiddish Theater Actors on Second Avenue,* September 1945 (16062.1993) (© Weegee / International Center of Photography)

step was bound up with memories of not long ago." The first place they passed was "the Café Royal, where Yiddish actors and writers had been steady guests."[135] It is difficult to tell whether the café was open, and Aaron decided not to go in—or it was already closed and lived only in his memory.

Indeed, in 1952, the time that Bashevis depicted in his novel, Café Royal finally closed. Soon after, the café became K&S Cleaners, which offered not only laundry services but also stories for people who came to visit the place without knowing that the café was gone. To a visiting journalist from the *New York Times,* the owner of the cleaning store explained what he said to nostalgic visitors returning to the place: "Well, the Café Royal isn't all gone. See the mirror there? That's your mirror from the café. You can still look in it and see yourself—just like the old days."[136] In an important article, "Yiddish Literateurs and American Jews: Have They Come to a Parting of the Ways?" (1954), Judd L. Teller wrote, "The decline of the literary café, or *kibitzarnya*, was an effect of the decline of Yiddish letters in New York. The cafés were kept going not by what writers spent in them, but by those more numerous patrons who liked to pass evenings where writers congregated. When the number of the patrons shrunk it was a portent of doom."[137] For Teller, the closing of Café Royal in 1952 symbolized the premature death of Yiddish culture in New York; it was like the "closing of the lid of the coffin."[138]

In spite of those poignant remarks, the closing of Café Royal did not mark the death of New York Jewish café culture or even of Yiddish culture. The postwar period brought many changes, but the city was still a major center of Jewish culture, not only for older Jews but also for second-generation and third-generation Jews who forged new types of Jewish identities during the 1930s and 1940s.[139] There was also much continuity between the cafeterias and the cafés of the East Side and Greenwich Village.

One prominent example of second-generation Jewish culture in New York was the presence of many Jewish students at the City College of New York (CCNY) in Harlem. A group of these students, among them Irving Howe, Alfred Kazin, Daniel Bell, Nathan Glazer, and Irving Kristol, eventually became known as the "New York Intellectuals." As Irving Howe observed, "Their social roots are not hard to trace. . . . They stem from the world of the immigrant Jews."[140] What is evident is their shared experience at City College, where much of the education took place not in class but in the cafeteria, more specifically in particular alcoves of the cafeteria, where students, self-divided by ethnicity and politics, ate lunches and argued endlessly about politics and everything else.[141] The budding New York Intellectuals occupied Alcove No. 1, that of the anti-Stalinist socialists. Alcove No. 2 was the home of the Stalinists. "It was between those two alcoves," Irving Kristol wrote in 1977, "that the war of the worlds was fought, over the faceless bodies of the mass of students, whom we tried desperately to manipulate into 'the right position.'"[142] After graduating from college, many of these young intellectuals found new homes in the cafeterias of the city. Daniel Bell described the atmosphere in the cafeteria as "kind of a heder."[143] Although the heyday of the Village as a bohemian space in the 1910s was largely gone, many of the new American newspapers and magazines were located there. Their writers and editors had a new place to gather: the cafeteria. William Phillips, the Jewish cofounder and editor of the *Partisan Review* since 1934, remembered, "Our favorite hangout was . . . Stewart's cafeteria on Sheridan Square, where for a dime you could get coffee and cake, and sit for hours arguing and solving the problems of the world."[144]

The novelist Saul Bellow, born in Canada and raised in Chicago, lived and worked in New York during most of the 1940s and 1950s. He published in the *Partisan Review* and *Commentary* and became part of the world of the New York Intellectuals. In his second novel, *The Victim* (1947), the main protagonist is Asa Leventhal, a second-generation New York Jew who suffered from unemployment during the Great Depression and finally found a job as an editor for a minor trade journal. The highly insecure Leventhal is haunted by a man named Kirby Allbee, who believes not only that his Jewish acquaintance is responsible for the loss of his job but also that Jews have taken New York (and America) away from the Protestants. Thus, the novel deals with the issue of anti-Semitism for second-generation American Jews. Leventhal is determined not only to call out the anti-Semite who hounds his every step but to resist the paranoia that such vigilance breeds. Chapter 10 of *The Victim* takes place in a cafeteria on Fourteenth Street. As Leventhal meets his friend Harkavy, he is introduced to a group of older migrant Jews who are involved in the theater and film industry. Among them is Schlossberg, a critic, who writes for a Yiddish newspaper. In the middle of a discussion of the virtues of actors, Schlossberg claims, "Good acting is what is exactly human. And if you say I am a tough critic, you mean I have a high opinion of what is human." This talk about acting turns into a discussion of morality and authenticity. Schlossberg's words are seen as the moral compass of the Jewish migrant, transmitted in the cafeteria to Leventhal, a second-generation Jew who is grounded in New York and America but is highly baffled by them: "It's bad to be less than human. . . . More than human, can you have any use of life? Less than human, you don't either." His final pronouncement, which seems to resonate with Leventhal's sense of loss, is "choose dignity."[145] It is not coincidental that this exchange between two generations of Jews in postwar America takes place in a cafeteria.

Cafeterias like the one described in Bellow's novel became common starting in the wake of the Great Depression. They were spaces with self-service, offering cheap food and drink that allowed customers to choose items without the assistance of waiters and servers. On the other hand, the eating and drinking space provided the habitué with a place to socialize and talk. From the mid-1940s to the 1970s, cafeterias attracted Jewish immigrants, Holocaust survivors, and even some American-born Jews and persisted on the Lower East Side and in other immigrant neighborhoods. These cafeterias served mostly as a bridge between the immigrant community, European Jews, and New York.[146] One of the best examples of such spaces was the Garden Cafeteria at 165 East Broadway, back on the Lower East Side, a few doors from where Herrick's and Sholem's used to be and where the editorial building of the Yiddish *Forverts* still operated, after the death of its great editor Abe Cahan in 1951. The Garden Cafeteria was established in 1941 by Charles Metzger, an Austrian Jew who had migrated to New York in 1911. Initially, he had a small cafeteria in East Harlem, where there was a substantial Jewish community, before moving it to East Broadway.[147] The Garden Cafeteria was open twenty-four hours a day and was quite successful from the beginning. Eventually, the management broke through one of the walls of the building to add more space. Like all American cafeterias at this time, and in contradistinction to Café Royal and the old cafés of the East Side, customers came in and took a ticket as they entered, with a man behind the counter punching the ticket with the price of what they ordered, and they paid when they left. The cafeteria system was built for efficiency, to accommodate as many customers as possible during meals.

The Jewish journalist and novelist Dan Wakefield wrote, "The Garden Cafeteria . . . is a crowded, noisy, American-style beanery, where customers shove their trays down a chromium counter and are hurriedly dipped out the specials of the day. The Garden is hardly different in outward appearance from a thousand cafeterias from Maine to California." But somehow, visitors to the Garden Cafeteria lingered there for hours. It was, according to Wakefield, "a refuge . . . of the spirit of the old East Side."[148] The new East Side of the 1950s had less than half the population it had in the early decades of the twentieth century. It was a patchwork of

Puerto Ricans, Jews (including many Holocaust survivors), Ukrainians, refugees, postwar émigrés, blacks, and Italians.[149] Still, many Jews came to the neighborhood because of the Jewish newspapers (*Forverts* and *Tog morgn zshurnal*) and other cultural institutions or because of nostalgia, and the Garden Cafeteria was its new social and intellectual center. According to Wakefield, "the particular kind of community sense which reached a peak at the Café Royal exists, in the shrunken Yiddish literary world that is left, in the Garden Cafeteria."[150] Isaac Bashevis Singer, the most well-known postwar Yiddish writer, who wrote for the *Forverts* for many decades, was a habitué of the Garden Cafeteria and described it as "a second home."[151]

Bashevis Singer wrote a number of stories that take place in cafeterias like the Garden. The most famous and powerful is "Di kafeterye" ("The Cafeteria," 1968).[152] In this story, the narrator, Aaron, an author and journalist who lives by himself, goes to the cafeteria, where he meets "the *landsleit* from Poland, as well as all kinds of literary beginners and readers who know Yiddish": "old bachelors like myself, would-be writers, retired teachers, some with dubious doctorate titles, a rabbi without a congregation, a painter of Jewish themes, a few translators—all from Poland or Russia." Aaron describes what he can talk about in the cafeteria: "about Yiddish literature, the Holocaust, the State of Israel, and often about acquaintances who were eating rice pudding or stewed prunes the last time I was here and are already in their graves."[153] Among the survivors whom the narrator meets in the cafeteria is a young woman named Esther. A few years after their meeting, the cafeteria burns down, and when it reopens, Esther and the narrator meet again. She tells him that her health is declining and that she might apply for reparation money from the Germans. One night Esther arrives at the narrator's apartment and confides that the night before the cafeteria burned down, she had a vision in which she went by the cafeteria and saw a scene she would never forget: "The tables were shoved together and around them sat men in white robes, like doctors or orderlies, all with swastikas on their sleeves. At the head sat Hitler." At first, the narrator simply assumes the woman is insane, but later he muses, "I thought about what Esther had told me of seeing Hitler in the cafeteria. It had seemed utter nonsense, but now I began to reappraise the idea."[154] The image of Hitler in the cafeteria reflects the dark side of the survivors' existence. Even Esther, the youngest and most optimistic among them, is caught in a net of evil, embodied in Hitler. In the story, Esther is transformed from an individual with a personal history into a vague shadow, a possible figment of the narrator's imagination.

Indeed, around the time Bashevis Singer published his story, the Lower East Side was changing dramatically, and the Garden Cafeteria ceased to be a center for Jewish writers, journalists, and artists. Still, it attracted many old Jewish habitués, old and vulnerable people on the margins of society. This is exactly what attracted Bruce Davidson, a photographer who immerses himself in a particular location. After making a film about Bashevis Singer, Davidson was drawn to the Garden for an extended period, taking photos and writing about the place. "Every day, for weeks," he wrote, "I went to Garden, took a check, got some coffee and sat down with people at the small tables along the wall."[155] Davidson did what Bashevis had been doing for years, namely, meeting and speaking with the Jewish habitués of the Garden, but instead of writing fictional stories about the place, he conveyed its human fabric in a moving photo essay.

Among the people whom Davidson spoke with and photographed was a man who worked for *Forverts* newspaper (fig. 5.15), who told him, "The place means to me a lot. . . . In the cafeteria I felt home, just like I would be in Warsaw, in 1939, before the war. . . . This was my refuge. . . . I found a gallery of living Jewish writers—Asch, Singer, Leivik—whom I adored." Davidson also spoke with Bessie Gakaubowicz, a seventy-seven-year-old Holocaust survivor who lived in the "projects" with "Spanish people, Italian people, colored people." "They are all nice," she told him.[156] Nevertheless, she came to the cafeteria every evening as a place of refuge. Davidson took a photograph of Mrs. Gakaubowicz holding a photo of herself and her husband, whom she lost before the war (fig. 5.16). In this photo, he captured not only each facial line on her face but also the deep sadness and sense of loss, as well as the solace that women such as her found in the Garden Cafeteria. The cafeteria, in other words, was a place where women could sit by themselves and socialize, just like men. Other photographs show old people who are worn and tattered, but with Davidson's focus on them, as they are surrounded by coffee, bagels, and rice pudding, he

Figure 5.15. Bruce Davidson, Garden Cafeteria, New York City, 1973 (© Bruce Davidson / Magnum Photos)

shows their strength and dignity, as well as the physical and social nurturing they found in the Garden Cafeteria. Apart from Bashevis, the people whom Davidson captured in the Garden were not writers or intellectuals but simple Jews (fig. 5.17).

Since the 1970s, there have been few, if any, cafés that were known as gathering places for Jewish writers. There continue to be many cafés in New York, but in the past fifty years, they have not been significant for the creation of Jewish culture. Part of the reason for this is the growing embourgeoisement of second- and third-generation Jewish intellectuals and writers, who lived in comfortable apartments that replaced the café as a thirdspace of exchange and discussion.

Hence, it is not surprising that the last great Jewish writer, thus far, to sit in and to reflect on New York cafés was Gabriel Preil, who was born in Lithuania in 1911 and migrated to New York in 1922. Preil started writing poetry both in Yiddish and in Hebrew under the influence of

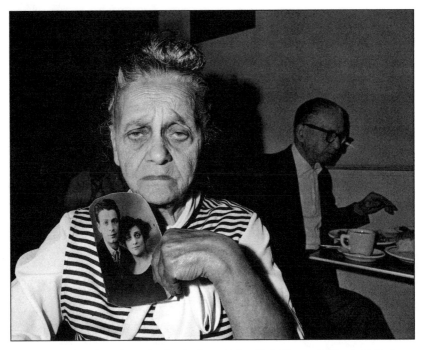

Figure 5.16. Bruce Davidson, Garden Cafeteria, New York City, 1966; Bessie Gakaubo-wicz, holding a photograph of her and her husband taken before World War II (© Bruce Davidson / Magnum Photos)

the In Zikh movement, but the majority of his poetry was written in Hebrew. While most Hebrew writers in New York, people such as Shimon Halkin, migrated to Israel in the 1950s or died in these years, Preil lived and wrote in the city until his death in 1993; the Israeli Hebrew poet Dan Pagis famously nicknamed him "The Duke of New York." Preil wrote in cafés around New York, and coffeehouses are a central locus of his urban, modernist poetics. While the young Preil knew Café Royal very well in the 1930s and 1940s and was part of the circles there, in latter decades, his café activity was mostly solitary. "The cafés of New York," observes Michael Weingrad, "were the launching pad of [Preil's] reclusive sensitivity, their windows his eyes to the world."[157] In 1954, Preil published an exquisite cycle of poems, "Shirim mi-beit ha-kafe" (Poems from the café), clearly in dialogue with Shimon Halkin's earlier cycle

Figure 5.17. Bruce Davidson, Garden Cafeteria, New York City, 1973 (© Bruce Davidson / Magnum Photos)

"Café Royal." The first poem in Preil's cycle, "Mishmeret eragon" (Watch of yearning), is dedicated to Halkin, and it begins with these lines:

> In this café, its ceiling is a sad, electric sunset
> Its walls spell the blooming of gardens, picking of fruit—
> I will be on my duty, a watch of yearning,
> with pencil drafts I will stir up the past,
> in my cup I will seek the shadows of the years.[158]

Unlike Halkin's "Sunset in New York," in which he evoked both nature's glory and the sexual energy of the city, Preil can only see an artificial, "sad, electric sunset" inside the New York café. Unlike the Zionist *shomer*, "watchman," or the solider in Israel's army, the poet's "duty" is a "watch of yearning." In his cup of coffee, he conjures both past and memory ("the shadows of the years") and yearning for a future. He is immersed in the "hesitating present" and is fully aware that the "now" is a "sealed gate," while the keys to the garden "were thrown in the lap of the past." At the same time, though, this sober ending brings us back to the opening of the poem and the image of the café's walls, which for the poet who can imagine the past and the future can conjure the "blooming garden" and even its "fruit."[159]

In the second poem of the cycle, "Lines for Avraham Mapu," the speaker evokes the nineteenth-century Hebrew novelist from Lithuania and identifies with him: "I, like you, am a Lithuanian Jew / who tried to bring forth from bland soil / sober trees in which a dream is set ablaze." But the speaker recognizes the difference between himself and Mapu. He dwells in a different time and space, "a café in which one can count many cups of loneliness." His New York poetic experience is one of a "different land, which vies with dreams; invents reality; / but the café will never quench the fires of solitude." This solitude can also be good, especially when the "coffee is steaming in the cup as usual."[160] In the sixth poem of the cycle, "Waiting for the Atomic Tomorrow," Preil's speaker highlights the strange comfort of "leisurely drinking coffee in a time of conflagration," the time in which the shadow of the Holocaust is mixed with the Cold War and the threat of the atomic bomb. In contrast to the destructive atom, there is a "wise energy" that is "hidden in the coffee bean" but is released when one brews and drinks it.[161] In fact, throughout the cycle, sitting in cafés and drinking coffee is much like the act of writing poetry. Both the world and the self are infused with this "wise energy," which can make everything seem more vivid, less tired, and full of potential and possibilities. In a later poem from the 1970s, Preil wrote, as if looking at himself from outside the New York café on a rainy day:

> Gabriel the rain-lover
> sits in a café
> thinking of the poem he's going to write,
> if not today, tomorrow.[162]

Indeed, Preil continued to write many poems in and about New York cafés, almost until his death in 1993. The readers of these poems, however, were mostly not in New York but in Israel. These readers, among them many important Israeli poets, writers, and intellectuals who found his Hebrew poetry new and refreshing, sat in cafés in Tel Aviv and Jerusalem. During the last decades of his life, Preil came to visit them many times and fostered a fruitful dialogue, and yet he always returned to New York, to his regular cafés and his "usual cup."

Preil, the Hebrew and Yiddish American poet, was drawn to these cafés on his own, without the company of migrant Jewish writers, intellectuals, actors, and artists who used to populate New York's cafés for many years. His silent solitude in New York cafés and cafeterias of the 1970s and 1980s stands in stark contrast to the noise that characterized the Jewish migrant experience in the period between the 1880s and the 1960s, an experience that transmitted eastern and central European cafés into America but also created a distinct American Jewish café culture. This culture was marked by the noise of various languages, the noise of kibitzing, socializing, and political activities in the cafés, the noise of artistic, theatrical, and literary business that intersected with aesthetics, the noise of creating new provisional homes and longing for lost ones.

6

Tel Aviv–Jaffa

The "First Hebrew City" or a City of Many Cafés?

Blessed be you, Oh Tel Aviv, city of *gazoz* and cinema.
Everywhere you turn around, coffeehouses call you,
come here!
—Avraham Shlonsky, 1934

In 1936, Sholem Asch—the most widely read Yiddish writer at the time and a habitué of cafés in Warsaw, Berlin, and New York—traveled to Palestine. "Before I came to Palestine," Asch reported, "some good people told me *not* to get my impressions about the country in Tel Aviv." Asch was well aware that Tel Aviv was at the center of controversies about the desired direction of the Yishuv, the Jewish community in Palestine. Some people believed that Tel Aviv represented the best of what this community had created in the early decades of the twentieth century; others believed the opposite. In spite of the warnings that Tel Aviv did not represent the Yishuv, Asch was very impressed with the young urban center. He claimed that "in Tel Aviv . . . there are more and better concerts than in any other Middle Eastern country, . . . the best theater . . . in the southern hemisphere, . . . the only European museum, . . . and a deluge of clubs, parties, and cafés."[1]

The cafés that Asch saw in Tel Aviv indeed seemed to multiply, from a handful in the early 1920s to 178 in 1934 and then to 422 in 1946.[2] The number of cafés and their visibility and centrality in Tel Aviv's cultural life during the 1930s and 1940s astonished many observers, both Jews and gentiles, in Palestine and around the world. Some of the surprise was due to the relatively small size of Tel Aviv. During these decades, the city had more cafés per capita than most European and American cities did. Even more significant is the fact that according to the fathers of Zionism—such figures as Theodor Herzl and Max Nordau—as well as the founders of "the first Hebrew City," Tel Aviv was not meant to have cafés at all. Tel Aviv's mythic story—a story of a city created ex nihilo, "out of the sands," by a group of sixty families—which was captured perfectly in Avraham Soskin's iconic photograph of 1909 (fig. 6.1), was all about leaving the perceived dirt and darkness of Jaffa and its Arab cafés, as well as the "decadence" of European cities where Jews lived as part of a minority and often found refuge and home in the café.[3] In Herzl's novel *Altneuland*, discussed in chapter 3, desperate young Jews like Dr. Löwenberg sat in Viennese cafés for hours with nothing to do or hope for. These cafés represented the "decadence" of Jews in Europe. When Löwenberg and his companion Kingscourt landed in Jaffa in 1902, they saw nothing but desolation. Simple Arab cafés, like the one in Jaffa (fig. 6.2), seemed to Löwenberg, and to Herzl, to be part of the "neglect," "filth," and "bareness" of Ottoman Palestine.[4]

In Herzl's novel, Löwenberg and Kingscourt returned to the port city of Haifa twenty years later, and it was transformed by Jewish migration to Palestine into an ultramodern, technologically advanced city. Jews went to the opera and theater, but cafés were nowhere to be found in the city of Herzl's utopian vision. When Akiva Arieh Weiss migrated from Łódź in Congress Poland to Palestine in 1906, during the period known

Figure 6.1. Avraham Soskin, photograph of the establishment of Ahuzat Bayit, 1909

Figure 6.2. Photograph of Shmuel Barkai and friends in Arab café in Jaffa, 1920s
(Courtesy of Beth Ha'ir, Tel Aviv Municipality, Barkai collection)

in Zionist historiography as "the Second Aliyah," he was inspired by
Herzl and especially enchanted by *Altneuland*.[5] Unlike other migrants
who dreamt about working the land in the colonies or creating a socialist kibbutz, Weiss came with a plan to establish a "garden suburb" outside the city of Jaffa. This was the neighborhood of Ahuzat Bayit, which
in May 1910 changed its name to Tel Aviv—the Hebrew translation of
Herzl's *Altneuland*. Ahuzat Bayit / Tel Aviv was initiated by mostly eastern European Jews such as Weiss who wanted to establish a substan-
tially different enterprise, contrasted both with Jaffa and with the earlier
neighborhoods on the outskirts of the old city that within a short period
took on the "crowded and oriental look" of Jaffa.[6]

The new neighborhood was indeed built as a garden suburb, with
neat family houses, each surrounded by a plot of land, in rows of straight
and relatively broad streets. Weiss and most of the founders were against
establishing any businesses, but this objection did not last for long. On
June 8, 1910, the neighborhood committee decided to approve the first
kiosk on the corner of Rothschild Boulevard and Herzl Street, "the
size of two by two meters," with a "permit to sell only cold drinks."[7]
For some people, this tiny kiosk selling *gazoz* (soda drinks) represented

the beginning of a slippery slope toward commercialization and urban decadence; for others, it was the beginning of a robust café culture in Tel Aviv that was essential to its modernity and urbanity. The mythography of Tel Aviv, which was deemed "the first Hebrew city," is full of firsts: the first house, the first school, the first kiosk, the first gas lamp, and so on.[8] However, in spite of the self-conscious attempts to tell the story of Tel Aviv as a story of separation and radical newness, Ahuzat Bayit and Tel Aviv grew out of Jaffa and out of diasporic Jewish urban culture. This complex story includes the history of Jaffa's and Tel Aviv's cafés.

Many years before Tel Aviv existed, Jaffa flourished, with numerous cafés lining its streets. Throughout the nineteenth and early twentieth centuries, Jaffa, known in Arabic as 'Arus al-bahr (Bride of the sea), was a mixed port city. Jews represented a significant and growing minority of the city's population. They resided among the Arab population and had daily contact with it. The period of 1841–1881 saw the first signs of Ottoman modernization in Jaffa, and many newcomers—Muslims, Christians, and Jews—arrived and settled, mostly outside the old city wall. The commercial and administrative center of the city moved to the east and the north, and new Arab neighborhoods were built. In 1869, the Templars, a messianic Protestant movement that originated in the German region of Württemberg, built their first colony near Jaffa. After 1882, a surge of development took place, with the construction of the Jaffa-Jerusalem railway and numerous public buildings by local and foreign governments and churches.[9] By 1888, due to efforts by the Ottoman Empire and local initiatives, the wall around the old city of Jaffa was completely demolished, and the city was in the midst of a building boom.[10] The construction of the predominantly Jewish neighborhoods of Neve Tzedek, Neve Shalom, Mahane Yosef, and Kerem Ha-teimanim was part of the growth of modern Jaffa, rather than a change toward the creation of an independent Jewish space separated from it. Moreover, Neve Shalom, established in 1890, was virtually mixed with the Arab neighborhood of Manshiyeh until the 1930s.[11] At the end of the nineteenth century, when the total population of modern Jaffa reached approximately thirty thousand, both Sephardi and Ashkenazi Jews who lived in Jaffa saw themselves as part of the local Arab-Jewish environment. The borders between the Jewish and Arab neighborhoods were fuzzy and not rigidly defined. In some buildings, Arab and Jewish families lived side by side. Small coffeehouses were a common feature in Jaffa, shared and enjoyed by all inhabitants.[12]

Early in the nineteenth century, cafés in Jaffa, like elsewhere in the Ottoman Empire, had been spaces to drink coffee and socialize, where one could find a public scribe to fill out official forms and petitions for a fee or where carriages picked up and discharged passengers. By the century's end, coffeehouses served a predominantly transient population. Jaffa's Arab cafés were similar to European and American cafés in some respects and different in others. In this port city, cafés served sailors, travel agents, customs officers, porters, and other itinerant workers. Jaffa cafés served recreational and entertainment functions, with games of cards and dominoes, the performance of music, the sale and consumption of alcohol, tobacco, and hashish, and occasionally the presence of prostitution. They also fostered the emergence of political and literary groups, a space in which members could hold unscheduled meetings, away from the watchful eyes of the Ottoman authorities.[13] When the local press gained ground in Palestine, especially after the Young Turk Revolution of 1908, cafés turned into locations of collective newspaper reading. Like cities elsewhere, owners of cafés enhanced the allure of their businesses by buying or subscribing to a range of papers. Visitors to the café enjoyed being able to read or to listen to other people reading several papers.[14]

We can see some of these changes in Jaffa's cafés of the late Ottoman period, as well as their attraction to Arabs and Jews of all backgrounds, in the memoirs of Yosef-Eliyahu Chelouche, born in Jaffa in 1870 to a local Jewish Sephardi family with roots in Algeria and Baghdad. The family was prominent in Jaffa because of Yosef-Eliyahu's father, Aharon, who was an established businessman. In the summer of 1880, Yosef-Eliyahu was kidnapped by a Muslim man who did business with his father and wanted to ransom the family. Hours after the boy's disappearance, his father started to search for him. Mehmet Tevfik Efendi, the *kaymakam* (governor) of Jaffa, offered his help. The whole city was informed, and volunteers set out to look for him, together with groups of soldiers, while Aharon went to the family synagogue to pray for the child's rescue. Meanwhile, the *kaymakam* sat "outside a café near the entrance to the old city, together with some government officials, waiting for further developments." Yosef-Eliyahu was rescued by a watchman in the orchards outside the city, and Theodor-George, a Christian Arab, discovered the kidnapper sitting in a café in one of Jaffa's new suburbs, where he was arrested.[15] Chelouche's experience was typical of Sephardi Jews in Palestine during this period. He was fluent in Arabic, French, and Hebrew, and his family had contacts with many Muslim and Christian Arabs. In the anecdote, we can also see how the presence of the highest-ranking Ottoman officials in a Jaffa café made it a respectable place, how quickly news and rumors could spread around Jaffa, and how coffeehouses could serve as places to gather and to exchange news.[16]

During the first years of the twentieth century, Jewish migration to Palestine increased together with the growth of Jaffa and its population. Between 1900 and the First World War, about thirty-five thousand Jews, mostly from eastern Europe, reached Palestine. Compared to Jewish mass migration to America or to large cities in Europe, the number of

Figure 6.3. Reuven Rubin, *Arab Café in Jaffa* (1923), oil on canvas (Rubin Museum Tel Aviv)

migrants was tiny, but these people became important in the creation of the new Yishuv. In spite of the Zionist emphasis on agriculture and manual labor in newly established kibbutzim, most of the migrants were not "pioneers." They settled in cities and many of them in the port of entry, Jaffa.[17] The city also attracted Jewish migrants who were active in journalism, literature, theater, and art and became a small center of Jewish culture, with prominent people such as Yosef Ḥayim Brenner, S. Y. Agnon, Dvora Baron, Sh. Ben-Zion, Ze'ev Smilansky, and Menaḥem Gnessin.

At that time, Bustros Street, the main commercial center of modern Jaffa, was full of cafés. This is where Gnessin and the "Lovers of Dramatic Art" circle were active. This circle of amateur actors operated in the school of girls in Jaffa, but they did not have a permanent place to stage readings of plays or productions. Their 1904 production—the first play preformed in Hebrew in Palestine—was a translation of *Uriel Acosta* by the German writer Karl Gutzkow. Gnessin tells how he was asked to play the leading role, and the company was looking for a place to stage it. They found it in an "Arab café in Jaffa that by chance had a stage in it." In his memoir, Gnessin reflected on the transformation of the café in terms that mostly reveal his cultural attitude toward Arab Jaffa and its cafés and the way European Jews changed them to be "dignified and clean" institutions: "The Arab café," wrote Gnessin, "was cleaned and purified from its age-old filth. . . . When the opening day arrived, Jaffa received a new, festive profile. Jews who never set a foot in the café went there majestically dressed. . . . The Arab café became in my view 'the center of the Yishuv' and suddenly was very dear to my heart."[18] A few years later, the group staged the historical drama *War and Love*. Yehudit Harari (Isenberg) wrote that the play was produced in the Arab Café Fadul on Bustros Street in Jaffa. "In this café," Harari wrote, "people play cards and dice games, smoke *nargila* [hookah], drink alcohol, and eat fried lamb chops; the space is full of smoke, dirt, and unpleasant smells. But the stage in the café is the largest in Jaffa, and behind the stage, there is a small room that could be used for changing costumes."[19] In the writing of Gnessin and Harari, we can see how Jaffa's café played an important role in the development of Jewish theater in Palestine of this period. They also stressed that these cafés were "redeemed" by the eastern European Jewish migrants, who assumed that they brought new cultural forms to "backward" Palestine.

It did not take much time for the eastern European Jewish migrants to establish their own café in Jaffa. Ze'ev Smilansky, who migrated from the Russian Empire to Palestine in 1903, conducted in 1905 a census of the Jewish community in Jaffa and wrote a detailed report with his findings. He highlighted the changes taking place due to the recent migration, which increased the number of hotels, inns, restaurants, and cafés in Jaffa. According to Smilansky, "the first Hebrew café was established at the end of the summer of 1905." Until then, there was "not even one coffeehouse belonging to Hebrews, while the number of cafés that belong to non-Jews rose to eighty." According to Smilansky, this café, owned by two Ashkenazi Jews from the Lifshitz family, was designed and arranged in "a European style and taste." This was done with the intention, said Smilansky, that "our fastidious brothers will feel comfortable going there."[20] Smilansky makes it clear that the owners made a conscious effort to give the café a European rather than Arab look and style. He wrote that many Jews doubted whether the café would be successful, because they thought that non-Jewish residents, especially Arabs, would not visit the café. In fact, Smilansky tells us, the business did quite well; about three-fourths of the income came from non-Jews, and the café often became a gathering place for people to meet and talk, especially at night. This new Jewish or "Hebrew" café in Jaffa was named after its owner, Lifshitz, but later it was called Café Levanon. Yehudit Harari remembered Café Levanon as a primitive and not particularly attractive place, with people drinking tea and eating cakes with dirt and flies around them.[21] Thus, it is quite possible that the transformation from Arab cafés to European cafés was not as decisive and complete as the Jewish immigrants wanted to imagine.

Agnon, the writer who, as we have seen, migrated to Jaffa in 1908, visited Café Levanon, as well as Arab and German cafés in Jaffa. In his masterpiece novel *Tmol shilshom* (*Only Yesterday*, 1945), the main protagonist, Yitzḥak Kumer, a dreamy-eyed youth impelled by Zionist rhetoric and ideology, comes to Palestine in the first decade of the twentieth century. Kumer dreams of working the land but winds up instead as a house painter. He is drifting between Jerusalem and Jaffa, where he discovers a number of cafés. One of the places he goes to is the fictional Café Hermon, modeled after Café Levanon:

> Café Hermon stands at the edge of Neve Shalom, near Bustros Street. You enter a hall where during the day in the doorway a pitch-black man sits bent over a green lattice table with large and small bills and coins, like those moneychangers who sit in the doorways of houses in the streets and count coins. Since we haven't got two pennies to rub to together, we will leave him and dwell on the café, where at night the café owner stands, his face red like a honey-cake and his beard flaming like a pomegranate bud, and his multicolored eyes stare at everyone who comes in or goes out.[22]

It is worth noting that Agnon insists on writing "café" in Hebrew as *beit ha-kahava* and not the more common *beit kafe* (common since the turn of the twentieth century), thus preserving the Arabic name *qahwa* and the origin of the institution of the coffeehouse. This is important because Agnon's narrator makes the same point that was implicit in Smilansky's account, namely, that "Café Hermon isn't like Arab cafés with their nargilas and gramophones and parrots." Agnon thus points to the fact that the eastern European Jewish migrants wanted a European café, different from the Arab places in Jaffa, without being aware that the café came to Europe from the Arab world in the first place. The irony is revealed later in the novel when Kumer and his friend Sonya go to Café Hermon and get weak coffee with milk. "If you want to taste real coffee," says Sonya, "go to the Arabs." The gap between Café Hermon and cafés in large European cities is also revealed when the narrator notes that the humble Café Hermon is very different from cafés that Kumer saw in European cities: "*nor* is it like the café in Lemberg with silver dishes and china dishes, and waiters stand like lords serving the guests." Still, from Kumer's point of view, in spite of its bad coffee and humble appearance, in Café Hermon, one finds a "higher virtue" because there one can see Jewish "writers, and teachers and clerks and activists."[23] Indeed, Café Levanon became a gathering place for the Jewish intelligentsia and a site for conducting business and politics in Jaffa. Chelouche even remembered the café as the place in which the very idea of establishing the neighborhood of Ahuzat Bayit, which soon became Tel Aviv, was born: in 1906, the idea of establishing a new settlement near Jaffa came up. . . . Weiss gathered around him a few friends and we gathered from time to time in Lifshitz's Café in Neve Shalom . . . for an entire year. We created various plans to build a magnificent neighborhood; the roads were marked, the sidewalks, beautiful buildings, etc."[24]

Apart from the eighty or so Arab cafés and the one European Jewish café, there was a new German café in early twentieth-century Jaffa. It was established in 1903 by Franz Lorenz in the German neighborhood Walhalla. It was one of the first buildings in the area to have electricity and was a place of mixture between Arabs, Germans, and Jews. In Agnon's *Tmol shilshom*, Yonatan Orgelbrand—a migrant from Russia and a clerk in the Anglo-Palestinian Company who "earns a good salary"— likes to visit Café Lorenz. Although Orgelbrand is described as a "comrade," a good friend of Kumer, he also becomes his erotic rival, as both of them are vying for Sonya's attention. "When Orgelbrand is in a generous mood, he invites Isaac to Lorenz Café, for Orgelbrand doesn't go into Café Hermon . . . but goes to Lorenz, where most of the customers are Germans . . . and even the Jews who come there want a break from business."[25] The Germans who operated Café Lorenz were quite resourceful. It was expanded in 1905, and in 1909, a spacious second floor was added where music was played, theater productions were staged, and films were screened. Thus, Café Lorenz became a place of modern European forms of entertainment and art and also a place of mixture among various languages spoken in Palestine: Arabic, German, Yiddish, and Hebrew.

Not surprisingly, this linguistic and ethnic mixture also caused tensions. This is evident in Agnon's novel and in the memoirs of such people as Eitan Belkind, one of the students who formed a "battalion" to defend Hebrew against other languages spoken in Palestine by locals and immigrants. He remembered an incident in Café Lorenz, where in 1914 a group of Jewish actors performed Goldfaden's historical plays, *Bar Kokhba* and *Shulamis*, in Yiddish. "We, the Hebrew Gymnasium students, were fanatics about the Hebrew language. We protested and threw stones into the hall in order to halt the play in Yiddish; with cries of 'only in Hebrew,' . . . we succeeded in dispersing the audience and caused the cancellation of the play."[26]

A few months after the incident that Belkind remembered, Ḥayim Zhitlovsky, the chief ideologist of Yiddishism and Jewish diaspora nationalism, traveled to Palestine from New York to give a number of lectures around the country. On July 4, 1914, one of Zhitlovsky's Yiddish lectures was planned in Café Lorenz. Apparently, the owners of other venues where lectures were given were afraid to host the Yiddish lecture, and Café Lorenz was chosen as a more "neutral" space between Jaffa and Tel Aviv, where several languages could live side by side. On the evening of the lecture, the main hall and the balconies of Café Lorenz were packed with advocates of Yiddish, eager to drink up every single word of Dr. Zhitlovsky. But here again, students from the Hebrew "battalion" along with their teacher from the Hebrew Herzliya Gymnasium, Ḥayim Bograshov, went to the house where Zhitlovsky was staying and tried to persuade him not to lecture in Yiddish. When they failed to do so, Bograshov tore his collar, a gesture associated with Jewish mourning, and the students waiting outside tore their shirts and shouted to Zhitlovsky, "Over our dead bodies."[27] There was some violence, and the Ottoman authorities had to intervene. The Yiddish lecture never took place, and Zhitlovsky left Tel Aviv and traveled back to New York City. However, this battle against Yiddish in Café Lorenz shows, more than anything else, how anxious were the Hebrew puritans in Jaffa / Tel Aviv about the mixture of languages and how cafés became multilingual spaces that defied attempts to achieve a monolingualism that some people believed was essential to a Hebrew national revival.

Amid this linguistic violence, Jaffa and the new small neighborhood of Tel Aviv were about to change drastically. In November 1914, the Ottoman Empire entered World War I on the side of the Central Powers. A month later, the Turks expelled the six thousand Russian Jews who resided in Jaffa. Many of them resettled in Alexandria, Egypt, or went to Europe or America. By January 1917, the British Army was about to attack the Ottomans in Palestine. Ahmed Jamal Pasha, the military governor of Ottoman Syria and Palestine, ordered the deportation of Tel Aviv's residents and many Jews in Jaffa. The cafés were empty. The writer and Zionist activist Moshe Smilansky wrote, "A deathly silence reigned throughout the streets. It seemed like a plague had stormed through the place."[28]

Bohemia and Bourgeoisie, Local and International in Small Tel Aviv's Cafés

In World War I, the British defeated the Ottoman Empire in the Levant. In November 1917, the British Empire issued the Balfour Declaration, with the promise of creating "a Jewish national home." A few years later, in 1921, Tel Aviv obtained from the British the status of "township," which implied a partial autonomy from Jaffa. This was seen as a great achievement for the Yishuv and the Zionist movement. Nevertheless, in 1921, Tel Aviv was still a small town, with a population of a few thousand residents, mostly new migrants from war-torn Europe, and still very much dependent on Jaffa. Then, in 1924 and 1925, sixty-five thousand migrants came to Palestine from economically troubled Poland. At least half of these migrants used to live in cities such as Warsaw and Łódź and might have made their way to New York City if the gates of American migration had not been closed to eastern European Jews in 1924. Instead, they settled in Tel Aviv. Soon, new streets and whole new neighborhoods grew, along with commercial, industrial, and cultural hubs that turned it into the urban center of the Yishuv in Mandatory Palestine.[29]

The 1920s and early 1930s also saw the birth of a nascent café culture in Tel Aviv, different from and independent of Jaffa's cafés. Most of these new cafés, owned by migrant Jews who came from Poland, Russia, and Hungary, operated in the courtyards or first floors of small residential buildings built in this period. Between 1921 and 1925, a number of such cafés were founded and were named after their owners: Café Izibitzky and the Hungarian Café on Nahalat Binyamin Street, Café Polak on Ahad Ha'am Street, Café Segal on Rothschild Boulevard, Café Gedansky and Café Shor on Herzl Street, and Café Bader on the corner of Hess and Allenby Streets.[30] Tziona Rabau-Katinsky, who grew up in Tel Aviv and was a student in the Herzliya Gymnasium, wrote in her memoirs about the Hungarian Café on Nahalat Binyamin Street, known also as Ha-gina (The garden): "There was a warm and intimate atmosphere in the café. Small tables stood in the different corners of the place, with chairs and small upholstered sofas." According to Rabau-Katinsky, the café was managed in "European style." The habitués were "young people with money in their pockets. People from the bourgeoisie, who were different from the workers and the pioneers. . . . In the Hungarian Café, real coffee was served in cups and milk in a special pitcher . . . and the cakes!"[31]

The "bourgeoisie" whom Rabau-Katinsky described sitting in the Hungarian Café was really a group of lower-middle-class migrants, who had little money to spare and a strong desire to replicate the cafés they knew and loved in Europe. But her sense of difference was still correct: the "workers" and "pioneers" did not go to these cafés. Thus, we can see the beginning of an attack on "decadent," urban Tel Aviv already in the mid-1920s, coming from the Socialist Zionists, which became the dominant political and ideological force in the Yishuv. The attack included the city's young cafés. Their growing popularity crystallized the fear, expressed in the press and in speeches, that Tel Aviv would became a second Odessa, Warsaw, or Łódź, or the "Jewish Ghetto" in New York, and would thus undermine the attempts to create a "New Hebrew Man," as part of a Zionist social reform of the Jewish nation that would be rooted in the land and engaged in agricultural labor and in cooperative settlement projects.

Those who were anxious about Tel Aviv's growth paid close attention to a specific café, which was very different from the humble cafés that sprouted in Tel Aviv's streets. This was a place initially called the Casino, which was not a place of gambling but a café, the first to be established on the beach of Tel Aviv, which was until then not utilized. The initiator of the café was Salomon Grigorivich Karzanovsky, who came to Palestine from Odessa in 1921. Inspired by beach cafés in the port city of Odessa (beach cafés were called "casinos" in European cities), Karzanovsky turned to David Izmojik, a family relative who was also a member of the town committee, with a request to build a new café on the beach in order to "foster the nightlife of Tel Aviv."[32] The Casino was planned by Yehuda Magidovitch, the first city engineer of Tel Aviv, who studied architecture in the School of Arts in Odessa. Since both Karzanovsky and Magidovitch were from Odessa, it was natural that they found inspiration for the new venture in the Ostrovsky Warsovian Café on Odessa's beach. The Casino was built with half the structure immersed in the waters of the Mediterranean Sea, which required special construction with reinforced concrete.[33]

When the Casino was completed and opened in May 1922, it was a large building with a bar and a hall, full of flourishes and ornaments, typical of the eclectic style in vogue in Tel Aviv at the time. When the café first opened, the owners complained that "families of sunflower-seed spitters with screaming children" sat there for hours without ordering anything and without paying. They claimed that "proper customers" could not find a free table and did not wish "to spend time in the same place with guests who only wanted a free place to sit."[34] In order to change that, the owners imposed a minimum charge for patrons, and later, they even demanded that the men who attended its weekend and afternoon dances wear jackets and the women dresses. The owners declared that the Casino could "compete with the most splendid drinking and eating establishments in European capitals."[35] As evident from the photographs (figs. 6.4 and 6.5), the décor of the Casino—both inside and outside—was unabashedly luxurious.

The writer Aharon Reuveni, who migrated to Palestine in the 1910s, wrote about the Casino in the story "She-a'hava nafshi" (Whom my soul loves, 1924). The story's protagonist is Nelly, a young woman who leaves her Hungarian family and comes alone to Tel Aviv. Everything is alien to her in Tel Aviv, and she doubts her decision to come. She goes out with a young man, Dushkin, a merchant's son, who invites her to a dance party in the Casino. The dances remind her of her days in London and bring a rush of memories and erotic longing: "The players found their places on the stage and started playing the waltz. Nelly and Dushkin danced, rested, and danced again until midnight. The face of the girl became hot,

Figure 6.4. Avraham Soskin, photograph of the interior of Café Casino Galei Aviv (Courtesy of Eretz Israel Museum, Soskin Collection)

Kasino „Galei-Aviv"   Casino „Galei-Aviv"   קזינו „גלי-אביב".

Figure 6.5. Photograph of Café Casino Galei Aviv, *Tel Aviv and Its Environments*, booklet, 1923 (Courtesy of the National Library of Israel)

her eyes shone. . . . Her soul was floating in the stream of the glances that enveloped her. The stream embraced her . . . and took her far away."[36] Later, Nelly discovers that Dushkin is engaged to another woman, and she meets Regalsky, the violin player at the Casino, with whom she has an affair. The Casino in Reuveni's story was experienced as a European island in the midst of Tel Aviv, one that elicits memories and longing.

The Casino also plays an important role in the story "Ha-bayta" (Going home) by Binyamin Tammuz, who migrated to Tel Aviv with his family in the 1920s. The protagonist of "Ha-bayta" is Ya'akov, a young man who comes back to Tel Aviv after living and working for a number of years at an agricultural colony in the Galilee. Penniless and dressed in simple worker clothes, Ya'akov cannot go into the Casino, but he can hear from outside the music and the dancing. He sees "the merchants of Tel Aviv" who come to the Casino with their wives or lovers and "the Arab merchants of Jaffa who come on their own." When the orchestra begins to play, "the Arab men would invite the Jewish women to dance waltz and tango." Ya'akov understands that both the merchants and the women come for this purpose, to advance their business. He knows that his own father used to do this when he tried to be a successful merchant, one who does business with "the east."[37] Tammuz's story shows us that around the Casino, the dichotomies of traditional and modern, Arabs and Jews, bourgeoisie and workers begin to break down. Indeed, as Tammuz describes, the Casino attracted not just Jews from Tel Aviv who longed for European style music, dance, food, and drinks but also Arabs from nearby Jaffa. In July 1922, the newspaper *Falastin* reported that Arabs from Jaffa visit the Casino and spend large amounts on drinks. The paper announced that the Jaffa municipality decided to build a large "casino" on Jaffa's beach so that Arabs would not go to the one in Tel Aviv.[38] This plan never materialized, but it makes it evident that Tel Aviv and its new cafés were attractive to some middle-class Arabs. The plan also shows the competition that began to erupt between Jaffa and Tel Aviv.

Although the Casino never became a "literary café," it attracted some well-known poets and intellectuals such as Ahad Ha'am and Bialik, who came to Tel Aviv in the mid-1920s, after spending much of their lives in Odessa, Berlin, and London. This is curious because, as mentioned in chapter 1, these "Sages of Odessa" were not enthusiastic about café culture in the port city by the Black Sea. However, when they arrived in Tel Aviv, they liked to visit the Casino that reminded them of Odessa and of Europe in general. The painter Ḥayim Gliksberg remembered a meeting with Bialik. "We entered the Casino. The hall was full of light and sun, and in its space was a smell of fresh paint mixed with the scent of the sea." When Bialik entered, he said, "You know, I love this place. Here you feel as if you sit in the ship at the heart of the sea." Gliksberg attested that around Bialik sat Arab businessmen and Jewish functionaries, like the one described in Tammuz's story. Although more Middle Eastern than most cafés in Odessa, the Casino nevertheless caused Bialik to remember and tell anecdotes from his childhood and his life in Odessa.[39]

As Tel Aviv fell into economic recession in 1926 due to rapid population growth and the cessation of Jewish capital entering Palestine, the Casino also fell into trouble. It did not help that the Casino was operating only between April and October and that new cafés were built in the

beach area. In 1927, the Casino was sold to a new owner, Naḥum Greenblat, who tried to make it profitable by adding plays and cabarets. The
new ownership and features brought new tensions of the kind we have
already encountered in Café Lorenz in Jaffa, namely, the issue of "foreign
languages" in the "first Hebrew city." What began as a small group of
high-school students grew into an activist movement that called itself
"The Battalion for the Defense of the Hebrew Language." On July 5, 1928,
Ya'akov Strod wrote a letter to the municipality of Tel Aviv on behalf of
the Battalion, making it aware that the Casino staged a performance in
German. "We see this," he wrote, "as a strong insult, not just to us, the
young and zealous, but also to each citizen of Tel Aviv, the first Hebrew
city."[40] The Battalion registered its protest not just to the owner of the
Casino but also to the authorities that allowed such performance to take
place. A few days later, Israel Rokach answered the letter on behalf of
Mayor Meir Dizengoff, announcing that the Tel Aviv municipality would
forbid the Casino to stage any performances or plays in any language
other than Hebrew. Dizengoff himself wrote to Greenblat in order to
enforce the monolingual policy of "only Hebrew," and Greenblat quickly
responded that the German performance was an oversight that would
never happen again. This incident shows how militant the Battalion had
become and how seriously it was taken by the authorities. At the same
time, the incident shows how the Casino continued to be a multilingual
space in the "Hebrew city" of Tel Aviv, which was, in fact, a city of mostly
migrants with many languages.

The Casino had become a landmark of Tel Aviv, beloved by some
people, hated by others. But in 1934, the city's engineer recommended
destroying the Casino because the salt water was causing dangerous deterioration. The deterioration of the Casino was delayed by renovation,
but the delay did not last long. In the final years before the eventual closing of the café and the destruction of the building in 1939, the Casino
looked dilapidated. The poet Nathan Alterman wrote a whimsical, loving feuilleton dedicated to the Casino in 1938. Alterman recognized that
the Casino was a place "whose form was entirely jest and whose fate was
entirely sorrow," but he also declared that it was "Tel Aviv's first poet, the
city's first original 'character,' a friend and counterpart of the town fool":
"the history of this city, its nights and its songs."[41]

By the time Alterman wrote his elegiac feuilleton, Tel Aviv was a much larger and more diverse city than it was when the Casino had opened. It also became the undisputed cultural center of the Yishuv. Alterman, who migrated to Tel Aviv from Warsaw and studied in Paris, was part of a large group of modernist Jewish writers and poets who came to Tel Aviv in the 1920s and 1930s from Europe and turned it into a city of newspapers, magazines, publishing houses, rival poetic groups, and "bohemian" cafés that fostered all this cultural activity. This process already had begun in the mid-1920s, when Tel Aviv's cafés were for the most part, unlike the Casino, simple and inexpensive. A journalist wrote that "shorts and pioneer [i.e., Russian] shirts were almost the uniform dress of café patrons, poetry was to tea as butter to bread."[42] This was true also of Café Bader, on the corner of Allenby and Hess Streets, where the poets and writers who were close to Bialik used to gather. The writer and educator Shlomo Tzemah remembered meeting in the café every Friday with the group of Bialik, Yosef Aharonovitz, Yitzhak Lufban, and Yitzhak Karni, as well as playing chess in the café with Ya'akov Shteinberg, a habitué of cafés in Warsaw and in Berlin.[43]

If Café Bader was known as the place of the "old guard," associated with Bialik and his followers, other cafés became bastions of young, modernist writers. The aforementioned Hungarian Café on Nahalat Binyamin Street was where Avigdor (Foyershtein) Hameiri and Arthur Koestler—who were born in Budapest and spent much time in Vienna and Berlin cafés—congregated. Koestler remembered that in 1926, he and Hameiri, who had already established his reputation for writing fiery modernist Hebrew poetry and fiction, felt that Tel Aviv was "a provincial and humorless place with no feeling for true genius." Both of them met daily in the Hungarian Café, which was, according to Koestler, "the main haunt of Tel Aviv bohemia," with the painters Reuven Rubin and Mane Katz and the poet Uri Zvi Greenberg, who migrated to Tel Aviv after spending much time in the Romanisches Café in Berlin.[44] In the Hungarian Café, Hameiri and Koestler came up with the idea to found a "politico-literary cabaret" with the name *Ha-kumkum* (The tea kettle), a name that came from the Yiddish expression *hakn a tshaynik* (to hit, strike, or hack at a tea kettle, meaning also to bother someone). The satirical cabaret preformed in 1927 and 1928, with most of its texts written by Avigdor

Hameiri, but it did not last for a long time because of differences between Hameiri and the actors. Soon after, a new cabaret, *Ha-matate* (The broom), which was modeled after *Ha-kumkum*, was established. This time, however, the main writer was Avraham Shlonsky, another young and fiery modernist Hebrew poet.

Although Shlonsky spent a few months of hard manual work in the Jezreel Valley when he migrated to Palestine in 1922, soon thereafter he moved to Tel Aviv, which, except for a year spent in Paris, became his hometown for the rest of his life. At that point, Shlonsky, a prolific poet, editor, translator, and writer, was at the heart of the new culture in Tel Aviv and became a habitué of a new café. Café Sheleg Levanon (Hebrew for "the snow of Lebanon"), on 15 Allenby Street (fig. 6.6), was noted for its cheap prices and popular menu and became a home of sorts for many young migrants—writers, artists, actors, and people from all walks of life who frequented it. Shlonsky remembered that people drank more tea than coffee in the café, because "the price of coffee was a whole *grush* (10 mills) and the price of tea was 3 or 5 mills at the most."[45] The habitués of this café frequented it mostly at night, when they used to sing Russian

Figure 6.6. S. Korbman, photograph of Café Sheleg Levanon, 1929 (By special permission of the Administrator General, The State of Israel, as the Executor of S. Korbman Estate & Eretz Israel Museum, Tel Aviv)

songs mixed with Hasidic tunes. Relations between the three owners, the waiters, and customers were warm and friendly, and people could sit in the café as long as they liked. Anyone who lacked money was allowed to drink tea on credit. "For hundreds of people, it was a space to rest, read the newspaper, conduct private and public conversations, do business, delve into literary questions, drink a decent glass of tea, eat, chat, and play chess."[46]

Sheleg Levanon became known as *the* bohemian café in Tel Aviv of the late 1920s. Uri Keisari—who was born to immigrant parents in Jaffa as Shmuel Kaiserman and studied in Paris between 1924 and 1926—was one of the young journalists who wrote for the nascent Hebrew press in Tel Aviv and was one of the café habitués. He claimed that Sheleg Levanon was adopted by the bohemians because it was close to the seashore.[47] The owners of the café wanted to capitalize on the fact that Tel Aviv's budding "bohemia" adopted the place as their own, and they advertised it as "the café of the artists, where singers and poets, painters, directors, and musicians all of kind meet."[48] The bohemian reputation was bolstered by the patronage of *Ha-matate* cabaret, by the new Ohel theater, and by writers, journalists, and others who spent their evenings in the café. In 1931, when Tel Aviv's municipality sought to enforce a midnight closing time for all cafés, a petition with no less than 411 signatures, including those of writers, poets, actors, and artists, asked that the closing order be rescinded for Sheleg Levanon. "Most of the habitués," the petition stated, "are people engaged in the arts, [who] work at various artistic institutions, theaters, and concert houses." They declared, "We meet in the café for a conversation and to socialize, not to consume alcoholic drinks. Among us there isn't anyone who could disturb the rest in any way. We ask to take into account the fact that we are busy during the day in various jobs, and for us, the night hours are the one time of pleasure, without which we cannot socialize or tend to our artistic affairs."[49]

The petition, with the idea that writers and artists do a different kind of "work" from pioneers and laborers, was convincing to the authorities. Sheleg Levanon, together with other cafés, was exempt from the closing-time provision and remained open and lively up to the small hours of the morning. The debate about work in Tel Aviv became the center of a caricature that showed the habitués sitting in the café all night until the street cleaners began their work early in the morning (fig. 6.7). The worker tells the bohemians that, as on Passover night, they have "fulfilled their duty" of sitting in the café, and it is time for them to go to another one.

Sheleg Levanon was also a place where poetic and artistic battles were fought. The artist Miron Sima, who migrated to Palestine from Germany, remembered that the café was full of painters. One of them, the modernist Yosef Zaritsky, asked Sima, "Have you come from Germany?" When Sima gave his positive answer, Zaritsky proclaimed, "The Germans have no art." "I told him," wrote Sima, "that there was much important art in Germany: the Bauhaus. Kokoschka, Paul Klee, Otto Dix. . . . I felt very alien. I saw that an abyss separated their artistic sensibility and our own less glamorous trend."[50] In the arena of literature, a different artistic battle took place in the cafés during the 1920s and 1930s. Shlonsky was cementing his status as the most important modernist Hebrew writer in Tel Aviv. He joined forces with Eliezer Steinman, who, we should recall, was a habitué of cafés in Warsaw and Odessa before his migration to Palestine in 1924. Shlonsky and Steinman edited an important Hebrew literary journal, *Ktuvim*, which was, since 1927, at the vanguard of fighting

Figure 6.7. Iza Hershkovitz, caricature of Café Sheleg Levanon, *Ha-hayim Ha-lalu*, April 1936

against the "old guard" of Hebrew literature, embodied in Bialik and his followers. The writer Ya'akov Horovitz, the critics Yiṯḥak Norman and Israel Zmora, and the poets Alexander Penn, Avraham Ḥalfi, and Nathan Alterman published in *Ktuvim*. They formed a poetic group called Yaḥdav (Together) and a new literary club, Amoda'im (the Hebrew word for "divers"). Their center was, for some time, in Sheleg Levanon, but then in 1932, they left the café and moved to another. According to Uri Keisari, poets and writers abandoned Sheleg Levanon because it was invaded by the "pseudo-bohemia," namely, by people who just wanted to meet for a drink and chat rather than engage in literary-cultural work.[51]

The new café that Shlonsky and his modernist group chose was at 37 Allenby Street, just a few blocks from Sheleg Levanon. Zvi Retzki and his wife opened it at the end of 1930, and initially it did not attract much attention. In an advertisement in the literary magazine *Turim* (fig. 6.8),

Figure 6.8. Advertisement for Café Retzki, *Turim*, May 1933

the owners promoted Café Retzki with a series of rhetorical questions: "Where is the place for artists to meet? Where are writers' groups being established? Where does one hear the verdict on theater productions? Where can one hear a review of a concert?" The answer to all these questions was the same: "In Café Retzki." The advertising, coupled with Retzki's attempts to accommodate writers and artists and make "bohemia" the allure of his business, seemed to have worked. Initially, the café was frequented by Bialik, who lived a few minutes away, and friends from his generation. By 1932, Shlonsky and the others who had abandoned Sheleg Levanon made Café Retzki their new home and dominated it.

The writer Ya'akov Ḥorgin remembered that Café Retzki became the headquarters of the group: "here over a cup of tea that cost 5 mills, they sat for hours and plotted the literary war, . . . [to] smash the gods and idols of contemporary Hebrew poetry. And the war was carried in the blaze of youth, with the pretension of last adjudicators, with much chutzpah."[52] Israel Zmora, one of the members of the Yaḥdav group who migrated to Tel Aviv in 1925 from Odessa and St. Petersburg, remembered that he and his friends spent many days and nights in Café Retzki. The poet Yehiel Perlmutter, better known by his pen name, Avot Yeshurun, grew up in Krasnystaw, a small town in eastern Poland. He migrated to Palestine in 1925 and began to write Hebrew poems. In 1934, Perlmutter came to Café Retzki because the "Yaḥdav group was there daily." Perlmutter approached Shlonsky in the café and asked him to read a poem he had written. Shlonsky read the poem and asked the unfamiliar poet if he had more. Perlmutter produced a collection of poems that were soon published in *Turim*, edited by Shlonsky.[53] This was Perlmutter's debut as a poet, one that was enabled by a meeting in Café Retzki. The café was also frequented by many actors from the Ohel and Ha-bima theaters. "It goes without saying," wrote Zmora, "that the café attracted numerous curious people, mostly young."[54] If this is true, it seems that, as in other cities and cafés, Café Retzki thrived on the curiosity of the young people who had turned Shlonsky and his group into cultural heroes.

While it seems that places such as Retzki were unique to Tel Aviv and to the Hebrew culture fostered there, many who visited there compared it to cafés in other cities around the world where Jewish culture thrived. Shlonsky himself wrote, in a 1933 article titled "Migrants in Their Homeland," about a Tel Aviv café that was a fictional version of Retzki, the place of gathering of "Hebrew artists" that reminded him of "Café La Coupole in Paris, and the Romanisches Café in the Berlin of yesteryear." He has a conversation with a certain "Hebrew actor," and he asks him whether he would subscribe to the literary weekly magazine *Turim*, but the answer is no. Instead, writes Shlonsky, "I saw in his hand the latest issue of *Poslednie Novosti*," the Russian émigré magazine published in Paris.[55] The concern about lack of enthusiasm for Hebrew literature that Shlonsky pointed to was real. Cafés were, on the one hand, bastions of a Tel Avivian Hebrew literature and culture, and on the other hand, they were similar to cafés in Europe and America where multilingual culture was created.

This lingual abundance is evident in the guest book of Café Retzki from the years 1932–1935, in which many people wrote their impressions in Hebrew (sometimes broken Hebrew), Yiddish, Russian, English, German, and Polish. Abraham Teitelbaum, a Yiddish actor who was active in Europe and in Maurice Schwartz's Art Theater in New York, wrote in the guest book in Yiddish: "Really, what would Eretz Yisroel be without Café Retzki, exactly like New York without Café Royal. So it's good this way."[56] The Polish Jewish journalist Moyshe Leyzerovich wrote, "We will continue Tłomackie 13 here, without Warsaw."[57] He was referring, of course, to the famous Warsaw café, in the building of the Association of Jewish Writers and Journalists. Yitzḥak Liponer from Warsaw wrote, "If I didn't know that I was in Tel Aviv, I would think that I was in sitting in Ziemiańska in Warsaw."[58] The Polish Yiddish writer Leyb Malakh wrote that "Café Retzki is the only place in which you forget that you are in . . . Asia."[59] For all these Jewish writers from Europe, the similarities and the connections between Romanisches, Café Royal, Tłomackie 13, Ziemiańska, and Café Retzki were obvious. For them, these cafés were all points on the silk road of modern Jewish culture; now Tel Aviv, the small but fast-growing city in the Middle East, was becoming a major stopping point along this road.

The similarities between Café Retzki and cafés in Europe and America became clear in another short text, written in the guest book of Café Retzki by the Yiddish journalist Aaron L. Riklis, visiting from Warsaw, who used the pen name Lyrik. He wrote that only when he came to Café Retzki did he begin "to believe in the future of Tel Aviv." Why? "Without cafés and without idlers," he wrote, "there is no urban culture."[60]

He argues that, by the 1930s, Jews who were skeptical of the ability of Tel Aviv, and of the Yishuv, to become not only a center of Zionist culture but also a major hub of Jewish culture had to reevaluate. The cafés were part of the realization of that promise. His statement is also a defense against the Labor-Zionist critique of Tel Aviv as a nonproductive place of "idlers." This term actually has roots in the Babylonian Talmud, *Megilla* 5a, where a city is defined as a place "in which there are ten idlers" who could, at any time, be available to create the quorum necessary for public prayer. Lyrik suggests that in the context of modern Jewish urban culture, you need these "idlers" just the same—writers or artists who can engage in cultural work. Instead of the synagogue, now the place of such "idlers" is the café.

Both the doubts about "small Tel Aviv" and the confidence in its bright future were tied to its cafés. This can be seen in a feuilleton, "Hollywood and the City," written by the poet Nathan Alterman in 1932, shortly after he returned from France. Alterman writes about how young and small Tel Aviv is: "fifty thousand souls, twenty years of existence, a few small industrial plants, . . . a day-old museum and beach and a port yet unborn. . . . A pedigree such as this would hardly grant any other city more than a mere dot in the garden of a map." Alterman enumerates the alleged "provincial" elements of Tel Aviv, evident in comparison to European metropolises. "True," Alterman admits, "Tel Aviv is small. In Tel Aviv all the artists and literati sit at Café Retzki and in Café Sheleg Levanon." However, claims Alterman, the fact that Tel Aviv is small, with a choice of just two major cafés, does not mean that it is provincial. Tel Aviv in 1932, according Alterman, is already a center, both for the Yishuv and for Jews elsewhere, who follow with much interest the culture created in Palestine. The writers, theaters, museums, and cafés of Tel Aviv are at the center of attention, he claims; everything new that is created in the center makes its way to the rest of the Yishuv and to the world at large. For this reason, concludes Alterman, "The city must grow. It cannot afford not to!"[61]

Builders, Speculators, and Migrants

Alterman's words had a prophetic ring to them, but it is doubtful that he knew how quickly his forecast would become a reality. In 1933, as

Hitler rose to power in Germany and as uncertainty grew across Europe, the largest wave of migration to Palestine began. Many of the migrants, especially those who came from central Europe's urban centers— especially Berlin, Vienna, and Prague—chose Tel Aviv as their new home. The city's population exploded, from approximately 46,000 in 1931 to 150,000 in 1936. The migrants were mostly educated and middle class. The city expanded to the north and to the west, partly follow- ing the plan that Patrick Geddes, the famous Scottish urban planner, devised. The years 1933 to 1936 saw Tel Aviv's biggest building boom yet; but the rate of building could hardly keep apace, and there was a housing shortage and a sharp rise in real-estate prices. The very nature of build- ing and Tel Aviv's urban space changed dramatically as well.

In 1933, three new migrants met in one of Tel Aviv cafés: Aryeh Sha- ron, who had just completed his studies at the famous Bauhaus School of Design, Architecture, and Applied Arts in Dessau, Germany; Yosef Neufeld, who before his migration worked with Erich Mendelsohn, the preeminent German Jewish modernist architect; and Zeev Rechter, who studied in France and was greatly influenced by the Swiss-French ar- chitect Le Corbusier. During this meeting in the café, these architects saw the opportunity in the building shortage and decided to introduce the International Style and to put its principles into practice in Tel Aviv. Unlike the earlier trend—epitomized in the Casino—of buildings in the "eclectic style," combining Oriental and European elements with orna- ments and flourishes, the new building was functional, fast to build, with clean lines and modern materials.[62] Many of these new buildings, both residential and commercial, were built in what became, in the late 1930s and 1940s, the new center of Tel Aviv, namely, Dizengoff and Ben- Yehuda Streets, north of the old center around Allenby and Herzl.

In this new center, dozens of new cafés were established. In 1934, David-Werner Senator from the Jewish Agency sent a letter to the Zi- onist leader Hayim Weitzman, in which he spoke about "a deluge of cafés" in Tel Aviv, most owned and operated by migrants from German- speaking countries.[63] Many, such as Café Sapphire, Café Atara, and Her- linger, were located in the first floor of International Style buildings and spilled outside onto the wide sidewalks, built to accommodate many tables and chairs. In 1936, the British traveler and writer John Gibbons wrote that Tel Aviv had "scores and scores of [cafés] for every sort of purse; and the cafés have open-air chairs and tables on the broad sidewalk."[64] Even some cafés that were established in the 1920s in the heart of "old Tel Aviv" changed owners as well as looks. A good example is Café Shor, on the corner of Herzl and Lilienblum Streets. Two brothers from the Shor family had established a simple and small café here in the mid-1920s. In 1934, two Jewish migrants from Germany—Karl Lewinstein and Edmund Hollander—who did not know much Hebrew and were looking for a way to make a living and to maintain social contact with their German Jewish community, decided to purchase Café Shor. They renovated the place, expanded it, opened it to the street, and gave it a more modernist, streamlined look. It is unclear how many German Jews became habitués of the café, but it is evident that it was thriving. In fact, it became the preeminent café for businessmen, especially for speculators who took advantage of Tel Aviv's hot real-estate market and attendant building boom.

In a 1935 article, published in *Davar*, a reporter wrote about "the principality of the speculators" that made its home in Café Shor. He

Figure 6.9. Aryeh Navon, caricature of Café Shor,
Davar, January 28, 1935

wondered what the "Zionist visionary Herzl and the Zionist realist Lil-ienblum" would think of what became of the café on the corner of the streets that are named after them. Would they be able to imagine that in this place, in the "first Hebrew city," speculation and real-estate dealing would become the norm? And who were these speculators? According to the reporter, the habitués of Café Shor were "migrants from Nalewki St. in Warsaw, Levantines, and intellectuals who realized that everything they believed in during their youth was worth nothing, the children of old *moshavot* who became rich, and people from the old guard of Jew-ish Jaffa whose mother tongue is Arabic."[65] The Socialist Zionist paper saw in the existence of this café and the activity that took place there an aberration, a deviation from the dream of the "New Hebrew Man" and the social revolution that the Zionist project was supposed to usher in.

The debates about Café Shor are also evident in literary depictions of the establishment; the most prominent was written by Y. D. Berkovitz. Berkovitz, the son-in-law of the great Sholem Aleichem, who had been active as a writer and translator since the early twentieth century, both in Europe and in New York. In 1928, Berkovitz migrated to Tel Aviv and be-came active in its literary and cultural life. He decided to bring the char-acter of Menakhem-Mendl back to life. Of course, Sholem Aleichem had died in New York in 1916, but Berkovitz felt that Menakhem-Mendl should continue his adventures and should write letters to his wife, Sheyne-Sheyndl, from Palestine. These letters were published in install-ments in 1934 and 1935, almost simultaneously in Yiddish and in He-brew. In the fifth letter, Menakhem-Mendl writes to his wife about his adventures in Tel Aviv: "May you know, my dear wife, that with the help of God I have already become a speculator like all the speculators in Tel Aviv, that is—I have already been honored to sit with the whole group of speculators in the hustle and bustle of the city, in the jolly café buzzing with people, whose doors and windows are open to two streets, Herzl Street and Lilienblum Street."[66]

For readers of Sholem Aleichem, Berkovitz's Menakhem-Mendl in Tel Aviv made much sense. If in Odessa, Menakhem-Mendl frequented Café Fanconi with the brokers, and in Warsaw, he sat in Kotik's Café with the journalists, in Tel Aviv, he would no doubt be attracted to Café Shor, with its speculators and businessmen. In this way, Berkovitz cap-tured the comic mastery of Sholem Aleichem, whose object of satire was always far-reaching. As in Sholem Aleichem's text, Berkovitz pokes fun at the naïve, traditional *shtetl* Jew and his schemes and plans to get rich soon after arriving in Tel Aviv. However, when Berkovitz located Menakhem-Mendl sitting in Café Shor, he also exposed the conceit of the Zionist project and the idea of Tel Aviv as the "first Hebrew city," supposedly an unprecedented phenomenon in Jewish history. The speculators of Café Shor might say that they engage in a pioneering Zionist activity, but in fact, they are "buying and selling lots and houses." In Tel Aviv, "just like in the whole world," observes Menakhem-Mendl, "a person doesn't lift a finger except for himself, does what he does only for the needs of his body and the good of his wife and children, and nevertheless, when we come to translate all that into the *local* language, we find that all of us, from the big to the small, among rich and poor, are helping to build the Land of Israel here."[67]

The fact that Café Shor is on the corner of Herzl and Lilienblum Streets does not escape Menakhem-Mendl's attention. Of course, he had heard of Herzl, but who was Lilienblum? "I thought that he was probably one of the big speculators in Tel Aviv, who helped build that street, and therefore the street was named after him, but when I asked my partner, . . . he burst out laughing: Lilienblum, he says, wasn't a speculator, but a great Hebrew writer and a devoted Zionist, one of the real Zionists who were in those days."[68] Berkovitz's Menakhem-Mendl thus brings the question of the place of Zionist ideology in the life of the people who actually live and work in the city of Tel Aviv. He insists that Zionist ideology and Tel Aviv reality are quite different from each other. The habitués of Café Shor, the speculators of Tel Aviv, are Jewish migrants, just as in other cities in Europe and America. As in those cities, they find in Tel Aviv cafés a place to do business, as well as a space of sociability and comfort in which they are contributing, in their own way, to the building of the city and of modern Jewish culture.

If Café Shor in the old center of Tel Aviv was renowned as a place of speculators, many of the new cafés that were established in the north on Dizengoff and Ben Yehuda Streets—or Ben Yehuda-Strasse as it was called by many people—became known as bastions of German Jewish culture. On January 12, 1934, Leopold von Mildenstein, a journalist who used the pen name Von Lim, wrote a very unusual article about Tel Aviv in German. The article was published in *Der angriff* (The attack), the

Nazi newspaper that Joseph Goebbels established in Berlin. The name of the article was "Die Stadt ohne Gojim" (The city without gentiles), a clear allusion to Hugo Bettauer's novel about Vienna as a "city without Jews." In the article, Mildenstein actually praised Tel Aviv as a city that is "a hundred percent Jewish," presumably in line with both Zionist ideology and the Nazi aim of driving Jews out of Europe. He noted that Tel Aviv could have been a success story but became a failure because of the Jews' love of financial speculation. Mildenstein paid much attention in his article to the Jews who emigrated from Berlin and other German cities. Trying to depict Tel Aviv from a German vantage point, he deemed the food to be tasteless and the city to be devoid of any amusement. The only exception he could find was a number of Tel Aviv cafés. "It is strange," he wrote, "but here one can encounter West Berlin again." While most of Tel Aviv is dominated by the workers, in these cafés, one can find intellectuals. "Their language of communication is not Hebrew but German. One can imagine he is in Kranzler or Romanisches Café rather than in Café Tarshish or Café Katte Dan."[69]

The point that the Nazi journalist made about Tel Aviv cafés was in fact a common one. Observers noted that new Tel Aviv cafés resembled cafés in Berlin, that they were advertised in German and other diasporic languages, and that the migrants continued to use these languages, rather than switch to Hebrew, as all migrants in Palestine were expected to do. These issues were very much in the center of attention not only in newspapers and works of literature but also in the activity of the municipality. In November 1934, the Tel Aviv municipality established a special committee that was in charge of "keeping the Hebrew character" of the city. The first activity of this committee was to create a list of Hebrew names for businesses in Tel Aviv. The list included many suggestions for Hebrew names for cafés and restaurants. Among the names suggested were Ariston, Ginati, Hinga, Tal-Yam, Kassit, Migdalor, Nogah, Kafe Kafu, Shevet Ahim, Sova, and Sasson.[70] The issue of Hebrew names was only part of the effort to "Hebraize" the cafés. Much more difficult was the enforcement of the monolingual regime of Hebrew on what was spoken by the habitués, the owners, and the servers of the cafés and written on the newspapers that were read there.

This issue can be seen in many caricatures published in the press. Good examples are the following two, published by A. Shlayn in the new magazine *Tesha ba-'erev* (Nine p.m.). One caricature (fig. 6.10) depicts a customer ordering in Hebrew, to the astonishment of the café habitués and the waiter. Another caricature (fig. 6.11) shows Tel Aviv café habitués reading newspapers in Russian, Polish, German, and English but none in Hebrew. The caption of this caricature is, "Hebrew, speak Hebrew!"—a familiar sign in many cafés and other similar spaces that was created and distributed by the Battalion of the Defenders of the Hebrew Language in Palestine.

In a study of language diversity in the Yishuv, Liora Halperin points out that cafés were spaces of contest over language practice. As in earlier years, in the 1930s and 1940s, Tel Aviv's cafés were occupied by habitués, guests, and servers who spoke different languages and had very different ideas about linguistic practices than those of the Hebrew activists and the official leadership of Tel Aviv and Palestine.[71] In July 1937, the municipality issued a proclamation: "Kol ha'ir ha-'ivrit le-toshavehah" (A message from the Hebrew City to its citizens). The writers of this text, which was signed by the new mayor of Tel Aviv, Israel Rokach, lamented the fact that the new migrants of the 1930s were taking longer than usual to "acclimate to the new environment" and to move from their diverse languages to Hebrew. As a result, "there are many holes in the wall of our Hebrew life. If these holes are not filled," they wrote, "everything

Figures 6.10 and 6.11. Adam Shlayn, caricatures of cafés in Tel Aviv, *Tesha ba-'erev*, 1938

that had been built could be ruined." Therefore, the municipality called on the city's citizens to fix the most visible problems, which included signs, posters, newspapers in cafés and similar businesses. They wrote that signs and advertisements written in many "foreign languages" make the city look like a "new Babel." They denounced the fact that cafés were flooded with newspapers in many languages, thus enabling both new and old migrants to continue their lifestyle before their migration, without needing to use Hebrew. They singled out especially those journals in German, the language of "our enemies." Finally, they asked owners of cafés, kiosks, and other businesses who do not know Hebrew to employ Hebrew-speaking servers.[72] The urgency and rhetoric of this official proclamation shows, of course, that the municipality was very anxious about language practices and quite limited in what it could do.

The issue of multilingualism was not limited to the "European" cafés in the center and north of Tel Aviv. There were also cafés in the south of Tel Aviv and on the border with Jaffa that raised tensions between Tel Aviv as a "Hebrew city" and the reality of Tel Aviv as a city of migrants. However, in the border area, the migrants were from Arab countries.[73] Although Tel Aviv separated itself from Jaffa in the 1920s, many Jews continued to live and work in Jaffa. Moreover, most of the older neighborhoods, Neve Tzedek, Neve Shalom, and Kerem Ha-temanim, were at that point populated largely by Jews from Arab countries who opposed being part of Tel Aviv and resisted it for some time. These neighborhoods and new ones that were established in the 1920s and 1930s— Florentin, Shapira, Ha-tikva, Neve Sha'anan—were in a border zone, south of Tel Aviv and north of Jaffa. The borderline was shifting and permeable. It did not fully separate between the Jews to its north and Arabs to its south but was an area of contact, crossing, and mixing.[74]

In the 1930s, cafés in the border zone continued to be prime areas of contact between Arabs and Jews from different locations. The poet and writer Haim Gouri (Gurfinkel), who was born in Tel Aviv in 1923, wrote in his semiautobiographical novel *Ha-sefer ha-meshug'a* (The crazy book) about both the attraction and the fear of Tel Aviv's Jews toward Jaffa and south Tel Aviv in the late 1930s:

> In the streets, the sun is setting. Streets of flies, of merchants, and shouts and shops, and stalls and cafés that bring out tables of *shesh-besh* [backgammon]

and stools. . . . Tiny cups of coffee, *nargilas*, chains of Amber. . . . I go
to the Jaffa of sticks and knives, of insane sermons from the mosque.
I go to Jaffa. . . . To Jaffa I'm going, the sea and turrets. . . . Don't go to
Jaffa! . . . Crazy! They'll butcher you there, don't you know? Crazy! . . . All
the shutters are closing. To Manshiyyeh I'm going.[75]

The cafés that Gouri described in border areas such as Manshiyyeh /
Neve Shalom were identified by most of Tel Aviv's European Jews with
"the East," thus blurring the distinction between "Jews of the East" and
the Arabs of Jaffa. Some of these cafés advertised their services, which
included drinks, food, and live music, in Jaffa's Arabic-language newspapers. These "Oriental cafés" were also the subject of complaints by
Ashkenazi neighbors who found their sounds, noises, and smells of-
fensive and disturbing. These European migrant Jews expressed their
infuriation with these cafés in letters to the municipality, in which they
complained about the habitués who "spend their days playing backgam-
mon, cards and other games, both legal and illicit. . . . The official language is Arabic. . . . The place attracts immoral traffic."[76] The language
used in these letters assumes that the Arabic language used by the Jews
and Arabs who frequented these cafés is inherently related to what they
saw as "low morals" and "noise."

Shabazi Street, running from Neve Tzedek through Neve Shalom
and Manshiyyeh, had numerous cafés, meeting grounds for these residents, who tended to move between the Jewish and the Arab realms.
Café Baghdadi, owned by the Jewish Ezra Shlomo, was one of several
cafés on Shabazi Street inspected by the Mandatory police. One of the
British policemen wrote in a report that "without a doubt this place is
the main attraction of Shabazi Street. All hours of the day it is crowded
with very shady characters, who sit and gamble, playing all manner of
card games and dominoes." He added that "many women, undoubtedly
prostitutes, gather in this café, and hang about, passing from table to
table."[77] In the late 1930s and early 1940s, the aforementioned Café Lorenz, the first German café in Jaffa, was still operating, but it was now
owned by Hinawi, from a well-known Arab family in Jaffa, and was run
by F. Nusbaum, an eastern European Jew. Café Lorenz was no longer
at the center of Jewish Jaffa but part of a border zone that attracted a
mixed crowd of Jewish men and women, Arabs, and British officers and

officials. It was another example of a café that disturbed the image of Tel Aviv as a "Hebrew city" but one that reflected well the complex reality and perception in a city of migrants, a city that is between the East and the West, the Mediterranean Levant and Europe.

A Modern (Jewish) Woman in the Café

While cafés in south Tel Aviv and Jaffa were places of border crossing between Arabs, Jews, and British, between the "Oriental" and the "European," and between men and women, the writers and intellectuals who made their home in Tel Aviv cafés in the 1930s and the 1940s were overwhelmingly Jewish men. In 1935, Retzki Café was abandoned by the bohemian circles, apparently because the owner refused to extend credit to writers and artists. Shlonsky and the modernist Yaḥdav group moved to the new café that was established in April 1935 at 59 Ben-Yehuda Street by Lyuba Goldberg and Ilana Mordekhovitz. Luyba Goldberg left Kassit at the end of 1937 and opened Café Ararat at 9 Ben-Yehuda Street, and many of the writers, artists, and journalists followed her there. Thus, a few women were owners and operators of these cafés but were rarely their habitués.

One of the very few women who did make the café a home was the poet and writer Leah Goldberg, who migrated to Tel Aviv in 1935 after living and studying in Kovno, Bohn, and Berlin, where, as we have seen, she visited many cafés and wrote about them. Soon after she arrived in Tel Aviv, she sent a letter to her friend in Europe, declaring, "Tel Aviv is a very European city. It is noisy, always in the process of being built, something between Berlin's West End and the old city of Kovno. For people without a large social circle, it is probably very unpleasant to live here."[78] Part of what made the life of Goldberg in Tel Aviv more tolerable was the existence of cafés in which she could widen her social circle, but being a woman writer made Goldberg's presence in these cafés much more complex. On April 22, 1937, the magazine *Tesha ba-'erev* dedicated its entire weekly issue to the topic of "the modern woman in Palestine." Part of this issue was a questionnaire that the editors posed to a number of women, asking them, "Who and what is the modern woman in our Yishuv?" Among others, they spoke with Goldberg, whom they called "the youngest and most modest of our poets." They met her during "the twilight hour in Café Kassit, the dwelling place of the writers, artists, and inspiration." To the question posed to her, Goldberg answered with the following words:

> It is my opinion that there are two kinds of modern women in the Yishuv. The first one is the working woman, and her place is in the Kibbutz. . . . The second one is the woman whose modernity is conveyed by her way of dressing and her sitting in fancy urban cafés. The life of the working woman is difficult, especially when she is intellectually developed; then her private life is especially hard! The second one is, thank God, a fleeting, short-lived phenomenon whose origin is the bourgeois society and its antimodern attitude to women.[79]

Since Goldberg herself was sitting in Café Kassit on Ben Yehuda Street when she gave her answer to the magazine's editors, she belonged, apparently, to the second category. But then she added that this kind of woman is a "fleeting, short-lived phenomenon"—a response that was ironic, even sarcastic, but had something genuine and serious in it. Goldberg's social circle included some of the most important writers and poets in Tel Aviv of the 1930s and 1940s, and they described her presence in these cafés in various ways. For example, the painter and illustrator Aryeh Navon wrote,

> When I came back to Tel Aviv from Paris, I found out that a new café named Kassit opened and went there in the evening. Shlonsky approached me, greeted me, and invited me to join the group. Among them sat a young delicate woman, somewhat tense with her eyes gazing as if expecting something. Shlonsky introduced her: Leah Goldberg. She used to sit in the afternoon in Café Herlinger. . . . I used to see her from the street, through the large window of the café. She would be revealed poring over her notebook, thin, her back rounded like a bow. Shrouded in a fog of cigarettes, she looked like she was made entirely of spirit.[80]

The editor and critic Israel Zmora wrote, "In most cases, the habitués of the café were all men. Women writers were very few. . . . Leah Goldberg was the exception. She used to go to the café almost daily, but on her own, and only occasionally mix with all of us in our cafés."[81] These two

Figure 6.12. A photograph of Leah Goldberg and the poet Ya'acov Horowitz in a Tel Aviv café, 1935 (Courtesy of the Ganzim Institute, Tel Aviv, and Yair Landau)

Figure 6.13. A. Shlayn, caricature showing Leah Goldberg with poets and writers, *Tesha' ba-'erev*, February 2, 1939

men, Navon and Zmora, emphasized Goldberg's singularity as a modern woman in the café. They saw her as different and separated from the collective, whether she was trying to be part of it or trying to find "a café of her own."

Goldberg herself gave very different testimonies about café culture in Tel Aviv and about her participation and role in it. In a 1954 essay, she remembered herself as part of the modernist group of Yaḥdav. She wrote in a somewhat apologetic tone, "Every evening a horse carriage used to pass by the small café in which we were meeting. . . . Later many people said that these *batlanim* [idlers] were spending day and night in 'Kassit.' . . . Well, these '*batlanim*' actually met there after an exhausting day of work. . . . All of us used to 'steal some time' in order to write poems. . . . In the evening, instead of laying down to sleep, we were allowing ourselves to be *batlanim*, sit in the café, converse, and argue."[82]

In Goldberg's answer to the questionnaire, she spoke about the regrettable woman "whose modernity is conveyed by her way of dressing and her sitting in fancy urban cafés." Her defense of idleness calls to mind Lyrik's comment that "without cafés and without idlers, there is no urban culture." But of course, this version of being idle and productive is thoroughly gendered. Women were not expected to be productive in the same way as men, and certainly not to be productive by writing poems. Goldberg detested and defied this expectation. Thus, it is not surprising that Goldberg also felt a real ambivalence about the café. On the one hand, she was attracted to what can be called cultural aristocracy and to the bourgeois gentility in which she grew up in Europe. On the other hand, Goldberg saw herself as a proletarian poet, not so much in the political socialist sense but in her rejection of the prominent notion that writers only write for themselves (or for each other) and in what she saw as a shallow bohemianism.[83] Being a woman in this homosocial environment made her ambivalent attitude much more complex. In this context, it is essential to look at a very different piece that Goldberg wrote about Tel Aviv cafés, a short poem that she inscribed in the guest book of Café Retzki:

> I, who am late for any occasion
> I was also late for this occasion of "sitting together."
> Every song of praise has preceded my own

so what is the value of me or my tribute?
And as always, this time I wouldn't know if the beginning of a period
    or its ending
I (like A.S. in "the banquet") today sign: Goldberg Leah.[84]

In spite of the lighthearted tone of this poem, the motifs of belatedness
and marginality are important, even crucial. Goldberg adopts a position of being late, which is related to her general position of being both
an outsider and an insider. Goldberg feels marginal and belated in Tel
Aviv's cafés, despite the fact that in the 1930s, Hebrew culture and café
culture in Tel Aviv were on the rise, not in their twilight. This position
surely has to do with the fact that Goldberg was a woman in a group of
male writers and with the fact that she did not understand herself as a
"poetic pioneer" in Palestine, a position that most important male poets
of the time adopted. Goldberg's sense of belatedness and marginality also
meant that, unlike some of her male counterparts, she wrote frequently
about both physical and cultural migration as a crisis. In poems and
short stories composed by Goldberg in the late 1930s and early 1940s, she
emphasized the simultaneous similarity and unbridgeable gap between
Tel Aviv and Europe. The gap is especially salient in a cycle of poems with
the title "Arba'ah shirim mi-beit kafeh" (Four poems from a café).[85]

Much of the cycle takes place in a café close to the beach of Tel Aviv,
where in the 1930s and 1940s numerous cafés dotted the streets close to
the seashore. As we have seen, there was a perception of a wide difference between the European and the Levantine-Arab café, and in these
café poems, Goldberg straddled Palestine and Europe, Orient and Occi-
dent, modern and biblical, as well as male and female. In the first poem,
the woman speaker tells readers about a certain man who is part of a
group of bohemians, writers, and artists, someone who "sat by the table
of friends and spoke about humans' death." The Tel Aviv café, with its
smoke and its modern, nontraditional jazz music—a new arrival in Tel
Aviv—seems to be the perfect setting for what this man is saying: "The
wine got warm in the café and on the radio the saxophone shrieked, /a
shadow was hanging and froze on an ancient wise face / and blushed the
paleness of someone who listens like me." The female speaker, perhaps
the poet Goldberg herself, is apparently only a passive listener; the jazz
tune is laughing at her, as if saying, "you will never, ever understand."[86]

The second part of the poem moves from the wise man to the speaker, who is revealed to understand what is being said, perhaps more than the wise man and his group of male friends do. Her understanding is ostensibly the result of her experience, which the poem describes as separation from "the one who promised to come—the one who is the closest of all." Her anguish at being the lone woman in the café, her love unrequited—and perhaps also being a new migrant, one who, in spite of her relatively young age, experienced the traumas of separation and migration—helps her to understand that "the small hand of the clock (the hour hand) is not mistaken." The speaker's understanding is double: she knows that the one she awaits will not come, but she also says, "Soon. The living? The dead? Those who are gone. / Those who are gone will not come."[87] Her disappointment and ultimate acceptance of her unrequited love are also an acceptance of death and those people in her life and in Jewish Europe who were gone.

The third poem in the cycle begins with a nocturnal description of the cityscape of Tel Aviv through the eyes of the speaker, who sits in a café not far from the beach.

> At night the boats sing to the storm
> and bodies sail toward the border of the *hamsin*
> and I sit in a café
> and count the movement of the lanterns—
>
> Twenty-nine. Thirty-two . . .
> A flame licks the darkness of the glass.
> Master of the Universe! You have spread heaven
> over a legendary eastern land.[88]

In contrast to these ships, which are able to sail away to the border of the *hamsin*—the summer's heat wave that Palestine is famous for and from which the European immigrants suffered—the stationary speaker sits in the café and counts the "pulse of the lanterns." This pulse is also the rhythm of Goldberg's years in Europe: 1929 and 1932, the years in which she completed her studies in Kovno and Berlin and moved on to different places. The ellipsis following the numbers expresses the break in Goldberg's life and its continuation in Tel Aviv. At the same time, "twenty-nine" and "thirty-two" are also the chapters in the book of Genesis in which Jacob meets Rachel and in which Jacob, Rachel, and Leah finally part from Laban.

The café on Tel Aviv's beach is a point in the present, but it is also frozen in time. It takes the speaker to a "legendary" time in Palestine, to the biblical story of Jacob and Rachel. The speaker creates a fascinating, ironic parallel between herself, the modern woman poet sitting in a Tel Aviv café, smoking and waiting, and the biblical matriarch Rachel, who yearns for Jacob. Of course, the irony here is double because Goldberg's name is Leah and not Rachel. Leah—or, rather, the female speaker of the poem, who is parallel to Rachel (described in Genesis 29:17 as "beautiful of form and appearance")—is the one whose "eyes are tender," presumably from crying, like the biblical Leah. But this modern-day Rachel, who does the watching, thinking, and feeling, is a very different female protagonist from the biblical Rachel, who is seen only from Jacob's point of view as a great beauty. Still, this active role of being the poetic I does not stop the modern-day Rachel—a woman poet—from sitting alone in the Tel Aviv café, smoking and waiting for the lover who, as she already knows well, will never come. Though the frustrating situation of the woman waiting for the man is familiar, going back to the Hebrew Bible and to Rachel and Leah, the speaker of the poem seems to accept her predicament and even exploits it for purposes of contemplation and poetic insight.

Tel Aviv cafés also play an important role in Goldberg's story titled "Ha-nes ha-shaḥor" (The black flag, 1938). The story is told from the point of view of Israel Nedanya, an older writer from Europe who has just arrived in Tel Aviv. It opens with Nedanya's recurring daily routine, a scene that highlights his sense of loss and estrangement in his new environment. He sits every day in a café, "on the spacious balcony overlooking the sea." Nedanya does not "direct his first gaze at the sea." Instead, he first notices the "white and red stripes of the fabric . . . and how they are reflected like the glass that covers the café tables. Then, his ear is finely tuned to the quiet and soft music of the spoons against the demitasse cups, the rustle of the newspaper, and the steps of the waiter." Only after "the hot cup of coffee is served to his table" can he "glance at the sea and the beach in front of him." The Tel Aviv beach café, which functions for Nedanya as a space for inner reflection and careful attention, is also his substitute for Europe. Nedanya's attachment to the daily rituals of the European-style café, more than anything else, marks the break in his world following his migration from Europe to Palestine. The black flag, which Nedanya sees in the background of the white sand, signaling danger on the stormy sea for swimmers, is also an expression of his predicament in Tel Aviv. It reminds him of a disturbing letter he received from Europe, which he cannot stop thinking about. The narrator recounts the story of the letter, as Nedanya meets a friend by the name of Anschel Dor, another new migrant to Palestine who has left a position as lecturer in ornithology at the University of Cologne and now sits in the Tel Aviv café. He "cannot even hear a shout" because he has lost his hearing.[89]

As the awkward conversation between these two European Jews continues, the reader learns that the disturbing letter sitting in Nedanya's pocket was actually written by Dor's daughter, the nineteen-year-old Agatha, who committed suicide in Vienna shortly after writing the letter. Nedanya is procrastinating, trying to avoid giving Dor the terrible news. Nedanya tries to talk about the black flag on the beach in an attempt to foreshadow the dark news, but Dor cannot guess what is about to come. He has a secret of his own about his daughter, namely, that when she was a young schoolgirl, she was secretly in love with Nedanya, who was then a Hebrew teacher at her Jewish school in Europe. The story ends abruptly when Nedanya finds out that he was the object of Agatha's unrequited love, with Dor on the verge of discovering that his daughter is not alive anymore. Unable to shout the news to him, Nedanya cannot bring himself to reveal the contents of the tragic letter. As the story ends, the two men sit opposite each other in the Tel Aviv café in a tense, charged silence. They probably do not need words to convey to each other the remorse and responsibility they both carry for the lost life of the young girl left behind in Europe.

The scene in the Tel Aviv café, centered around the young girl as a symbol of a Europe that in 1938 was on the brink of war, highlights the demise of European culture and the irreparable break that older European migrants in Tel Aviv felt. This break also appears in a feuilleton that Goldberg wrote and published under the pseudonym Ada Grant in 1944. In it, Goldberg describes a visit to the Tel Aviv zoo:

> I'm walking between the cages of the exotic birds, the water birds and the land birds. The more I look at them, the more I feel that I happened to be in an Immigrant Society House. Such alienated creatures! And each one of them carries a testimony of its past life. Anyone who visits a large café in Tel Aviv will see something akin to this will. Each bird shows in its face a mark of the past with a foreign landscape and longing for the world it had to leave. Without much choice they are adapted to the new environment, but how pronounced is the fact that they were forced to do so.[90]

Although this feuilleton seems to be a less personal text that Goldberg published about Tel Aviv café, it beautifully reveals her status both as a European migrant and as a woman in this space. It also shows us the position of Tel Aviv and its cafés as a place of refuge for many European Jews as the old world was consumed by war.

The Last "Jewish" Café?

When Goldberg described the alienated creatures who carried a testimony of their past life in a Tel Aviv café, she was likely describing people such as Zusman Segalovitsh, the Polish Yiddish writer from Warsaw. Segalovitsh, we should recall, was a prominent figure in Jewish Warsaw's writing circles, and the literary café of Tłomackie 13 was his second home for years. When the Nazis invaded Warsaw in September 1939, Segalovitsh fled the city, and following a journey through Lithuania, Russia, Bulgaria, Turkey, and Syria, he arrived in Tel Aviv in 1941. In his Yiddish memoir *Mayne zibn yor in Tel Aviv* (My seven years in Tel Aviv), Segalovitsh wrote, "I'm going to Tel Aviv. Why Tel Aviv? Because in Tel Aviv there are Jews from the diaspora, . . . and I yearn for them, since the entire European diaspora is confined to the ghetto." In his memoir, Segalovitsh describes how he arrived in Tel Aviv as "a battered refugee" and a "wanderer" who on the way "lost the best strength, lost might, faith." Instead, he brought with him "great horror; the Jews of Poland are in captivity, what will become of them?"[91]

In order to overcome the horror, Segalovitsh anchored himself; namely, he "found a coffeehouse, occupied a *shtamtish* [a regular table] for a whole seven years." His choice was Café Ginati on the corner of Ben Yehuda and Allenby Streets.[92] Café Ginati was established in 1936 by two German Jews and was renovated and redesigned in 1941 by the architect Heinz (Ḥayim) Fenchel, as a spacious café with tables and chairs in the large hall, as well as on a sidewalk that was designed like a little garden. There, Segalovitsh established his regular table, "with the permission of the café owner": "That was my only ground, my only territory." For Segalovitsh and for other refugees from Europe who found themselves in Tel Aviv, Café Ginati was a harbor, a safe haven that enabled them to find people in similar situations and to talk. "In those days," writes Segalovitsh, "it was necessary to talk; you had to have a friend. Without them, you just sink. . . . You think of suicide." The conversation was in "a couple dozen languages. It's no wonder. Jews came to Palestine from forty-three countries and brought forty-three languages." The people who were drawn to Segalovitsh's table spoke and read mostly Yiddish. "There was no new book in Yiddish that couldn't be found on this table."[93]

Figure 6.14. Hans Pinn, *A Saturday Morning at the Ginati Café on Ben Yehuda St. Tel Aviv* (Courtesy of Israel Government Press Office)

For Meyer Weisgal, the Zionist activist who was born in the Russian Empire and migrated to New York as a child, Café Ginati was "the gathering place." In Ginati, Weisgal was drawn to the crowds, in which he found people he thought had "long passed into the great beyond," where they were "sipping tea or coffee, putting the world in order and arranging the Jewish future."[94] Whether they were Zionists like Weisgal or Bundists like Segalovitsh, Ashkenazi diaspora Jews were attracted to Tel Aviv cafés during and after World War II. Tel Aviv was far from the horror of the battles and the ghettos, and while many people followed with great concern the news from Europe and the fate of its Jews, most people in the city's cafés were busy "arranging the future" of the Yishuv, its culture and politics.

Even amid the war, Dizengoff Street was becoming the new center for commerce and for café culture. This was mainly because of one institution, Café Kassit. In 1942, Café Kassit, which had closed its doors on Ben-Yehuda Street, reopened at 117 Dizengoff Street under the ownership of Lyuba Goldberg. At that point, Dizengoff was still a new street at the northern edge of Tel Aviv, and Kassit was just a small café. In the summer of 1944, Goldberg sold Kassit to Yehezkel (Khatskl) Weinstein. Weinstein was born in Rzeszów, a city in Galicia. While many members of his family migrated to New York—including his brother-in-law Berish Weinstein, who became a well-known Yiddish poet—Khatskl made his way to Palestine in 1924. He worked as a dishwasher, a server, a cook, and a manager in a number of Tel Aviv cafés and operated a small late-night club for waiters from other cafés and restaurants. When the opportunity to acquire Café Kassit came up, he seized it. Kassit became successful very quickly, and Khatskl acquired the nearby shop and expanded the café. Much of Kassit's success had to do with Khatskl's personality and the warm atmosphere he created there. The owner and his café became so intertwined with each other that Weinstein changed his last name to Ish-Kassit (the man of Kassit). Within a short time, prominent figures who were habitués of other cafés—the writers Avraham Shlonsky, Nathan Alterman, Leah Goldberg, Avraham Halfi, Alexander Penn, Ya'akov Orland, Menashe Levin, and Avot Yeshurun; the actors Hannah Rovina, Aharon Meskin, and Raphael Klatzkin; and the painters Reuven Rubin and Yosef Zariztki—all frequented Café Kassit on a regular basis.

Café Kassit also became a gathering place for the new generation of writers and poets who, starting in the 1940s, published in a Hebrew journal called *Yalkut ha-re'im* (The friends' satchel). This was the generation of the sabras (natives) Ḥayim Gouri, Moshe Shamir, Sholomo Tanai, and Yigal Mosinzon, who were born in Palestine to migrant eastern European parents. These young people eventually spent much of their time in the socialist youth movement, the paramilitary units of the Haganah and Palmaḥ, and in kibbutzim. However, most of them grew up in Tel Aviv and were drawn to Kassit and to older writers such as Shlonsky and Alterman who still dominated the literary and artistic scene.

In one of Moshe Shamir's early stories, "Mafteḥot avudim" (Lost keys, 1946), the narrator takes the readers inside "Café Lulyan, the coffeehouse of the writers and artists"—a thinly veiled reference to Café Kassit. In the story, Assaf Ya'akovi, a young poet from a kibbutz, visits Tel Aviv and is

Figure 6.15. Boris Carmi, photograph of the poet Avraham Shlonsky and friends, Café Kassit, 1947

magnetized by Café Lulyan. Ostensibly, the reason for visiting the café is to find and meet "the maestro," who is indeed "sitting and focusing hard on what happens on his table, . . . the lion in the group, the greatest poet, who played chess."[95] Anyone who ever visited Café Kassit knew that the reference was to Shlonsky, who was a fixture in the café, often playing chess (see fig. 6.15). In Shamir's story, the poet with the unmistakably sabra appearance and name tries to get the older poet's attention with the hope of being able to publish some of his poems in the established Hebrew journals and books. He manages to speak with the Shlonsky character but fails to truly interest him in his new poems, which are very different from the "poems about the urban café, about the smoke of the cigarettes, the loneliness, and the cruelness of the clock." At the end of the story, the young sabra poet from the kibbutz loses the keys to the apartment in which he stays during his visit in Tel Aviv and returns to the café in the middle of the night, to witness the late-night "bohemian"

Figure 6.16. Advertisement of Café Kassit, *Davar*, September 10, 1945

scene full of writers, editors, and artists who "sit here day in, day out, for many hours" and discuss "the awe-inspiring events."[96]

Indeed, Café Kassit was in its heyday amid the drama of the 1940s: when World War II came to an end and its full devastation became apparent; when, in 1947, the UN voted to divide Palestine into a Jewish state and an Arab state, effectively causing the end of the British Mandate; when David Ben-Gurion announced the establishment of the State of Israel—in Dizengoff's house in Tel Aviv. All these dramatic events were marked in Café Kassit, but in 1948, the country, and Tel Aviv, was plunged into war. Jaffa, the largest and most important Arab city in Palestine, was completely destroyed, with most of its population sent into exile. Now, Jaffa, the city from which Tel Aviv separated, was subsumed under the municipality of Tel Aviv, which officially changed its name to Tel Aviv–Jaffa.

While in the period following 1948, a new generation of sabra writers became very prominent, millions of new migrants to Palestine arrived and transformed the population. Most of the migrants were Holocaust survivors from Europe and Jews from Arab countries, who found themselves refugees in a new state with enormous military and economic hardships. A new policy of economic austerity was implemented to control and oversee distribution of necessary resources and to ensure equal rations for all Israeli citizens. Tel Aviv and its citizens did not deal very well with these policies, and their pain was felt, perhaps more than elsewhere, in the cafés and shops of Dizengoff Street.[97] Perhaps the most glaring contradiction between the austerity policies and the life of bourgeois Tel Aviv was the establishment of a new café, Café Rowal (or Roval), almost opposite Kassit, on 111 Dizengoff Street. Café Rowal was established by two central European migrants, Gustav Rosenberg and Karl Waller (the name Rowal was the combination of their two last names). It was huge—six hundred seats inside and hundreds more outside, in a yard and on the sidewalk. It advertised itself unabashedly as a "luxurious café" that catered to Tel Aviv's middle and upper-middle class, mostly women from central Europe and Poland, as well as young people who came after they visited the cinemas and shops of Dizengoff.[98]

While Café Rowal was constantly mentioned in the gossip and society sections of Israel's newspapers, some people resented the scene of consumption and commodity spectacle. The poet Erez Bitton, born in Algeria, a resident of transit camps around Tel Aviv, and one of the first poets in Israel who gave voice to the trauma of Arab migrants, was particularly vocal. One of his most well-known poems is "Shir kniyah be-Dizeongoff" (Shopping song on Dizengoff):

קָנִיתִי חֲנוּת בְּדִיזֶנְגּוֹף	I bought a shop on Dizengoff
כְּדֵי לְהַכּוֹת שֹׁרֶשׁ	to strike some roots
כְּדֵי לִקְנוֹת שֹׁרֶשׁ	to buy some roots
כְּדֵי לִמְצֹא מָקוֹם בְּרוֹוָל	to find a spot at Rowal
אֲבָל	but
הָאֲנָשִׁים בְּרוֹוָל	the crowd at Rowal
אֲנִי שׁוֹאֵל אֶת עַצְמִי	I ask myself
מִי הֵם הָאֲנָשִׁים בְּרוֹוָל	who are these folks at Rowal
מַה יֵּשׁ בָּאֲנָשִׁים בְּרוֹוָל	What's with these people at Rowal
מַה הוֹלֵךְ בָּאֲנָשִׁים בְּרוֹוָל,	What's going on with these people at Rowal
אֲנִי לֹא פוֹנֶה לָאֲנָשִׁים בְּרוֹוָל	I do not turn to the people of Rowal
כְּשֶׁהָאֲנָשִׁים בְּרוֹוָל פּוֹנִים אֵלִי	When the people at Rowal turn to me
אֲנִי שׁוֹלֵף אֶת הַשָּׂפָה	I unsheathe my tongue
מִלִּים נְקִיּוֹת,	with clean words,
כֵּן אֲדוֹנִי,	Yes sir,
בְּבַקָּשָׁה אֲדוֹנִי,	please sir,
עִבְרִית מְעֻדְכֶּנֶת מְאֹד,	A very up-to-date Hebrew
וְהַבָּתִּים הָעוֹמְדִים כָּאן עָלַי	And the buildings looming over me here
גְּבוֹהִים כָּאן עָלַי,	tower over me here,
וְהַפְּתָחִים הַפְּתוּחִים כָּאן	and the openings open here
בִּלְתִּי חֲדִירִים לִי כָּאן.	are impenetrable to me here.
בְּשָׁעָה אַפְלוּלִית	At dusk
בַּחֲנוּת בְּדִיזֶנְגּוֹף	I pack my things
אֲנִי אוֹרֵז חֲפָצִים	in the shop on Dizengoff
לַחֲזֹר לַפַּרְוָרִים	to head back to the outskirts
וְלָעִבְרִית הָאַחֶרֶת.	and the other Hebrew[99]

When the speaker says that he bought a shop on Dizengoff Street, he does it in order to "strike roots" in urban Israel. Finding your roots by buying them is, of course, very problematic, and this is highlighted by the fact that the speaker's acquired "roots" are expressed by his desire "to find a spot at Café Rowal." The meaning of the Hebrew word *makom* (place) is double: to find a spot to sit in the café, which is presumably difficult because the place is full, and to find a place in the new Israeli urban existence of Tel Aviv. Café Rowal becomes a metonym for Israeli society, but one in which the speaker cannot find a place, one in which he cannot even communicate. The colloquial language of his repeated lament—"Who are these folks at Rowal?"—shows his increasingly alienated position. He finally abandons his attempts at "up-to-date Hebrew" (which is of course a Hebrew spoken by local and European immigrants) and goes back to the "outskirts," where there is an "other Hebrew," a low-brow Hebrew, mixed with Arabic, but a language more authentic and more powerful than the one heard in Café Rowal.

Throughout Rowal's debated emergence, Café Kassit remained—physically and symbolically—on the other side of Dizengoff. It established itself as the city's undisputed bohemian café. What this "bohemia" really meant in the context of the young State of Israel is a complex matter. While the café was frequented by both old and young writers, artists, journalists, and the many people who came to see them, the owner Khatskl, so identified with his café, had the appearance and the demeanor of a middle-class Jew from Poland. There is also a clear tension between the notion of Kassit as an incubator of new, distinctively Israeli-Hebrew culture and the fact that Khatskl and many of the habitués of the café were Jews who spoke, read, and wrote Yiddish (and other languages), including many Holocaust survivors who came to Palestine as refugees. These Yiddish speakers were marginalized in a society determined to be strong and sure of itself and to reject the Jewish diaspora, which was associated with passivity and weakness. These Yiddish speakers found in Kassit a warm house, because it was a café, very much like other "Jewish" cafés in prewar Europe and in New York. Yiddish writers, poets, and actors such as Dzigan and Shumacher—who survived the Holocaust and migrated to Tel Aviv in 1950—were Khatskl's closest friends.

The New York Yiddish actor and writer Moyshe Nudelman, who lived in Tel Aviv in the 1940s and early 1950s, described Kassit using the familiar New York Yiddish expression "the *kibetzarnya*." He saw Kassit as a place "always bursting" with guests, who were Yiddish speakers from eastern Europe, as were, he reminds us, many of the Hebrew poets and writers. Everybody was sitting and talking in Kassit until late at night, because the café was open until three a.m. and only closed for a few hours before reopening for breakfast.[100] He remembered one night when Dzigan and Shumacher sat down at one of the tables outside and asked the waiter inside for a lemonade. Dzigan cried out, "Shema Yisroel!" (Hear O Israel). "If you think," Nudelman wrote, "that Dzigan was saying the [central Jewish prayer of] Shema, you're mistaken; he was just calling the waiter, who's named Yisroel."[101] This little story invokes much of the unique and seemingly contradictory atmosphere of the thirdspace of Café Kassit, between Israeli-Hebrew and diasporic Yiddish, between reality and imagination, between outside and inside. The story also shows that for many people, habitués and occasional visitors, Kassit of the 1940s and 1950s was a point in the silk road of modern Jewish culture, a crucial node in that network of cafés in Europe, America, and the Middle East. This fact becomes clear when one reads examples in the Hebrew, Yiddish, and English press in which Café Kassit was compared to New York's Café Royal. In fact, when Khatskl visited New York in July 1950, he was brought to Café Royal by a group of Yiddish journalists, writers, and actors and was asked to create "a New York Kassit," by reviving and reorganizing Café Royal, which was, as mentioned in chapter 5, in a time of decline before it closed down.[102]

The food in Kassit was eastern European food; the most popular drink was tea (as well as vodka and brandy at night). Gradually, the décor of the café became composed of paintings by the habitué artists Moyshe Bernshtein and Yosl Bergner. Bergner was the son of the Yiddish poet Melech Ravitsh, who, we should recall, was a café habitué in Vienna and Warsaw. Bergner migrated to Australia in the 1930 and largely escaped the devastation of the Holocaust. He migrated to Israel in 1950 and, after a few years of living in Safed, made a permanent home in Tel Aviv—and in Café Kassit. Bergner's paintings were first seen by Israeli critics and artists as too "diasporic" and too "literary," as they did not adhere either to the tendency to depict Israel and its inhabitants or to the new abstract style that was in vogue in the 1950s. But Bergner painted, in his signature expressionist style, figures that looked like they were coming out of the shtetl or the Jewish neighborhood of Warsaw or out of Yiddish stories by Sholem Aleichem or Y. L. Peretz, mixed with surreal figures from Kafka's stories. This style can clearly be seen in the large-scale painting that Bergner created in 1957, which covered almost one entire wall of Café Kassit (fig. 6.17). Bergner tells how he used to sit with Khatskl and fall asleep in the café. When Khatskl asked Bergner to do the painting, in exchange for a bottle of brandy, he immediately agreed and created the most recognizable icon of Kassit. The painting itself shows a wall with many windows, with people and objects seen through the windows and sometimes coming out of the windows into the forefront, as if moving into the café itself. The only clearly recognizable figure in the painting is Khatskl, the owner, as he sleeps in the café, a position that became familiar to the late-night habitués. The other figures in the painting can be understood as artistic representations of the café habitués, some of them with masks, others with musical instruments or clown hats. Indeed, the

Figure 6.17. Yosl Bergner, mural on the wall of Café Kassit, 1950s (Courtesy of Charlie and Nadine Hollander)

fact that many poets, writers, and artists sat in front of Bergner's painting blurs the border between art and reality. In this way, Bergner created a visual representation of the thirdspace of the café that trespasses the boundary between the inside and outside, the real and the imaginary.

One of Bergner's new friends in Tel Aviv who might be represented in the painting is the aforementioned poet Avot Yeshurun. After the Holocaust, Yeshurun discovered that almost all of his family had perished. The mourning for the loss of his family and millions of eastern European Jews, as well as his deep grief over the lost lives of Arabs and Jews in the 1948 war, caused him to change his poetic style. From the 1950s until his death, Yeshurun wrote complex poems that mixed Hebrew with Yiddish, Arabic, and Polish and mixed everyday language with traditional Jewish texts. One of Yeshurun's poems, "Eḥad be-yanur, layla" (January 1, night), takes place in a café reminiscent of Kassit:

בְּבֵית קָפֶה, מִצַּד הָרְחוֹב	In a café, by the side of the street.
מִי שֶׁהָיוּ פֹּה – אֵינָם.	Those who were here—are gone.
מִי שֶׁחָשׁוּב כְּמֵת	He who is numbered as dead
וּמִי שֶׁחָשׁוּב כְּנָם.	and he who's numbered as slumber.
רַק סַדְרָן זָקֵן מִן הַקּוֹלְנוֹעַ	Only an old usher from the cinema
עִם לָבָן זָקֵן מִן "הַבִּימָה".	with the white old from "Ha-bima"
וְהַדֻּבָּה הַגְּדוֹלָה עַל הַגַּג	and the Great Bear on the roof
מְצִיצָה אֵלֶיהָ פְּנִימָה.	glancing at it inside.
מְשַׂחֲקִים שָׁח. הַבַּיִת	Playing chess. The coffee
קָפֶה מָלֵא דֶּצֶמְבֶּר.	house is full December.
שׁוֹמְעִים גֹ'ון בָּאֶז	Listening to Joan Baez
שָׁרָה אִי רִימֶמְבֶּר.	singing I Remember.
יד טבת תשלב, 1 ינואר 1972	January 1, 1972[103]

Yeshurun's short, ostensibly simple, but quite enigmatic poem captures beautifully the ruptures and absences felt at Tel Aviv cafés such as Kassit.

The poem is about memory and remembrance. It is about those "who are gone," whether they are the migrants who came to Tel Aviv and are gone, the Holocaust survivors who found their way to Tel Aviv, or those with family members and others who perished in the war. These might be well-known people or someone like "the old usher from the cinema." All of them are making their way to the café. Some of those people are numbered as dead, and others are "numbered as slumber"—perhaps a reference to Khatskl and his famous sleeping in the café. The playing of chess and the conversation in the café cannot cover the immense sense of loss and absence. This becomes mostly clear in the third stanza, in which the speaker separates the Hebrew combination *beit-kafe* (coffee-house) into two words in two separate lines. Moreover, instead of using the regular compound construction *beit*, Yeshurun writes *bayit*, which means "house" or "home." Why does he do it? This is the place where it becomes evident that something is broken in the house, and the sense of brokenness is related to the old people who populate Tel Aviv and the sense of loss about which Joan Baez was also singing in the song "For Sasha": "And I remember the Holocaust / I remember all we lost / The families torn and the borders crossed."[104] It is typical of Yeshurun not to mention explicitly the Holocaust but to evoke it gently in a poem about a Tel Aviv café, in which the habitués are overcome by a sense of loss and absence.

Yeshurun's employment of the space of the café in his poem is related to how Café Kassit appears in Yoram Kaniuk's masterful novel *Ha-yehudi ha-aḥaron* (*The Last Jew*, 1981). Kaniuk was born in Tel Aviv in 1930 to parents who came from eastern Europe and from Germany. His father was Dizengoff's secretary, and he grew up in Tel Aviv. He fought and was injured in the 1948 war, after which, shocked and unhinged, Kaniuk lived for a decade on New York's Lower East Side; there he encountered many Holocaust survivors and older Jews who made him examine his own sense of Jewishness and Israeliness, which he explores in the novel. Kaniuk resembles one of the novel's protagonists, Boaz Schneerson, who fought and was shell-shocked in the 1948 war. After his traumatic war experience, Boaz goes to Café Kassit and hangs a poster with the words, "I know dead people." He sits in the café, ready to give testimonies, but almost nobody is interested in him, as he appears to be out of his mind. After three days in Kassit, Boaz walks toward the house of Obadiah

Henkin, a Tel Aviv Hebrew teacher who is mourning the loss of his son Menahem in the war. Boaz sees in Henkin "a scarecrow of a man drying himself."[105] Henkin is the founder of a local "Committee for Bereaved Parents," devoted to honoring fallen soldiers and hosting somber visits from Israeli political figures and occasional European authors. Surrounded by parents clamoring for memories of their lost children, Boaz is driven to produce fake poems and letters, including a forged poem that Boaz gives Henkin, claiming that it was written by his son before he was killed in the war.

Later in the novel, when Henkin wants to meet with Jordana, a representative from the Israeli government, in order to plan an outing for the group, they look for a café in which they can hold the meeting, away from home and the family. Henkin tells Jordana, "I'm no expert in the new cafés, and I remembered Café Kassit, *once* a meeting place for writers and artists, and I said: What about Kassit, and she said, Fine. I went there and thought that if I had sat in Kassit, I would have met Boaz, who sat there then and waited for me." Henkin realizes that after all the years he has not set foot in Kassit, "the waiters were still expecting those artists." He also remembers the exact place where Khatskl used to sit, half asleep, as well as a certain man, Mr. Soslovitch, an eastern European migrant Jew who used to frequent Kassit with wife and friends and sing sad songs in Yiddish, Russian, and Hebrew. Mr. Soslovitch was a habitué with a regular table. "Now," Henkin realizes, "a stranger sits there, and that's a sign that Mr. Soslovitch is dead."[106]

Kaniuk's novel, like Yeshurun's poem, is about constructed memory and about how the Holocaust and the near annihilation of European Jewish culture is bound up with the rise of Israel and with the continuing violence that mars that rise. When Henkin remembers Khatskl and Mr. Soslovitch, he identifies Kassit with those new European Jewish migrants; many of them are survivors who lost their families in the Holocaust, as well as their sons in Israel's wars. Kaniuk's novel and Yeshurun's poem relate this memory with the decline of Kassit as a Jewish cultural institution. Khatskl's health deteriorated in the late 1960s. Both Nathan Alterman and Leah Goldberg died in 1970. Avraham Shlonsky died in 1973. The journalist Aharon Bakhar wrote that "the end of Kassit took place when it closed down for two hours during Alterman's funeral."[107] Indeed, in the 1970s, Kassit lost its appeal. If between the late 1940s and

Figure 6.18. Micha Bar-Am, legendary Café Kassit after midnight
with its owner Khatskl dozing at the entrance (© Micha Bar-Am)

1960s, the café was open and full of people and life until very late at
night, by the 1970s, it closed down at nine p.m.

Then, on December 29, 1979, Khatskl died. His coffin stood in Kassit,
and the municipality of Tel Aviv closed down Dizengoff Street for traffic to allow the funeral procession, which was attended by a crowd of
thousands. When Khatskl was buried in the Kirayt Shaul cemetery, the
eulogy was given in Yiddish by the Polish Jewish actor Shimen Dzigan.

Kassit did not close down and continued to be operated by Khatskl's sons until the end of the twentieth century, but it was a mere shadow of itself. Bakhar wrote that Kassit became "full with people who did not know where they had come and for what. They sat at the tables of Shlonsky, Alterman, and Leah Goldberg and did not know them."[108] The editor and critic Gabriel Moked elaborated further: "The place of Alterman, Shlonsky, and Penn was taken by people from the underworld and melancholic night birds." Instead of conversations about poems, claimed Moked, there were conversations about how to open boutiques, how to fake fire that looks like arson and get money from the insurance company.[109]

The question that Moked and Bakhar posed is the question of why: why did a place like Kassit stop being culturally important? Khatskl himself gave part of the answer, when he said before he died, "People used to be friends. . . . After the theater, the actors used to come with flowers, excited, drinking, eating, speaking. . . . Today, they don't want to be together. There is no communication, not between me and them and not among themselves."[110] Khatskl seems to be making a psychological argument about how people's desire to communicate and be together in a café had changed over time. This point is also evident in photographs from the late 1970s and early 1980s, which the photographer Barry Frydlender took of people sitting at Kassit on Friday afternoons (fig. 6.19).

In an analysis of these photographs, Nissan Perez, the curator of an exhibition of Frydlender's photographs, wrote that "basic sadness pervades . . . the images; a strong feeling of alienation." The reason for this is that "although these people are sitting, drinking and talking, there seems to be no contact between them." Each person seems to be "locked into his own tiny bubble." Peretz made another crucial point about the people who still frequented Kassit in its twilight years: "They want to be the new Shlonskys and Leah Goldbergs, but they are not. They are a different generation. . . . They were all native-born Israelis, and there lies the difference."[111] Although a sense of alienation was a common theme in earlier writings about Tel Aviv cafés and in cafés of other cities, Frydlender's photographs of Café Kassit of the 1970s exhibit Israelis who are not connected to the immigrants who populated these cafés. After the death of Khatskl and the generation of the Jewish migrants who were connected to cafés and cities in Europe and America, Café Kassit was more of a relic of bygone days than a living institution.

Figure 6.19. Barry Frydlender, untitled, Café Kassit, 1982 (Israel Museum Catalogue, 1985; courtesy of Barry Frydlender)

Indeed, similar shifts took place during the same years in Tel Aviv and in New York. In both cities, cafés continued to exist, and people visited—and still visit—them; but in both cities, cafés are no longer central to Jewish culture, at least not in the same way. In Kassit's heyday, between the mid-1940s and the 1960s, it epitomized the culture of Tel Aviv. At the same time, Kassit was a "Jewish" café, perhaps the last one that resembled the many cafés explored in this book in Europe and America. It was owned by Khatskl, an eastern European migrant who was a shrewd businessman and at the same time a man who was enamored with Jewish art, literature, and theater, in Yiddish, Hebrew, and other languages. Kassit was the last "Jewish" café because the habitués who made it famous, and made it their second home, were mostly migrants who carried with them the active memory of migration and the network of Jewish cafés that offered respite and familiarity along their journeys. It seems as if when these Jewish migrants died, the café as an institution significant for modern Jewish culture also died with them.

Conclusion

Closing Time

Where have all these cafés gone? Did they survive? Are there any cafés that are still significant to Jewish culture today? These are the questions I have received again and again as I have told colleagues, students, friends, and others about the book I am writing. I have asked myself these same questions repeatedly. Indeed, the answers are far from obvious. Of course, there are still cafés in the cities we have explored. In fact, thanks to international chains of coffee shops such as Starbucks and our obsession with overpriced caffeinated beverages, there are far more cafés in the world now than there have been at any point in human history. Many more people pass through their doors every day. And yet, when we compare the spaces explored in this book to current ones, we sense that the institution of the café and its function are very different now.

Moreover, it is clear that the confluence of modern Jewish culture and urban cafés that existed in European cities until World War II and in New York and Tel Aviv until the 1960s and 1970s does not exist anymore. It is hard to think of significant poetic or intellectual groups meeting in cafés on a regular basis, nor can you find many Jewish writers, journalists, actors, artists, political figures, and others socializing, arguing, and creating in cafés. The only exceptions I can think of are the Mizraḥi group ʿArs Poetica in Café Albi in south Tel Aviv and the literary activities in Café Tmol Shilshom in Jerusalem (named after Agnon's novel).[1] Perhaps there are a few others, but, by and large, cafés in Europe, America, and the Middle East no longer constitute the silk road of modern Jewish creativity that this book has traced. Contemporary urban cafés cannot be considered significant sites for the production of modern Jewish culture, despite the fact that Jewish culture exists, perhaps even thrives, today in many cities.[2] What are the reasons for this change?

To attempt to answer these questions and to reflect on what this book has explored and revealed, we turn briefly to three contemporary Jewish writers and producers of culture who have contemplated and responded to them. The first is Aharon (Erwin) Appelfeld, the great Jewish novelist who was born in Bukovina in 1931 and lives today in Jerusalem. Appelfeld is one of the few contemporary Jewish writers who has made the café a center of his literary activity since the 1950s. He has written many of his stories and novels in cafés, and he has written about cafés as well. In 2001, Appelfeld published a memoir in Hebrew, 'Od ha-yom gadol, which was translated into English as A Table for One.[3]

Appelfeld, who survived the Holocaust and came to Palestine as a refugee in 1946 after spending a few years in a displaced persons camp, tells us in the memoir about how he finally found his place during the 1950s and 1960s in Jerusalem cafés. Appelfeld describes vividly his first visit to Café Peter, in the German Colony neighborhood of Jerusalem, when he was a twenty-three-year-old student: "no sooner was I through the doorway than I knew these people," the habitués of the café, "were my lost uncles and cousins." In Café Peter, Appelfeld found not only a kind of provisional home but also his voice after drifting for a few years as a Holocaust survivor in various European and Israeli camps and institutions. When reflecting on the reasons for his affinity for the café and finding a home there, Appelfeld writes, "My attraction to cafés probably goes back to the beautiful cafés of Czernowitz, in Bokovina, where I was born." He tells us that several Jerusalem cafés—Café Peter, Café Rehavia, Café Atara, Café Vienna, and Café Hermon—"retained something of the aromas and manners of European cafés."[4] This is where he met people like Leah Goldberg, S. Y. Agnon, U. Z. Greenberg, and Gershom Scholem, as well as many other Hebrew, German, and Yiddish writers, including Holocaust survivors like himself.

None of these places, notes Appelfeld, exist today. "It should be said," he further reflects, that "most cafés nowadays are not so much cafés but more like large, crowded spaces. . . . Don't try to find any quiet there, or something mysterious, or that furtive connection with those surrounding you. . . . Cafés of this sort are not inviting, nor are they intended for sitting or lingering. You'd like to get out of them as quickly as possible."[5] Appelfeld's memoir provides a multifaceted answer to our questions. First, by connecting Jerusalem cafés in the

Figure C.1. Café Vienna, Jerusalem, 1950, in *Jerusalem, Living City*
(Jerusalem: Government of Israel, 1950)

1950s and 1960s to the European cafés he still had a chance to visit in his childhood and about which he had read and heard, he points to what we have explored as the silk road of modern Jewish culture—the transnational network of cafés that extended across and between European, American, and Middle Eastern cities. This network of Jewish cafés existed as long as large-scale Jewish migration was taking place, and the connection between various cities of significant Jewish migration was profound and meaningful.

Appelfeld also claims that the institution of the café has changed, that what he calls "real cafés" do not exist anymore. This is because most of the contemporary cafés that replaced them are something else altogether, spaces in which communication, exchange, and contemplation do not take place. At first glance, it appears that Appelfeld's judgment might contain a certain sentimentality, a longing for bygone days and for shuttered places. But Appelfeld is consciously aware of this danger. "A café," he writes cautiously, "is not a sentimental place. Those who sit in cafés are generally people who find their own homes cramped, or for whom loneliness is a frequent companion, people from foreign parts who have gathered so they can speak their native tongue and share memories. In cafés you can sometimes hear words cold as ice, or worlds full of longing and a fierce loyalty."[6]

Indeed, our journey through the cafés of Odessa, Warsaw, Vienna, Berlin, New York City, and Tel Aviv–Jaffa has shown them to be central to modernity and modern Jewish culture. As we have seen, these urban cafés constituted not only the nexus of cultural migrant networks but spaces of refuge for people who could not find home elsewhere, spaces or shelters of cosmopolitan multilingualism that the pressure of nationalism and monolingualism threatened and sometimes destroyed. We have also seen how cafés were spaces of contested identities and conflicted narratives, spaces that were experienced as "cold as ice" and at the same time "full of longing." Cafés were those places that seem to be coming from elsewhere, not rooted in the soil, places where people from "foreign parts" gathered. Moreover, although Appelfeld does not use the term "thirdspace," he is aware of the café's position between reality and imagination. For him, the café is "a port to which all gates of the imagination are open." Finally, when Appelfeld writes that "towards evening, a café can resemble a secular prayer house in which people are immersed in observation,"[7] he reiterates the link that existed—for so many people and for so long—between traditional Jewish spaces and the modern café as a "Jewish space" in a time of radical transformations.

The café as a significant cultural institution and as crucial to modern Jewish culture is now gone in Appelfeld's estimation. I tend to agree with him. Perhaps, as my students have pointed out to me, cafés as centers of communication and exchange have been replaced in the late twentieth and early twenty-first century by technology, by the Internet and social media, which serve the function of "virtual cafés." However, there are some people, including some Jews, who are still attracted to cafés exactly for the reasons that Appelfeld mentioned. Some even try to create, or rather re-create, the cafés of bygone days but find it difficult, perhaps impossible, to do so. One such person is Michael Idov, who was born in 1976 to a Jewish family in Riga, Latvia. Idov arrived in the United States with his family in 1992, and after graduating from the University of Michigan, he moved to New York City and became a journalist. In early 2005, he and his wife decided to open a Viennese-style café on Orchard Street on the Lower East Side. At the end of that year, he wrote about his experience, "You know that charming little café on New York's Lower East Side that just closed after a mere six months in business—where coffee was served on silver trays with a glass of water and a little chocolate cookie? . . . Yeah, that one was mine."[8]

Four years later, Idov published a novel called *Ground Up*, a fictional text about Mark Scharf, a young American book reviewer from a Russian Jewish family who opens a café that soon fails miserably. In the novel, as Mark and his wife, Nina, consider possible names for their future café, they search for a "cozy cluster of letters, something that would sound lived in, settled, verging on quaint but not quite there yet, slightly east European but well short of Soviet kitsch, bookish but not overbearingly so . . . with a couple of those extra z's or w's, or four consonant runs that ravage Polish and German tongues."[9] The name they come up with is Café Kolschitzky, which, as we should recall, is based on the name of the mythological Polish translator and spy who was, and still is, mistakenly believed to have established Vienna's first café. After deciding on the name, Mark and Nina look for a location in the city. They look everywhere in Manhattan and Brooklyn but find a place only on the gentrifying Lower East Side, where "Puerto Ricans in hiphop gear, themselves relatively recent arrivals who had taken the place of the decamped Jews, mingled with the straw-thin, tragic-haired children of privilege." Mark begins to realize that "in its own odd way . . . the LES was the most European-feeling neighborhood." He is thrilled with "the idea of setting up shop in a place practically synonymous with immigration."[10]

After our own tour through six cities and a century and a half of café life, it is clear that Café Kolschitzky is a re-creation of a re-creation, which makes the name, indeed, very fitting for a Viennese-style café in

New York during the 2000s in a novel by an American-Russian Jewish writer. In other words, what Mark and Nina were attempting to create, and what Michael Idov is writing about, is yet another thirdspace, located between the real and the imaginary, between the reality of the present and the memory of the past. In this case, that thirdspace comes in the form of a postmodern novel, in which even the attempt to re-create a re-creation fails. The collapse of the re-creation of the Viennese café begins with the appearance of a "six-foot-ten Israeli with a glass eye" property owner, a man who came to the real-estate business "in a classic Lower East Side manner, through the clothing business."[11] The landlord is an embodiment of the gentrifying neighborhood of the early twenty-first century, which has little to do with Mark's nostalgic idea of the Lower East Side as a "European neighborhood" that is synonymous with immigration. The novel becomes much grimmer toward the end, when, instead of educating the locals on "authentic café culture," Mark and Nina are forced to close it down, and their marriage collapses together with the dream of the café.

If *Ground Up* shows the impossibility of re-creating a Viennese café on the Lower East Side of the twenty-first century, even in a fictional novel, the 2015 documentary film *Café Nagler* invites us to think about Jewish café culture with a trip to contemporary Berlin via Tel Aviv.[12] Mor Kaplansky, who codirected *Café Nagler* with her husband, grew up in Israel hearing stories from her grandmother Naomi Kaplansky about the café. Café Nagler, in Moritzplatz, in the Kreuzberg neighborhood of Berlin, was owned by Kaplansky's great-grandparents in the 1910s and 1920s, before they migrated to Palestine and closed it down. Kaplansky was raised on tales of a grand and culturally important café, at the center of the intellectual and social world of Weimar Berlin, where writers and artists met, chatted, and argued. Armed with a few photographs and many stories, she decided to travel to Berlin to find out more about the place. Soon she discovered that the spot where the café had been located was bombed during World War II and is now a small park. Searching in vain for anyone who remembered the place, she met one man who shared his memories of Café Nagler, only to find out that he was a fraud, as he was born the same year it closed.

The more Kaplansky delved into the city's history, the more difficult it became to reconcile the details about a café that nobody remembers—and that was of no particular cultural importance—with the stories she heard in her childhood. She was devastated and struggled with what and how to tell her beloved grandmother about her findings. She also did not know what direction the documentary film, which was supposed to be about a successful journey to the past, would take. In the end, she decided to turn the documentary into something akin to a mockumentary: to create a re-creation of the café with the help of friends in Berlin and with the power of the camera and storytelling. This she did with a group of young Berliners with deep longing for Weimar Berlin, who organize 1920s-style parties. She asked them to re-create if not the space, at least the atmosphere of Café Nagler for her in an old Berlin apartment that survived World War II. She also asked her friends to tell a personal story from their family histories in front of the camera and to insert Café Nagler fictionally into their own preexisting family memories. One of the participants told her that the 1920s were the last period in which they, as Germans, can take pride. And so the film succeeded in its re-creation, in bringing back to life, even if only for a few moments in front of the camera, the "legendary" Café Nagler or at least its image as reflected in the stories of both the Nagler family in Israel and the Germans in contemporary Berlin.

These three twenty-first-century Jewish texts—Appelfeld's memoir, Idov's novel, and Kaplansky's film—offer us varied, but complementary, answers to the questions of where all these cafés have gone and why cafés are no longer significant spaces of contemporary Jewish culture. They also give us a hint as to what has gone with them. The fact that the creators of these three texts are either migrants—Idov is part of a new Jewish diaspora, the migration from the Soviet Union and the former Soviet Union—or descendants of migrants is surely significant and not coincidental.[13] Moreover, all three texts deal with displacement, diaspora, and the multiplicity of Jewish and non-Jewish languages, as well as the memory of the past and its place in the present and its possible future.

These three Jewish texts also afford us good ways to reflect on the nostalgia that lurks beneath them, as well as—it must be admitted—beneath this book. Here it might be useful to think together with Svetlana Boym, another Jewish migrant from the former Soviet Union, about what she called in 2001 the "future of nostalgia." Boym defines nostalgia as "longing for a home that no longer exists or has never existed." She makes a crucial distinction between "restorative" nostalgia and "reflective" nostalgia: "Restorative nostalgia stresses *nostos* (home) and attempts a transhistorical reconstruction of the lost home. Reflective nostalgia thrives on *algia* (the longing itself) and delays the homecoming—wistfully, ironically, desperately."[14]

This is a crucial distinction in thinking about Jewish café culture in the present moment. However, "reflective nostalgia" might also be a helpful concept to use to think about the period covered in this book. It seems that much of what took place in the café, and especially what was written about it, is a form of "reflective nostalgia," the longing that ironically and desperately delays the homecoming even as it facilitated sociability and the circulation of ideas in service of a budding modernity in Jewish life. In this view, the café emerges as a quintessential modern diasporic Jewish space, shaped by identities that are "constantly producing and reproducing themselves anew, through transformation and difference."[15] This reflection sends us from the twenty-first century back to Agnon's life and novel, with which we began our journey. In Agnon's writing, the early twentieth century's longing for the café is a diasporic one both for a past and for a future. It is a longing for a substitute for home. What Agnon called in Hebrew *beit kahava* (coffeehouse) is not the "lost home" but rather a diasporic, preliminary, contingent one, a thirdspace that mediates between reality and imagination, inside and outside, past and present. It is alluring and comforting but also temporary and ephemeral, without the false promise of homecoming. If Appelfeld's, Idov's, and Kaplansky's works are illustrative of something larger than themselves and their experiences, they might be telling us that contemporary Jewish writers and filmmakers are engaged in such nostalgic diasporic desire, playfully re-creating the thirdspace of the café, despite the absence of a physical structure or site.

ACKNOWLEDGMENTS

The seed of this book was sown many years ago in a series of short articles I have written in Hebrew for *Ha'aretz* newspaper. I owe a debt of gratitude to Benny Mer, the editor who initiated, edited, and published these articles. The enthusiastic response I received from many people for this publication made me realize that the topic merits a full-length study, thus initiating a long and unexpected journey of research, translation, lectures, teaching, writing, and editing. This book is the outcome of that scholarly journey, and I am happy to acknowledge the numerous people and institutions who supported me along the way.

Charlotte Ashby, Verena Dohrn, Gertrud Pickhan, and Anne-Christin Saß invited me to present my work in conferences in London and Berlin and then to contribute to volumes they were editing. W. Scott Haine and Mark Wollaeger invited me to contribute to volumes on café culture and on global modernisms. I have drawn on materials from these publications in chapters 1, 3, and 4 of this book. I thank the editors and the presses that published these volumes for allowing me to use these materials. Giddon Ticotsky invited me to give a lecture on Leah Goldberg and the coffeehouse and shared with me many materials and insights, for which I am very grateful. Kenneth Moss invited me to submit an article on the topic to *Jewish Social Studies*, parts of which have been incorporated into chapters 4 and 6. I thank the editors and the journal for their permission to use these materials. Thanks also go to Sandee Brawarsky, who solicited a short article on cafés and Jewish culture for the *New York Jewish Week* and suggested the title for this book.

I conducted research for this book at the Tel Aviv Municipality Archive, New York City Municipal Archives, Gnazim Archive, the National Library of Israel, the New York Public Library, the YIVO Institute, the Leo Baeck Institute, the American Jewish Historical Society, and the International Center of Photography. I thank the helpful staff of all these institutions for their support.

For help at different stages of the research and writing of this book in all kinds of ways, I would like to thank Robert Alter, Israel Bartal, Ya'ad Biran, Natan Cohen, Hasia Diner, Sidra Ezrahi, Matan Hermoni, Tal Hever-Chybowski, Avner Holtzman, Barbara Kirshenblatt-Gimblett, Chana Kronfeld, Avraham Novershtern, Eddy Portnoy, Paul Reitter, Naomi Seidman, Marci Shore, Rebecca Stanton, Tamara Sztyma-Knasiecka, Scott Ury, Suzanne Wasserman, Beth Wegner, and Sarah Wobick-Segev. For help with translation of texts from Polish, Russian, Yiddish, German, and Hebrew, I would like to thank Maria Blackwood, Nick Block, Sara Feldman, Calder Fong, Barbara Harshav, Alexandra Hoffman, Adriana X. Jacobs, Deborah Jones, Zuzanna Kołodziejska, Joanna Mazurkiewicz, Kai Mishuris, and William Runyan.

I would like to thank the people who invited me to give talks on topics related to the book: Lily Kahn and Andrea Schatz at UCL and King's College London, Vered Shem Tov at Stanford University, Chana Kronfeld at UC Berkeley, Rachel Seelig and Sidra Ezrahi at the Hebrew University, Hana Wirth-Nesher at Tel Aviv University, Na'ama Roken and Anna Band at the University of Chicago, Ranen Omer-Sherman and Shelley Salamensky at the University of Louisville, Melissa Weininger and Diane Wolfthal at Rice University, and Dell deChant at the University of South Florida. I learned much from the various audiences that engaged with the materials and helped me to understand them better.

I am grateful to graduate students at the University of Michigan who took my seminar on Jewish modernism—Nadav Linial, Yael Kenan, and Ya'akov Herskovitz—and commented on drafts from the book. I thank Ya'akov and Erin Platte for their help with images and permissions. Thanks to the undergraduate students who took my course "Urban Cafés and Modern Jewish Culture." I learned much from their questions, comments, and attempts to make sense of these materials. I was fortunate to work on this book as a fellow of the Frankel Institute for Advanced Judaic Studies during the academic years 2013–2014 and 2016–2017. I thank the fellows for their comments and suggestions on earlier drafts of chapters of this book. I am happy to acknowledge the financial support for this project that came from the Associate Professor Support Fund at the LSA College, the University of Michigan, as well as a Publication Subvention from the OVPR office at the University of Michigan.

For reading parts of the manuscript at various stages and giving me invaluable feedback, I would like to thank Naomi Brenner, Deborah Dash Moore, Ofer Dynes, Todd Endleman, Liora Halperin, Anita Norich, Derek Penslar, Allison Schachter, Rachel Seelig, Sasha Senderovich, Lisa Silverman, Karolina Szymaniak, and Jeffery Weidlinger. For expert help with editing drafts of the entire manuscript, I thank David Lowenstein. At NYU Press, my sincere gratitude goes to Jennifer Hammer. Jennifer was enthusiastic about this project from the day I met her. She read and commented on drafts of the book proposal and the book and helped me to move smoothly through the process of editing and publishing this book. Her editorial guidance and professionalism are highly appreciated. Thanks go also to Amy Klopfenstein and the production team at NYU Press.

My children, Yotam and Niv, have been growing up throughout the process of research and writing the book. I am thrilled with the fact that my older son, Yotam, now a freshman at Indiana University, read the entire manuscript and gave me invaluable feedback that helped to improve it. My greatest debt of gratitude is for my wife, Amanda Fisher, who helped this book and its author in more ways than I can think of. In fact, my love for and fascination with cafés and café culture go back to the time I first met Amanda, who was making her initial steps in the culinary world. A few years after, she became the founding chef of a café, working with my good friend David Ehrlich, the writer and owner of the bookstore-café Tmol-Shilshom in Jerusalem. I dedicate this book to Amanda and to David with love and appreciation.

NOTES

INTRODUCTION

1. Dan Laor, *Ḥaye Agnon* (Tel Aviv: Schocken, 1998), 34–48.
2. On the urban landscape of Lemberg at that time, see Markian Prokopovych, *Habsburg Lemberg: Architecture, Public Space, and Politics in the Galician Capital, 1772–1914* (West Lafayette, IN: Purdue University Press, 2009).
3. Shachar Pinsker, *Literary Passports: The Making of Modernist Hebrew Fiction in Europe* (Stanford, CA: Stanford University Press, 2011), 63–65.
4. On the flowering of modern Jewish culture in Lemberg and Habsburg Galicia in this period, see Joshua Shanes, *Diaspora Nationalism and Jewish Identity in Habsburg Galicia* (New York: Cambridge University Press, 2012).
5. S. Y. Agnon, *Tmol shilshom* (Tel Aviv: Schocken 1945), 13; English translation in Agnon, *Only Yesterday*, trans. Barbara Harshav (Princeton, NJ: Princeton University Press 2000), 9.
6. David Biale, *Cultures of the Jews: A New History* (New York: Schocken Books, 2002), 726.
7. Ibid., 725.
8. Tamara Chin, "The Invention of the Silk Road, 1877," *Critical Inquiry* 40, no. 1 (2013): 194–219.
9. For a discussion of the concepts of "network" and "mobility" in Jewish modernity, see Todd S. Presner, *Mobile Modernity: Germans, Jews, Trains* (New York: Columbia University Press, 2007); Laurence Roth, "Networks," in *The Routledge Handbook of Contemporary Jewish Cultures*, ed. Nadia Vlaman and Laurence Roth (London and New York: Routledge, 2014), 195–209.
10. For a discussion of "space" in Jewish culture and scholarship, see Barbara Mann, *Space and Place in Jewish Studies* (New Brunswick, NJ: Rutgers University Press, 2012).
11. Ralph S. Hattox, *Coffee and Coffee Houses: The Origin of a Social Beverage in the Medieval Near East* (Seattle: University of Washington Press, 1985).
12. Ulla Heise, *Coffee and Coffeehouses* (West Chester, PA: Schiffer, 1997); Markman Ellis, *The Coffee House: A Cultural History* (London: Weidenfeld and Nicolson, 2004); Brian W. Cowan, *The Social Life of Coffee: The Emergence of the British Coffeehouse* (New Haven, CT: Yale University Press, 2005).
13. Cowan, *Social Life*, 25.
14. Elliot Horowitz, "Coffee, Coffee-Houses, and the Nocturnal Rituals of Early Modern Jewry," *AJS Review* 14, no. 1 (1989): 17–46; Francesca Bregoli, *Mediter-*

ranean Enlightenment: Livornese Jews, Tuscan Culture, and Eighteenth-Century Reform (Stanford, CA: Stanford University Press, 2014), 152–180; Maoz Kahana, "The Shabbes Coffeehouse: On the Emergence of the Jewish Coffeehouse in Eighteenth-Century Prague," *Zion* 78, no. 1 (2013): 5–50.

15. Robert Liberles, *Jews Welcome Coffee: Tradition and Innovation in Early Modern Germany* (Waltham, MA: Brandeis University Press, 2012).

16. Brian Cowan, "Café or Coffeehouse? Transnational Histories of Coffee and Sociability," in *Drink in the Eighteenth and Nineteenth Centuries*, ed. Susanne Schmid and Barbara Schmidt-Haberkamp (London: Pickering and Chatto, 2014), 35–46.

17. On the relations between taverns and Jews in Poland, see Glenn Dynner, *Yankel's Tavern: Jews, Liquor, and Life in the Kingdom of Poland* (Oxford: Oxford University Press, 2014).

18. Shmuel Feiner, *The Origins of Jewish Secularization in Eighteenth-Century Europe* (Philadelphia: University of Pennsylvania Press, 2010), 48–56.

19. Cowan, "Café or Coffeehouse?," 38.

20. Sarah Wobick-Segev, "Buying, Selling, Being, Drinking: Jewish Coffeehouse Consumption in the Long Nineteenth Century," in *The Economy in Jewish History: New Perspectives on the Interrelationship between Ethnicity and Economic Life*, ed. Gideon Reuveni and Sarah Wobick-Segev (Oxford, UK: Berghahn Books, 2011), 115–134; Steven Beller, "'The Jew Belongs in the Coffeehouse': Jews, Central Europe and Modernity," in *The Viennese Café and Fin-de-Siècle Culture*, ed. Charlotte Ashby, Tag Gronberg, and Simon Shaw-Miller (Oxford, UK: Berghahn Books, 2013), 50–58; Marci Shore, *Caviar and Ashes: A Warsaw Generation's Life and Death in Marxism, 1918–1968* (New Haven, CT: Yale University Press, 2006).

21. Derek Penslar, "Introduction: The Press and the Jewish Public Sphere," *Jewish History* 14, no. 1 (2000): 3–8l; Jeffrey Veidlinger, *Jewish Public Culture in the Late Russian Empire* (Bloomington: Indiana University Press, 2009); Scott Ury, *Barricades and Banners: The Revolution of 1905 and the Transformation of Warsaw Jewry* (Stanford, CA: Stanford University Press, 2012).

22. Jürgen Habermas, *Strukturwandel der Öffentlichkeit: Untersuchungen zu einer Kategorie der bürgerlichen Gesellschaft* (Neuwied, Germany: Hermann Luchterhand, 1962); English translation in Habermas, *The Structural Transformation of the Public Sphere*, trans. Thomas Berger (Cambridge, MA: MIT Press, 1989), 30–32.

23. See Craig J. Calhoun, ed., *Habermas and the Public Sphere* (Cambridge, MA: MIT Press, 1992); James Van Horn Melton, *The Rise of the Public in Enlightenment Europe* (New York: Cambridge University Press, 2001), 226–251.

24. Markman Ellis has questioned Habermas's understanding of the English coffeehouse. Joan Landes critiqued Habermas from a feminist perspective, decrying the public sphere as essentially masculine. See Markman Ellis, "The Coffee Women, *The Spectator*, and the Public Sphere in the Early-Eighteenth Century," in *Women, Writing and the Public Sphere, 1700–1830*, ed. Elizabeth Eger, Charlotte Grant, Clíona Ó Gallchoir, and Penny Warburton (Cambridge: Cambridge University Press, 2001), 27–52; Joan B. Landes, *Women and the Public Sphere in the Age of*

the French Revolution (Ithaca, NY: Cornell University Press, 1988). See also Brian Cowan, "What Was Masculine about the Public Sphere?," *History Workshop Journal* 51 (2001): 127–157; Emma Clery, "Women, Publicity and the Coffee-House Myth," *Women: A Cultural Review* 2, no. 2 (1991): 681.

25. Habermas, *Structural Transformation*, 181–195.

26. In the transformed public sphere, spatial and social experiences were mediated through what Oskar Negt and Alexander Kluge call "public spheres of production." Oskar Negt and Alexander Kluge, *Öffentlichkeit und Erfahrung: Zur Organisationsanalyse von bürgerlicher und proletarischer Öffentlichkeit* (Frankfurt am Main: Suhrkamp, 1972).

27. Walter Benjamin, *Berliner Chronik* (Frankfurt am Main: Suhrkamp Verlag, 1972); English translation in Benjamin, "A Berlin Chronicle," in *Selected Writings*, vol. 2, ed. Michael W. Jennings, Howard Eiland, and Gary Smith (Cambridge, MA: Harvard University Press, 1999), 595–637.

28. The basic division between "place," defined as the physical setting, and "space," defined as an abstraction, the outcome of social processes by which human beings make sense of and negotiate place, has been the foundation of geography but was challenged by the field of cultural geography. This challenge is central to "the spatial turn" in the humanities and social sciences in general.

29. Henri Lefebvre, *The Production of Space* (Oxford, UK: Blackwell, 1991); Edward Soja, *Thirdspace: Journeys to Los Angeles and Other Real-and-Imagined Places* (Oxford, UK: Blackwell, 1996). Soja was one of the scholars who called attention to the "spatial turn" in historical and literary studies, a turn that began to influence Jewish studies in recent years.

30. For a discussion of homosociality, see Eve Kosofsky Sedgwick, *Between Men: English Literature and Male Homosocial Desire* (New York: Columbia University Press, 1985). For a discussion of homosociality in modern Jewish literature and culture in Europe, see Todd Presner, *Muscular Judaism: The Jewish Body and the Politics of Regeneration* (New York: Routledge, 2007); Pinsker, *Literary Passports*, 185–204; Naomi Seidman, *The Marriage Plot: Or, How Jews Fell in Love with Love, and with Literature* (Stanford, CA: Stanford University Press, 2016).

31. Wealthy Jewish women were central in salons in Berlin and Vienna. See Hilde Spiel, *Fanny Von Arnstein: A Daughter of the Enlightenment, 1758–1818* (New York: Berg, 1991); Deborah Hertz, *Jewish High Society in Old Regime Berlin* (New Haven, CT: Yale University Press, 1988).

32. George Steiner makes a similar proposal to map what he calls "the idea of Europe": "Draw the coffeehouse map and you have one of the essential markers of 'the idea of Europe.'" George Steiner, *The Idea of Europe* (Tilburg, Netherlands: Nexus Institute, 2004), 17.

33. Jacob Katz, *Out of the Ghetto: The Social Background of Jewish Emancipation, 1770–1870* (Cambridge, MA: Harvard University Press, 1973); Jacob Katz, *Tradition and Crisis: Jewish Society at the End of the Middle Ages* (New York: Schocken, 1993).

34. On processes of Jewish acculturation and integration, which are distinct from the ideological and problematic term "assimilation," see Todd M. Endelman, "Assimilation," in *YIVO Encyclopedia of Jews in Eastern Europe*, July 2010, www .yivoencyclopedia.org. See also David Sorkin, "Emancipation and Assimilation: Two Concepts and Their Application to German-Jewish History," *Leo Baeck Institute Yearbook* 35 (1990) 17–33; Jonathan Frankel, "Assimilation and the Jews in Nineteenth-Century Europe: Towards a New Historiography?," in *Assimilation and Community: The Jews in Nineteenth-Century Europe*, ed. Jonathan Frankel and Steven J. Zipperstein (Cambridge: Cambridge University Press, 2004), 1–37. The classic discussion of these terms is in Milton M. Gordon, *Assimilation in American Life: The Role of Race, Religion and National Origins* (New York: Oxford University Press, 1964).

35. On diasporic Jewish culture, see Daniel Boyarin and Jonathan Boyarin, *Powers of Diaspora: Two Essays on the Relevance of Jewish Culture* (Minneapolis: University of Minnesota Press, 2008). On modernist diasporic Jewish literature, see Allison Schachter, *Diasporic Modernisms: Hebrew and Yiddish Literature in the Twentieth Century* (New York: Oxford University Press, 2011).

36. Rebecca Kobrin, *Bialystok and Its Diaspora* (Bloomington: Indiana University Press, 2010); A. F. Kahn and Adam Mendelsohn, *Transnational Traditions: New Perspectives on American Jewish History* (Detroit: Wayne State University Press, 2014). See also Moshe Rosman, "Jewish History across Borders," in *Rethinking European Jewish History*, ed. Jeremy Cohen and Moshe Rosman (Portland, OR: Littman Library of Jewish Civilization, 2009), 15–29.

37. As the Boyarins write, "From the standpoint of territorial states, 'migrancy' is an intolerable situation: people are either 'im-migrants' or 'e-migrants,' but in either case there is a crossing of a juridical boundary, a reclassified jurisdiction." Boyarin and Boyarin, *Powers of Diaspora*, 27.

38. Dan Miron, *From Continuity to Contiguity: Towards a New Jewish Literary Thinking* (Stanford, CA: Stanford University Press, 2010).

39. Malcolm Bradbury, "The Cities of Modernism," in *Modernism: A Guide to European Literature, 1890–1930*, ed. Malcolm Bradbury and James McFarlane (London: Penguin, 1991), 96.

40. Michael Rössner, ed., *Literarische Kaffeehäuser: Kaffeehausliteraten* (Vienna: Böhlau, 1999); Leona Rittner, W. Scott Haine, and Jeffrey H. Jackson, eds., *The Thinking Space: The Café as a Cultural Institution in Paris, Italy, and Vienna* (Farnham, UK: Ashgate, 2013).

41. Scott Spector, "Modernism without Jews: A Counter-historical Argument," *Modernism/Modernity* 13, no. 4 (2006): 617.

42. For an exploration of Jewish café culture in Lemberg/Lwów, see Józef Mayen, "Gawędy o Lwowskich Kawiarniach" (1934), available at www.lwow.com.pl; on Budapest, see Mary Gluck, "The Budapest Coffee House and the Making of 'Jewish Modernity' at the Fin de Siècle," *Journal of the History of Ideas* 74, no. 2 (2013): 289–306.

43. On Sephardi Jews and cafés in North African cities and Paris, see Ethan Katz, *The Burdens of Brotherhood: Jews and Muslims from North Africa to France* (Cambridge, MA: Harvard University Press, 2015). For cafés in Tangier, see Susan Gilson Miller, "Making Tangier Modern: Ethnicity and Urban Development," in *Jewish Culture and Society in North Africa*, ed. Emily R. Gottreich and Daniel Schroeter (Bloomington: Indiana University Press, 2011), 128–149. On Baghdad, see Stacy E. Holden, *A Documentary History of Modern Iraq* (Gainesville: University Press of Florida, 2012). On Cairo, see Alon Tam, "How Cairo's Cafés Made Egypt's 1919 Revolution," *Ha'aretz*, January 14, 2017.

44. Zvi Karniel, *Ha-felyeton ha-'ivri: Hitpatchuto shel ha-felyeton ba-sifrut ha-'ivrit* (Tel Aviv: Alef, 1981); Hildegard Kernmayer, *Judentum im Wiener Feuilleton (1848–1903): Exemplarische Untersuchungen zum literarästhetischen und politischen Diskurs der Moderne* (Tübingen, Germany: Niemeyer, 1998); Katia Dianina, "The Feuilleton: An Everyday Guide to Public Culture in the Age of the Great Reforms," *Slavic and East European Journal* 47, no. 2 (2003): 187–210.

CHAPTER 1. ODESSA

1. Leon Feinberg, *Der farmishpeter dor: Roman in fir tayln* (New York: L. Faynberg yoyvl-komitet, 1954).

2. Studies of the history and culture of Odessa and its Jews in this period include Steven Zipperstein, *The Jews of Odessa: A Cultural History, 1794–1881* (Berkeley: University of California Press, 1985); Patricia Herlihy, *Odessa: A History, 1794–1914* (Cambridge, MA: Harvard University Press, 1986); Charles King, *Odessa: Genius and Death in a City of Dreams* (New York: Norton, 2011); Jarrod Tanny, *City of Rogues and Schnorrers: Russia's Jews and the Myth of Old Odessa* (Bloomington: Indiana University Press, 2011); and Rebecca J. Stanton, *Isaac Babel and the Self-Invention of Odessan Modernism* (Evanston, IL: Northwestern University Press, 2012).

3. Herlihy, *Odessa*, 1–20.

4. King, *Odessa*, 100.

5. Ibid., 106.

6. Zipperstein, *Jews of Odessa*, 96–116.

7. Oleg Gubar and Alexander Rozenboim, "Daily Life in Odessa," in *Odessa Memories*, ed. Nicolas V. Iljine (Seattle: University of Washington Press, 2003), 102.

8. John Moore, *A Journey from London to Odessa: With Notices of New Russia* (Paris: Delaforest, 1833); Patricia Herlihy, "Odessa: Staple Trade and Urbanization in New Russia," *Jahrbücher für Geschichte Osteuropas* 21, no. 2 (1973): 184–195.

9. Quoted in David Magarshack, *Pushkin: A Biography* (New York: Grove, 1968), 139. About Greek and Turkish coffeehouses, see Gubar and Rozenboim, "Daily Life in Odessa," 86.

10. Robert Sears, *An Illustrated Description of the Russian Empire* (New York: R. Sears, 1855), 167.

11. Russian supplement to *Ha-carmel*, December 8, 1861, 91–92.

12. Osip Rabinovich, "Istoriia a tom, kak Reb Khaim-Shulim Feige puteshestvoval iz Kishineva v Odessu, i chto s nim sluchilos" (1865), in *Izbrannoe* (Jerusalem: Institute of Russian Jewry, 1985), 247–248.

13. Perez Smolenskin, *Simchat ḥanef* (Vilnius: Katsenelenbogen, 1905), 10.

14. Katz, *Tradition and Crisis*, 162.

15. A. A. Kabak, *Toldot mishpaḥa aḥat* (Tel Aviv: Devir, 1998). For an analysis of Kabak's historical novel and Smolenskin's role in it, see Ruth Shenfeld, "Sipur Bli Giborim: Al roman Odessi shel A.A. Kabak," *Jerusalem Studies in Hebrew Literature* 9 (1986): 215–238.

16. Kabak, *Toldot mishpaḥa aḥat*, 1032–1033.

17. Ibid., 1035.

18. Ibid., 1037.

19. Herlihy, *Odessa*, vii.

20. Cited ibid., 279.

21. Karl Baedeker, *Russland: Handbuch für Reisende* (Leipzig: Baedeker, 1888); H. Tiedeman, *The Continent by Queenboro', viâ Flushing! A Comprehensive Handbook for English and American Tourists Abroad* (London: Iliffe and Son, 1894), 512–513.

22. Steven Zippertstein, "How It Was Done in Odessa?" in *Homage to Odessa*, ed. Rachel Arbel (Tel Aviv: Beth Hatefutsoth, 2002), 78.

23. Quoted in Herkihy, *Odessa*, 259–260.

24. Gubar and Rozenboim, "Daily Life in Odessa," 102–103.

25. Dan Miron, "The Odessa Sages," in Arbel, *Homage to Odessa*, 62–81. See also Steven Zipperstein, "Remapping Odessa, Rewriting Cultural History," *Jewish Social Studies* 2, no. 2 (1996): 21–36.

26. Elḥanan Leib Lewinsky, "Ir shel ḥaiym," *Ha-tsfirah*, 1896, reprinted in Lewinsky, *Kitve E. L. Lewinsky*, vol. 2 (Tel Aviv: Dvir, 1935), 452–456.

27. Ibid. Lewinsky actually visited cafés in Odessa, Warsaw, and other European and Middle Eastern cities and wrote about his experiences in a number of feuilletons he published in the 1890s and early 1900s.

28. Beseda was a club established by Odessan Jews in 1864 in order to foster fellowship and understanding between Jews, non-Jews, and "assimilated Jews." Membership was unrestricted, and everybody was encouraged to join. Beseda was hailed in the Jewish press, and a notice about it was published in the *Odeski vestnik*. But it probably closed within its first year and was only resurrected at the turn of the twentieth century. See Zipperstein, *Jews of Odessa*, 110.

29. In these "salons," there was even a hierarchy of reading texts and speaking. The first to speak were the older and more established writers, followed by the younger writers who came to Odessa. See Lea Beirach, "From Space to Symbol: The Memories of Hebrew Odessa, 1881–1914" (master's thesis, Tel Aviv University, 1991).

30. John Klier, *Imperial Russia's Jewish Question, 1855–1881* (Cambridge: Cambridge University Press, 1995).

31. Nahma Sandrow, *Vagabond Stars: A World History of Yiddish Theater* (New York: Limelight, 1986), 51–56.

32. Yacob P. Adler, "40 yor oyf der bine, mayn lebens-geshikhte un di geshikhte fun idishen theater," *Di varhayt* (New York), April 30, 1916–February 22, 1919; English translation in Jacob P. Adler, *A Life on the Stage: A Memoir* (New York: Knopf, 1999).
33. Adler, *Life on the Stage*, 54–60.
34. "Night after night we met at Akiva's Restaurant on Rivnoya Street, never guessing that in this very room where we sat and dreamt of it, the first Yiddish performance would take place." Ibid., 73.
35. Ibid., 112.
36. Barbara J. Henry, *Rewriting Russia: Jacob Gordin's Yiddish Drama* (Seattle: University of Washington Press, 2011).
37. Jacob Gordin, *Safo*, in *Dramen* (New York: Soyrkel fur Ya'akov Gordin's fraynt, 1911). The play was performed on the Russian stage, especially by the Korsh troupe, under the name "Dos odeser lebn" (The Odessa life). In 1912, "Sappho," under the name "Di yidishe safo," was published in Odessa in the Russian translation of D. Rosenblit (Yiddish Theater Lexicon). For more about the play, see Beth Kaplan, *Finding the Jewish Shakespeare: The Life and Legacy of Jacob Gordin* (Syracuse, NY: Syracuse University Press, 2007), 91–94.
38. Gordin, *Safo*, 33.
39. John Klier, *Russians, Jews, and the Pogroms of 1881–1882* (Cambridge: Cambridge University Press, 2011), 24–25. There were pogroms, or waves of anti-Jewish violence, in Odessa in 1881, in 1903, and the largest one in 1905.
40. "Ma'sim be-khol yom," *Ha-melits*, August 10, 1887, 4.
41. Bar-Katsin, "Ma'asim be-khol yom," *Ha-melits*, August 23, 1887, 3.
42. Ibid.
43. Ibid.
44. These tensions between rich and poor were also present in S. Y. Abramovitch's enlarged and revised version of his novel *Fishke der krumer* (Fishke the lame), published in Odessa in 1888. Abramovitch added to the novel new chapters in which the beggar Fishke arrives in Odessa and is bewildered by it. He says, "there's also plenty of your modern type, high-tone almsmen; all shave their faces and prefer to rub shoulders with other Jewish men who dress like French and sit around in cafés." S. Y. Abramovitch, *Ale ksovim fun Mendele Moykher Sforim*, vol. 2 (Odessa, 1907), 228.
45. The first part of the epistolary novel was written in Odessa in 1892 under the name *London: A roman fun der Odeser kalyner berze*. Menakhem-Mendl had briefly appeared in an epistolary feuilleton in 1887 as a young husband still living with his in-laws.
46. Sholem Aleichem, "Londons," in *Ale verk fun Sholem Aleykhem*, vol. 3 (Buenos Aires: Ikuf, 1952), 23; English translation in Sholem Aleichem, *The Letters of Menakhem-Mendl and Sheyne-Sheyndl*, trans. Hillel Halkin (New Haven, CT: Yale University Press, 2002), 8.
47. Sholem Aleichem, "Londons," 24; Sholem Aleichem, *Letters*, 10–11.

48. See also the Russian short story by Sholem Aleichem, "Characters from the 'Small Bourse'" (Tipy "maloi birzhi"), in *Yiddish Fiction and the Crisis of Modernity, 1905–1914*, by Mikhail Krutikov (Stanford, CA: Stanford University Press, 2001), 54.

49. Sholem Aleichem, *Letters*, 11.

50. Ibid., 14.

51. Ibid., 13.

52. Ibid., 16.

53. Robert Weinberg, *The Revolution of 1905 in Odessa: Blood on the Steps* (Bloomington: Indiana University Press, 1993), 20–23.

54. Caroline Humphrey, "Odessa: Pogroms in a Cosmopolitan City," in *Post-cosmopolitan Cities: Explorations of Urban Coexistence*, ed. Caroline Humphrey and Vera Skvirskaya (Oxford, UK: Berghahn Books, 2012), 17–62; Rebecca Stanton, "'A Monstrous Staircase': Inscribing the Revolution of 1905," in *Rites of Place: Public Commemoration and Celebration in Russia and Beyond*, ed. Julie Buckler and Emily D. Johnson (Evanston, IL: Northwestern University Press, 2013), 59–80.

55. Barry Scherr observes regarding Odessa's role in the novel, "with its stimulating intellectual and cultural life, its cafés and lively downtown streets, the rich mix of nationalities, the distinctive environs, and even the peculiarities of the local speech, the city does not just provide the novel's main setting, but seems integral to the lives of the major characters, including the narrator." Barry Scherr, "An Odessa Odyssey: Vladimir Jabotinsky's *The Five*," *Slavic Review* 70, no. 1 (2011): 94–115.

56. Vladimir Jabotinsky, *The Five: A Novel of Jewish Life in Turn-of-the-Century Odessa* (Ithaca, NY: Cornell University Press, 2005), 58.

57. Ibid., 26.

58. Israel Trivus, "Etsel Ambarazaki," *Ha-mashkif*, May 5, 1941, 3.

59. Ambarzaki and other Greek cafés appear in Jabotinsky's novel *The Five*, in which the narrator is enjoying "a cup of Turkish coffee and some Turkish delight in his favorite Greek café on the corner of Krasnyi Lane" (12). Greek cafés are mentioned in the writings of another Russian-Jewish Odessan writer, Lev Slavin, who wrote in his memoir "My Hometown Odessa" (1968), "Branching off from De-ribasovskaya St. was a small shady bystreet immersed in acacias. It had retained its old name of Krasny Lane. Here, I remembered, had been numerous cafés kept by the Greeks, and no sooner had I stepped into the lane than the pungent smell of coffee hit my nostrils." Lev Slavin, "My Hometown Odessa," *Soviet Life* 6 (June 1970): 38–39.

60. Café Libman is mentioned in the autobiographical novel of the writer Valentin Kataev, *A Small Farm in the Steppe* (*Khutorok v stepi*, 1956).

61. Paul Avrich, *The Russian Anarchists* (Princeton, NJ: Princeton University Press, 1967), 61–63.

62. Anke Hilbrenner, "Der Bombenanschlag auf das Café Libman in Odessa am 17. Dezember 1905: Terrorismus als Gewaltgeschichte," in *Jahrbücher für Geschichte Osteuropas* 58, no. 2 (2010): 210–231.

63. A. Kuprin, *Gambrinus: And Other Stories*, trans. Bernard G. Guerney (New York: Adelphi, 1925), 11–73.

64. Ibid, 63.

65. Ibid., 72–73.

66. Ya'akov Rabinovitz, *Neve kayits* (Tel Aviv: Mitzpe, 1934).

67. Ibid., 155–156.

68. Ibid., 191.

69. Sholem Aleichem, *Ale verk fun Sholem Aleykhem*, vol. 7 (Buenos Aires: Ikuf, 1952), 286.

70. Ibid., 288.

71. Ibid., 290–294.

72. Tanny, *City of Rogues and Schnorrers*, 80.

73. Semyon Yushkevich, *Leon Drei* (Berlin: Izdatelstvo Grzhebina, 1923), 48.

74. Ibid., 49–50.

75. William E. Curtis, *Around the Black Sea: Asia Minor, Armenia, Caucasus, Circassia, Daghestan, the Crimea, Roumania* (New York: Hodder and Stoughton, 1911), 329.

76. Sydney Adamson, "Odessa—The Portal of an Empire," *Harper's Magazine*, November 1912, 902–913.

77. Ibid., 906.

78. Roshanna Sylvester, *Tales of Old Odessa: Crime and Civility in a City of Thieves* (DeKalb: Northern Illinois University Press, 2005), 11–13.

79. Grigory Moskvich, *Putevoditel' po Odesse* (Odessa: Tip. "Tekhnik," 1913), 47–49.

80. Sylvester, *Tales of Old Odessa*, 5.

81. Quoted ibid., 114.

82. "Zvuki dnia," *Odesskiy listok*, August 11, 1912, 2; English translation in Sylvester, *Tales of Old Odessa*, 117–118.

83. "Zvuki dnia: Damskaia boltovnia," *Odesskiy listok*, April 7, 1912, 3; English translation in Sylvester, *Tales of Old Odessa*, 112.

84. Sylvester, *Tales of Old Odessa*, 114.

85. Satana, "O tom, o sem: Robinisti," *Odesskaia pochta*, October 17, 1915, 3; English translation in Sylvester, *Tales of Old Odessa*, 115.

86. Eliezer Steinman, *Ester Ḥayut* (Warsaw: Stybel, 1922–1923).

87. Ibid., 79.

88. Ibid., 81.

89. Ibid., 139.

90. Ya'akov Fichman, *Sofrim be-chayehem* (Tel Aviv: Massada, 1942), 69–70.

91. See Kenneth Moss, *Jewish Renaissance in the Russian Revolution* (Cambridge, MA: Harvard University Press, 2009).

92. Isaac Babel, "Odessa," in *The Complete Works of Isaac Babel*, trans. Peter Constantine (New York: Norton, 2001), 78.

93. See Efraim Sicher, *Jews in Russian Literature after the October Revolution: Writers and Artists between Hope and Apostasy* (Cambridge: Cambridge University Press,

1995); Rebecca J. Stanton, *Isaac Babel and the Self-Invention of Odessan Modernism* (Evanston, IL: Northwestern University Press, 2012).

94. The critic Max Erik was probably the first to note the "variants on Menakhem-Mendl in Babel's heroes of the Odessa stories." See Max Erik, "*Menakhem-Mendl* [A Marxist Critique]," *Prooftexts* 6, no. 1 (1986): 23–39. For a discussion of Babel's Jewishness and the place of Yiddish and Hebrew literature and culture in Babel's work, see Efraim Sicher, *Babel' in Context: A Study in Cultural Identity* (Boston: Academic Studies Press, 2012).

95. The first sketch about Odessa was published in *Vecherniaia zvezda* (Petrograd) on March 19, 1918; the second sketch was published in the same newspaper on the March 21, 1918. Both sketches appeared under the title "Listki ob Odesse." Isaac Babel, *Sobranie sochinenii*, vol. 1 (Moscow: Vremia, 2006), 536–538; English translation of the second sketch in Babel, "The Aroma of Odessa," in *Complete Works*, 80–82.

96. Babel, "Aroma of Odessa," 82.

97. Isaac Babel, "The End of the Almshouse," in *Complete Works*, 176.

98. Isaac Babel, *Sunset*, in *Complete Works*, 760.

99. Efraim Sicher, "Isaac Babel's Jewish Roots," *Jewish Quarterly* 25 (Autumn 1977): 25–27.

100. Leonid Utesov, *Spasibo serdtse* (Moscow: Vagrius, 1999), 132.

101. Tanny, *City of Rogues and Schnorrers*, 88.

102. Quoted ibid., 115.

103. Ilya Ilf and Evgeny Petrov, *The Golden Calf: A Novel*, trans. Konstantin Gurevich and Helen Anderson (Rochester, NY: Open Letter, 2009), 136–137.

104. Ibid., 137.

CHAPTER 2. WARSAW

1. Glenn Dynner and François Guesnet, eds., *Warsaw. The Jewish Metropolis: Essays in Honor of the 75th Birthday of Professor Antony Polonsky* (Leiden: Brill, 2015).

2. See Stefan Kieniewicz, "The Jews of Warsaw, Polish Society and the Partitioning Powers 1795–1862," in *The Jews in Warsaw*, ed. Władysław T. Bartoszewski and Antony Polonsky (Oxford, UK: Basil Blackwell, 1991), 151–170.

3. Anthony Polonsky, "Warsaw," in *The YIVO Encyclopedia of Jews in Eastern Europe*, December 13, 2010, www.yivoencyclopedia.org.

4. Kazimierz W Wójcicki, *Kawa literacka w Warszawie* (Warsaw: Gebethner i Wolff, 1873); Antoni Magier, *Estetyka miasta stołecznego Warszawy* (1830), ed. Hanna Szwankowska (Wrocław: Zakład Narodowy im. Ossolińskich, 1963). See also Marta Jazowska, "Café Culture in 18th Century Poland," Culture.pl, October 10, 2014, http://culture.pl.

5. Halina Goldberg, *Music in Chopin's Warsaw* (New York: Oxford University Press, 2008), 292–296.

6. Jacob Shatzky, *Geshikhte fun Yidn in Varshe*, vol. 1 (New York: Yidisher visinshaflekher Institut, hisorishe sektsie, 1947), 295, 307. For an overview of the Jewish

participation in the anti-Russian uprising, see Yisrael Bartal and Magdalena Opalski, *Poles and Jews: A Failed Brotherhood* (Hanover, NH: University Press of New England, 1992).

7. See Nathan Cohen, "Distributing Knowledge: Warsaw as a Center of Jewish Publishing, 1850–1914," in Dynner and Guesnet, *Warsaw*, 180–206; Shachar Pinsker, "Warsaw in Hebrew Literature 1880–1920: New Perspectives," *Studia Judaica* 35, no. 1 (2015): 105–137.

8. Franciszek Galiński, "Z gawęd i wspomnień o starej Warszawie: Dziatwa Appolina w mleczarni Udziałowej," *Stolica*, no. 37 (1958): 14; Andrzej Z. Makowiecki, *Warszawskie kawiarnie literackie* (Warsaw: Iskry, 2013), 62–73.

9. The Polish-Jewish writer Bernard Singer wrote that in the early twentieth century, an "invisible wall that separated the district from the rest of the city" still existed. Many Polish children spoke about it with fear, and their elders treated it with contempt. Bernard Singer, *Moje Nalewki* (Warsaw: Czytelnik, 1959), 45.

10. Dovid Pinski, "Geshikhte fun di *Yontev bletlekh*," *Di tsukunft* 50, no. 5 (1945): 321–324.

11. Ben Avigdor, "El hovevei sfat-ever ve-sifruta," in *Leah moheret ha-dagim* (Warsaw: Ben Avigdor, 1891), i.

12. David Frishman, *Otiyot porhot* (Warsaw: Ben Avigdor, 1892), 23–32.

13. Dynner and Guesnet, introduction to *Warsaw*, 9.

14. For an account of Jewish readership in this period, using statistics from libraries and other sources, see Jeffrey Veidlinger, *Jewish Public Culture in the Late Russian Empire* (Bloomington: Indiana University Press, 2009), 67–113.

15. On Peretz's "salon," see Yitzhak Dov Berkowitz, *Undzere rishoynim: Zikhroynes-dertseylungen vegn Sholem-Aleichem un zayn dor* (Tel Aviv: Ha-Menorah, 1966), 56–65. For an overview of these salons, see Ela Bauer, "From the Salons to the Street: The Development of a Jewish Public Sphere in Warsaw at the End of the 19th Century," *Jahrbuch des Simon-Dubnow-Instituts* 7 (2008): 143–159.

16. See Elhonan Zeitlin, *In a lierarisher shtub* (Buenos Aires: Tsentral farband fun Poylishe Yidn in Argentine, 1946).

17. Ya'akov Fichman, *Ruhot menagnot* (Jerusalem: Mosad Bialik, 1952), 9–10.

18. Quoted in Scott Ury, "In Kotik's Corner: Urban Culture, Bourgeois Politics and the Struggle for Jewish Civility in Turn of the Century Eastern Europe," in Dynner and Guesnet, *Warsaw*, 207.

19. Scott Ury, *Barricades and Banners: The Revolution of 1905 and the Transformation of Warsaw Jewry* (Stanford, CA: Stanford University Press, 2012), 146–153; Ury, "In Kotik's Corner," 207–226.

20. Abraham Teitelbaum, *Varshever heyf: Mentshn un geshenishn* (Buenos Aires: Tsentral-farband fun Poylishe Yidn in Argentine, 1947), 140.

21. Sholem Asch, *Varshe* (Warsaw: Kultul Lige, 1930), 242–244. The novel is the second part of Asch's trilogy, *Farn mabl* (Before the deluge), translated into English by Willa and Edwin Muir as *Three Cities* (New York: G. P. Putnam's Sons, 1933).

22. Avrom Reyzen, *Epizodn fun mayn lebn* (Vilna: B. Kletskin, 1927), 212.

23. Ibid., 217.

24. About Kotik, who later in life wrote an important biography of his childhood and early life in the shtetl, see Yekhezkel Kotik, *Journey to a Nineteenth-Century Shtetl: The Memoirs of Yekhezkel Kotik*, ed. David Assaf (Detroit: Wayne State University Press, 2008).

25. A. Litvin, "Yehezkel Kotik un zayn kawiarnia," in *Yudishe neshomes*, vol. 4 (New York: Folksbildung, 1917), 1.

26. Shlomo Shrebrek, *Zikhronot ha-motzi le-or Shlomo Shrebrek* (Tel Aviv: Shrebrek, 1955), 143.

27. Ibid., 144.

28. Litvin, "Yehezkel Kotik," 2–3.

29. Avrom Reyzen, *Epizoden fun mayn lebn*, vol. 1 (Vilna: B. Kletzkin, 1929), 215.

30. Ibid.

31. Litvin, "Yehezkel Kotik," 4.

32. On April 25, 1913, Sholem Aleichem wrote to Kotik, "To my very dear friend, Reb Khatskl Kotik! This is the name my Menakhem-Mendl has bestowed upon you in his second letter, published in *Haynt*, and he will not forget you, God willing, in any of his letters to Sheyne-Sheyndl. Every Friday, God willing, he will mention you and I hope you are not angry with either him or with me." Quoted in David Assaf, introduction to *Journey to a Nineteenth-Century Shtetl*, 45.

33. Sholem Aleichem, *Menakhem-Mendl: Nyu York–Varshe–Vin–Yehupets* (Tel Aviv: Sholem Aleichem House, 1977); English translation in Sholem Aleichem, *The Further Adventures of Menakhem-Mendl*, trans. Aliza Shevrin (Syracuse, NY: Syracuse University Press, 2001).

34. Sholem Aleichem, *Further Adventures*, 8, 14.

35. Ury, "In Kotik's Corner," 214.

36. Sholem Asch, *Ha-tsfirah*, May 19, 1901, 2–3.

37. L. Shapiro, "Berte," in *Di yudishe melukhe un andere zakhn* (New York: Farlag Yidish lebn, 1929), 253–266; English translation in Shapiro, "Bertha," trans. Golda Werman, *Fiction* 12 (1994): 147–155.

38. Shapiro, "Bertha," 148.

39. Ibid., 152–153.

40. Eliezer Steinman, *Sehor, sehor, Ha-tekufah* 1 (1918): 125.

41. Zalman Shneour, *Ha-tsfirah*, June 29–July 1, 1903.

42. We find a similar situation in Sholem Asch's Yiddish story *Der kleyner daytsh* (The little German, 1926).

43. Avrom Reyzen, *Fermashken't zikh aleyn: Ertseylung* (Warsaw: Ferlag Bikher-far-ale, 1905).

44. Ephraim Kaganowski, *Yidishe shrayber in der heym* (Paris: Oyfsnay, 1956), 45.

45. Ibid., 37.

46. Ibid., 43.

47. Ibid., 46.

48. Litvin, "Yehezkel Kotik," 6.

49. Sholem Aleichem, *Menakhem-Mendl*, 165; Sholem Aleichem, *Further Adventures*, 90.

50. Isaac Bashevis Singer, "Concerning Yiddish Literature in Poland" (1943), English translation in *Prooftexts* 15, no. 2 (1995): 113–127.

51. About Hebrew literary life in interwar Warsaw, see Nathan Cohen, *Sefer, sofer ve-'iton: Merkaz ha-tarbut ha-yehudit be-varshah, 1918–1942* (Jerusalem: Magnes, 2003), 142–159.

52. After raising some funds, the association was located at 1 Leszno Street and then at 11 Tłomackie. Only after more than two years, on October 25, 1918, did the association find a home in the second floor of a building at the nearby 13 Tłomackie Street.

53. Cohen, *Sefer*; Nathan Cohen, "Association of Jewish Writers and Journalists in Warsaw," *YIVO Encyclopedia of Jews in Eastern Europe*, July 2017, www.yivoency-clopedia.org.

54. Eliyahu Shulman, *Getselten* 3, nos. 13–14 (1947): 55.

55. Isaac Bashevis Singer, "Der shrayber klub," *Forverts*, January 13–December 28, 1956.

56. Isaac Bashevis Singer, "Figurn un epizodn fun literatn Fareyn," *Forverts*, June 28, 1979, 3.

57. Bashevis Singer, "Der shrayber klub," *Forverts*, January 13, 1956.

58. Kaganowski, *Yidishe shrayber*, 455–463.

59. Isaac Bashevis Singer, "Concerning Yiddish Literature," 122.

60. Ibid.

61. Melech Ravitch, *Dos mayse-bukh fun mayn lebn*, vol. 3 (Tel Aviv: Farlag Y. L Per-etz, 1962), 309–336.

62. Ibid., 317–320.

63. Zusman Segalovitsh, *Tlomatske 13: Fun farbrenṭen nekhtent* (Buenos Aires: Tsentral-farband fun Poylishe Yidn in Argenṭine, 1946), 9–10.

64. Kadya Molodowsky, "Fun mayn altern zaydn," *Svive* 34 (1971): 40–42.

65. Kaganowski, *Yidisher shrayber*, 456.

66. Nakhmen Mayzl, *Geven amol a lebn: Dos yidishe kultur-lebn in poyln tsvishn beyde velt-milkhomes* (Buenos Aires: Tsentral farband fun poylishe yidn in argentine, 1951), 143–144.

67. See Aleksandra Geller, "Shvu'onim te'omin: *Wiadomości literackie* ve *Literar-ishe bleter*: Behina hashva'atit," in *Historyah mitnageshet ve-kiyum meshutaf: Perspektivot hadashot 'al ha-mifgash ha-Yehudi-Polani*, ed. Daniel Blatman (Tel Aviv: Open University Press, 2015), 171–185.

68. Mieczysław Grydzewski, "Brylanty," *Wiadomości*, December 15, 1968.

69. Grydzewski edited the journal of the group, with the name *Skamander*.

70. Aleksander Wat, *Dziennik bez samogłosek*, ed. Krzysztof Rutkowski (London: Polonia, 1986), 180.

71. On the Jewishness of Słonimski and Tuwim, see Marci Shore, "The Spring That Passed: The Pikador Poets' Return to Jewishness," *Polin* 22 (2002): 414–426; Antoni Polonski, "Julian Tuwim: Confronting Antisemitism in Poland," in *The Individual in History: Essays in Honor of Jehuda Reinharz*, ed. Chae-Ran Y. Freeze,

Sylvia F. Fried, and Eugene R. Sheppard (Waltham, MA: Brandies University Press, 2015), 384–402; and Magdalena Opalski, "*Wiadomosci literackie*: Polemics on the Jewish Question, 1924–1939," in *The Jews of Poland between Two World Wars*, ed. Yisrael Gutman, Ezra Mendelsohn, and Jehuda Reinharz (Hanover, NH: University Press of New England, 1989).

72. Quoted in Czeslaw Miłosz, *The History of Polish Literature* (Berkeley: University of California Press, 1983), 385–386.

73. Antoni Słonimski, *Alfabet wspomnień* (Warsaw: PIW, 1975).

74. Jan Żyznowski, "Pod Picadorem," *Świat*, December 14, 1918, 7.

75. Kazimierz Wierzyński, *Pamietnik poety* (Warsaw: Interim, 1991), 83.

76. Quoted in Miłosz, *History of Polish Literature*, 385–386.

77. Makowiecki, *Warszawskie kawiarnie literackie*, 109–110.

78. Ron Nowicki, *Warsaw: The Cabaret Years* (San Francisco: Mercury House, 1992).

79. Beth Holmgren, "Acting Out: Qui Pro Quo in the Context of Interwar Warsaw," *East European Politics and Societies and Cultures* 27, no. 2 (2013): 205–223.

80. Nowicki, *Warsaw*, 65–76.

81. See the poems "Melodia" by Julian Tuwim, translated by Pacze Moj, Pacze Moj's blog, January 22, 2011, http://paczemoj.blogspot.com; and "In a Literary Café" by Aleksander Wat, translated by Leonard Nathan, in *With the Skin: Poems of Aleksander Wat* (New York: Ecco, 1989), 95.

82. Marci Shore, *Caviar and Ashes: A Warsaw Generation's Life and Death in Marxism, 1918–1968* (New Haven, CT: Yale University Press, 2006), 11–13.

83. Witold Gombrowicz, *Polish Memories*, trans. Bill Johnston (New Haven, CT: Yale University Press, 2004), 109.

84. Ibid., 178.

85. Shore, *Caviar and Ashes*, 2.

86. Aleksander Wat, *My Century: The Odyssey of a Polish Intellectual*, trans. Richard Lourie (New York: Norton, 1988), 293, 116.

87. Ibid., 224. Wat also wrote, beautifully and enigmatically, about Jewishness and about cafés in short stories with kabbalistic undertones, such as "The Eternally Wandering Jew" and "Has Anyone Seen Pigeon Street?" The latter story is about a man named Raphael who discovers one day that the street in which he lives, as well as his wife and son, have suddenly disappeared. His searches bring him to a certain café on Silver Street, where he meets a set of characters who talk about the nature of contemporary café culture. See Aleksander Wat, *Bezrobotny Lucyfer* (Warsaw: Hoesick, 1927); English translation in Wat, *Lucifer Unemployed*, trans. Lillian Valee (Evanston, IL: Northwestern University Press, 1990), 41–52.

88. Julian Tuwim, "Wspomnienia o Łodzi," *Wiadomości literackie*, August 12, 1934, 11.

89. Antoni Słonimski, "Wspomnienie," *Wiadomości literackie*, September 2, 1928, 4.

90. Antoni Słonimski, "O drażliwości Żydów," *Wiadomosci literackie*, August 31, 1924, 3; English translation by Mariusz Wesolowski at www.zabludow.com.

91. Antoni Słonimski, *Kroniki tygodniowe 1927–1931* (Warsaw: LTW, 2003), 69.
92. Antoni Słonimski, *Wiersze zebrane* (Warsaw: Wydawnictwo J Przeworskiego, 1933), 70. English translation in Eugenia Prokop-Janiec, *Polish-Jewish Literature in the Interwar Years* (Syracuse, NY: Syracuse University Press, 2003), 283.
93. Antoni Słonimski, *Alfabet wspomnień* (Warsaw: Państwowy Instytut Wydawn, 1975), 82–85.
94. Shimen Dzigan, *Der koyekh fun yidishn humor* (Tel Aviv: Der gezelshaftlekher komitet tsu fayern 40 yor tetikayt fun Shimen Dzigan oyfder yidisher bine, 1974), 131–132.
95. Ibid., 132.
96. Ibid., 134.
97. Ibid., 135.
98. Yitzhak Katzenelson, *Ketavim* (Kibbutz Lohame ha-getaot, Israel: Bet lohame ha-getaot, 1982), 176.
99. Y. Y. Trunk, *Poyln: Zikhroynes un bilder*, vol. 7 (New York: Farlag unzer tsayt, 1953), 235–236.
100. Ibid., 236.
101. Ephraim Kaganowski, *Poylishe yorn* (Warsaw: Yidish bukh, 1956), 342.
102. Segalovitsh, *Tlomatske 13*, 228. On the end of *Tlomatske 13*, see Cohen, *Sefer*, 297–303. On Café Piccadilly, see Dzigan, *Der koyekh*, 120.
103. Ravitch, *Dos mayse-bukh*, 3:336.
104. Cohen, *Sefer*, 305.
105. Ibid., 311.
106. Jonas Turkow, *Azoy iz es geven: Khurbn varshe* (Buenos Aires: Tsentral-farband fun Poylishe Yidn in Argentine, 1948), 198.
107. Ibid., 196.
108. Emanuel Ringelblum, *Notes from the Warsaw Ghetto: The Journal of Emmanuel Ringelblum* (New York: McGraw-Hill, 1958), 93.
109. Moshe Fass, "Theatrical Activities in the Polish Ghettos during the Years 1939–1942," *Jewish Social Studies* 38, no. 1 (1976): 54–72.
110. Shirli Gilbert, *Music in the Holocaust* (Oxford: Oxford University Press, 2005), 25.
111. Mary Berg, *The Diary of Mary Berg: Growing Up in the Warsaw Ghetto*, ed. S. L. Shneiderman (Oxford, UK: Oneworld, 2007), 51.
112. Quoted in Lucjan Dobroszycki, *The Chronicle of the Łódź Ghetto, 1941–1944* (New Haven, CT: Yale University Press, 1984), 58.
113. Michel Mazor, *The Vanished City: Everyday Life in the Warsaw Ghetto* (New York: Marsilio, 1993), 41.
114. Berg, *Diary of Mary Berg*, 52.
115. Turkow, *Azoy iz es geven*, 81.
116. Yaakov Tselemensky, *Mitn farshnitenem folk* (New York: Farlag Unzer Tsayt, 1963), 73–74.
117. Władysław Szpilman, *The Pianist: The Extraordinary True Story of One Man's Survival in Warsaw, 1939–45*, trans. Anthea Bell (New York: Picador USA, 1999), 13.

118. Berg, *Diary of Mary Berg*, 30. Some artists performed in cafés such as Sztuka for good salaries but worked at soup kitchens as well.

119. "Władysław Szlengel—The Forgotten Star of Warsaw," Jewish Historical Institute blog, May 8, 2015, www.jhi.pl.

120. Fass, "Theatrical Activities," 59.

121. Berg, *Diary of Mary Berg*, 104.

122. Mazor, *Vanished City*, 43.

CHAPTER 3. VIENNA

1. Austrian Commission for UNESCO, "Austrian Inventory: Intangible Cultural Heritage in Austria," http://immaterielleskulturerbe.unesco.at.

2. After "Vienna Coffeehouse Culture" was put on the UNESCO list, Turkey applied with success, but as a country, not a specific city. Buenos Aires tried to include its café culture on the list as well, but so far without success.

3. Friedrich Torberg, "Traktat über das Wiener Kaffeehaus," in *Das Wiener Kaffeehaus: mit zahlreichen Abbildungen und Hinweisen auf Wiener Kaffeehäuser*, ed. Kurt-Jürgen Heering (Frankfurt: Insel, 1993), 18–32; English translation in Torberg, *Tante Jolesch, or The Decline of the West in Anecdotes*, trans. Amria Poglitsch Bauer (Riverside, CA: Ariadne, 2008), 205–213.

4. Karl Teply, *Die Einführung des Kaffees in Wien: Georg Franz Koltschitzky, Johannes Diodato, Isaak de Luca* (Vienna: Verein für Geschichte der Stadt Wien, 1980).

5. Heise, *Coffee and Coffeehouses*, 104–105.

6. Tag Gronberg, "Coffeehouse Orientalism," in Ashby, Gronberg, and Shaw-Miller, *Viennese Café*, 59–77.

7. Joseph II, "Edict of Tolerance (January 2, 1782)," in *The Jew in the Modern World: A Documentary History*, ed. Paul Mendes-Flohr and Jehuda Reinharz (Oxford: Oxford University Press, 1980), 42–45.

8. Eisig Silberschlag, "Hebrew Literature in Vienna 1782–1939," in *The Great Transition: The Recovery of the Lost Centers of Modern Hebrew Literature*, ed. Glenda Abramson and Tudor Parfitt (Totowa, NJ: Rowman, 1985), 75–90.

9. W. Scott Haine, introduction to Rittner, Haine, and Jackson, *Thinking Space*, 5.

10. Heise, *Coffee and Coffeehouses*, 96.

11. *Das Wiener Kaffeehaus* (Vienna: Museen der Stadt Wien, 1980), 79; Herbert Lederer, "The Vienna Coffee House: History and Cultural Significance," in Rittner, Haine, and Jackson, *Thinking Space*, 31.

12. See Hilde Spiel, *Fanny von Arnstein: A Daughter of the Enlightenment, 1758–1818* (New York: Berg, 1991).

13. Sigmund Mayer, *Die Wiener Juden* (Vienna: R. Loewit, 1918), 275–277; Ludwig A. Frankl, *Zu Lenaus Biographie* (Vienna: Keck and Pierer, 1854), 3–7.

14. Mayer, *Die Wiener Juden*, 224–230. See also Ruth Beckermann and Teifer Hermann, *Die Mazzesinsel: Juden in der Wiener Leopoldstadt 1918–1938* (Vienna: Löcker, 1984).

15. John Strang, *Germany in 1831*, vol. 2 (London: T. Foster, 1836), 243.

16. Until 1848, there were only three daily newspapers in Vienna, and they were either government controlled or heavily censored. See Charlotte Ashby, "The Cafés of Vienna: Space and Sociability," in Ashby, Gronberg, and Shaw-Miller, *Viennese Café*, 15.

17. Gilbert Carr, "Austrian Literature and the Coffee-House before 1890," *Austrian Studies* 16 (2008): 156.

18. Heise, *Coffee and Coffeehouses*, 151.

19. Jonathan Sperber, *The European Revolutions, 1848–1851* (Cambridge: Cambridge University Press, 2005).

20. Werner J. Cahnman, "Adolf Fischhof and His Jewish Followers," *Leo Baeck Institute Year Book* 4 (1959): 111–139.

21. Marsha Rozenblit, *The Jews of Vienna, 1867–1914: Assimilation and Identity* (Albany: State University of New York Press, 1983), 10–11.

22. Ibid., 17.

23. Steven Beller, *Vienna and the Jews, 1867–1938: A Cultural History* (Cambridge: Cambridge University Press, 1989), 114–187. Beller argues that most of the acculturated Viennese Jewish intellectuals of the fin de siècle articulated a deeply moral point of view derived from the kind of education they received: a mixture of Enlightenment idealism and Jewish tradition.

24. Rozenblit, *Jews of Vienna*, 147–174.

25. Carl E. Schorske, *Fin-de-Siècle Vienna: Politics and Culture* (New York: Knopf, 1981). Schorske's powerful but also contested thesis is that modernism in Vienna became a kind of political surrogate for a marginalized liberal bourgeoisie. See also Jacques Le Rider, *Modernity and the Crisis of Identity: Culture and Society in Fin-de-Siècle Vienna* (New York: Continuum, 1993); Jürgen Nautz and Richard Vahrenkamp, eds., *Die Wiener Jahrhundertwende: Einflüsse, Umwelt, Wirkungen* (Vienna: Böhlau, 1993); Steven Beller, ed., *Rethinking Vienna 1900* (Oxford, UK: Berghahn Books, 2001).

26. Ashby, "Cafés of Vienna," 9.

27. Ibid., 11–13.

28. Carr, "Austrian Literature."

29. Gilbert Carr, "Time and Space in the Café Griensteidl and Café Central," in Ashby, Gronberg, and Shaw-Miller, *Viennese Café*, 33–35.

30. Franz Werfel, *Barbara oder die Frömmigkeit* (Berlin: Zsolnay, 1929), 424.

31. Anton Kuh, "Central und Herrenhof," in Heering, *Das Wiener Kaffeehaus*, 170; English translation in Harold B. Segel, ed. and trans., *The Vienna Coffeehouse Wits, 1890–1938* (West Lafayette, IN: Purdue University Press, 1993), 348.

32. Carr, "Time and Space," 35; Harold B. Segel, "Introduction: The Vienna Coffeehouse in Society and Culture," in Segel, *Vienna Coffeehouse Wits*, 22–25.

33. Leon Trotsky, *My Life* (New York: Scribner, 1930), 206–207.

34. Quoted in Slavoj Žižek, "Trotsky's Terrorism and Communism, or, Despair and Utopia in the Turbulent Year of 1920," in *Terrorism and Communism: A Reply to Karl Kautsky*, by Leon Trotsky (London: Verso, 2007), vii.

35. See Edward Timms, *Karl Kraus, Apocalyptic Satirist* (New Haven, CT: Yale University Press, 1986), 4–10.

36. Edward Timms, "Coffeehouses and Tea Parties: Conversational Spaces as a Stimulus to Creativity in Sigmund Freud's Vienna and Virginia Woolf's London," in Ashby, Gronberg, and Shaw-Miller, *Viennese Café*, 199–219.

37. Stefan Zweig, *Die Welt von Gestern* (Stockholm: Bermann-Fischer, 1942); English translation in Zweig, *The World of Yesterday: An Autobiography* (New York: Viking, 1943), 39.

38. Peter Altenberg, *Mein Lebensabend* (Berlin: S. Fischer, 1919), 19; English translation in Segel, *Viennese Coffeehouse Wits*, 123–124.

39. Hermann Bahr, "Loris" (1894), in *Hermann Bahr Buch* (Berlin: Fischer, 1913), 253–260.

40. Schorske, *Fin-de-siècle Vienna*, 7.

41. Peter Hall, *Cities in Civilization: Culture, Innovation, and Urban Order* (London: Phoenix Giant, 1998), 5.

42. Beller, *Vienna and the Jews*, 22.

43. Le Rider, *Modernity*, 3. See also Abigail Gillman, *Viennese Jewish Modernism: Freud, Hofmannsthal, Beer-Hofmann, and Schnitzler* (University Park: Pennsylvania State University Press, 2009).

44. Beller, *Vienna and the Jews*, 40–41.

45. Segel, "Introduction," 12.

46. Timms, *Karl Kraus*, 5.

47. Arthur Schnitzler, *Jugend in Wien: Eine Autobiographie* (Vienna: Molden, 1968); English translation in Schnitzler, *My Youth in Vienna* (New York: Holt, Rinehart and Winston, 1970), 82.

48. Theodor Herzl, *Feuilletons* (Berlin: B. Harz, 1919).

49. Theodor Herzl, "Das Kaffeehaus der neuen Richtung," in *Neues von der Venus: Plaudereien und Geschichten* (Leipzig, 1887), 79–95.

50. Reuven Brainin, *Peretz ben moshe Smolenskin: Ḥayav u-sefarav* (Warsaw: Tushiya, 1896), 95–96.

51. Robert S. Wistrich, *The Jews of Vienna in the Age of Franz Joseph* (Oxford: Oxford University Press, 1989), 350.

52. Peretz Smolenskin, *Sipurim ve-filitonim* (Vilna: Bet mishar ha-sefarim M. Katsenelenbogen, 1901), 6–10.

53. Gabriele Kohlbauer-Fritz, "Yiddish as an Expression of Jewish Cultural Identity in Galicia and Vienna," *Polin* 12 (1999): 166.

54. Andrea Portenkirchner, "Die Einsamkeit am 'Fensterplatz' zur Welt: Das literarische Kaffeehaus in Wien 1890–1950," in *Literarische Kaffeehäuser, Kaffeehausliteraten*, ed. Michael Rössner (Vienna: Böhlau Verlag, 1999), 31–65.

55. Schorske, *Fin-de-Siècle Vienna*, 119.

56. Ibid., 75.

57. "Ein antisemitischer Straßentumult," *Neue Freie Presse*, December 3, 1895, 6.

58. Ibid.

59. Beller, "Jew Belongs." See also Torberg, *Tante Jolesch.*

60. Andreas Huyssen, *Miniature Metropolis: Literature in an Age of Photography and Film* (Cambridge, MA: Harvard University Press, 2015), 1–22.

61. Alfred Polgar, an accomplished feuilletonist, emphasized the hybridity of the genre, specifically its "mixture of ur-Jewishness and ur-Aryanness, of melancholy of the synagogue and alcohol atmosphere of the Grinzinger." In Segel, *Vienna Coffeehouse Wits,* 250. See also Hildegard Kernmayer, *Judentum im Wiener Feuilleton (1848–1903): Exemplarische Untersuchungen zum literarästhetischen und politischen Diskurs der Moderne* (Tübingen: Niemeyer, 1998).

62. Timms, *Karl Kraus,* 179–180.

63. Karl Kraus, *Die demolirte Literatur* (Vienna: Verlag A. Bauer, 1897); English translation in Segel, *Vienna Coffeehouse Wits,* 65–85.

64. Ibid., 66.

65. Paul Reitter, *The Anti-Journalist: Karl Kraus and Jewish Self-Fashioning in Fin-de-Siècle Europe* (Chicago: University of Chicago Press, 2008), 75–76.

66. Carr, "Time and Space," 43.

67. Bruce F. Pauley, *From Prejudice to Persecution: A History of Austrian Anti-Semitism* (Chapel Hill: University of North Carolina Press, 1992), 35–36.

68. Kraus, *Die demolirte Literatur,* in Segel, *Vienna Coffeehouse Wits,* 81.

69. Le Rider, *Modernity,* 251.

70. Karl Kraus, *Eine Krone für Zion* (Vienna: M. Frisch, 1898), 13.

71. Reitter, *Anti-Journalist,* 76.

72. On Nordau, see Michael Stanislawski, *Zionism and the Fin-de-Siècle: Cosmopolitanism and Nationalism from Nordau to Jabotinsky* (Berkeley: University of California Press, 2001); Shulamit Volkov, *Germans, Jews, and Antisemites: Trials in Emancipation* (Cambridge: Cambridge University Press, 2006).

73. Max Nordau, "Muskeljudentum," *Jüdische Turnzeitung,* June 1900, 10–11. See also Erich Burin, "Das Kaffeehaus Judentum," *Jüdische Turnerzeitung,* May–June 1910, 5–6.

74. Theodor Herzl, *Altneuland* (Leipzig: Seemann, 1902), 1; English translation in Herzl, *Old-New Land,* trans. Lotta Levensohn (New York: Bloch, 1960), 3.

75. Beller, "Jew Belongs," 56–57.

76. Herzl, *Alteuland,* 54. See Michael Gluzman, *Ha-Guf ha-tsiyoni* (Tel Aviv: Hakibbutz Hameuchad, 2007).

77. Jacques Le Rider has described the confluence of crises in fin-de-siècle Viennese culture: a crisis of modernist identity, of masculinity, and of Jewishness that are interrelated. See Le Rider, *Modernity and Crisis.* Michael Pollak has argued that the disappearance of the literary salons and their replacement with cafés in the late nineteenth century resulted in the loss of the (Jewish) woman, who played a maternal and protective role. According to Pollak, the last literary salon disappeared with the death of Josephine von Wertheimstein in 1894. See Michael Pollak, *Wien 1900: Eine verletzte Identität* (Konstanz, Germany: Univ.-Verlag, 1997), 160–164.

78. Much of *Lieutenant Gustl* (1901) takes place in the Viennese café, which is a space of crisis due to Gustl's confusion about his masculine identity and honor. Gustl's rival may or may not be Jewish himself. Anti-Semitism becomes in the novella a psychological affair, heightening consciousness about one's identity, on behalf of both the aggressor and the victim, an identity that is spatially mapped on various cafés in Vienna. See Arthur Schnitzler, *Leutnant Gustl: Novelle* (Berlin: S. Fischer, 1910).

79. Arthur Schnitzler, *Der Weg ins Freie: Roman* (Berlin: S. Fischer, 1913), 109; English translation in Schnitzler, *The Road into the Open*, trans. Roger Byers (Berkeley: University of California Press, 1992), 69.

80. Schnitzler, *Der Weg ins Frie*, 174–175; Schnitzler, *Road into the Open*, 112–113.

81. Schnitzler, *Der Weg ins Frie*, 175; Schnitzler, *Road into the Open*, 113.

82. Torberg, *Tante Jolesch*, 136.

83. On these aspects of the Talmudic culture and the masculine ideal of the "house of study," see Daniel Boyarin, *Unheroic Conduct: The Rise of Heterosexuality and the Invention of the Jewish Man* (Berkeley: University of California Press, 1997).

84. Walter Benjamin made another such attempt in the Berlin café, discussed in chapter 4.

85. Alfred Polgar, "Theorie des Café Central," in Heering, *Das Wiener Kaffeehaus*, 149.

86. Ibid., 151–153. See also the description of Café Central seen through the eyes of Ferdinand, the non-Jewish protagonist of Werfel's novel, as "an exclusive seat of power," full of "cloud-drift cigarette smoke," where the habitués "suited the place, the light, the air." Werfel, *Barbara*, 425.

87. Lisa Silverman, *Becoming Austrians: Jews and Culture between the World Wars* (New York: Oxford University Press, 2012), 5.

88. Meir Henisch. "Galician Jews in Vienna," in *The Jews of Austria*, ed. Josef Fraenkel (London: Valentine, Mitchell, 1967), 361–373; Klaus Hödl, *Als Bettler in die Leopoldstadt: Galizische Juden auf dem Weg nach Wien* (Vienna: Böhlau, 1994).

89. Beckermann and Hermann, *Die Mazzesinsel*, 9–23.

90. Joseph Roth, *Juden auf Wanderschaft* (Berlin: Die Schmiede, 1927), 39; English translation in Roth, *The Wandering Jews* (New York: Norton, 1976), 66.

91. Melech Ravitch, *Dos mayse-bukh fun mayn leben*, vol. 1 (Buenos Aires: Tsenral-Farband fun Poylishe Yidn in Argentine, 1962), 181.

92. On Zionism in Vienna in this period, see Michael Berkowitz, *Western Jewry and the Zionist Project, 1914–1933* (Cambridge: Cambridge University Press, 1997). On Yiddish and diaspora nationalism, see Thomas Soxberger, "Literatur und Politik—Moderne jiddische Literatur und 'Jiddischismus' in Wien (1904 bis 1938)" (PhD diss., Universität Wien, 2010). On Yiddish Theater in Vienna, see Brigitte Dalinger, *Verloschene Sterne: Geschichte des jüdischen Theaters in Wien* (Vienna: Picus, 1998).

93. Allan Janik and Hans Veigl, *Wittgenstein in Vienna: A Biographical Excursion through the City and Its History* (Vienna: Springer, 1998), 188–189.

94. Ravitch, *Dos mayse-bukh*, 1:209–211; Daniel Charney, *Di velt iz kaylekhdik* (Tel Aviv: Y. L. Peretz 1963), 160–165; Michael Weichert, *Zikhroynes*, vol. 1 (Tel Aviv: Farlag Menorah, 1960), 229–248.

95. Charney, *Di velt iz kaylekhdik*, 160–165.

96. Meir Henisch, *Mi-bayit u mi-ḥuts: Pirke zikhronot* (Tel Aviv: Ahdut, 1961), 145–147. The Yiddish poet Melech Chmelnitzki, who migrated to Vienna in 1912, wrote an impressionist sonnet about the Votivkirche as he looked at it from Café Arkaden. See Melech Chmelnitzki, *Ru un umru* (New York: Ignatoff Foundation, 1948), 31. Café Arkaden continued to exist until the 1930s. In the interwar period, it was also the location of cabaret shows and a meeting place for directors and actors of silent films, such as *Sodom and Gomorrah* (1922). The Jewish physician Richard Berczeller played the biblical character Lot in the film and met with the director in Café Arkaden. See Richard Berczeller, "Sodom and Gomorrah," *New Yorker*, October 14, 1974, 48–54.

97. See David Rechter, *The Jews of Vienna and the First World War* (London: Littman, 2001); Marsha L. Rozenblit, *Reconstructing a National Identity: The Jews of Habsburg Austria during World War I* (Oxford: Oxford University Press, 2001).

98. Rechter, *Jews of Vienna*, 25.

99. David Rechter, "Galicia in Vienna: Jewish Refugees in the First World War," *Austrian History Yearbook* 28 (1997): 113–130.

100. Joseph Roth, *Werke*, vol. 1 (Cologne: Kiepenheuer and Witsch, 1956), 572–576; English translation in Roth, *The Spider's Web and Zipper and His Father*, trans. John Hoare (Woodstock, NY: Overlook, 2003).

101. Roth, *Spider's Web and Zipper*, 143.

102. Ibid., 174.

103. Ibid., 174–175.

104. Ibid., 175.

105. Silverman, *Becoming Austrians*, 16–27.

106. Ibid., 21–22.

107. Hugo Bettauer, *Die Stadt ohne Juden* (Hamburg: Achilla Presse, 1996), 16–17; English translation in Bettauer, *The City without Jews*, trans. Salome Nuemark Brainin (New York: Bloch, 1927), 12.

108. Bettauer, *Die Stadt ohne Juden*, 6–7; Bettauer, *City without Jews*, 3–4.

109. See, for example, Dorothy Thompson, "The Passing of the Vienna Coffee House," *Philadelphia Public Ledger*, May 9, 1922.

110. Hans Veigl, *Wiener Kaffeehausführer* (Vienna: Kremayr u. Scheriau, 1989), 52–54.

111. Anton Kuh, "'Central' und 'Herrenhof'" (1926), in Heering, *Das Wiener Kaffeehaus*, 157–166; English translation in Segel, *Viennese Coffeehouse Wits*, 347–352.

112. Quoted in Beller, "Jew Belongs," 53.

113. See Soxberger, "Literatur und Politik." For a study of Hebrew fiction in Vienna, see Pinsker, *Literary Passports*, 87–104.

114. Ravitch, *Dos mayse-bukh fun mayn lebn*, 1:363–369. Soxberger, "Literatur und Politik," 106–108.

115. Mikhail Krutikov, *From Kabbalah to Class Struggle: Expressionism, Marxism, and Yiddish Literature in the Life and Work of Meir Wiener* (Stanford, CA: Stanford University Press, 2011), 54–56.

116. Peter Altenberg, *Ktavim nivḥarim*, trans. Gershon Shofman (New York: Shtybel, 1921).

117. After the war, Ben-Yitzhak briefly served as secretary of the Palestine Department of the Zionist Organization in London but resigned in 1921. He stayed in Vienna until his emigration to Palestine in 1938, serving as the director of the Hebrew Teachers' Seminary (Pedagogium).

118. Elias Canetti, *The Play of the Eye* (New York: Farrar, Straus and Giroux, 1999), 132–162.

119. Krutikov, *From Kabbalah*, 102.

120. A. M. Fuchs, *Unter der brik un Andere Dertseilunge* (Warsaw: Kultul-Lige, 1924), 78–79.

121. Michel Foucault, "Of Other Spaces," *Diacritics* 16 (Spring 1986): 22–27.

122. Fuchs's Café Glazer should be compared with Meir Wiener's Viennese café in his unpublished novel *Der groyser roman* (The great novel), written in the late 1920s. Meir Wiener Archives, NNUL, 4°, 1763/16, 39. English translation in Krutikov, *From Kabbalah*, 70.

123. David Vogel, *Ḥaye nisu'im* (Tel Aviv, 1929–1930); English translation in Vogel, *Married Life*, trans. Dalya Bilu (London: P. Halban, 1988).

124. Vogel, *Married Life*, 23.

125. Ibid., 26.

126. Lilach Nethanel, who discovered the manuscript and then edited and published the novel, estimates that Vogel began to write the text in the late 1910s and completed it in the early 1930s. See Lilach Nethanel, "David Vogel's Lost Hebrew Novel, Viennese Romance," *Prooftexts* 33, no. 3 (2013): 307–332.

127. David Vogel, *Roman Vina'y* (Tel Aviv: Am Oved, 2012); English translation in Vogel, *Viennese Romance*, trans. Dalya Bilu (Brunswick, Austral.: Scribe, 2013).

128. Vogel, *Roman Vina'y*, 26; Vogel, *Viennese Romance*, 25.

129. Vogel, *Roman Vina'y*, 40; Vogel, *Viennese Romance*, 41.

130. Vogel, *Roman Vina'y*, 27; Vogel, *Viennese Romance*, 26.

131. Vogel, *Roman Vina'y*, 40; Vogel, *Viennese Romance*, 41.

132. Vogel, *Roman Vina'y*, 210; Vogel, *Viennese Romance*, 237.

133. Vogel, *Roman Vina'y*, 5; Vogel, *Viennese Romance*, 3.

134. Melech Chmelnitzki, *Oyf shtiler steshke* (Vienna: Kval farlag, 1921), 58.

135. Werfel, *Barbara*.

136. Vicki Baum, *It Was All Quite Different: The Memoirs of Vicki Baum* (New York: Funk and Wagnalls, 1964), 164. See Lisa Silverman's analysis of Jewish women (and Jewish women writers) in interwar Vienna. Silverman, *Becoming Austrians*, 66–102.

137. Veza Canetti, *Die gelbe Straße: Roman* (Munich: Hanser, 1990); English translation in Canetti, *The Yellow Street*, trans. Ian Mitchell (New York: New Directions Books, 1990).

138. V. Canetti, *Yellow Street*, 97.

139. Ibid., 100–101.

140. Ibid., 111.

141. Silverman, *Becoming Austrians*, 135–137.

142. For a discussion of these Jewish writers in postwar Vienna, see Hillary Hope Herzog, *"Vienna Is Different": Jewish Writers in Austria from the Fin de Siècle to the Present* (New York: Berghahn Books, 2011). On the role of café culture in the late twentieth century in the lives of Jews in Vienna, see Matti Bunzl, "The City and the Self: Narratives of Spatial Belonging among Austrian Jews," *City & Society*, 1996, 50–81.

143. Torberg, *Tante Jolesch*, 170.

CHAPTER 4. BERLIN

1. Leah Goldberg, *Mikhtavim mi-nesi'a meduma* (Tel Aviv: Davar, 1937), 15–16.

2. Ibid., 16.

3. Andreas Nachama, Julius H. Schoeps, and Hermann Simon, *Jews in Berlin* (Berlin: Henschel, 2002), 18–29.

4. Melton, *Rise of the Public*, 241.

5. Johann D. E. Preuss, *Die Lebensgeschichte des großen Königs Friedrich von Preußen* (Berlin: Nauck, 1837), 13.

6. Moses Mendelssohn and Georg B. Mendelssohn, *Moses Mendelssohn's gesammelte Schriften, nach den Originaldrucken und Handschriften*, vol. 5 (Leipzig: Brockhaus, 1845), 214.

7. Ibid., 215.

8. Rainer Falk, "Gelehrtes Kaffeehaus," in *Handbuch der Berliner Vereine und Gesellschaften 1786–1815*, ed. Uta Motschmann (Berlin: De Gruyter, 2015), 17–19.

9. Ludwig Geiger, "Briefe von, an und über Mendelssohn," in *Jahrbuch für jüdische Geschichte und Literatur* 1 (1917): 129.

10. Uta Motschmann, "Montagsklub," in Motschmann, *Handbuch der Berliner Vereine*, 160–168.

11. Alexander Altmann, *Moses Mendelssohn: A Biographical Study* (Alabama: University of Alabama Press, 1973), 76.

12. *Der Chamäleon: Eine moralische Wochenschrift* (Berlin: Birnstiel, 1759).

13. The *Spectator* was translated into German, and *moralische Wochenschriften* attained the height of their popularity in the German-speaking sphere between 1740 and 1780, when at least fifty were published. Melton, *Rise of the Public*, 95–96.

14. Wolfgang Martens, *Die Botschaft der Tugend: Die Aufklärung im Spiegel der deutschen moralischen Wochenschriften* (Stuttgart: Metzler, 1971).

15. Habermas, *Structural Transformation*, 42.

16. Brian Cowan, "Mr. Spectator and the Coffeehouse Public Sphere," *Eighteenth-Century Studies* 37, no. 3 (Spring 2004): 345–366.

17. Altmann, *Moses Mendelssohn*, 78. Although Mendelssohn never identified himself as the author and co-editor of *Der Chamäleon*, Müchler published these pieces and attributed them to Mendelssohn in Moses Mendelssohn, *Kleine philosophische Schriften* (Berlin: Vieweg, 1789).

18. For the original Hebrew version of the text, see Meir Gilon, *Kohelet musar le-mendelson 'al rek'a ekufato* (Jerusalem: ha-Akademyah ha-le'umit ha-Yiśre'elit le-mada'im, 1979); English translation in Edward Bruer and David Sorkin, "Moses Mendelssohn's First Hebrew Publication: An Annotated Translation of the Kohelet Mussar," *Leo Baeck Institute Yearbook* 48 (2003): 3–23.

19. Jonathan Karp, "The Aesthetic Difference: Mendelssohn's *Kohelet Musar* and the Inception of the Berlin Haskalah," in *Renewing the Past, Reconfiguring Jewish Culture: From al-Andalus to the Berlin Haskalah*, ed. Ross Brann and Adam Sutcliffe (Philadelphia: University of Pennsylvania Press, 2004), 93–120.

20. Karp, "Aesthetic Difference," 95; Jeremy Dauber, *Antonio's Devils: Writers of the Jewish Enlightenment and the Birth of Modern Hebrew and Yiddish Literature* (Stanford, CA: Stanford University Press, 2004), 114–138.

21. Karp, "Aesthetic Difference," 95.

22. Christian Wilhelm Dohm, "Über die Kaffeegesetzgebung," *Deutsches Museum* 2 (1777): 123–145. For a discussion of Dohm, coffee, and Jewishness, see Jonathan M. Hess, *Germans, Jews and the Claims of Modernity* (New Haven, CT: Yale University Press, 2002), 25–27; Liberles, *Jews Welcome Coffee*, 32–33.

23. Friedrich Nicolai, *Beschreibung der Königlichen Residenzstädte Berlin und Potsdam, aller daselbst befindlicher Merkwürdigkeiten, und der umliegenden Gegend*, vol. 2 (Berlin: Nicolai, 1779), 975. On Nicolai, see Pamela E. Selwyn, *Everyday Life in the German Book Trade: Friedrich Nicolai as Bookseller and Publisher in the Age of Enlightenment, 1750–1810* (University Park: Pennsylvania State University Press, 2000).

24. In the 1760s and 1770s, Jewish and gentile intellectuals as well as members of the Berlin Jewish elite gathered for discussion in Mendelssohn's home. Other wealthy Jewish families such as the Itzigs, the Meyers, and the family of Levin Markus also entertained non-Jewish guests. Steven M. Lowenstein, *The Berlin Jewish Community: Enlightenment, Family, and Crisis, 1770–1830* (New York: Oxford University Press, 1994), 104–105.

25. Isaak Euchel, *Reb Henoch, oder: Woss tut me damit: Eine jüdische Komödie der Aufklärungszeit*, ed. Marion Aptroot (Hamburg: Buske, 2006), 139–140, 181–183.

26. Hertz, *Jewish High Society*, 1–22.

27. Lowenstein, *Berlin Jewish Community*, 105–106.

28. Liliane Weissberg, "Literary Culture and Jewish Space around 1800: The Berlin Salon Revisited," in *Modern Jewish Literatures: Intersections and Boundaries*, ed. Sheila Jelen, Michael P. Kramer, and L. Scott Lerner (Philadelphia: University of Pennsylvania Press, 2011), 24–43.

29. Katy Heady, *Literature and Censorship in Restoration Germany: Repression and Rhetoric* (Rochester, NY: Camden House, 2009), 11–13.

30. Fedor Zobeltitz, *Chronik der Gesellschaft unter dem letzten Kaiserreich* (Hamburg: Alster, 1922), 58–61; Wolfgang Jünger, *Herr Ober, ein' Kaffee! Illustrierte Kulturgeschichte des Kaffeehauses* (Munich: W. Goldmann, 1955), 187–202.

31. Adolph von Schaden, *Berlins Licht- und Schattenseiten* (Dessau: Schlieder, 1822), 151–153.

32. A. F. Thiele, *Die jüdischen Gauner in Deutschland*, vol. 1 (Berlin: Reimarus, 1843), 248–251.

33. Wolfgang Kaschuba, "German *Bürgerlichkeit* after 1800: Culture as Symbolic Practice," in *Bourgeois Society in Nineteenth-Century Europe*, ed. Jürgen Kocka and Allan Mitchell (Oxford, UK: Berg, 1993), 393–421.

34. Leopold von Zedlitz-Neukirch, *Neustes Conversations-Handbuch für Berlin und Potsdam zum täglichen Gebrauch der Einheimischen und Fremden aller Stände* (Berlin: Eisersdorff, 1834), 139.

35. Ibid., 140.

36. Adolf Glassbrenner, *Berliner Volksleben*, vol. 2 (Leipzig: W. Engelmann, 1847), 48.

37. Jeffrey L. Sammons, *Heinrich Heine: A Modern Biography* (Princeton, NJ: Princeton University Press, 1979).

38. Heady, *Literature and Censorship in Restoration Germany*, 70.

39. Karl Kraus, *Heine und die Folgen* (Munich: A. Langen, 1910), 7. See Hildegard Kernmayer, *Judentum im Wiener Feuilleton (1848–1903): Exemplarische Untersuchungen zum literarästhetischen und politischen Diskurs der Moderne* (Tübingen: Niemeyer, 1998).

40. Heinrich Heine, *Sämtliche Schriften*, vol. 2 (Munich: C. Hanser, 1968), 11.

41. Ibid., 14–15.

42. Siegbert Salomon Prawer, *Heine's Jewish Comedy: A Study of His Portraits of Jews and Judaism* (Oxford: Oxford University Press, 1985), 47–58.

43. Deborah Hertz, *How Jews Became Germans: The History of Conversion and Assimilation in Berlin* (New Haven, CT: Yale University Press, 2007), 173–177.

44. Heine, *Sämtliche Schriften*, 17–18.

45. Ibid., 36.

46. Quoted in Hertz, *How Jews Became Germans.* 179.

47. Heine, *Sämtliche Schriften*, 41.

48. Mary L. Townsend, *Forbidden Laughter: Popular Humor and the Limits of Repression in Nineteenth-Century Prussia* (Ann Arbor: University of Michigan Press, 1992), 2.

49. Jefferson Chase, *Inciting Laughter: The Development of Jewish Humor in 19th Century German Culture* (Berlin: de Gruyter, 2000), 17.

50. Karl von Holtei, *Vierzig Jahre*, vol. 4 (Berlin, 1944), 284–290.

51. Moritz Gottlieb Saphir, *Conditorei des Jokus: oder, scherzhafte Bonbons, Früchte und Confitüren für spassliebende Näscher und lustige Leckermäuler* (Leipzig: C. Focke, 1828), 63.

52. Ibid., 65.

53. Townsend, *Forbidden Laughter*, 35–45.

54. Eduard Maria Oettinger, *Charivari*, January 1, 1848.

55. Ernst Dronke, *Berlin* (Frankfurt am Main: Literarische Anstalt, 1846), 45–46.

56. Friedrich Arnold Steinmann, *Briefe aus Berlin*, vol. 2 (Hanau, Germany: Friedrich König, 1832), 133.

57. Dronke, *Berlin*, 47–48.

58. Friedrich Saß, quoted in Georg Hermann, *Das Biedermeier im Spiegel seiner Zeit: Briefe, Tagebücher, Memoiren, Volksszenen und ähnliche Dokumente* (Berlin: Bong, 1913), 61–62.

59. Robert J. Hellman, *The Red Room and White Beer: The Free Hegelian Radicals in the 1840s* (Washington, DC: Three Continents, 1990), 5–25.

60. Isaiah Berlin, *The Life and Opinions of Moses Hess* (Cambridge, UK: W. Heffer, 1959), 228.

61. Hermann, *Das Biedermeier*, 63.

62. Nachama, Schoeps, and Simon, *Jews in Berlin*, 80–88; Michael Brenner, introduction to *German-Jewish History in Modern Times*, vol. 2, *Emancipation and Acculturation: 1780–1871*, ed. Michael A. Meyer (New York: Columbia University Press, 1997), 3.

63. Iain B. Whyte and David Frisby, eds., *Metropolis Berlin: 1880–1940* (Berkeley: University of California Press, 2012).

64. Monika Richarz, "Demographic Developments," in *German-Jewish History in Modern Times*, vol. 3, *Integration in Dispute, 1871–1918*, ed. Michael A. Meyer (New York: Columbia University Press, 1997), 27.

65. Emily D. Bilski, introduction to *Berlin Metropolis: Jews and the New Culture, 1890–1918*, ed. Emily D. Bilski (Berkeley: University of California, 1999), 5.

66. Sarah E. Wobick-Segev, "German-Jewish Spatial Cultures: Consuming and Refashioning Jewish Belonging in Berlin," in *Longing, Belonging, and the Making of Jewish Consumer Culture*, ed. Gideon Reuveni and Nils Roemer (Leiden: Brill, 2010), 39–60.

67. Henry Vizetelly, *Berlin under the New Empire: Its Institutions, Inhabitants, Industry, Monuments, Museums, Social Life, Manners, and Amusements* (London: Tinsley Bros., 1879), 343.

68. Ibid., 190.

69. Peter Pulzer, "The Return of Old Hatreds," in Meyer, *German-Jewish History in Modern Times*, vol. 3, 221–222.

70. Norbert Kampe, "Jews and Antisemites at Universities in Imperial Germany: (II) The Friedrich-Wilhelms-Universitat of Berlin: A Case Study on the Students' 'Jewish Question,'" *Leo Baeck Institute Yearbook* 32, no. 1 (1987): 43–101.

71. Paul Lindau, *The Great Streets of the World* (New York: C. Scribner's Sons, 1892), 201.

72. See Renate Petras, *Das Café Bauer in Berlin* (Berlin: Verlag für Bauwesen, 1994).

73. Lindau, *Great Streets*, 203.

74. "Berlin's Tower of Babel," *New York Times*, February 14, 1884.

75. Wobick-Segev, "German-Jewish Spatial Cultures," 49–50.

76. Hans Ostwald, *Berliner Kaffeehäuser* (Berlin: Seemann Nachfolger, 1905), 4.

77. Reinhold Heller, "'Das schwarze Ferkel' and the Institution of an Avant-Garde in Berlin, 1892–1895," in *Künstlerischer Austausch—Artistic Exchange*, ed. Thomas W. Gaehtgens, vol. 3 (Berlin: Akademie, 1993), 509–519; Roy F. Allen, *Literary Life*

in German Expressionism and the Berlin Circles (Ann Arbor, MI: UMI Research Press, 1983), 68, 180.

78. Allen, *Literary Life*, 150–154; Ernst Pauly, *20 Jahre Café des Westens. Erinnerungen vom Kurfürstendamm* (Berlin: Richard Labisch, 1914).

79. Hans Ostwald, "Berlin Coffeehouses," in Whyte and Frisby, *Metropolis Berlin*, 186.

80. Jürgen Schebera, *Damals im Romanischen Café: Künstler und ihre Lokale im Berlin der Zwanziger Jahre* (Frankfurt: Büchergilde Gutenberg, 1988), 17–24; Sigrid Bauschinger, "The Berlin Moderns: Else Lasker-Schüler and Café Culture," in Bilski, *Berlin Metropolis*, 78–79.

81. Pauly, *20 Jahre*, 18–22.

82. Ibid., 51–53; Bauschinger, "Berlin Moderns," 62–63.

83. Schebera, *Damals*, 23; Allen, *Literary Life*, 67–73.

84. See John Höxter, *So lebten wir: 25 Jahre Berliner Bohème* (Berlin: Biko-Verl, 1929); Erich Mühsam, *Unpolitische Erinnerungen* (Berlin: Volk und Velt, 1961), 101–105.

85. Quoted in Trust (pseud.), "Der Sumpf von Berlin," *Der Sturm* 2, no. 82 (October 21, 1911): 651–652.

86. Ibid.

87. Henry Pachter, "Expressionism and Café Culture," in *Passion and Rebellion: The Expressionist Heritage*, ed. Stephen E. Bronner and Douglas Kellner (New York: Universe Books, 1983), 43–54.

88. Ernst Blass, "Das alte Café des Westens," *Die literarische Welt* 4, no. 35 (1928): 3–4; English translation in Blass, "The Old Cafe des Westens," in *The Era of German Expressionism*, ed. Paul Raabe, trans. J. M. Ritchie (London: Calder and Boyars, 1974), 27–32.

89. Blass, "Old Cafe des Westens," 30.

90. Hans Tramer, "Der Expressionismus: Bemerkungen zum Anteil der Juden an einer Kunstepoche," *Bulletin des Leo Baeck Instituts* 2, no. 5 (1958): 33–46; Paul Mendes-Flohr, *Divided Passions: Jewish Intellectuals and the Experience of Modernity* (Detroit: Wayne State University Press, 1990), 413–423.

91. Martin Buber, "Jüdische Renaissance," *Ost und West* 1 (1901): 7–10.

92. Mendes-Flohr, *Divided Passions*, 79–109.

93. Donna K. Heizer, *Jewish German Identity in the Orientalist Literature of Else Lasker-Schüler, Friedrich Wolf, and Franz Werfel* (Columbia, SC: Camden House, 1996), 32–33.

94. Stanley Nash, *In Search of Hebraism: Shai Hurwitz and His Polemics in the Hebrew Press* (Leiden: Brill, 1980).

95. Steven Aschheim, *Brothers and Strangers: The East European Jew in German and German Jewish Consciousness, 1800–1923* (Madison: University of Wisconsin Press, 1982), 44–45.

96. Itamar Ben-Avi, *'Im shaḥar atzma'utenu* (Tel Aviv: Magen, 1961), 146–156.

97. Ibid., 147.

98. Aharon Hermoni, *Be-'ikvot ha-biluyim* (Jerusalem: Reuven Mass, 1951), 151.

99. Reuven Brainin, "Shpatsiergeyng durkh Berlin," *Der Yud* 23 (1902): 6–8.

100. Z. Durlitsh, "Café Monopol," *Der Moment*, August 8, 1911, 3.
101. Shmaryahu Gorelik, "Dos kafe monopol," *Der fraynd*, September 15, 1913, 3. Sholem Asch also wrote about Café Monopol in his novel *Der veg tsu zikh* (1917).
102. Y. D. Berkovitz, *Ha-rishonim ki-vney adam* (Tel Aviv: Dvir, 1966), 1088–1090.
103. "'Osey ha-dramot," *Ha-'olam*, March 18, 1908, 7–9.
104. Ibid., 7.
105. Immanuel Ben-Gurion, *Reshut ha-yachid* (Tel Aviv: Reshafim, 1980), 64–72. See also Berdichevsky's German diary of these years published in *Ginzey Micha Yosef* 7 (1997): 90–113.
106. Benjamin, *Berliner Chronik*, 43–45.
107. Cristanne Miller, *Cultures of Modernism: Marianne Moore, Mina Loy, and Else Lasker-Schüler, Gender and Literary Community in New York and Berlin* (Ann Arbor: University of Michigan Press, 2005), 36.
108. Else Lasker-Schüler, *Mein Herz: Ein Liebesroman mit Bildern und wirklich lebenden Menschen* (Munich: Verlag Heinrich F. S. Bachmair, 1912), 15. English translation in Else Lasker-Schüler, *My Heart: A Novel of Love*, trans. Sheldon Gilman and Robert Levine (Amsterdam: November Editions, 2016), 8.
109. Georg Zivier, *Das Romanische Café. Erscheinungen und Randerscheinungen rund um die Gedächtniskirche* (Berlin: Haude and Spener, 1965), 8–20; Schebera, *Damals*, 33–37.
110. Else Lasker-Schüler, "Unser Café," in *Prosa, 1903–1920* (Frankfurt am Main: Jüdischer Verlag, 1998), 291.
111. Ibid., 292.
112. Peter Pulzer, "The First World War," in Meyer, *German-Jewish History in Modern Times*, vol. 3, 364–384.
113. Gershom Scholem, *Walter Benjamin: The Story of a Friendship* (New York: New York Review Books, 2001), 24. See also Gershom Scholem, *From Berlin to Jerusalem: Memories of My Youth* (New York: Schocken Books, 1980).
114. Benjamin, *Berliner Chronik*, 605.
115. S. Y. Agnon, *'Ad hena*, in *Kol sipurav shel S. Y. Agnon*, vol. 7 (Tel Aviv and Jerusalem: Schocken, 1960), 5–170.
116. Ibid., 80.
117. Michael Brenner, *The Renaissance of Jewish Culture in Weimar Germany* (New Haven, CT: Yale University Press, 1996).
118. Quoted in Peter Gay, "The Berlin-Jewish Spirit: A Dogma in Search of Some Doubts," *Leo Baeck Memorial Lecture* 15 (1972): 3.
119. Gennady Estraikh, "Introduction: Yiddish on the Spree," and Shachar Pinsker, "Deciphering the Hieroglyphics of the Metropolis: Literary Topographies of Berlin in Hebrew and Yiddish Modernism," in *Yiddish in Weimar Berlin: At the Crossroads of Diaspora Politics and Culture*, ed. Gennady Estraikh and Mikhail Krutikuv (London: Modern Humanities Research Association, 2010), 1–53.
120. Alfred Rath, "Berliner Caféhäuser (1890–1933)," in *Literarische Kaffeehäuser, Kaffeehausliteraten*, ed. Michael Rössner (Vienna: Böhlau, 1999), 116.

121. Schebera, *Damals*, 41.

122. Ibid., 44–45.

123. Eric D. Weitz, *Weimar Germany: Promise and Tragedy* (Princeton, NJ: Princeton University Press, 2007), 77–78.

124. Joseph Roth, "Richard ohne Königreich," *Neue Berliner Zeitung*, January 9, 1923; English translation in Roth, *What I Saw: Reports from Berlin, 1920–1933*, trans. Michael Hoffmann (New York: Norton, 1996), 135–139.

125. Benjamin, *Berliner Chronik*, 19.

126. Mühsam, *Unpolitische Erinnerungen*, 78.

127. Paul E. Marcus, "Romanisches Café: Der Berliner Olymp der brotlosen Künste," *Münchner Illustrierte*, April 14, 1929, quoted in Schebera, *Damals*, 40.

128. Ilya Ehrenburg, *Visum der Zeit* (Leipzig: P. List, 1929), 44.

129. Matheo Quinz, "Das Romanische Cafe," *Der Querschnitt* 6, no. 8 (1926): 608–610; English translation in Quinz, "The Romanic Café," in *The Weimar Republic Sourcebook*, ed. Anton Kaes, Martin Jay, and Edward Dimendberg (Berkeley: University of California Press, 1994), 415–417.

130. The German writer Wolfgang Koeppen described meeting in Romanisches Café "a son of a wonder rabbi from Miropolye in Galicia, who glided by the patio like a starving angel, where the discussants believed to have a future or at best permanence in the present. The son of the wonder rabbi wore a greasy and dusty fur cap and uttered a Yiddish or Hebrew word; I have forgotten it, and then again I have not; it sounded like *hevter*, and it signified sand or wind or sand in the wind." Wolfgang Koeppen, *Romanisches Café: Erzählende Prosa* (Frankfurt am Main: Suhrkamp, 1972), 9.

131. Naḥum Goldmann, *The Jewish Paradox* (New York: Fred Jordan Books, 1978), 21.

132. Avrom Nokhem Stencl, "Arop funem yarid," *Loshn un lebn* 10–11 (1968): 25.

133. Lev Bergelson, "Memories of My Father: The Early Years (1918–1934)," in *David Bergelson: From Modernism to Socialist Realism*, ed. Joseph Sherman and Gennady Estraikh (Oxford, UK: Legenda, 2007), 85.

134. Daniel Charney, *A yortsendlik aza: 1914–1924* (Tel Aviv: Y. L. Peretz, 1963), 335.

135. Gennady Estraikh, "The Berlin Bureau of the New York *Forverts*," in Estraikh and Krutikov, *Yiddish in Weimar Berlin*, 145.

136. Daniel Charney, *Oyfn shvel fun yener velt: Tipn, bilder, epizodn* (New York: Marstin, 1947), 36.

137. Israel Rubin, "Bay di tishlekh fun romanishn kafe," *Literarishe bleter*, January 10, 1930, 28.

138. Bal Dimyen, "Feliton, literatur (siluetn fun romanishes cafe)," *Dos fraye vort* 5 (1923): 31.

139. Quoted in Delphine Bechtel, "Babylon or Jerusalem: Berlin as Center of Jewish Modernism in the 1920s," in *Insiders and Outsiders: Jewish and Gentile Culture in Germany and Austria*, ed. Dagmar C. G. Lorenz and Gabriele Weinberger (Detroit: Wayne State University Press, 1994), 116.

140. Peretz Markish, "Biznes, Moskve—Berlin," *Khalyastre* 1 (1922): 62.

141. For a recent study of multilingual Jewish literature in Weimar Berlin, see Racehl Seelig, *Strangers in Berlin: Modern Jewish Literature between East and West, 1913–1933* (Ann Arbor: University of Michigan Press, 2016).

142. Sima Ingberman, *ABC: International Constructivist Architecture, 1922–1939* (Cambridge, MA: MIT Press, 1994).

143. Quoted in Martin Hammer and Christina Lodder, *Constructing Modernity: The Art and Career of Naum Gabo* (New Haven, CT: Yale University Press, 1994), 101.

144. U. Z. Greenberg, "Dvorah be-shivya," in *Kol-Ktavav*, vol. 15 (Jerusalem: Mosad Bialik, 2001), 127.

145. Yeshurun Keshet, *Maskiyot* (Tel Aviv: Dvir, 1953), 138.

146. Ya'akov Shteinberg, "Sonnetot mi-beit ha-kafe," in *Kol-Kitvei Ya'acov Shteinberg* (Tel Aviv: Dvir, 1959), 67.

147. Ibid., 68.

148. Leah Goldberg, *Avedot* (Tel Aviv: Sifriat Poa'lim, 2010), 280.

149. Ibid., 284.

150. Donald L. Niewyk, *The Jews in Weimar Germany* (Manchester: Manchester University Press, 1980), 79.

151. Koeppen, *Romanisches Café*, 10.

152. See Leah Goldberg, *Pegisha 'im meshorer: 'Al Avraham Ben-Yitshak* (Tel Aviv: Sifriyat po'alim, 1988), 42–44.

153. Egon Erwin Kisch, "Wir gehen ins Café, weil . . . ," *Hamburger illustrierte Zeitung* 11 (March 15, 1930): 5.

CHAPTER 5. NEW YORK CITY

1. Alfred Polgar, *Anderseits: Erzählungen und Erwägungen* (Amsterdam: Querido Verlag, 1948), 94.

2. William H. Ukers, *All about Coffee* (New York: Tea and Coffee Trade Journal, 1922), 115–124; Mary R. M. Goodwin, *The Coffee-House of the 17th and 18th Centuries* (Williamsburg VA: Colonial Williamsburg Foundation Library, 1956).

3. Howard B. Rock, *Haven of Liberty: New York Jews in the New World, 1654–1865* (New York: NYU Press, 2015), 126–130.

4. Ibid., 158.

5. Christine Stansell, "Whitman at Pfaff's: Commercial Culture, Literary Life and New York Bohemia at Mid-century," *Walt Whitman Quarterly Review* 10 (1993): 107–126.

6. Menken's writings were collected in the volume *Infelicia: by Adah Isaacs Menken* (London: H. L. Williams, 1868).

7. Sven Beckert, *The Monied Metropolis: New York City and the Consolidation of the American Bourgeoisie, 1850–1896* (Cambridge: Cambridge University Press, 2001), 58.

8. Harmonie Club, *Harmonie Club of the City of New York: One Hundred Years, 1852–1952* (New York, 1952); Annie Polland and Daniel Soyer, *Emerging Metropolis: New York Jews in the Age of Immigration, 1840–1920* (New York: NYU Press, 2012), 207–212.

9. Francis B. Thurber, *Coffee from Plantation to Cup: A Brief History of Coffee Production and Consumption* (New York: American Grocer Publishing Association, 1881), 44.

10. In the period discussed here, the area was known mostly as the "East Side." It is hard to tell when, how, and why the name "Lower East Side" became prevalent or what exactly its borders are. See Hasia Diner, *Lower East Side Memories: A Jewish Place in America* (Princeton, NJ: Princeton University Press, 2002), 14; Beth S. Wenger, "Memory as Identity: The Invention of the Lower East Side," *American Jewish History* 85, no. 1 (1997): 3–27.

11. Tony Michels, *Fire in Their Hearts: Yiddish Socialists in New York* (Cambridge, MA: Harvard University Press, 2005), 43.

12. S. L. Blumenson, "From the American Scene: Culture on Rutgers Square," *Commentary*, July 1, 1950.

13. James Huneker, *Steeplejack* (New York: Scribner, 1920), 10.

14. Emma Goldman, *Living My Life*, vol. 1 (1931; repr., New York: Dover, 1970), 5.

15. Mario Maffi, *Gateway to the Promised Land: Ethnic Cultures on New York's Lower East Side* (New York: NYU Press, 1995).

16. Barbara Henry, *Rewriting Russia: Jacob Gordin's Yiddish Drama* (Seattle: University of Washington Press, 2011), 24.

17. Leon Kobrin, *Eraynerungen Fun a Idishen Dramaturg* (New York: Komitet far kobrins shriftn, 1925), 111–113.

18. Beth Kaplan, *Finding the Jewish Shakespeare: The Life and Legacy of Jacob Gordin* (Syracuse, NY: Syracuse University Press, 2007), 137–138.

19. "Passing of Zeitlin's," *Sun*, December 13, 1908, 6.

20. S. L. Blumenson, "The Golden Age of Tomashefsky: At the Tables Down at Schreiber's," *Commentary*, April 1, 1952; Irving Howe, *World of Our Fathers* (New York: Simon and Schuster, 1976), 237.

21. *Der Nayer gayst* 1 (1898).

22. Mordecai Soltes, "The Yiddish Press: An Americanizing Agency," *American Jewish Year Book* 26 (1924): 165–372.

23. S. L. Blumenson, "From the American Scene: Utopia on Columbia Street," *Commentary*, October 1, 1948.

24. Tony Michels, "The Lower East Side Meets Greenwich Village: Immigrant Jews, Yiddish, and the New York Intellectual Scene," in *Choosing Yiddish: New Frontiers of Language and Culture*, ed. Shiri Goren, Hannah Pressman, and Lara Rabinovitch (Detroit: Wayne State University Press, 2012), 69–85.

25. Van Wyck Brooks, *Scenes and Portraits: Memories of Childhood and Youth* (New York: E. P. Dutton, 1954), 152.

26. Abraham Cahan, *Bleter fun mayn leben*. vol. 2 (New York: Forverts, 1926), 131.

27. Lincoln Steffens, *The Autobiography of Lincoln Steffens: Complete in One Volume* (New York: Harcourt, Brace, 1931), 317–318.

28. *Sun*, September 26, 1898, 4.

29. "Riot on the East Side," *New York Times*, September 27, 1898.

30. Hutchins Hapgood, *The Spirit of the Ghetto: Studies of the Jewish Quarter in New York* (New York and London: Funk and Wagnalls, 1902), 90.

31. Ibid., 42–43.

32. Michael A. Lerner, *Dry Manhattan: Prohibition in New York City* (Cambridge, MA: Harvard University Press, 2008); Marni Davis, *Jews and Booze: Becoming American in the Age of Prohibition* (New York: NYU Press, 2012).

33. "In the East Side Cafés," *New York Tribune*, September 30, 1900, 1.

34. Maurice Fishberg, "Health and Sanitation," in *The Russian Jew in the United States: Studies of Social Conditions in New York, Philadelphia and Chicago, with a Description of Rural Settlements*, ed. Charles S. Bernheimer (Philadelphia: JC Winston, 1905), 291.

35. Abraham H. Fromenson, "Amusements and Social Life: New York," in Bernheimer, *Russian Jew in the United States*, 222.

36. Louis H. Pink, "The Café—A Substitute for the Saloon," *Independent*, March 6, 1906.

37. Henry James, *The American Scene* (New York: Harper, 1907), 127.

38. Jonathan Freedman, *The Temple of Culture: Assimilation and Anti-Semitism in Literary Anglo-America* (Oxford: Oxford University Press, 2002), 117.

39. James, *American Scene*, 137.

40. Ibid., 138.

41. Sabine Haenni, *The Immigrant Scene: Ethnic Amusements in New York, 1880–1920* (Minneapolis: University of Minnesota Press, 2008).

42. James, *American Scene*, 195–196.

43. Ibid., 135.

44. Donald Weber, "Accents of the Future: Jewish American Popular Culture," in *The Cambridge Companion to Jewish American Literature*, ed. Michael Kramer and Hana Wirth-Nesher (Cambridge: Cambridge University Press, 2003), 129–148.

45. Bernard G. Richards, *Discourses of Keidansky* (New York: Scott-Thaw, 1903), 199.

46. Ibid., 203.

47. Abraham Cahan, *The Rise of David Levinsky: A Novel* (New York: Harper and Bros., 1917), 454.

48. Ibid., 455.

49. Ibid., 461.

50. Ibid., 457.

51. Ibid., 456–457.

52. Shmuel Niger, quoted in Mikhail Krutikov, *Yiddish Fiction and the Crisis of Modernity, 1905–1914* (Stanford, CA: Stanford University Press, 2001), 132. See Krutikov's analysis of the novel in the context of "the crisis of immigration" (ibid., 133–138).

53. Leon Kobrin, *Di imigrantn, a roman oys dem lebn fun rusishe yidn in Amerike* (New York: Hebrew Publishing Company, 1909).

54. Ibid., 74.

55. Sholem Aleichem, *Blonzhende shtern* (Warsaw: Tsental, 1913), 169.

56. Kobrin, *Di imigrantn*, 74.

57. Ibid., 80.

58. Sholem Aleichem, *Blonzhende shtern*, 170.

59. Quoted in Ruth Wisse, "Di Yunge: Immigrants or Exiles?," *Prooftexts* 1, no. 1 (1981): 44.

60. Advertisement in *Der groyser kibitzer*, February 5, 1909.

61. Melech Epstein, *Pages from a Colorful Life: An Autobiographical Sketch* (Miami Beach: Block, 1971), 51.

62. L. Feinberg, "Di Yunge," *Vokh*, March 21, 1930, 13, 15.

63. *Forverts*, November 20, 1910.

64. Ibid. For English translation and discussion of this feuilleton, see Marc Miller, *Representing the Immigrant Experience: Morris Rosenfeld and the Emergence of Yiddish Literature in America* (Syracuse, NY: Syracuse University Press, 2007), 39–40.

65. The novel was first published in *Shriftn*.

66. David Ignatov, *In keslgrub: Roman in dray teylen mit tsvey epilogen* (New York: Inzel 1918), 28.

67. Ibid., 32–34.

68. A. Raboy, "In a kafe-hoyz," *Der arberter*, April 20, 1907, 5.

69. Reuben Iceland, *Fun unzer friling* (New York: Farlag Inzl, 1954).

70. Ibid., 187.

71. Ibid., 189.

72. Avraham Novershtern, *Kan gar ha-ʿam ha-yehudi: Sifrut Yidish be-artsot ha-brit* (Jerusalem: Magnes, 2015), 17–76.

73. Moyshe L. Halpern and Menahem Boreisho, *Ist Brodvey: Zamelbukh* (New York: Literarisher Farlag, 1916), 3.

74. Ibid., 13–14.

75. Zishe Weinper, *Moyshe-Leyb Halpern* (New York: Farlag Oyfkum, 1940), 91–92; Iceland, *Fun unzer friling*, 73–74.

76. L. Miller, autobiographical note, in Lamed Shapiro, *Ksovim* (Los Angeles: L. Shapiro Ksovim Komitet, 1949), 11. This was not the last time something like this happened. In the 1920s, Moyshe Nadir, the writer and humorist who was loosely affiliated with Di Yunge, opened a café called Nakinka, an acronym of "Nadir's kinstler kafe" (Nadir's artists' café), but it also closed down very quickly for not being economically viable.

77. Konrad Bercovici, *Around the World in New York* (New York: Century, 1924), 79.

78. B. Botwinik, "Der kafe vu es ferzomelen zikh yidish aktioyren," *Forverts*, November 14, 1916, 4.

79. Chaver Paver, *Gershn in Amerike* (Warsaw: Ikuf farlag, 1963), 178.

80. Ibid.

81. Ibid., 182.

82. Ruth R. Wisse, *A Little Love in Big Manhattan* (Cambridge, MA: Harvard University Press, 1988), 4.

83. Eve Kosofsky Sedgwick, *Between Men: English Literature and Male Homosocial Desire* (New York: Columbia University Press, 1985); Naomi Seidman, *The Mar-*

riage Plot: Or, How Jews Fell in Love with Love, and with Literature (Stanford, CA: Stanford University Press, 2016), 297–298.

84. Paver, *Gershn in Amerike, 178–179.*

85. This abandoning one desire for the another is related to the discomfort that David Levinsky feels in Cahan's novel, as a businessman having abandoned one type of desire (Torah and text) for another (money and capitalism).

86. Iceland, *Fun unzer frining,* 191–193.

87. Fromenson, "Amusements and Social Life," 225.

88. For an analysis of the intersections between gender, sex, class, and ethnicity in New York of this period, see Christine Stansell, *City of Women: Sex and Class in New York* (New York: Knopf, 1986); and Sharon Zukin, "Urban Lifestyles: Diversity and Standardization in Spaces of Consumption," *Urban Studies* 35, nos. 5–6 (1998): 825–839.

89. Hapgood, *Spirit of the Ghetto,* 301.

90. Ibid., 307.

91. Ibid., 312.

92. Avraham Novershtern, "Anna Margolin—Materialn tsu ir poetisher geshtalt," *YIVO Bleter* 1 (1991): 151.

93. See the fictionalized account of the café debates about Margolin (under the name Ada), in Rochelle Weprinski, *Dos kreytsn zikh fun di hent* (Tel Aviv: Y. L. Peretz, 1971), 94.

94. Anna Margolin, "In kafe," *Di naye velt* 2, no. 3 (1922): 6, reprinted in Anna Margolin, *Lider* (Jerusalem: Magness, 1991), 77–78; the following English translation of the poem is by Barbara Mann, in "Picturing the Poetry of Anna Margolin," *Modern Language Quarterly* 63, no. 4 (2002): 521–522. See also Kathryn Hellerstein, "From 'Ikh' to 'Zikh': A Journey from 'I' to 'Self' in Yiddish Poems by Women," in *Gender and Text,* ed. Anne Lerner, Anita Norich, and Naomi Sokoloff (New York: Jewish Theological Seminary of America, 1992), 113–144.

95. Mikhail Krutikov, "Cityscapes of Yiddishkayt: Opatoshu's New York Trilogy," in *Joseph Opatoshu: A Yiddish Writer between Europe and America,* ed. Sabine Koller, Gennady Estraikh, and Mikhail Krutikok (Oxford, UK: Legenda, 2013), 149–160.

96. Yoysef Opatoshu, *Hibru* (New York: Mayzel, 1920), 96.

97. Ibid., 99–101.

98. Christine Stansell, *American Moderns: Bohemian New York and the Creation of a New Century* (New York: Metropolitan Books, 2000), 6. This proximity might be related to the fact that garment factories had moved up Broadway and stood just to the east of Greenwich Village. The Triangle shirtwaist factory was located two blocks east of Washington Square Park.

99. Joanna Levin, *Bohemia in America: 1858–1920* (Stanford, CA: Stanford University Press, 2009), 339.

100. Randolph Bourne, "The Jew and Trans-National America," *Menorah Journal* 2 (December 1916): 277–284.

101. On Frank and Lewisohn, see Julian Levinson, *Exiles on Main Street: Jewish American Writers and American Literary Culture* (Bloomington: Indiana University Press, 2008), 56–92. It should be noted that Lewisohn grew up in Charleston in a very assimilated Christian environment, while Bercovici grew up in Europe and moved to New York.

102. Michels, "Lower East Side Meets Greenwich Village." See also Cristanne Miller, "Tongues 'Loosened in the Melting Pot': The Poets of Others and the Lower East Side," *Modernism/Modernity* 14, no. 3 (2007): 455–476; Victoria Kingham, "The *Pagan*, Joseph Kling, and American Salon Socialism," *Journal of Modern Periodical Studies* 1, no. 1 (2010): 1–37.

103. Matthias Newman, "Jewish Bohemia," *American Jewish Chronicle*, October 4, 1918, 531.

104. Opatoshu, *Hibru*, 141.

105. For the history of *Ha-do'ar* and other American Hebrew newspapers and magazines of this period, see Michael Gary Brown, "All, All Alone: The Hebrew Press in America from 1914–1924," *American Jewish Historical Quarterly* 59 (December 1969): 153–156.

106. S.H. (Shimon Halkin), "Al beit ha-kafe," *Ha-do'ar*, year 5, vol. 41 (1926): 804.

107. Ibid., 806.

108. Ibid., 807.

109. Daniel Persky, "Beit kafe 'ivri," *Ha-do'ar*, year 5, vol. 42 (1926): 836.

110. In a late interview in Tel Aviv, Halkin said, "I remembered Café Royal, in which part of the new New York bohemia met, and there gather the American and Yiddishist modernists. I, in spite of being loyal to Hebrew poetry, used to like the bohemians, and I would sit and argue with them about modernist poetry." Quoted in Moshe Dor, *Legalot le-a'adam acher* (Tel Aviv: Hakkibutz Hameuchad, 1974), 34.

111. Sh. Halkin, *Al ha-'i* (Jerusalem: Mosad Bialik, 1945), 229–245. On Halkin's poetry, see Alan Mintz, *A Sanctuary in the Dessert* (Stanford, CA: Stanford University Press, 2012), 274–297.

112. Halkin, *Al ha-'i*, 229.

113. Ibid., 232.

114. Ibid., 230–231.

115. Wenger, "Memory as Identity."

116. Edna Nahshon, ed., *New York's Yiddish Theater: From the Bowery to Broadway* (New York: Columbia University Press, 2016).

117. Some of the poetry of the In Zikh poets refers to or takes place in New York cafés. See, for example, A. Leyeles's poem "Nyu-yorker nekht" ("New York Nights"). I use the first three lines of the English translation by Zackay Sholem Berger in the epigraph to this chapter.

118. Curt L. Heymann, "Hymie the First," *New York Times*, March 1, 1942, X2.

119. Lulla A. Rosenfeld, *Bright Star of Exile: Jacob Adler and the Yiddish Theatre* (New York: T. Y. Crowell, 1977), 338.

120. Judd L. Teller, *Strangers and Natives: The Evolution of the American Jew from 1921 to the Present* (New York: Delacorte, 1968), 51.

121. Paver, *Gershn in Amerike*, 410.

122. Epstein, *Pages from a Colorful Life*, 52.

123. Leo Rosten, "Café Royal," *New Yorker*, April 10, 1937, 45.

124. Herman Yablokoff, *Der Payatz: Around the World with Yiddish Theater* (Silver Spring, MD: Bartleby, 1995), 188–190.

125. Baruch Glasman, *In goldenem zump: Novele in tsvey teyln* (New York: Yidishe Bukh-Gezelshaft, 1940), 46.

126. Ibid., 68–70.

127. Isaac B. Singer, *Lost in America* (Garden City, NY: Doubleday, 1981), 121.

128. Nathan Ausubel, "Hold Up the Sun! Kaleidoscope: The Jews of New York," Works Progress Administration Historical Records Survey: Federal Writers' Project, Jews of New York, New York Municipal Archives, box 7, microfilm 176, MN 21175, 270–288.

129. Suzanne Wasserman, "Re-creating Recreations on the Lower East Side: Restaurants, Cabarets, Cafés, and Coffeehouses in the 1930s," in *Remembering the Lower East Side*, ed. Hasia Diner, Jeffrey Shandler, and Beth Wenger (Bloomington: Indiana University Press, 2000), 155–178.

130. Ausubel, "Hold Up the Sun," 275. See also the parody of Café Royal written in Yiddish by "Der Ashmeday" (Shmuel Adler), "Café Loyal," *Newyorker vokhnblat*, June 21, 1940, 12–13.

131. Ausubel, "Hold Up the Sun," 270. Visiting East Side cafés as tourists was not new. In Cahan's novel *The Rise of David Levinsky*, he writes, "To spend an evening in some East Side café was regarded as something like spending a few hours at the Louvre." Cahan, *Rise of David Levinsky*, 284.

132. Montague Glass, "East Side Cafés," *Saturday Evening Post*, January 9, 1932, 110–137.

133. H. S. Kraft, *Cafe Crown: Comedy in Three Acts* (New York: Dramatists Play Service, 1952).

134. Jacob Fishman, "Café Royal Is Rediscovered," *Chicago Sentinel*, December 3, 1942, 7.

135. Isaac Bashevis Singer, *Meshugah* (New York: Farrar, Straus and Giroux, 1994), 10.

136. Harrison E. Salisbury, "Return of Show Business to Second Avenue Comes Too Late to Save Old Café Royal," *New York Times*, September 30, 1955, 19.

137. Judd L. Teller, "Yiddish Litterateurs and American Jews," *Commentary*, July 1, 1954, 32.

138. Teller, *Strangers and Natives*, 253.

139. About these processes, see Deborah Dash Moore, *At Home in America: Second Generation New York Jews* (New York: Columbia University Press, 1981); Eli Lederhendler, *New York Jews and the Decline of Urban Ethnicity, 1950–1970* (Syracuse, NY: Syracuse University Press, 2000).

140. Irving Howe, "The New York Intellectuals," *Dissent*, October 1, 1969, www.dissentmagazine.org.

141. Meyer Liben, "CCNY—A Memoir," *Commentary*, September 1965, 68.

142. Irving Kristol, "Memoirs of a Trotskyist," *New York Times Magazine*, January 23, 1977, 51.

143. Michael Kaufman, "Daniel Bell, Obituary," *New York Times*, January 24, 2011.

144. William Phillips, "New York Intellectual Life in the 1930s," *New York Times*, January 4, 1978, 21.

145. Saul Bellow, *The Victim* (New York: Penguin, 1947), 133.

146. Another place that served as a bridge in the 1950s and 1960s was Café Éclair on 141 West Seventy-Second Street. See Robert Thomas, "A. M. Selinger Dies at 91" (obituary), *New York Times*, January 19, 1998, 15.

147. Emma Jacobs, "Garden Cafeteria," *Place Matters*, accessed July 19, 2012, www.placematters.net.

148. Dan Wakefield, "New York's Lower East Side Today," *Commentary* 27 (1959): 461.

149. Christopher Mele, *Selling the Lower East Side: Culture, Real Estate, and Resistance in New York City* (Minneapolis: University of Minnesota Press, 2000), 140.

150. Wakefield, "Lower East Side Today," 463.

151. Bruce Davidson and Isaac Bashevis Singer, *Isaac Bashevis Singer and the Lower East Side* (Amherst, MA: Mead Art Museum, 2004), plate 1.

152. The Yiddish version was first published in *Di tsukonft* 73, nos. 3–4 (1968): 121–129. The English version, translated by Bashevis Singer and Dorothea Strass, was published in the *New Yorker*, December 28, 1968, 27–33.

153. Bashevis Singer, "The Cafeteria," 28.

154. Ibid., 33.

155. Bruce Davidson, "The Cafeteria," *New York*, October 15, 1973, 40.

156. Ibid.

157. Michael Weingrad, *American Hebrew Literature: Writing Jewish National Identity in the United States* (Syracuse, NY: Syracuse University Press, 2011), 206–207.

158. Gabriel Preil, *Mi-tokh zman ve-nof: Shirim mekubatsim* (Jerusalem: Mosad Bialik, 19), 148–149.

159. Ibid.

160. Ibid., 149–150.

161. Ibid., 152.

162. Gabriel Preil, *Adiv le-ʿatsmi: Shirim 1976–1979* (Tel Aviv: Hakibbutz hameuchad, 1980), 60.

CHAPTER 6. TEL AVIV–JAFFA

1. Sholem Asch, "Tel Aviv," in *Yediot ʾirityat Tel Aviv* 7, nos. 3–4 (1936): 116–117.

2. Gidon Biger and Yaʾakov Shavit, *Ha-historia shel Tel Aviv*, 4 vols. (Tel Aviv: Tel Aviv University Press, 2001), 2:270.

3. Hizky Shoham, "Tel Aviv Foundation Myth: A Constructive Perspective," in *Tel Aviv: The First Century*, ed. Ilan Troen and Maoz Azaryahu (Bloomington: Indiana University Press, 2011), 34–59.

4. Herzl, *Altneuland*, 45–57.

5. Akiva Arieh Weiss, *Reshita shel Tel Aviv* (Tel Aviv: Ayanot, 1957), 34–35.

6. Deborah S. Bernstein, "Contested Contact: Proximity and Social Control in Pre-1948 Jaffa and Tel-Aviv," in *Mixed Towns, Trapped Communities: Historical Narratives, Spatial Dynamics, Gender Relations and Cultural Encounters in Palestinian-Israeli Towns*, ed. Daniel Monterescu and Dan Rabinowitz (Farnham, UK: Ashgate, 2007), 219.

7. Quoted in Mordechai Naor, *Tel Aviv be-reshita* (Jerusalem: Yad Ben-Zvi, 1984), 36. Ilan Shḥori, *Ḥalom she-hafakh li-kherakh: Tel-Aviv, ledah u-tsemiḥah* (Tel Aviv: Avivim, 1990), 81.

8. Maoz Azaryahu, *Tel Aviv: Mythography of a City* (Syracuse, NY: Syracuse University Press, 2007).

9. Ruth Kark, *Jaffa, a City in Evolution, 1799–1917* (Jerusalem: Yad Ben Zvi Press, 1990), 53–107.

10. Mark Levine, *Overthrowing Geography: Jaffa, Tel Aviv, and the Struggle for Palestine, 1880–1948* (Berkeley: University of California Press, 2001), 55–56.

11. Or Aleksandrowicz, "Paper Boundaries: The Erased History of Neve Shalom," *Teorya u-bikoret* 41 (2013): 197.

12. Menahem Klein, *Lives in Common: Arabs and Jews in Jerusalem, Jaffa and Hebron* (New York: Oxford University Press, 2014); Abigail Jacobson and Moshe Naor, *Oriental Neighbors: Middle Eastern Jews and Arabs in Mandatory Palestine* (Waltham, MA: Brandeis University Press, 2016).

13. Salim Tamari, *Mountain against the Sea: Essays on Palestinian Society and Culture* (Berkeley: University of California Press, 2009), 176–190.

14. Ami Ayalon, *Reading Palestine* (Austin: University of Texas Press, 2004), 103.

15. Yosef Eliyahu Chelouche, *Parashat Ḥayay* (Tel Aviv: Stroud, 1930), 23–42.

16. Johann Büssow, *Hamidian Palestine: Politics and Society in the District of Jerusalem, 1872–1908* (Leiden: Brill, 2011).

17. Gur Alroey, *An Unpromising Land: Jewish Migration to Palestine in the Early Twentieth Century* (Stanford, CA: Stanford University Press, 2014).

18. Menaḥem Gnessin, *Darki ʿim Ha-Teaṭron Ha-ʿivri, 1905–1926* (Tel Aviv: Hakibutz ha-meʾuḥad, 1946), 20–21.

19. Yehudit Harari, *Ben Ha-Keramim* (Tel Aviv: Devir, 1947), 224–225.

20. Zeeʾv Smilansky, "Ha-yishuv ha-ʿivri be-Yafo," *Ha-ʿOmer* 1 (1907): 66.

21. Quoted in Shimshon Ḥalfi, *Ḥolmim ba-ḥolot* (Tel Aviv: Misrad ha-bitaḥon, 2001), 236.

22. Sh. Y. Agnon, *Tmol shilshom* (Tel Aviv: Schocken, 1966), 129; English translation in Agnon, *Only Yesterday*, trans. by Barbara Harshav (Princeton, NJ: Princeton University Press, 2000), 133.

23. Agnon, *Tmol shilshom*, 130–133; Agnon, *Only Yesterday*, 133–136.

24. Chelouche, *Parashat Ḥayay*, 130. There are various versions about the location of the meetings and the process that brought the establishment of Ahuzat Bayit. See Shoham, "Tel Aviv Foundation Myth."

25. Agnon, *Tmol shilshom*, 164–165; *Only Yesterday*, 189–189.

26. Eitan Belkind, *Kakh zeh hayah: Sipuro shel ish Nili Eitan Belkind* (Tel Aviv: Ministry of Defense, 1977), 46.

27. Leo Heiman, "The Struggle for Yiddish in Israel," *Chicago Jewish Forum* 17, no. 4 (1959): 229–253; Ya'akov Zerubavel, *Bi-yemei milḥama u-mahapeḥa* (Tel Aviv: Y. L. Peretz, 1966), 40–42; A. Leyb Pilowsky, *Tsvishn yo un neyn: Yidish un Yidish-literatur in Erets-Yisroel, 1907–1948* (Tel Aviv: Veltrat far Yidish un Yidisher kultur), 1986.

28. Quoted in Tom Segev, "When Tel Aviv Was a Wilderness," *Ha'aretz*, April 3, 2009.

29. Biger and Shavit, *Ha-historia shel Tel Aviv*, 1:152–191.

30. Batya Carmiel, *Batei ha-kafe shel Tel Aviv* (Jerusalem: Yad Ben Zvi, 2007), 32–50.

31. Tziona Rabau, *Be-Tel Aviv al ha-ḥolot* (Ramat Gan: Masada, 1973), 41–42.

32. Dov Gavish and Roi Raviv, "The Casino of Tel Aviv," *Ariel* 48–49 (1987): 134–139.

33. Sosh Rotem, "I'm ha-panim la'yam" (master's thesis, Tel Aviv University, 2005), 54, 67–68.

34. Tel Aviv Municipality Archive, 2–59. See also Anat Helman, *Young Tel Aviv: A Tale of Two Cities* (Waltham, MA: Brandeis University Press, 2010), 122.

35. Advertisement, in *'Ir be-moda'ot: Yafo ve-Tel-Aviv, 1900–1935*, vol. 3, ed. Reḥvam Ze'evy (Tel Aviv: Eretz Israel Museum, 1988), 516.

36. Aharon Reuveni, *Sipurim* (Tel Aviv: Devir, 1951), 243.

37. Binyamin Tammuz, *Reḥo ha-mar shel ha-geranyum* (Tel Aviv: Hakkibutz Hameuchad, 1980), 189.

38. Quoted in "Yediot Aḥaronot," *Do'ar ha-yom*, July 22, 1922, 3.

39. Haim Gliksberg, *Bialik yom yom* (Tel Aviv: Hakkibutz Hameuchad, 1945), 101.

40. Tel Aviv Municipality to the Battalion of the Defenders of Hebrew Language, July 5, 1928, Tel Aviv Municipality Archive, 4–140A.

41. Nathan Alterman, "Batim u-mabatim: Ha-kasino," *Tesha Ba-'erev*, January 21, 1938.

42. Sh. Samet, "Lifeni 'eser shanim," *Tesha ba-'erev*, April 8, 1937, 12.

43. Shlomo Žemaḥ, *Sipur Hayai* (Jerusalem: Devir, 1983), 142.

44. Arthur Koestler, *Arrow in the Blue* (London: Collins, 1952), 169–170.

45. Hagit Halperin, *Ha-ma'estro, ḥayav ve-yetzirato she Avraham Shlonsky* (Tel Aviv: Hakkibutz Hameuchad, 2011), 280.

46. Emil Foyershtein, "Sirtutim Tel Aviviyim," *Tesha ba-'erev*, April 8, 1938, 7.

47. Uri Keisari, "Ksatot u'gvi'im," *Do'ar ha-yom*, October 28, 1934, 3.

48. Carmiel, *Batei ha-kafe*, 219.

49. Petition to the Tel Aviv Municipality, June 14, 1931, Tel Aviv Municipality Archive, 4–3023.

50. Quoted in Gideon Ofrat, "Tel Aviv and Jerusalem Art," *Ariel* 47 (1978): 53.

51. Keisari, "Ksatot u'gvi'im."

52. Ya'akov Ḥorgin, "Le-Tel Aviv: "Tsror ziḥronot," *Gazit* 33, nos. 9–12 (1984): 19–20.

53. Avot Yeshurun, *Homograph* (Tel Aviv: Hakkibutz Hameuchad,1985), 66.

54. Israel Zmora, "Batei ha-kafe ha-sifrutiuyim she shnot ha-20 ve ha-30" (part 1), *Yediot Aḥaoront*, Literature and Culture Supplement, December 23, 1977, 1, 5.

55. Avraham Shlonsky, "Mehagrim ba-moledet," *Turim*, July 6, 1933, 1.

56. Mordechay Naor and Shula Vidrich, *Bet-kafe, makom kaṭan ko! bet-kafe, davar adir! Kafe Retzki, kafe sifruti be-Tel Aviv, 1932–1935* (Ben Shemen: Modan, 2006), 58.

57. Ibid., 77.

58. Ibid., 129.

59. Ibid., 103.

60. Ibid., 47.

61. Natan Alterman, "Hollywood ve-ha'ir," *Ha'aretz*, November 16, 1932; English translation in Alterman, "Hollywood and the City," in *Little Tel Aviv* (Tel Aviv: Hakibbutz Hameuchad, 1981), 21–25.

62. Nathan Harpaz, "Mi-bataei ḥalomot le-batei kufsa'ot—ha-mahapakh ha-adrikhali shel shnot ha-shloshim be-Tel Aviv," in *Tel Aviv be-reshita*, ed. Yossi Ben-Artzi (Jerusalem: Yad Ben Zvi, 1948), 91–106; Michael D. Levin. *White City: International Style Architecture in Israel* (Tel Aviv: Tel Aviv Museum, 1988).

63. Biger and Shavit, *Ha-historia shel Tel Aviv*, 2:270.

64. John Gibbons, *The Road to Nazareth* (London: Hale, 1936), 82.

65. Y. Ro'eh, "Nesikhut ha-safsarut," *Davar*, January 28, 1935, 5.

66. Yiddish version in Y. D. Berkovitz, *Menakhem Mendl in Erets-Yiśroel* (Tel Aviv: Sholem Aleichem House, 1973); Hebrew version in Berkovitz, *Kitvei Y. D. Berkovitz*, vol. 2 (Tel Aviv: Devir, 1952), 38.

67. Berkovitz, *Kitvei*, 44.

68. Ibid., 40.

69. Von Lim, "Die Stadt ohne Gojim," in *Tel Aviv: Hatzi yovel*, ed. Maoz Azaryahu Arnon Golan and Aminadav Dikman (Jerusalem: Carmel, 2009), 68–73.

70. *Yediot Iriyat Tel Aviv* 7 (1937): 97.

71. Liora Halperin, *Babel in Zion: Jews, Nationalism, and Language Diversity in Palestine, 1920–1948* (New Haven, CT: Yale University Press, 2015), 46–48.

72. "Kol ha-'Ivrit le-Toshaveha," July 1937, Tel Aviv Municipality Archive, 4–2640. See also, Anat Helman and Yael Reshef, "Kol ha-'Ir ha-'Ivrit le-Toshaveha: Moda'ot 'Ironiyot be-Tel Aviv ha-Mandatorit," *Israel: Studies in Zionism and the State of Israel, History, Society, Culture* 11 (2007): 64–70.

73. Ḥayim Feierberg, "Mizrah pogesh ma'arav: Bate ha- kafe be- shule Tel Aviv 1936–1960," in Carmiel, *Batei ha-kafe*, 296–300.

74. Deborah Bernstein, "South of Tel Aviv and North of Jaffa—The Frontier Zone of 'In Between,'" in Troen and Azaryahu, *Tel Aviv*, 115–137.

75. Ḥayim Gouri, *Ha-sefer ha-meshugah* (Tel Aviv: Am Oved, 1972), 98–99.

76. Letters to the municipality from October 1938, quoted in Deborah Bernstein, "Contested Contact: Proximity and Social Control in Pre-1948 Jaffa and Tel-Aviv," in Monterescu and Rabinowitz, *Mixed Towns, Trapped Communities*, 229.

77. Ibid., 231.

78. Leah Goldberg, *Ne'arot 'ivriyot: Mikhteve Leah Goldberg min ha-provintsyah, 1923–1935*, ed. Yfaat Weiss and Giddon Ticotsky (Tel Aviv: Sifriat po'alim, 2009), 230.

79. "Ha'ankita shel 9 ba-erev: H-isha hamodernit be-eretz Israel," *Tesha ba-'erev*, April 22, 1937. For the background on this questionnaire that was created by the editors

as a response to a "public sentence" on the status of women in the Yishuv initiated by WIZO (the Women's International Zionist Organization), see Oz Almog, *Preida mi-srulik*, vol. 2 (Or Yehuda: Zmora Bitan, 2004), 866–869.

80. Aryeh Navon, *Be-kav u be-khtav: Pirkei ḥayim* (Tel Aviv: Am Oved, 1996), 85.
81. Israel Zmora, "Batei ha-kafe shel Tel Aviv," *Yedioth Aharonot*, June 11, 1973.
82. Leah Goldberg, "Pgishot Aḥerot: Pireki zikhronot ve-hirhurim," *Al Ha-mishmar*, November 12, 1954, 5–6.
83. Giddon Ticotsky, "Aharit davar," in *Kol ha-sipurim*, by Leah Goldberg, ed. Yfaat Weiss and Giddon Ticotsky (Tel Aviv: Sifriat Poalim, 2009), 208.
84. Naor and Vidrich, *Beit-kafe*, 146.
85. Leah Goldberg, "Arba'ah shirim mi-beit kafeh," *Davar*, March 19, 1937, Weekend Supplement, 5. Poems 1, 2, and 4 were republished in Goldberg, *Shirim*, vol. 3 (Tel Aviv: Sifriat Poalim, 1986), 132–135. The third poem was published (with the title "Jacob and Rachel") in Goldberg, *Shirim*, vol. 1 (Tel Aviv: Sifriat Poalim, 1986), 163–164.
86. Goldberg, *Shirim*, vol. 3, 132.
87. Ibid.
88. Goldberg, *Shirim*, vol. 1, 163.
89. Goldberg, *Kol ha-sipurim*, 62.
90. Ada Grant, "Meagadot ha-ḥay: Me-'inyan le-'inyan," *Mishmar*, May 3, 1944, 2.
91. Zusman Segalovitsh, *Mayne zibn yor in Tel-Aviv* (Buenos Aires: Tsentral-Farband fun Poylishe Yidn in Argentine, 1949), 23.
92. Ibid., 43.
93. Ibid., 200.
94. Meyer Weisgal, *So Far: An Autobiography* (New York: Random House, 1972), 152–153.
95. Moshe Shamir, *Sefer yalkut ha-r'eim* (Jerusalem: Bialik Institute, 1992), 15.
96. Ibid., 243–244.
97. Orit Rozin, "Austerity Tel-Aviv: Everyday Life, Supervision, Compliance, and Respectability, in Tel-Aviv," in Troen and Azaryahu, *Tel Aviv*, 165–188.
98. Carmiel, *Batei ha-kafe*, 275–287.
99. Erez Bitton, *Minḥah markoa'it* (Tel Aviv: Eked, 1979), 42.
100. In 1949, dozens of writers, artists, actors, and journalists wrote a petition to the municipality of Tel Aviv, asking to let Kassit stay open late at night. See Carmiel, *Batei ha-kafe*, 231.
101. M. Nundelman, *Lakht a Yid in Eretz-Yisroel* (New York: Shulsinger Brothers, 1956), 80–87.
102. "Kassit, gam be-New York," *Ma'ariv*, July 21, 1950, 2.
103. Avot Yeshurun, *Ha-shever ha-suri afrikani* (Tel Aviv: Siman Kri'ah, 1974), 58.
104. Joan Baez, "For Sasha," *Honest Lullaby* (CBS Records, 1979).
105. Yoram Kaniuk, *Ha-yehudi ha-aḥaron* (Tel Aviv: Hakibutz Hameuchad, 1981), 21; English translation in Kaniuk, *The Last Jew*, trans. Barbara Harshav (New York: Grove, 2006), 22.

106. Kaniuk, *Ha-yehudi ha-aharon*, 364–365; Kaniuk, *Last Jew*, 397.
107. Aharon Bakhar, "Kafe Kassit: Zavit re'iya ketsat shona," *Yedioth Aharonot*, July 11, 1975, 16.
108. Ibid., 17.
109. Gabriel Moked, "Kasit be-tahapukhotea'h," *Gazit* 33 (1984): 9–12; 34 (1984): 1–12.
110. Quoted in Yehonatan Gefen, *Homer tov* (Lod: Devir, 2002), 35.
111. Nissan N. Perez, "Photography: Café Kassit," *London Magazine* 27, no. 5 (August 1, 1987): 143.

CONCLUSION

1. On 'Ars Poetica, see Ayelet Tsabari, "Mizrahi Artists Are Here to Incite a Culture War," *Forward*, March 16, 2016; on Café Albi ("My heart" in Arabic) and the photographs of Nino Herman, see "Nino Herman, Café Albi," *L'oeil de la photographie*, December 31, 2016, www.loeildelaphotographie.com.
2. For a discussion on contemporary Jewish culture, see Caryn Aviv and David Shneer, *New Jews: The End of the Jewish Diaspora* (New York: NYU Press, 2005); James Loeffler, "The Death of Jewish Culture," *Mosaic*, May 2014, https://mosaic magazine.com, and the responses to this essay.
3. Aharon Appelfeld, *'Od ha-yom gadol* (Jerusalem: Keter, 2001); English translation in Appelfeld, *A Table for One*, trans. Aloma Halter (New Milford, CT: Toby, 2005).
4. Appelfeld, *Table for One*, 3.
5. Ibid.
6. Ibid.
7. Ibid., 4.
8. Michael Idov, "Bitter Brew: I Opened a Charming Neighborhood Coffee Shop. Then It Destroyed My Life," *Slate*, December 29, 2005, www.slate.com.
9. Michael Idov, *Ground Up* (New York: Farrar, Straus and Giroux, 2009), 49.
10. Ibid., 51.
11. Ibid., 61.
12. *Café Nagler*, dir. Mor Kaplansky and Yariv Barel (Tel Aviv, 2015).
13. For an exploration of Jewish migration from the former Soviet Union, see Zvi Gitelman, ed., *The New Jewish Diaspora: Russian-Speaking Immigrants in the United States, Israel, and Germany* (New Brunswick, NJ: Rutgers University Press, 2016).
14. Svetlana Boym, *The Future of Nostalgia* (New York: Basic Books, 2001), xviii.
15. Stuart Hall, "Cultural Identity and Diaspora," in *Identity: Community, Culture, Difference*, ed. Jonathan Rutherford (London: Lawrence and Wishart, 1990), 235.

INDEX

Note: Locators in *italic* indicate pages with illustrations.

ABOUT THE AUTHOR

Shachar M. Pinsker is Associate Professor of Hebrew Literature and Culture at the University of Michigan. He is the author of the award-winning *Literary Passports: The Making of Modernist Hebrew Fiction in Europe*, the editor of *Where the Sky and the Sea Meet: Israeli Yiddish Stories* and *Women's Hebrew Poetry on American Shores: Poems by Anne Kleiman and Annabelle Farmelant*, and the co-editor of *Hebrew, Gender, and Modernity: Critical Responses to Dvora Baron's Fiction*.